LEADING QUESTIONS

Malcolm Peet
&
David R   son

Nelson

For Elspeth and Jude. You can come home now.

Thomas Nelson and Sons Ltd
Nelson House Mayfield Road
Walton-on-Thames Surrey
KT12 5PL UK

Thomas Nelson Australia
102 Dodds Street
South Melbourne
Victoria 3205 Australia

Nelson Canada
1120 Birchmount Road
Scarborough Ontario
M1K 5G4 Canada

© Judith Wainwright and Jackie Hutton 1992

Cover illustration: Pippa Sterne

First published by Thomas Nelson and Sons Ltd 1992

I(T)P   Thomas Nelson is an International
        Thomson Publishing Company

I(T)P   is used under licence

ISBN 0-17-432337-9
NPN 9 8 7 6 5

Printed in China

Contents

Contents

Preface

We are writing this preface on Shakespeare's 437th birthday. This week, Prince Charles said that it was a shame and a scandal that, in what he quaintly termed 'Shakespeare's land', huge numbers of pupils and students left school with little or no familiarity with Our Great Poet's work. On the same day, the Artistic Director of the English Shakespeare Company said that the ideal birthday present for Shakespeare would be a ten-year ban on teaching his work in schools. Earlier this month, a respected Professor published a fierce little article arguing that the traditional A-Level Literature examination is narrow, depressing and non-creative. His word-processor was still warm when the Secretary of State for Education got to his feet and urged the return to traditional methods of teaching and examining.

Clearly, there's no longer a comfortable consensus of opinion as to what the A-Level curriculum should be, nor about how it should be examined (and therefore taught). Behind this general discord there is the equally important, if less public, debate as to what criticism is, and what it should try to do. All this is to the good, no doubt, and the issues raised are interesting. (One of the things this book tries to do is encourage students to give these issues some serious thought.) But it poses problems for writers of books such as ours. Our desire is that our book should be, above all else, practical; that it should be useful to students who will have to sit an A-Level exam in Literature, no matter what form that exam might take.

To ensure that *Leading Questions* remains useful over a period of time, we have used, as the basic building block of the book, the close questioning of particular texts. Clearly, this is the one activity which seems most likely to survive the current debates. As its title suggests, this book is about this close questioning of texts. And we have tried to write a book which is flexible in use, which lends itself to a variety of teaching and learning strategies: private reading, class discussion, group work, coursework, and other written assignments. Our book invites – indeed, it depends upon – the active participation of the reader. *Leading Questions* does not pretend to be a 'course' in literary criticism. It is not structured in prescriptive steps; readers and teachers should feel free to use our materials in whatever way best suits their needs and interests.

Leading Questions has three main elements:

1 Chapters which introduce and discuss 'technical' aspects of criticism, such as rhythm, metaphor, narrative position, and so on. Whenever possible, these matters are discussed within the context of particular genres of writing, such as crime fiction, the pastoral, travel writing. These chapters are not intended for passive reading. They are 'hands-on' pieces, with tasks and activities for readers to try.

2 Chapters offering approaches to new or 'unseen' texts; our intention here being to suggest ways in which students may develop their initial responses into the kind of critical writing sought after by examiners.

3 A sequence of practice exercises.

In the final chapter, we have attempted a brief account of the critical theories challenging conventional thinking about literature and criticism. We hope, too, that *Leading Questions* will be read as an anthology; it contains well over one hundred verse and prose passages. Some of them are by William Shakespeare.

Books

From the heart of this dark, evacuated campus
I can hear the library humming in the night,
an immense choir of authors muttering inside their books
along the unlit, alphabetical shelves,
Giovanni Pontano next to Pope, Dumas next to his son,
each one stitched into his own private coat,
together forming a low, gigantic chord of language.

I picture a figure in the act of reading,
shoes on a desk, head tilted into the wind of a book,
a man in two worlds, holding the rope of his tie
as the suicide of lovers saturates a page,
or lighting a cigarette in the middle of a theorum.
He moves from paragraph to paragraph
as if touring a house of endless, panelled rooms.

I hear the voice of my mother reading to me
from a chair facing the bed, books about horses and dogs,
and inside her voice lie other distant sounds,
the horrors of a stable ablaze in the night,
a bark that is moving toward the brink of speech.

I watch myself building bookshelves in college,
walls within walls, as rain soaks New England,
or standing in a bookstore in a trench coat.

I see all of us reading ourselves away from ourselves,
straining in circles of light to find more light
until the line of words becomes a trail of crumbs
that we follow across a page of fresh snow;

when evening is shadowing the forest,
small brown birds flutter down to consume them
and we have to listen hard to hear the voices
of the boy and his sister receding into the perilous woods.

Billy Collins

1
The Name of the Game

Presumably you are reading this because you have decided to study English Literature to A- or AS-Level. Perhaps you have already discovered that it is a rather odd subject. It is like other academic subjects in that it involves you in the activities of finding, sifting and assessing evidence, but it seems to lack a hard core of 'facts' or certainties. Many students feel unnerved by this absence of a factual core of knowledge and wish that there were more factual stuff to hold on to. It might be laborious to learn mathematical formulae, the names of fossils, or the theory of Money Supply, but at least you know what you're doing and you can know whether you've got them right or wrong. Studying literature denies you these crumbs of comfort. There are, of course, facts about writers – Shakespeare's father was a glovemaker, George Eliot was a woman, Virginia Woolf preferred to write standing up, Joseph Conrad was a Polish ex-mariner whose real name was Korzeniowski – but these facts may or may not tell you something about what these people wrote.

And there are facts about writing that your teachers will expect you know: what Chaucer meant by the word 'nice', perhaps, or how many lines there are in a sonnet, or that a line in a poem by T. S. Eliot is a quotation from *Hamlet*. You will also be told, we expect, that knowing these things will not in itself make you a competent student of literature, any more than being given a set of spanners will make you a competent engineer. The question that any sensible A-Level Literature student will be asking at the beginning of the course is 'What am I supposed to be doing?'

With that very basic question in mind, we decided not to write the usual sort of Introduction to this book: the kind of thing that would say what we thought literature was all about and why studying it is Good For You. Instead we thought it might be a good idea to ask Literature students in our area what they thought they were doing and why. The first question we asked was the obvious one: 'Why did you decide to study English Literature at A-Level?' The answers we got were remarkably varied, as you will see. A selection follows; the least original come first.

A I wanted to do a third A-Level subject, so I chose Literature because it's easier than sciences or foreign languages.

B I chose English because I enjoyed it at school and I got a good grade at GCSE.

C I decided to study English Lit at A-Level because I enjoy reading.

D I think that if you study literature you learn more about people and what actually motivates them.

E There are many great writers, like Dickens, whose books I want to read because they are full of interesting ideas about the world.

F I think that reading poetry and some novels makes you a more informed person about moral issues.

G I want to be a journalist, so I thought that it would be a good idea to study how writers use words.

H I want to study as many women writers on this course as possible because I am very interested in women and their writing at the moment.

I I want to study literature because I write poetry myself.

You might like to look at these replies and ask yourself which of them corresponds most closely with your own reasons for enlisting as an A-Level Literature student. You'll no doubt find that your motives are a mix of some of the above. Perhaps your motives are simultaneously lofty ('I want to be a novelist') and pragmatic ('I couldn't cope with Physics'). Just possibly, your reasons are personal and quirky ('The English teacher is excessively attractive and witty and generous with the marks'). In any event, our list of responses is, we think, fairly representative of what goes on in the minds of most students who choose Literature as one of their 'options'.

Far more of the replies we received were 'sensible' rather than idealistic or inspired. It is, probably, a good idea to follow up a subject that you had some success with and enjoyed at GCSE level. Sadly, however, students whose motives resemble answers A, B and C often get a nasty shock early on in their A-Level course when they discover that the sort of 'reading' they have to do is far more intense and demanding than they realised it would be, that Literary Studies requires a kind of reading that is radically different from the fairly elementary skill that enables you to escape into a novel for an hour or two. This book's main task is to show you how close and critical reading of a text differs from ordinary reading.

Our survey was not particularly scientific, and our interests were not in the least sociological. We wanted to identify the kind of issues that needed confronting: the kind of issues raised, in fact, by the latter six answers (D to I) on our list. If you look at them again, it should occur to you that they involve assumptions that invite a closer look. We think that the questions they raise are important. We think that you should ask, discuss and think about these questions not merely for a few moments right now, but throughout the time you are studying literature. Here they are:

1 Is it true that poets and novelists are more perceptive than 'ordinary' people? How are they? In what sorts of ways? What sorts of things are they more perceptive about?

2 If you are reading books by 'perceptive' writers, will that make you more perceptive than you might otherwise be? Will the writer's perceptive powers gradually infect you so that you have them as well? If reading does this, how does it do it?

3 Does reading about fictional characters help you to understand real people? What are the differences between fictional characters and real people?

4 Where would you turn to if you wanted to find an accurate account of human motivation: to a novel or to a textbook written for A-Level Psychology students? Is this a silly question? If it is, why is it?

5 If you wanted to find out what the French Revolution was all about, and what the experience of living through it felt like for many of the people involved, would you ask your local librarian for a historical novel or a history book? Is *this* a silly question?

6 Someone who reads a lot of books may be better informed about the world, but will he or she be a 'better person', in the moral sense? If you read a lot of poems and novels and plays is it likely, or even possible, that doing this will make you a more open, generous, tolerant and kind human being? If you do think that the activity of reading is a kind of ethical training, how does this training work?

7 Is studying Literature just a matter of studying words and how they can be efficiently assembled to obtain certain effects? Or is there more to it than that? If so, what is the 'more to it than that'?

8 Why are there nearly always more female than male students on A-Level Literature courses? Is this a Good Thing or a Bad Thing?

9 Do you think that studying and writing about poetry will help you become a better poet? How might it? If you do think that examining other people's poetry will make you a better writer, does it disturb you to be told that a great many poets refuse to criticise other poets' work on the grounds that doing so damages their own writing? Or are poets who say this just being precious?

It's pretty obvious that these questions do not have simple answers. Or perhaps it would be more accurate to say that they have two kinds of answer: the straightforward kind and the more involved kind. For instance, fictional characters differ from real people in that you cannot touch or smell them, they aren't really alive (except in our heads), they go to the toilet very infrequently, and they often seem far more witty and articulate than ourselves. But then these straightforward observations spawn more interesting problems which have to do with this troublesome word 'real'. What sort of 'reality' do fictional characters possess? How and where do they 'come alive'? In the author's mind? On the printed page? In the reader's mind? All three? For now, let's postpone these questions by saying that fictional characters are purely linguistic creations; they exist entirely as words.

It's likely that you found others of those questions equally ambiguous. If you discussed them, you almost certainly came to the conclusion that they cannot have 'right' or 'wrong' answers because they are 'philosophical' questions. But the way you feel about them is very likely to affect the way you read – and therefore write – about literature.

When we asked students why they had decided to study English Literature at A-Level, we also asked them to say what they thought was the hardest task they had found themselves facing during the first two terms of their course, what was especially hard about it, and what changes they would like to see in the course they were studying. A clear majority of students said that they had the most trouble with 'Unseens'. In case you don't already know, the 'Unseen' is the popular term for a rather unpopular exercise. It involves being given a poem or prose passage you have not seen before and being told to write a criticism (or 'appreciation') of it. Most of you will have to do this as part of your final exam, and some of you will have to do it against the clock. Your teachers may ask you to do it, too – perhaps as part of your coursework. So will this book. 'Doing Unseens' is an exercise in **Practical Criticism**. We'll have more to say about that in the next chapter. By way of introduction to its delights, here is part of the transcript of a recording of a discussion between two students at a Sixth Form College. We've made them sound a little more articulate by editing out a few 'ums' and 'ers' and the odd expletive.

RACHEL: Well, I think that going in 'cold' like that is horrendous. There's nothing like it in GCSE. It's not just what the poet says, is it? I mean, it's the way those things are said as well. It's difficult to get all the meanings out, all at the same time, and then have to write an essay about them, work out your ideas, understand the words, all at the same time. I mean, within one hour.

JO: Well, I think that if we have to write on an unseen poem or whatever then there ought to be lots to choose from, that's all … It's the most difficult thing to do because, well, if you don't get the content, you can kiss goodbye to the rest, right? I never know what's right, really. I mean, you can totally miss the whole point of a poem, can't you? What is a poem's real meaning, anyway? Is it the poet's original meaning, or the one that you give it? I'm confused …

RACHEL: Yes, and you know all those technical terms, and somehow you never get the chance to use them, do you? … I don't think you can, really, teach anyone how to analyse a poem because each one is different, isn't it? Besides, you don't really get marks for your own ideas – you always have to write out stuff that pleases them. Well, you do, don't you?

JO: Well, you're meant to be objective about poetry, aren't you? Well, yeah, that and subjective as well …

RACHEL: But how do they test what people write? Because different people understand different things in each poem. I find this weird, actually … when you have to do this stuff with poetry, sometimes you can use your imagination quite a lot, and sometimes you can't. At least with a play there's characters and plot and so on. But with a poem they can be really obscure, can't they?

JO: I think that the problem with poems is that they're so short, and you have to get so much out of them really. I usually like most poems initially, when I read them. But then it becomes a sort of academic thing. Well, doesn't it? I suppose we have to go into so much detail because every word's chosen very carefully. Obviously. But you can ruin it that way. Well, I think so.

RACHEL: No, I quite like that part of it, really. What I find hardest is getting what I want to say into some sort of shape. Sometimes when I read through what I've written, it sounds ... vague. As if I hadn't understood the poem, even though I did, actually ... I think.

JO: Well, I think it's odd, really. All of it. None of my family reads poetry. They wouldn't even know what one looked like. I mean, nobody does, do they, out of school? Still, it broadens your horizons, as they say.

RACHEL: You know what the worst thing is? The next day! You suddenly realise all those things you wanted to say and didn't. Don't you?

We want to spend some time discussing what these students have to say, although it's probably more 'educational' if first you do this yourself with some of the other people in your group. You might like to decide which of the points raised are the more important ones, and which ones you think they should have discussed further.

Perhaps the most important thing that Rachel has realised is that the way a poem is written (its form) is usually just as significant as what it has to say (its content). These elements of a piece of writing are nearly always inseparable from, or integral to, each other. If you gain nothing else from this book, we hope you will take on board this one central idea: that form and content work together, and that writing which lacks either of these elements cannot create meaning. (That's why there are so many chapters on form in this book.) Writing about these things simultaneously and discussing the way they interrelate is a very difficult thing to do, and it requires a lot of practice. Performing such a complex and subtle task under timed conditions is, as Rachel says, horrendous. It is possible, though, and it gets easier. Nevertheless, it is a very odd and stressful way of finding out whether you can write about words and meanings.

Jo is probably right when she says that the first and most fundamental thing you have to do is simply to understand what you're reading before you go on to do anything else more mysteriously 'literary'. Jo does seem to think, however, that a poem must have only one real meaning ('I mean, you can totally miss the whole point of a poem, can't you?'), rather than levels or a series of meanings. (This is a common 'heresy' which this book examines in more detail in Chapter 3.) Jo hasn't yet realised that analysing a poem or a passage of prose is a gradual, exploratory process – during which you will inevitably make mistakes, as we all do. She seems to imagine that getting to grips with a poem is some sort of weird alchemical procedure: that by knowing the secret spell she will suddenly discover the hidden, true meaning ('the whole point of the poem'). This may sound like a very attractive and exciting way of describing the mental processes involved in reading and understanding a poem but, sad to say, it's very rarely like that.

Jo has, in fact, raised the biggest and hardest question of all: 'What is a poem's real meaning, anyway? Is it the poet's original meaning, or the one you give it? I'm confused ... ' Don't trust anyone who tries to sell you a simple answer to this problem. It happens to be one of the Great Mysteries of the Universe. Jo has inadvertently wandered into the dark woods of Linguistic Philosophy, where topics such as The Meaning of 'Meaning' are endlessly puzzled over, written about, and left unresolved; and there are as yet no clear answers available to us all as to what 'meaning' actually is. One way through this murky area might be this: what we can say is that when Jo is reading a poem, the meaning that occurs is taking place in her mind and nowhere else. Her eyes, and thus her mind, are stimulated by a set of visual signs (words) on a piece of paper, and so, in a very real sense, she is providing the meaning of the poem. Its meaning is, if you like, within her and not 'out there'. Or to put it another way: if a poem spent its entire existence buried in a tin box, it would be strange to say that it still had meaning. So Jo is probably wrong to think that a poem has a 'real', 'original' meaning and wrong to believe that the meaning she gives to it is necessarily a 'second-class' or inaccurate kind of meaning. She is the person reading the poem, and she is the one who is giving it meanings.

This is one of the points (one of the many points) in this book where you should say 'hang on a minute'. Because if that's the case, then why shouldn't a poem (or anything else) mean anything we want it to mean? The short answer to this is that language is not your private property. It's in public ownership. In effect, this means that while you are perfectly free to use language – and interpret other people's language – in any way you choose, you are likely to make difficulties for yourself if the way you do that deviates wildly from the way all other people do. You could find yourself in the locked ward of a Caring Institution. Or fail A-Level English. The English language and its conventions are the common ground for all of us, and so it naturally follows that poets writing in English are using the same language that the rest of us use. (Students often disbelieve this, but it's true.) While it is true that a few (very few) poets and prose writers are deliberately obscure, the fact is that most writers are not using language as a private code that only they can understand. There wouldn't be much point, would there, in publishing poems in books if you wanted to keep what you had to say secret. It follows from all this that Jo is quite right to concern herself with 'getting' a poem's 'original' meaning. She's worried that her understanding of a poem might not be what the poet intended her to understand. What's more, she thinks that maybe the examiners do know what the poet 'really' meant, and that they'll knock off marks if she gets it wrong. Well, they don't. Really, they don't. Let's spend a moment or two trying to destroy a myth.

Somewhere in Paris, we are told, there is a length of metal which is the perfect, the definitive metre length. If you suspect that your ruler or tape measure is not quite accurate, you could nip over there and compare it with this length of metal. If the match is not exact, then your ruler or tape measure is faulty. There is no such test for interpretations of poems. And if there were, poets would form themselves into a small army and set out to destroy it. This is because poets like – no, rely – on their poems meaning slightly, or even greatly, different things to different readers. If their poems didn't do this, they could not have any universal appeal, and they could not continue to interest readers over long periods of time. This means that you must rid your mind of that nasty suspicion that while you're sitting there struggling with a poem, The Perfect Definitive Poet-Approved Interpretation is locked away in the Chief Examiner's safe. It isn't. This does not mean, of course, that you have a general licence to impose upon a poem any crazy interpretation that strikes your fancy. If you read a poem that began 'I must go down to the sea again ... ' and you decided that this meant 'I must strive to overthrow the Capitalist system', you would need superhuman powers of persuasion to convince an examiner that you were not completely daft. It is part of your job to decide what you think a poem is saying, and you will be rewarded for doing this rationally and skilfully. The fact is that no-one (not even, oddly enough, the poet who wrote it) can say with absolute certainty that he or she knows the 'correct' interpretation of a poem. This is something that should reassure you, not fill you with panic. It means that there *is* room for your own views, your own subjective responses. And this takes us back to something that Rachel said.

Rachel said ' ... you always have to write out stuff that pleases them ... But how do they test what people write?' A fair point and a good question. It's easy enough to understand how examiners can mark answers which have the potential for being correct or incorrect, but not at all easy to understand how they can assess answers which express value judgements and personal feelings. Rachel feels that she rarely gets rewarded for her own ideas, and knows that in order to survive she has to regurgitate received opinions and accepted wisdoms. Well, it's true that the Literary Establishment does tend to generate a set of subtle and unquestioned value judgements about writing, and it is also true that students often pick them up almost unconsciously from their teachers and from books they read (including this one). Poets get put in order of rank, for example, as if they were examination candidates themselves. Somehow, a subtle consensus of opinion gets established and then filters down to us. What this means is that teachers and examiners probably do have views about what counts as 'Good' in literature and what counts as 'Bad'. It's reasonable to assume that the set texts you'll study – Shakespeare, Lawrence or whatever – have been selected by the Examining Boards because they are considered to be Good in some way. Yet it is not – emphatically not – compulsory to pretend to think that all the writers you'll come across are perfectly brilliant. But if you happen to think that some of their work, or some aspect of it, is feeble or ugly or offensive, it is compulsory to say why you think so, and to argue your case well. That just happens to be one of the rules you're playing by. So it's worth wondering what Rachel means by her 'own ideas'. If she means that the rules of the game frequently smother her original and profound insights, then yes, that's an outrage. But if she means she gets low marks because she merely voices her prejudices and doesn't justify her views, that's fair enough. But then how do examiners judge her work, be it good or awful?

Examiners are often fairly secretive about the way they mark essays. They frequently say that it's more of an art than a science – which is a way of saying that they're not really sure. Nevertheless, what they are essentially interested in is finding out from your work whether or not you can read in depth, whether or not you are aware of the different sorts of patterns that writers can put words into, and whether or not you can express yourself with confidence and clarity. The main thing to remember is that you are marked for what you say as an individual, and that your work is not assessed by comparing it with that mythical 'Ideal Literary Response'.

Another thing that Rachel seems to believe is that examiners expect you to use lots of technical vocabulary ('you know all those technical terms and you never get the chance to use them, do you?'). She would probably think that this sort of thing is rather wonderful:

> The emphasis the caesura gives in the iambic line is further reinforced by the impudence of the plosive consonance subsequently modified by the sinister sibilance of the echoic effect discovered in the poem's near-rhymes.

Sounds good, doesn't it? Its meaning is about as clear as a muddy hole on a foggy night, however. Divorced from its context – the words it is describing – this sort of stuff is completely meaningless. Even within its context it would sound too clever by half. What your examiners are looking for is an intelligent and perceptive understanding of language, not a catalogue of jargon. Rachel is probably wrong to think that she lets herself down badly when she fails to use her 'technical terms' in an essay. But there's no denying that it is useful to have at your disposal a few technical words that help you to get across your ideas easily and quickly. It's simply more efficient to say 'metaphor' than it is to burble on about 'the kind of language that compares one thing with another'. In short, don't be frightened or over-impressed by Lit-Crit terminology, but don't ignore it either. Examiners do not give marks for jargon, but they do enjoy reading work that has a 'professional' feel to it. What you will find (partly, we hope, from this book) is that there are certain skills in writing about writing, and that you get better at it the more practice you get. The trick is to know what questions to ask about a poem or piece of prose. Knowing what an iambic pentameter is does not necessarily make you a good reader.

Finally, we come to Jo's rather mournful conclusions: 'I usually like most poems initially when I read them, but then it becomes a sort of academic thing ... None of my family reads poetry. They wouldn't even know what one looked like. I mean, nobody does, do they, out of school. Still, it broadens your horizons, as they say.' It's hard to know how to respond to sad comments like these. Perhaps there is a case, after all, for not teaching literature as a 'subject', on the grounds that when reading becomes work it ceases to be a pleasure. But then work and pleasure are not mutually exclusive terms. Well, they needn't be. It is true, and tragic, that thousands of people have been put off literature not so much by the way that they've been taught it, but because that teaching has been directed towards cramming them through examinations. And those examinations have been oppressive. It is also true that too many students have had to struggle with writing that may well have been dull and remote from their lives (although most teenagers seem to find poems about teenage life pretty awful, on the whole). For what it's worth, the writers of this book happen to believe that, despite all of this, it is worthwhile to study literature – not least because the skills you can acquire, the skills involved in critical reading and self-expression, are genuinely valuable; their usefulness is not limited to writing essays on poetry. We think that yes, there is a difference between studying literature and simply enjoying it, but these two activities are not necessarily at odds. There is not, in our opinion, much to be said for making students write, under examination conditions, about works of literature they have enjoyed. If John Keats could have witnessed the ugly spectacle of a school hall full of students, under the baleful gaze of the clock, all sweating away at essays on his *Ode to a Nightingale*, he would, we suspect, have been tempted to pack in poetry altogether and go back to being a surgeon. Still, things are getting better, gradually. Methods of examination are becoming more humane. And while we hope this book will be of some use to you when it comes to getting through your exams, it's just as important to us that it leaves the pleasure you get from reading intact.

2
Seeing Through Language

We all encounter literature in a variety of ways. Our parents read us bedtime stories. We progress to comics, to stories, to whole novels. Perhaps you acquire a taste for science fiction or bodice-ripping romances. Your teachers may get you to read novels or poems as background to history or sociology. Or possibly you discover how pleasant it is to escape from tedious reality into the 'world' of a book.

In the previous chapter, we suggested that studying Literature at A-Level differs from these normal encounters with literature in two ways. The first is that the books you study are not determined by your own taste but by the Examiners and what they consider Good. The second is that you are asked not only to read critically but to write critically too. You will be expected to discuss not only *what* a writer writes, but also *how* that writer writes. In other words, you are being asked to try your hand at literary criticism. As you are probably aware, there are different kinds of literary criticism (which have different sets of rules). There is, for example, the kind of essay you will have to write on your set texts ('Is Hamlet really mad?' and that sort of thing). There are learned books on the works of one particular author. There are those daunting books with titles something like *Concepts of Nature in Eighteenth-Century English Verse*. And then there's the kind of criticism this book is mostly about: the kind that, for convenience, we will call by its traditional name, Practical Criticism. This is the kind of criticism you'll need some skill in when you are asked to write about particular poems or particular pieces of prose.

What is Practical Criticism?

'Practical Criticism' has a no-nonsense, sleeves-rolled-up, hands-on sort of a sound to it; and that's appropriate enough, in a way, because it involves the close, careful scrutiny of individual poems and prose extracts. It's a way of getting to the meanings of a piece of writing by looking at the way it's put together. It's a technique that grew from a book called *Practical Criticism* by a scholar called I. A. Richards, published in 1929. You will not be surprised to learn that the technique has been rethought and revised a good deal since then. Let's begin by summarising the basic principles of Practical Criticism as evolved by Richards and other critics associated with him. Very briefly, they are these:

1 The text (of a poem, especially) is self-contained and self-defining. It is what it is, and it contains its meanings within itself.

2 The text is what we might call 'organic'. That is to say, its various elements (the meanings of individual words, their sounds, their rhythms when grouped together, and so on) relate to and depend on each other. As critical readers, we should be trying to understand the 'internal dynamics' of the piece and the way these various elements work together.

3 The way to an understanding, an appreciation, of a work of literature is through a close reading, or scrutiny, of its language.

These principles are a bit hard to grasp at first, but never mind. The ideas that lie behind them, though, are rather important, and you should give them some thought. In the same order, they are:

1 The historical, social and political influences upon a work of literature are largely irrelevant. So are the details of the writer's life. Accordingly, if we are reading a poem by Shakespeare, it doesn't matter a hoot when and where he was when he wrote it, or what his political views were, or who he was married to. In fact, it wouldn't make any difference – to the poem – if 'Shakespeare' was someone else altogether. What matters is what is there, in the poem.

2 A good reader is an analytical reader. If a reader is to appreciate how the different elements of a piece of writing interact (and this applies especially to poetry) then that reader has to be able to separate these elements out. Equally

importantly, that reader must be able to put them back together again, because that's how you arrive at a 'reading' of the poem as a whole.

3 Whatever else a written work may be, it is primarily a linguistic structure. It is an organisation of words.

Principle number 1 and Idea number 1 are no longer widely accepted, and there's no need for you to accept them either. What they suggest, after all, is that something called 'literature' exists independently of the people who create it. They suggest that the personality of the writer, and the society in which that writer lives or lived, are unimportant when we read and think about what he or she wrote. The implication is that literature exists at some sort of 'pure' level, detached from history, politics, sex, money and all the other messy things that surround any writer's life. Theoretically, according to this view of literature, it is largely irrelevant whether the writer of a poem or novel is a man or a woman. This is not a view that is taken very seriously nowadays. It is fairly obvious that, for all its uniqueness, any literary work must be related in some way to its social and historical context; and this means that this context must be relevant to its meaning. It is also fairly obvious that any poem or novel or whatever is, in a loose sense, autobiographical, because writers write from their own experience and view of the world. This means that the events and circumstances of the writer's life may well be important when it comes to trying to understand his or her work. However, the idea of the 'self-contained text' is useful in one respect: it warns us against the temptation of trying to 'explain' a writer's work in simple biographical terms. In other words, while it is, of course, likely that a writer's life-experiences influence the way that person writes, we shouldn't assume that these experiences are a 'key' to anything. It would be silly to think that a poem about loneliness, let's say, can be easily understood if we know that the poet's mother ran off with a soldier when the poet was nine years old. In practice this means that if you do dig into a writer's life and times, and you come up with something you think illuminates one of that writer's poems, you will be expected to argue your case quite carefully.

We're left with the remaining two principles of Practical Criticism and their implications. These are more important to you because they still apply; examiners will expect you to understand and respect these ideas, especially when you are writing about individual poems or pieces of prose. We'll take them one at a time.

To say that a poem is 'organic' is to say that it resembles an organism (a living thing) more than it resembles a machine. You can take the fan belt off a car engine and what you have left is still recognisably a car engine. If you chop out a line or a stanza of a poem (or abridge or censor a novel) you change it radically. This is because poems (especially, but it's true of prose works as well) are highly *integrated*; their component parts are interdependent. To give a very crude example, you could replace a word in a line of poetry with another word or phrase which means much the same thing, and the sense of that line would remain the same. But the effect on another element of the poem might be quite drastic. If instead of

The curfew tolls the knell of parting day

you wrote

The curfew tolls the knell at the end of the day

you wouldn't change the meaning but you would destroy the *rhythm* of the line.

Practical Criticism demands that you be abnormally aware of the way that these different elements of a piece of writing interrelate. It requires a close attention to detail. You have to accept from the outset that it is a specialised sort of a task which requires specialist skills.

Now for the third of these Principles and Ideas: that understanding a piece of writing depends upon a close and careful scrutiny of its language, because all literary works are, first and foremost, words on a page. This may seem ridiculously obvious, yet many students are reluctant to accept it. One reason for this (and here you have to imagine the authors of this book smugly stroking their long grey beards) is that students are still young enough to be in a hurry. They – you – are impatient to get 'through' the language in order to get at 'Meanings', to get at 'Ideas', 'Interpretations', 'Insights into Life' and whatever. (This is the 'message-hunting' approach to literature, about which more later.) The destination, they feel, is more important than the journey. It isn't. There may not be a destination. Another reason is that grappling with language is hard work; strangely enough, it is much easier to ramble on about the philosophical or political implications of a poem than it is to struggle to see how the poet put the thing together. Another problem is that we can only describe what language does by using language. This means that in order to discuss how someone else uses language, you have to develop a pretty sophisticated language of your own – and that too is hard work.

Is there such a thing as 'literary language'?

There was a time when there was such a thing as 'poetic language'. It was full of musical sound-effects, the lines always rhymed, it was heavily figurative (it contained lots of metaphors and similes), there would be capital letters at the beginning of every line (and liberally scattered about elsewhere, too), and its subject would be some noble or tragic feeling. Something like this, in fact:

> It was a dismal and fearful night:
> Scarce could the Morn drive on th'unwilling Light,
> When Sleep, Death's image, left my troubled breast
> By something liker Death possest.

We can no longer expect literary language to announce itself so loudly or signal to us so energetically. Certainly in much modern writing the distinction between 'literary' and 'ordinary' language is very blurred. We think it would be best to abandon the idea of a special literary language, a language peculiar to imaginative writing. It will be much more useful for you to have a few flexible techniques for getting at what writers do with language. Here are four ideas for you to consider:

1 In literature, language tends to draw attention to itself:

> Even on Central Avenue, not the quietest-dressed street in the world,
> he looked about as inconspicuous as a tarantula on a slice of angel food.

Raymond Chandler: Farewell My Lovely

In other words, he was loudly dressed. In the novel from which this is taken, it is preceded by ninety words describing this character's outfit, so we know that already. But the phrase 'as a tarantula on a slice of angel food' isn't there to convey information. It jumps off the page at you. (Critics sometimes use the word 'foregrounding' to describe this technique.) It shocks, and it grabs your attention (which may have been wandering). Like the man's clothes, it is 'loud': the extremely different associations of 'tarantula' and 'angel' collide with a bang. And perhaps you stop for a moment while across your mind scuttles the thought of what it would be like to be served a dessert with a huge hairy spider sitting on it. The phrase also contains suggestions about this character which might become relevant as the story progresses: poisonous, dangerous, out of place.

2 Language is sometimes transparent, sometimes opaque.

A Slice an onion and fry it in a little oil until lightly browned.

B An odour of frying wafts at the opening of the page, of onion in fact, of onion being fried, a bit scorched, because in the onion there are veins that turn violet and then brown, and especially the edge, the margin, of **each little sliver of onion becomes black before golden, it is the juice of** the onion that is carbonised, passing through a series of olfactory and chromatic nuances, all enveloped in the smell of simmering oil.

Italo Calvino: If On A Winter's Night A Traveller ...

The purpose of transparent language is to convey information or instruction. Reading sentence A in a cookery book, there would be no point dwelling on its language. You look 'through' the language, so to speak, at the things – onion and oil – and what you are supposed to do with them. In that sort of situation, language that drew attention to itself would simply get in the way, would hold you up, and dinner would never get cooked.

While still on the subject of onions, sentence B could hardly be more different. Here it is the language itself which is noticeable. We look (at first, anyway) *at* it rather than through it; it is much more opaque. The language in this sentence draws attention to itself by being so very busy. We'll not go on at length about it, but you should perhaps notice a few things. First of all, there is the way the sentence moves, the way it hurries along from comma to comma not quite able to stop. Then there is the insistent repetition of the word 'onion', and the way the writer seems so eager to make everything very precise. If one word doesn't do the job well enough, he helps it along with another: 'onion being fried, a bit scorched' and 'the edge, the margin'. There are strong contrasts in the 'feel' of different words and phrases: compare the bluntness of 'a bit scorched' with the elaborate phrase 'a series of olfactory and chromatic nuances' (which means 'shades of smell and colour'). This sentence is playing a game, sharing a joke with the reader: this description of onions being fried is, the writer pretends, so concrete and realistic that smell actually 'wafts' off the page. (And the fact that it doesn't, really, is his way of pointing out that words on a page remain only words on a page no matter how hard we work them.)

3 The meaning of words depends on and changes with the words' context.

At a simple level, this is obvious. Many English words are capable of a number of different meanings. It is only in conjunction with other words that they achieve a particular meaning:

bar
colour bar
bar one
gold bar
bar sinister
wine bar

You can probably think of hundreds more examples. You might like to see how many variations you can make on the meanings of *post, fire, house, water*.

Here is an example of how meaning can be modulated by context in a more subtle way. The following short extract describes how the first warnings of the Indian Mutiny reach an outpost of the British Empire.

> The first sign of trouble at Krishnapur came with a mysterious distribution of chapatis, made of coarse flour and about the size and thickness of a biscuit; towards the end of February 1857 they swept the countryside like an epidemic ...
>
> The Collector was busy at that time. In addition to his official duties, which had become swollen and complicated by the illness of the Joint Magistrate, he had a number of domestic matters on his mind; his wife, too, had been in poor health for the past few months and must now be sent home before the hot weather.
>
> *J. G. Farrell: The Siege of Krishnapur*

The words 'swollen and complicated' can be taken at face value as meaning that the Collector's work-load had increased and become more difficult. ('Collector' here means Chief Administrator, by the way.) But the phrase occurs in a passage which also contains the words 'epidemic', 'illness' and 'poor health', and it takes on an extra shade of meaning. To overstate it a little, there's the suggestion that the Collector's duties have been infected by disease. In this way, the phrase contributes to the picture being built up of a colonial society that is 'sick' – perhaps in more ways than one.

4 Language can be used as a code.

A code is 'a language familiar to both writer and reader (or speaker and listener)'. This does not mean simply English or Arabic, say, as those languages would be understood by the people that happen to speak them. It also means the way that language is used by members of the same group, or class, or profession, for example, when addressing each other. Codes of this sort imply shared interests, experiences or values. Judges and barristers have a language code (which the rest of us are not meant to understand). So do Rastafarians. And Freemasons. It is possible that your family uses a code which outsiders would not fully understand. The language code of *The Sun* is obviously different from the language code of *The Guardian*. As an A-Level student, you will be expected to understand the language code of teachers and examiners (and the authors of textbooks).

In literature, certain words or phrases or grammatical forms may contain meanings that are different from, or more than, their literal meanings. They can conjure up ideas or associations in the minds of readers who 'know what they mean'. With this in mind, look at the following four sentences, and before we say anything about them, spend a minute or two thinking about what they convey to you:

A She had blue eyes and blonde hair.

B She was a blue-eyed blonde.

C Blue-eyed, blonde-haired Michelle Williams, 24, told the Court that on the night in question she had stayed at home doing the *Times* crossword.

D Azure were her eyes, golden her hair.

Sentence A is seemingly 'transparent'. It appears to refer neutrally to objective facts about a person's appearance. But it also operates as a code, because blue eyes and blonde hair is one of the clichés, or stereotypes, of female attractiveness. It is an image, or 'trigger', that men are conditioned to respond to. The sentence is thus capable of the hidden meaning 'she was sexually attractive'. In this particular sentence, however, the 'coded message' is optional, because the way that the sentence is constructed does not exclude the possibility that she had other things as well – a degree in Political Science, or a wet nappy, or whatever. In other words, she is not completely trapped within the sentence.

Now try these questions:

1 The structure of sentence B is only slightly different to that of sentence A. What effect does this slight change have on the code that it carries?

2 Where would you expect to find sentence C? How do you respond to the statement it makes? Do you take this sentence to be 'neutral' or 'objective' reportage? Do you think that its writer intended you to take it as neutral, objective reportage?

On the face of it, sentence D does not seem to belong with the others. Simply 'translated', it means the same as sentence A, but you probably recognised straight away that it is meant to be 'poetic'. It clearly signals its poetic intentions with certain linguistic devices, which are inverted syntax ('were her eyes' instead of 'her eyes were'); the omission of 'was' between 'golden' and 'her': the use of the more melodious 'azure' rather than plain 'blue'; putting a sort of rhythm into the line (two emphases, or 'beats' before the comma, on 'azure' and 'eyes', and two after the comma, on 'gold' and 'hair'). Also, 'azure' is a much more opaque or attention-seeking word than 'blue'. As well as being another name for the colour, it is also another name for the precious stone lapis lazuli; it also means, the dictionary tells us, 'the clear blue of the unclouded sky' and 'the unclouded vault of heaven'. The associations of gold are obvious. Clearly, then, the writer of sentence D is manipulating language a great deal. You could say that he is 'interfering' with the 'plain' language of sentence A. Why is he? Well, what this writer is trying to do – rather desperately – is block or 'intercept' the coded messages we get from sentences A and B. He doesn't want the vulgar interpretation 'she was sexually attractive' put on his words. Instead, he is trying to convey a message something like 'she was rare, heavenly, a treasure'. Unfortunately for him, however, he has merely replaced a sexual cliché with a poetic one; he has tried to refresh a tired old descriptive cliché – and failed.

Now let's try applying those four ideas – language drawing attention to itself, transparency/opacity, meaning changing with context, and code – to a poem.

You may remember those simple Reading Scheme books for very young children. They starred a rosy-cheeked middle-class brother and sister called Janet and John (or Peter and Jane). They had a large yellow dog of some sort. The language of these books was, naturally, elementary and repetitious: 'Here is Janet. Here is John. Here is the dog', and so on. A language so 'plain' and 'transparent' it seems completely devoid of poetic possibilities. Here is what Wendy Cope does with it:

Reading Scheme

Here is Peter. Here is Jane. They like fun.
Jane has a big doll. Peter has a ball.
Look, Jane, look! Look at the dog! See him run!

Here is Mummy. She has baked a bun.
Here is the milkman. He has come to call.
Here is Peter. Here is Jane. They like fun.

Go Peter! Go Jane! Come, milkman come!
The milkman likes Mummy. She likes them all.
Look, Jane, look! Look at the dog! See him run!

Here are the curtains. They shut out the sun.
Let us peep! On tiptoe Jane! You are small!
Here is Peter. Here is Jane. They like fun.

I hear a car Jane. The milkman looks glum.
Here is Daddy in his car. Daddy is tall.
Look, Jane, look! Look at the dog! See him run!

Daddy looks very cross. Has he a gun?
Up milkman! Up milkman! Over the wall!
Here is Peter. Here is Jane. They like fun.
Look, Jane, look! Look at the dog! See him run!

Wendy Cope

It's fairly obvious that Wendy Cope is making comedy here by shuffling together two very incongruous clichés: the easy-to-read style of the children's book and the corny old joke about Mummy doing Something Naughty with the milkman and being caught at it by Daddy. Try answering the following questions about the poem:

1 What is your first reaction to the opening lines, finding them in an adult poem in this book rather than in an 'Early Reader'?

2 What do you notice about the rhymes in the poem?

3　What do you notice about the use of repetition?

4　At what point in the poem do you begin to suspect that something odd is going on?

5　Who speaks line 7?

6　Who might 'them all' in line 8 refer to?

7　Does the word 'fun' have the same meaning at the end of the poem as it did at the beginning?

Here are the answers. (If you haven't tried working them out for yourself yet, don't read them!)

1　Quite simply, you ought to be surprised. You ought to do a 'double-take'.

2　There are only two: words that rhyme with 'fun' and those that rhyme with 'ball'.

3　There's a lot of it, and it is arranged in a formal pattern. The lines that begin with 'Here is Peter' and 'Look, Jane' alternately end each 'verse' and form a final couplet.

4　At lines 7 and 8.

5　Mummy. She's telling Peter and Jane to get lost, and inviting the milkman in.

6　'Them all' might mean Peter, Jane, the dog and the milkman; or all milkmen; or all the men who come calling (if you've got a suspicious mind).

7　No. At the end of the poem, 'fun' has come to include what Mummy does with the milkman, and also the spectacle of seeing Daddy, armed with a gun, chasing an adulterous milkman over the garden wall. Not the same thing at all.

Now let's try and make some connections between these answers and the ideas about language that we put to you earlier.

One way that language – or anything else, for that matter – can draw attention to itself is by being out of context (like that tarantula). In its 'proper place' – in a Reading Scheme book – the sentence 'Here is Peter' carries very little meaning. Its only function is to point to a picture of Peter. As language, it is 'transparent'. But when this sentence appears in a collection of poems for grown-ups (and without a picture of Peter) we do not simply look through it. We look at it. We suspect that it has something other than its normal significance.

The first lines of this poem operate as a kind of code. The primitive sentences 'Here is Peter. Here is Jane. They like fun' conjure up, or evoke, the world depicted in those early Reading Scheme books. It is a world in which healthy, improbably well-behaved, fair-haired children frolic about with their bouncy golden retriever in a sunlit, peaceful suburban garden while Mummy is in the kitchen and Daddy is at the office. A world, in short, of security, respectability, niceness, and – above all – innocence. (Needless to say, if you never read those books as a child you won't 'get' all this. But then, as we said earlier, that is characteristic of codes; you have to be a member of a group 'in the know' to get the message.)

The simple rhyme-scheme and the insistent repetition mimic the language of the Reading Scheme book. Before long, we realise that this is a **parody**. This should 'click' with you when you begin to think that Mummy's relationship with the milkman is not quite what it should be.

In the context of the poem, the meaning of the innocent word 'fun' is undermined. It becomes much more ambiguous and loses its association with 'harmless'.

If we add all this up, we can get to a 'reading' of the poem. What Wendy Cope does is set up the idealised, fanciful world of the Reading Scheme books and then subvert it by introducing the sordid adult activities of infidelity, jealousy and violence. She does this, presumably, because she believes that world and its 'innocence' to be phoney, dishonest. This may be taking a jokey poem too seriously for your taste. Perhaps it is. One last observation, then: this poem is a story of sexual misbehaviour told in the simple, naïve language of children. The language is inappropriate to its subject. Put another way, there is a deliberate discrepancy, or conflict, between subject and language. This is a form of irony – but we'll come to that later. In the meantime, try writing just a few sentences on the strange things writers are doing with language in each of these brief extracts:

A Compare   'She was not very upset by the death of her husband'
      with   'Her hair has turned quite gold with grief'.

B Tell me, O Octopus, I begs,
       Is those things arms, or is they legs?
       I marvel at thee, Octopus;
       If I were thou, I'd call me Us.

Ogden Nash: The Octopus

C When as in silks my Julia goes,
       Then, then (methinks) how sweetly flows
       That liquifaction of her clothes.

Robert Herrick: Upon Julia's Clothes

D He snorted and hit me in the solar plexus.
       I bent over and took hold of the room with both hands and spun it.
       When I had it nicely spinning I gave it a full swing and hit myself on
       the back of my head with the floor. This made me lose my balance
       temporarily and while I was thinking about how to regain it a wet
       towel began to slap at my face and I opened my eyes. The face of
       Henry Eichelberger was close to mine and bore a certain appearance
       of solicitude.

Raymond Chandler: Pearls Are A Nuisance

E One humid afternoon a visitor did arrive to disturb Rottcodd as he
       lay deeply hammocked, for his siesta was broken sharply by a
       rattling of the door handle which was apparently performed in lieu of
       the more popular practice of knocking at the panels. The sound
       echoed down the long room and then settled into the fine dust on the
       boarded floor. The sunlight squeezed itself between the thin cracks of
       the window blind.

Mervyn Peake: Titus Groan

3
Who's Who and What's What

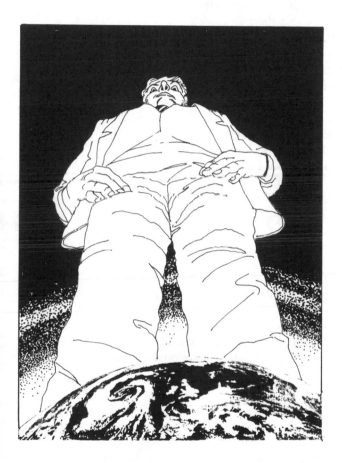

In the first chapter of this book, as you may recall, two students discussed something called The Unseen – the exercise that involves writing about poems or prose passages which you have not seen before. For some, this can be an examination ordeal; for others a more leisurely piece of coursework. This chapter is about this kind of exercise. We'll have a look at different responses to the same poem, and we will try to offer some advice about dealing with the problems and the pitfalls that you are almost certain to come across.

The most important thing to remember is that the kind of critical writing being asked of you is a specific sort of writing, and it requires what we might call a 'house style' which has a bit of polish to it. And, of course, you are expected to show that you have bucketsful of perception and imagination. One problem, particularly for those who have not taken GCSE in English Literature, is that you may well have been taught to write about poetry in a variety of ways which are not very appropriate for A or AS Level work. The easiest way to make this clear is to dive straight in and read a poem by W. H. Auden called *Who's Who*:

Who's Who

A shilling life will give you all the facts:
How Father beat him, how he ran away,
What were the struggles of his youth, what acts
Made him the greatest figure of his day:
Of how he fought, fished, hunted, worked all night,
Though giddy, climbed new mountains, named a sea:
Some of the last researchers even write
Love made him weep his pints like you and me.

With all his honours on, he sighed for one
Who, say astonished critics, lived at home;
Did little jobs about the house with skill
And nothing else; could whistle; would sit still
Or potter round the garden; answered some
Of his long marvellous letters but kept none.

W. H. Auden

(Note: a 'shilling life' is a cheap, brief biography.)

Congratulations if you recognised that this is a sonnet (i.e. a poem of fourteen lines with a systematic rhyme-scheme). Before you read on, you should make a few notes of your own on the poem.

What follows is a series of four very different responses to this poem, which we will call A, B, C and D. When you have read each one, and before you read what we have to say about each one, we would like you to ask yourself the following questions:

1 Did reading that help me understand Auden's poem?

2 Was that easy to read or was it confusing?

3 Do I agree with it or not?

You might also like to play examiner and award grades to each one. Here's the first:

A I like this poem because it reminds us that famous people are often mythologised, but we don't know anything about them really. I can imagine this famous man climbing mountains and having his photograph in all the papers. He seems a very determined person. The poem says that he 'works all night' and, although he suffers from vertigo (he's 'giddy') he is still determined to conquer mountains because they're 'new'. He's obviously a famous explorer, and these mountains and seas are somewhere far away and remote, like Africa or South America. There is something fantastic and impressive about having a whole sea named after you. He's so famous, in fact, that that researchers have written books about him and there are biographies and even a paperback shilling life.

What's odd about him though is his wife, who isn't famous at all but who does 'little jobs' about the house and 'potters' in her garden, and doesn't realise how important her husband is. I can see her cheerfully whistling away while she sows seeds in the garden and puts up shelves. She's middle-aged and quite independent, and not at all interested in fame and glory like her husband. She probably spends a lot of time dusting all his books and the photographs which show him on top of the Himalayas or shaking hands with other famous people. Perhaps she grumbles as she polishes all his cups and trophies lined up on the shelves of his study, angrily glinting at her while he's away. She's quite happy leading an ordinary life, like most of us. Perhaps the poem is saying that she's a better person than her husband. She certainly doesn't have to prove herself like he does (in the first part of the poem) and she seems fairly indifferent towards him. She doesn't keep any of his letters, and I suspect that this is because she doesn't really love him any more. He's really a stranger to her because he's never there. What's interesting about this poem though is that it implies that he needs her. She reminds him of home and security, things he secretly needs when he's off exploring remote regions of the world. The poem's message is probably something like that — we all need love and security, even though we often pretend that we don't, or worse, have to pretend that we don't.

Try asking those questions about this piece. And then: what do you think it is trying to achieve? What do you think the writer of it wanted it to do? (You might look carefully at those phrases 'I can see her ... ' and 'I can imagine ... ') The second paragraph is different in character from the first. How?

We'll come back to response A in a moment. Here's something completely different. It contains a good deal that you will probably not understand (unless you are already an Auden fan), but don't let that worry you. We're concerned here with the kind of response it is, not its precise meaning.

B This sonnet (from 'Look Stranger', 1936) contains many of the standard themes and obsessions that we have met before in Auden poems from this period. In the same year that 'Look Stranger' was published, Auden had collaborated with Christopher Isherwood in the writing of the fascinatingly eccentric 'Ascent of F6', which has a mountaineer, Michael Ransome, as its protagonist. (Ransome is persuaded by his mother to save the declining reputation of England by climbing a remote Himalayan peak — the F6 of the title. He does so, after conversations with various Tibetan Holy Men on the way, only to die after meeting the mountain's 'demon', which turns out to be a disturbing and peculiarly Freudian vision of his own mother crooning a lullaby. Auden's attitude towards his protagonist seems strangely ambivalent.) Ransome, like the airmen of other Auden poems, is an idealised Byronic figure, an individual who escapes from the petty struggles for power of those who live at lower altitudes, and yet a fool who lacks any powers of analysis or knowledge of the self.

Similar preoccupations are evident in the octet of this sonnet. The heroic figure climbs 'new mountains', names a sea, is an obsessive worker and becomes the 'greatest figure of his day'. The familiar obsessions with heroics and Freudian analysis are also evident. What spurs the hero to achieve is clearly the beatings by his archetypal Father and the miseries of his adolescence. (This examination of the driving force behind the man is implied rather than stated.) The central point of the poem is that the famous man is one whose fame derives from his acts and not from his thoughts, and these acts are more like responses which are conditioned and involuntary. The famous man is a victim of life, and not at all a man in charge of his own destiny.

It is, of course, the sestet that measures these heroics against the ordinary lives of 'you and me'. The hero's lover lives a life of domestic contentment and mundane routine, achieves only 'little jobs', can 'whistle', and 'potter' and, perhaps most importantly of all, can 'sit still'. This portrait of quiet ease and self-confidence not only calls heroics into question, but also suggests that only those who suffer from some kind of inner turmoil are likely to achieve recognition in life.

The sonnet has all the verbal dexterity and poetic skill that one expects to find in an early Auden poem; many of his poems of this time are full of direct oratorical address and colloquial directness: the 'shilling life gives you all the facts', the hero cries 'like you and me'. Nevertheless this sonnet is quieter in tone than much of the other work of the period; it is neither publicly strident, nor mysteriously prophetic. In this respect it points more towards many of the post-war poems that focus on the sorrows and joys of a more private and enclosed life.

Don't concern yourself (not yet, anyway) with 'Freudian visions' and 'archetypes' and the like. You have just read one fairly typical example of Advanced Critspeak, and you need not bother yourself about not understanding all of it. Ask yourself those basic questions about it: was it helpful, was it confusing, do you agree? And then ask yourself these questions: where would you expect to find an extract like this? Is it a critical appreciation of the poem? If it isn't, what is it?

Let's pause at this point and re-examine these first two pieces in more detail. Whatever else is clear or cloudy in your mind, you should have seen that they are very different kinds of response to the same poem. The reason for their being so different has to do not so much with the different abilities of the writers, as with the different purposes for which they were written.

Response A is an interesting and quite lively piece of writing which sets out to be creative and imaginative rather than analytical in any way. It is a *reaction* to the poem, not a *discussion* of it. The writer thinks that the instruction 'Write about this poem' really means 'Write a short story of your own using this poem as a starting-point.' Consequently, he has felt quite free to add large amounts of 'extra information' for which there is no evidence at all in the poem. The fleshing out of the 'wife' who spends her time dusting her husband's trophies is the most blatant example of this inventive spinning-off from the text itself. As a piece of creative writing, it's quite good, in fact: the writer can empathise in an imaginative way with his fictional character, notably in his vision of the trophies 'glinting angrily'. His last sentence is interesting, too, although its relevance to the poem is remote: 'We all need love and security, even though we often pretend that we don't, or worse, have to pretend that we don't.' In short, this is a piece of work which might well get a reasonable mark as a GCSE English essay responding to a question which invited a flight of fancy. There is no doubt in the candidate's mind as to what he is up to – look at the way he says 'I can imagine ... ' But Response A is not an A-Level piece of work. Your teachers and examiners are looking for creativity, yes – but a different kind of creativity, a kind that is more analytical and more firmly anchored in the text itself.

Now for Response B. Let's begin with the questions we posed at the end of it. You might expect to find this passage in a textbook or a very long essay on the poetry of W. H. Auden. The very first sentence tells us that this is an extract from a longer work ('This sonnet ... contains many of the standard themes and obsessions that we have met before ... ') Reading it, we learn that the sonnet *Who's Who* can usefully be seen in conjunction with other work written by the poet during the same period and also later in his life. Apart from one or two remarks, though, it is short on specific textual detail. It is, obviously, a professional job, bursting at the seams with knowledge and information. The writer's purpose, however, is less immediately obvious than the purpose behind Response A. What this critic wants to do is *contextualise* the poem, to show us how this sonnet fits with other work that is 'Audenesque' in similar ways: it has themes also found in a play of his, it makes references to psychoanalysis, it depicts heroism in an ambiguous way, and so forth. *But* fascinating though this may or may not be, this passage is performing a specific and scholarly task in which a detailed examination of one particular poem is not of great importance. Clever as it may be, this is no more an acceptable A-Level essay on *Who's Who* than Response A is. An examiner who got this from a candidate would be fairly flabbergasted; but, going strictly by the rules of the game, he probably couldn't award it a very good mark.

If Responses A and B are, in their very different ways, inappropriate as pieces of **A-Level work**, what *are* you expected to produce? We'll approach this question in a back-to-front way, in the belief that the best way to learn is from your mistakes. Or, better still, from someone else's. The student who wrote this next piece had only recently started his AS course and was still in a state of bewilderment. His effort is wonderfully disorganised and anarchic. You can almost hear the sighs of pain as he desperately tries to make a start.

C This poem is by W. H. Auden who was one of the writers in the 1930s interested in politics and the rise of Fascism in Europe. It is a very moving poem because it points out that ordinary people are more important than political leaders, which is very true. The poem is about a fascist dictator who had a hard life when young, and this has made him bitter. He has 'struggled' and 'fought' and 'worked all night' in order to reach the top. The poet says that he was 'the greatest figure of his day', which is only true if you accept that politicians are 'great figures'.

The second section of the poem is about his wife. Critics of the dictator are astonished that he could love someone like her because she lives at home and doesn't support her husband politically. The poet is surprised that she didn't answer some of his letters. It is not clear to me why these letters are 'marvellous'.

The poet depicts the wife more clearly than her husband. She works all day cooking and keeping the house clean and seems very happy, because she whistles. She is very patient, because she can sit still and read, unlike her husband who is always off climbing mountains and giving his names to seas, like Stalin did. She 'potters' around her garden, which means that she is rather bored, perhaps, or certainly doesn't achieve very much. She probably has a large garden to look after, though, which is why she spends a lot of time looking after it, or, more likely organizing a team of gardeners to do it. The poet implies that they do all the real work while she only 'potters'

The poet seems to admire the dictator at times. Even though he can 'weep his pints' and 'sigh' and has had a hard life as a child, this is no excuse. You cannot forgive dictators just because they had unhappy childhoods. Dictators always think they know what is right, but Democracy is better because mistakes come out into the open and get corrected.

I like this poem because it is wonderfully descriptive about these two different people. When I first read it, I found it off-putting and difficult, but when I read it again it made more sense, especially the contrast between the two people. There are still a few things I don't understand. Why does Auden write that the researchers 'even write' that he cried? Why are the critics astonished? Maybe Auden is trying to make the reader think that dictators are not just hard unfeeling people who are not supposed to show their feelings. Dictators have to wear masks. They have to if people are to follow them. Perhaps that's why this one keeps his wife hidden away in the country somewhere.

'Though giddy, climbed new mountains, named a sea.'

This is one example of how the poet uses rhythm. It shows the effort required to climb mountains. The poem's rhyme-scheme is ABABCDCD and then ABCCBA, which is like a mirror image.

I really enjoyed this poem. It is like the letters the dictator wrote to his wife — marvellous as well as clever. You hardly notice that the lines rhyme at all.

We hope you enjoyed reading that. It's the kind of essay that makes teachers feel they would be happier being in charge of a school crossing on the M25. What do you think is wrong with it?

One of the problems here – quite apart from all the whacky stuff about dictators – is that it lacks any semblance of organisation. It's not completely hopeless, but it reads like a random collection of thoughts and comments that might, just possibly, have been pruned and polished into a critical essay.

Eight popular heresies

No doubt you were able to see that Response C was pretty awful, but perhaps you find it more difficult to pin down its specific kinds of awfulness. What we could do with is some means of identifying and categorising these mistakes so that they can be pruned out, leaving the good stuff to be polished.

Given that writing about a poem can be a difficult experience, there are several strategies that all of us – students and teachers alike – will adopt to avoid the hard work involved in reading and thinking carefully. (Some of us will expend a huge amount of effort in the attempt to avoid hard work.) The student who wrote Response C has tried nearly all of these strategies and has thus produced at least one example of each of the most common errors made by students. What we have done is make a list of the errors, or 'heresies' that make Response C fairly dreadful. You don't have to agree with or accept all of them, but you'll probably find that most teachers and A-Level examiners have this kind of 'checklist' in their heads when they assess your work.

Heresy One: The Eureka Solution
This can be, and often is, the most disastrous error of all, so we should deal with it

first. The Eureka Solution is the extreme version of the 'code-cracking' approach to poetry which we mentioned in Chapter 1. It is the mistaken idea that a poem has one – and only one – meaning, and that this meaning can suddenly reveal itself like a blaze of light in a dark tunnel. The student who suffers from this hallucination will then ignore all linguistic evidence that doesn't fit his or her 'insight' and mercilessly shove and squeeze the poem into this single 'interpretation'.

The Eureka approach to poems has, we believe, something to do with the mysterious status of Unseens in the A-Level exams and coursework. There is a suspicion among students that sitting Unseens is a form of psychological warfare. For many students, poems are like secret messages, and the faceless Examiners are waiting to see if these poetic messages can be deciphered – by the brightest and best only. This is not so. While there may be some poems which lend themselves to this 'decoding' approach (those which are allegorical, for example), beware: they are very rare. And once you get into this way of thinking, once you set out on this road, there's no getting off or turning back. If you make up your mind, at the start, straight away, that the poem you are reading is about dictators, for example, then the chances are that you will be wrong, that the rest of your essay will be a mess, and that your examination or coursework grade will come somewhere below the last letter of the last word of this sentence.

The antidote for the Eureka syndrome is essentially simple: be careful, be exploratory, don't be dogmatic. Examine a poem's specific linguistic details and allow the meanings it contains to emerge gradually. A very great number of poems – including this one – have layers of meaning, not just one meaning. Poems often present shifting points of view; they may even present different and opposing arguments. This means that writing a good essay about a poem is often a two or three stage drafting process, not a sudden burst of furiously enlightened scribble. Sorry, but there it is. (Chapter 18 of this book is about this 'drafting' process.)

Heresy Two: The Waffle

Quite often this takes the form of providing irrelevant or useless facts to do with the poet's life. Many students like to begin their essays with such stuff and try to pass it off as an 'introduction'. It also serves the useful purpose of saving them the effort of actually reading the poem and thinking about it: 'W. H. Auden was one of the writers in the 1930s interested in politics and the rise of fascism ... ' For the writer of Response C, this smattering of background knowledge proved deadly: it set him off down the bleak road of half-baked and erroneous 'interpretation' from which there was eventually no escape.

Heresy Three: The Gush

This takes the form of making flattering judgements of no real worth and offering no evidence for them, e.g. 'It is a very moving poem ... ' Is it? Why? What exactly are these powerful emotions that were stirred in you, and what did the poet do to bring you to this verge of tears? A nastier version of this particular heresy is the Full Gush. There is an example in C: 'It is like the letters the dictator wrote to his wife – marvellous, as well as clever'. Writing critically is not the same thing as oozing compliments, and your examiners will not be tricked by fulsome praise into thinking that you are a wonderfully sensitive human being: 'This is ever such a magical, extraordinary and perceptive and moving poem. Can I have my grade B now, please?'

Heresy Four: The Running Commentary or Continuous Translation

A great many students begin writing about a poem with the intention of 'talking through it' line by line. This is really a version of the Eureka Heresy, because it assumes that it is necessary to 'translate' a poem into a continuous narrative in plain language: 'She is very patient, because she can sit still and read ... She potters about the garden, which means she's rather bored'. An even more lazy (or desperate) version of this is the blatant stringing together of quotes without any commentary at all: 'He has 'struggled' and 'fought', 'worked all night', in order to reach the top'.

Poetry tends to suggest, to invoke, to play with words and their meanings. There can be several valid interpretations, or readings, of a poem, even though there may be one which you personally favour. If you plod along with your running commentary you are likely to miss the way that one line is 'set off' against another, or the way that meanings are changed by their contexts. There may also be patterns of imagery and cross-references within the poem. Using the Running Commentary route, you will see the trees, but you'll fail to notice the wood.

Heresy Five: The Flight of Fancy

The purest version of this is to be found in Response A – remember the wife dusting her husband's trophies? This heresy involves the production of extra 'creative' material which may well be an imaginative response to the poem but which is completely irrelevant to and unsupported by what is actually there. But at least the writer of Response A genuinely believes in what *she* is doing, whereas the writer of C is going in for a bit of 'padding' because he doesn't have much else: 'She works all day keeping the house clean ... she spends a lot of time organising a team of gardeners.'

Heresy Six: Getting on the Soapbox

This afflicts the kind of student who has only to see the word 'whale' in a poem before he sets off at a gallop on the subject of ecology, or seeing the word 'black' preaches a sermon on racism. This heresy usually stems from one or both of two delusions, which are 1) that the poet has particular political and social views and writes poetry in order to express them, and that any political and social views contained in that poet's work must inevitably be that poet's own; 2) that teachers and examiners are eager to see what effect the poet's views have upon a student and are keen to read the student's more perceptive and profound comments on, say, dictatorship. Point 1 is only sometimes true; 2 never is.

One can have a good deal of sympathy with the soapbox heretic. His convictions are often deeply held and he often has a strong need to convert others. Writer C is undoubtedly sincere when he says that 'Dictators always think they know what is right. Democracy is better because mistakes come out into the open and get corrected.' This is an interesting (and highly debatable) comment which is well worth discussing. Unfortunately, it has nothing whatever to do with *Who's Who* by W. H. Auden. An extreme version of this tendency is the Autobiographical Socio-Political Reminiscence: 'I once had an auntie Doreen who was a dictator.'

Heresy Seven: The Interior Monologue or Ramble

An A- or AS-Level essay should be a finished product, not a record of what happened to flit across your mind while you were reading a poem. The person who looks at your work is going to expect something fairly professional, with a bit of shine to it, not a chatty letter to your pen-pal: 'It's not clear to me why these letters are 'marvellous', 'When I first read it I found it difficult and off-putting, but when I read it again I saw that it made more sense ... ' What is the point of this? Is an examiner meant to be impressed that this writer read the poem twice? It's also advisable to avoid the cheap device of the rhetorical question: 'Why are the critics astonished?' In short, avoid chatty language and take some pride in your work.

The Eighth and Last Heresy: Muddle

Lack of organisation is perhaps the commonest failing in A-Level essays on poetry. It is a compound of elements of all the other heresies and is perhaps the hardest to avoid. Most of us, when we start to write appreciations, stagger desperately from one isolated point to another like someone urgently seeking signposts in the fog. There is no single item of advice that can prevent this happening. For many students it is a long time before they begin to see what kind of approach, planning, and execution are necessary to produce something good. If it takes you a long time, don't panic. There are, of course, a few things you can do. For instance, you could (and should) make fairly detailed preliminary notes before you start – either as 'marginalia' around the poem itself or on a separate piece of paper. You might even grit your teeth and write out a complete first draft of your essay and then revise and re-order it. (More about this in Chapter 18.) Remember that you are writing something that another human being will have to read (and like you that person may well be working against the clock). If your work is incoherent and disorganised and doesn't develop, that person is likely to suffer deep feelings of hostility towards you and your essay. Examiners and teachers are under no obligation to get a headache from trying to sort out what you are trying to say. The writer of Response C will provoke such hostile reactions in anyone who reads his essay. There is no coherence in it, no design. Most of the time he doesn't stop to read (really *read*, not just glance at the words) before he writes. He realises that he should make some comments on the form of the poem, but he tacks these on at the end, as if the poem's form was incidental. He displays the same attitude when he assumes that rhyme is a technical nuisance to be overcome whenever possible: 'You hardly notice that the lines rhyme at all.' He employs quotations with a deep reluctance, as if there were a tax on inverted commas, and he hasn't grasped the fact that the function of quotation is to *illustrate*; so he misses the point that quotations are really useful only if they follow, rather than precede, the critical comment being made. (Look at the one-line quotation towards the end of his essay.)

Enough said. There is such a thing as a good bad example, and writer C has kindly provided one. While we have been at pains, more than once, to point out that there is no such thing as a perfect answer, there is such a thing as a very imperfect one, and you might find it useful to recall writer C and our list of heresies when you are asked to attempt a similar exercise.

The Good One

We have arrived, finally, at the point where we ought to offer you something we do consider to be an accomplished, high-grade A-Level poetry appreciation – something with qualities you might aspire to. Response D, which follows, shows confidence, is based squarely on the text, and avoids the eight popular heresies. We are well aware that this kind of thing can be intimidating or (even worse) depressing – especially if you are at any early stage of your course and still feeling your way. In which case, it may reassure you a little to know that we've cheated. Unlike Responses A and C, Response D is not the work of a beginner, and it was not written against the clock. The writer was a gifted Mature Student at the end of her two-year A-Level course, and the essay was entered as one of her pieces of coursework, which means it was not written under exam conditions. This being so, please do not be dismayed by (for example) the fluent way she handles technical terms and critical concepts with which you are unfamiliar (in time, you will be). Don't be distracted by particular words you don't understand: the important thing to notice is the way that ideas are put together.

D The title of this poem seems to me to be both ambiguous and ironic. 'Who's Who' is the title of a reference book which lists all the famous people alive in Great Britain, usually those who are members of the Establishment. The hero of this sonnet would obviously be included. As far as Auden's poem is concerned, though, the title also refers to the obvious point that the facts about a man's public life (his social mask, so to speak) rarely reveal much about the real, inner, private person. In that sense, the title is almost a question: 'Who's Who?' The two 'Who's also suggest, perhaps, that we should choose between the two lives presented to us by the poem.

The ironies of the first line of the sonnet's octet (which is one long sentence) imply that in fact no human being can be explained away so easily as a cheap potted biography (a 'shilling life') pretends it can. We can never possess 'all the facts' about something as hidden and complex as a whole life and the inner drives that created it. 'Facts' are public and 'scientific'; human lives are private and frequently mysterious.

Auden calls this smug confidence of the 'shilling life' into question stylistically: six out of the first eight lines are bluntly end-stopped, and the rhymes are simple, blatant and monosyllabic. The emphasis that the rhyme places upon 'facts' and 'acts' demonstrates that both are crude, external and public: what can be 'known' about a man are only those things that can be observed and recorded by 'researchers'. The telegrammatic, idiotic abbreviations of the potted biography are sent up by the way the lines have a broken, stuttery rhythm, departing from any regular iambic pattern:

How Father beat him, how he ran away,
What were the struggles of his youth, what acts
Made him .... *

Auden seems to imply that this man's fame derives from a furious and almost psychotic need to conquer the world and its creations. This is emphasised by the frantically busy rhythm of the following lines, hurried along by the alliterations:

(*These little ticks and dips are scansion marks, used to indicate stressed and unstressed syllables and thus the rhythm of a line. We'll come back to these later in this book.)

... <u>f</u>ought, <u>f</u>ished, hunted, worked all night,
Though giddy, climbed <u>n</u>ew mountains, <u>n</u>amed a sea ...

Whether or not these 'acts' of hunting and so forth are metaphorical doesn't seem to me to be very important. It is the 'greatness' of the achievements that Auden is stressing. The meaning of the words is probably quite literal.

The idiocy of those who go in for that kind of hero-worship, who can refer to someone as 'the greatest figure of his day' is soon undermined by the irony of the last two lines of the octet. It is only the 'last researchers' (presumably those who are slightly better informed and less awe-struck) who are prepared to admit that this hero could 'weep his pints'. The bathos of this colloquial phrase emphasises that the man was after all only human 'like you and me'. (This being so, I think that the use of 'even' in the previous line – 'Some of the last researchers even write ... ' – is a bit heavy-handed with the irony, perhaps just a bit patronising toward the reader.)

As is to be expected, the sestet of the sonnet (another single sentence) takes a change in direction. Failing to see the absurdity of medals and decorations ('all his honours on') the critics are 'astonished' by the real, ordinary emotions of this public figure, who 'sighed'.

Only one line of the sestet (apart from the last line) is end-stopped. The effect of this enjambment is to stress the continuity of a life very different from that of our hero – a life of contented private and domestic routine. The famous one's lover can perform only 'little' tasks, is one who 'potters' amateurishly (rather than strives feverishly) and answers only 'some' of his letters. Even more 'astonishing', she (or he) can remain wholly inactive ('would sit still') for periods of time – and not engaging in deep contemplation, either. (Whether the domesticated loved one is male or female is of no significance as far as the poem is concerned; but the fact that Auden was homosexual may account for the rather coy absence of any reference to the lover's gender.)

The clipped rhythm and short vowel sounds of

'Did little jobs about the house with skill'

hint at a slight fussiness as well as adroitness in the domestic routine. The slight rhythmic clumsiness of

' ... or potter round the garden'

forms a contrast and hints at a rather casual and aimless life. The most obvious rhythmic contrast, though, is in the last line of the sonnet. We all know that the love letters of the famous dead are either burned or published. This hero's correspondence is clearly now in the public domain; but the gushing tone of the 'long marvellous letters' is cut short (and maybe sent up) by the blunt double stress of 'kept none'.

In the sestet, rhyme is less intrusive, and this has several effects. It reduces the finality of the sonnet (there's no Shakespearian rhyming couplet as a closer) and this seems to make it trail off, remain more open-ended, less final. Also, the private, unrecorded details of this other kind of life – the lover's life – are less forcefully presented to us: this life is a collection of vague everyday generalities, not specific 'acts' and 'facts'. Auden's technical skills are deployed here to emphasise the differences between the two kinds of life.

It seems fairly clear to me that Auden does not expect us to 'choose' between these two kinds of life-style (despite what I said in the first paragraph). His sonnet seems, in the end, to suggest that 'great' men are those who are driven by deep and powerful psychological forces — or simply by anxieties. Yet they are often exciting and admirable beings whom we all admire for their bravery, their dedication and their talent. Most of us would, I suspect, 'weep pints' and 'sigh' if we could have a sea named after us. However, most of us — including myself, I suppose — will 'potter' and 'whistle' and, even if we dream of greatness, live at home and lead ordinary and unremarkable lives. Perhaps this sonnet suggests a common illusion which we all share: that we have a choice between fame and obscurity, when we probably don't, in fact. The poem is perhaps in this sense determinist: our childhoods determine the kinds of life we lead as adults. I'd like to think this isn't true.

I thought the poem's strength lay partly in this kind of ambiguity and puzzling uncertainty. It's probably what we are bound to feel about a poem that compares dramatically two kinds of life. It is a very accessible poem. Its language is direct and colloquial. This may well be because the two characters in the poem are themselves symbolic, and any additional use of metaphor might have obscured their significance.

Apart from the odd moment when the irony seemed a bit heavy-handed and condescending, I thought this was a very accomplished poem, technically very polished and thought-provoking. I enjoyed it.

This essay would brighten the day of any teacher or examiner. It is an analytical essay in that it shows some knowledge of the sonnet form, it is prepared to discuss the poet's use of individual words or phrases, it tackles tricky matters like rhythm and rhyme. What is much more important than any of this is that the writer is able to use this 'technical' stuff to make her points, to bring out, for example, Auden's use of irony. The technical stuff, in other words, is not dealt with as if it were something extra to be shoved on to the end of the essay as an afterthought. What she shows us is that what the poem is about (its content) and how it is written (its form) are not issues that can be separated one from the other and written about in different parts of the essay.

It is a very good piece of work. It's not perfect – there's no way that it could be – but it's both impressive and personal; reading it, one feels that it was written by a human being with her own feelings and opinions. If you wanted to criticise it adversely, you could say that she does seem to assume at times that her job is to discover the 'real philosophy' of Auden by examining the poem. (This is, although in a mild form, a symptom of what professionals call the Intentionalist Fallacy – the assumption that all works of literature are autobiographical, no matter how cunningly disguised.) She also seems to feel obliged to give Auden an end of term report in the concluding paragraph of her essay (which makes it sound just a bit pompous). Nevertheless, it's a good piece of work by an intelligent and perceptive student. What gives it that 'A-Level flavour' is not simply her grasp of a few technical terms (*octet*, *sestet*, *end-stopped*, *enjambment*, and the like); what this student has been encouraged and taught to do (and clearly has some talent for) is to read a poem very carefully – microscopically, you might say. She examines the language of the poem in great detail (for example, she was the only student in her group to comment on the poem's title, even though that might seem a fairly obvious thing to do). She looks closely at individual words to discover their ambiguities and ironies, and maps out the ways in which rhyme and rhythm contribute to what is, for her anyway, the meaning of the poem. She provides plenty of evidence for her ideas, which are expressed clearly but not heavy-handedly or dogmatically. She knows a few facts about the poet (that he was homosexual, for instance) but she does not let this information lead her off up some blind alley. (One dreads to think what the writer of Response C would have said had he known of Auden's sexual inclinations.) In a nutshell, what she does is ask herself questions about the poem like 'Why does the rhythm go all over the place in the first few lines?' and she comes up with good answers. The thing is, of course, that the good answers only come if the right questions are asked. What the good questions are, and where and when to ask them, is what much of this book is about.

4

A Traveller's Guide to Words

One problem that faces all writers working in the English language is the immense range of vocabulary at their disposal. English presents any writer with a huge choice of closely-related words which have different shades of meaning. These semantic differences are often extremely subtle. What writers have to do is find those words which generate the shades of meaning that function correctly and appropriately in a specific piece of writing. That may sound all rather theoretical, but it is actually a very practical matter, as should become clear when we look at some samples of writing in a moment. A major challenge for any writer (including you) is that single words can generate meanings of different 'strengths'. There are relatively few words in the English language whose meaning is as straightforward as, let's say, triangle. 'Triangle' means 'a three-sided figure', and that is all it means: the word and its meaning have a one-to-one relationship. Most words though, fortunately for writers, do not have a single transparent meaning in the way that 'triangle' does. Let's try and clarify this by dipping into a dictionary of synonyms:

> **Travelling:** wayfaring, globe-trotting, touring, journeying, making an odyssey, going on a pilgimage, making an expedition, going on safari, trekking, exploring, visiting, tripping, promenading, gallivanting, roving, rambling, making an excursion, sunseeking.

As far as the dictionary is concerned all the above words and phrases are 'synonymous' with the word 'travelling'; but even a sleepy glance at the list should tell you that they do not really mean the same thing. Here's a simple exercise for you to do. Divide those 'synonyms' for 'travelling' into three lists. List 1 should consist of words which suggest or imply a serious or professional approach to the business of travelling; list 2 should consist of words which suggest a more relaxed or amateurish attitude; in list 3 put words or phrases that seem to be 'neutral' in meaning (or which are difficult to place in the other two categories).

We ended up with four entries in list 1, eleven in list 2 and three in list 3. Compare your lists with other people's and discuss why you put words where you did. There isn't a right or wrong answer to this list-making exercise, although there will almost inevitably be a measure of agreement about what belongs where. Anyone who puts 'gallivanting' into list 1, for example, is either weird or perverse or metaphorically-minded. Most people would not refer to an explorer 'tripping' around the Brazilian forests (or what's left of them), and only if we were being heavily ironic would we speak of 'going on a pilgrimage' to Blackpool (unless we happened to be tower or sticky rock enthusiasts).

Now have another look at your lists and decide which words or phrases you would choose to describe a journey made by

A a bored millionaire to the world's major cities;

B someone who wanted to make real discoveries about places and perhaps about himself or herself;

C a frivolous woman who has no particular destination but is determined to enjoy herself.

We came up with 'globe-trotting', 'making an odyssey' and 'gallivanting' respectively, although there are other words from our lists that might have done the job equally well.

These two very artificial little exercises should at least have begun to reveal to you the sorts of problems and choices faced by writers; we have left the uncontaminated semantics of 'triangle' far behind.

So, individual words and phrases generate different – sometimes quite subtly different – shades of meaning. (What are the differences between 'touring' and 'tripping' and 'making an excursion', for example?) These differences of meaning are often a matter of implication and insinuation rather than definition. For most of us, the word 'rambling', for example, has a 'core', or central meaning – something like 'walking about for pleasure with no great urgency or particular destination'; but at the same time the word evokes a number of 'side meanings', or associations – rucksacks, thick brown socks, big boots with mile-long laces, country lanes, healthy environmentally-conscious folks on high-fibre diets, and so on, not to mention all the connotations of 'rambling' speech or thought. This semantic complexity is one of the things which make English one of the more fertile of all languages. (This is unlikely to console a foreign student grappling with its slippery hordes of near-synonyms.)

Literary critics and linguistic philosophers – and even humble writers – have tried to analyse and classify the mysteries of words and their meanings, with mixed success. The usual view is that most words have a 'core' meaning (which is the 'definition' that dictionaries usually fasten onto, sometimes with a certain degree of desperation); and then, subsequently, a collection of 'side meanings', connotations and 'emotional meanings' – a collection sometimes referred to as a 'sphere of significance'.

While the associations of a particular word will be to some extent subjective and private, the fact is that, to a large extent, they are determined by the sort of social and cultural conditioning which also affects the way you see the world around you and the way you describe and understand it. Such conditioning is not, of course, just a matter of where you live, but also a matter of when you live: words change in significance over time, as well as distance, as any reader of Shakespeare knows. The word 'pilgrimage' no longer has the same powerful and uniquely religious meanings it once possessed, although it has not lost such meanings altogether. Another specific example of conditioned meaning has to do with the word 'war'. The writer of this chapter is an Englishman of early (as I like to see it) middle age who has spent most of his life living in various parts of England during the latter half of the twentieth century. This means that for me the word 'war' has connotations merely of television programmes, distant places, films, books, and perhaps a vague fear of future nuclear obliteration. But for my father, who fought in the Second World War, or for someone of my own age living in Vietnam or Nicaragua, the word has more fiercely immediate associations. And, in fact, for English people alive during most of the previous twenty centuries, 'war' would have signified things that are far more devastating and real than they are for me. That happens to be my good fortune, but perhaps my 'meanings' for the word are very limited and ignorant – because, ultimately, war is something that happens to other people. And the meanings of words are not things you can evade or choose – any more than you can choose being born English or Vietnamese. Such meanings are very much controlled by the society in which we live, and by where it is, and by how it is organised politically and culturally; and by our status within that society. Only among certain groups in certain societies could the phrase 'globe-trotting' have meaning, because its meaning depends upon the possession of some concept of wealth, leisure and freedom. The phrase would earn you some blank looks in Peking or Soweto.

The Englishman abroad

We are all to some extent trapped mentally and perceptually within the societies in which we live. That is why travel writing acts, in a very real sense, as a form of positive escape and mental liberation for those who read it. Travel writing can provide us with a special kind of freedom by allowing us to realise that most of what we regard as normal and natural is, in fact, socially conditioned and artificial. The lovely truth that foreigners do everyday things quite differently is what makes travel writing often so stimulating and thought-provoking. It's this kind of 'cultural relativism' which often makes anybody's first trip across the Channel the most exciting. (For me, it was the telegraph poles. I can remember my astonishment at discovering that the French telegraph pole was a metal skeleton-like thing, rather than a wooden pole. I had always considered the British telegraph pole the 'natural' way of carrying wires. In fact, I thought it was typically extravagant of the French to actually manufacture telegraph poles, when it was clearly more sensible simply to chop a tree down. But I was young then.)

Describing and celebrating different cultural norms is not, of course, the sole purpose of good travel writing. What we hope to get from it is, above all, a powerful, almost physical sense of place and what it's like to be there. And it all has to be done with words. Here's Robert Byron, in Baalbek, Syria, trying to get the right words in the right order to describe something rather more impressive than telegraph poles:

> Baalbek is the triumph of stone; of lapidary magnificence on a scale whose language, being still the language of the eye, dwarfs New York into a home of ants. The stone is peach-coloured, and is marked in ruddy gold as the columns of St Martin-in-the-Fields are marked in soot. It has a marmoreal texture, not transparent, but faintly powdered, like bloom on a plum. Dawn is the time to see it, to look up at the Six Columns, when peach-gold and blue air shine with equal radiance, and even the empty bases that uphold no columns have a living, sun-blest identity against the violet deeps of the firmament. Look up, look up; up this quarried flesh, these thrice-enormous shafts, to the broken capitals and the cornice as big as a house, all floating in the blue. Look over the walls, to the green groves of white-stemmed poplars; and over them to the distant Lebanon, a shimmer of mauve and blue and gold and rose. Look along the mountains to the void: the desert, that stony, empty sea. Drink the high air. Stroke the stone with your own soft hands. Say goodbye to the West if you own it. And then turn, *tourist*, to the East.
>
> We did, when the ruins closed. It was dusk. Ladies and gentlemen in separate parties were picknicking on a grass meadow, beside a stream. Some sat on chairs beside marble fountains, drawing at their hubble-bubbles; others on the grass beneath occasional trees, eating by their own lanterns. The stars came out and the mountain slopes grew black. I felt the peace of Islam.

> *Robert Byron: The Road to Oxiana (1937)*

We hope you enjoy a splash of purple prose now and then. See if you can come up with reasonable answers to the following questions before you read on:

1 What are the feelings that Byron is hoping to arouse in his readers?

2 What do you think are the key words in this passage, the ones that are doing the work of attaining your interest and evoking feelings?

3 Are these key words similar in any way, and if so, are they patterned in some way?

Byron clearly wants his readers to share his enthusiasm for the architectural splendours of the Middle East. He wants you to empathise with his own emotional responses to the ethereal beauties of dawn and dusk in Syria, and he's seeking to achieve that by appealing to your senses of sight and touch. The key words in the passage would seem to be all those colour adjectives: peach, gold, plum, peach-gold, blue, violet, green, white, mauve, blue, gold, rose, black. Byron was an artist as well as a writer, and this fact comes through strongly in his writing. Notice also how, by using those 'fruity' colour words, he makes the architecture almost taste wonderful; and how he gives it a sensual, almost sexual quality when he urges you to 'stroke' the stone's 'quarried flesh'. At the same time, his diction has another, different effect, because words like 'faintly', 'radiance', 'floating', 'shimmer' insinuate something dreamlike and insubstantial. And, of course, like most enthusiasts, he has just a touch of the bully about him, ordering his readers to 'look up' and 'stroke'.

There are two words in the last extract that you probably had to look up: 'lapidary' and 'marmoreal' – and they lead us conveniently into another short digression about words and choice. Because English is a mongrel language, cobbled together from Anglo-Saxon, Greek, Latin, French, Hindi, Gaelic and any number of other tongues, a writer often has the opportunity to choose words which have similar meanings but which have different etymological roots. The main choice for an English writer is between Anglo-Saxon and Latinate words. Anglo-Saxon words tend to be simple, clear and concrete, whereas Latinate words tend to be longer and more abstract. (That's a generalisation, obviously, but compare, for examples, *clot*, *think* and *bright* with *coagulate*, *cogitate* and *luminous*.) Latinate diction frequently gives the impression that the person using it has some kind of learning or scientific expertise or sophistication. (Please note that we are generalising here.) Robert Byron was an expert on architecture and a lover of words – of their sounds, as well as what they mean. By using the words 'lapidary' and 'marmoreal' instead of 'carved' and 'marble' he can signal the intricacy and the delicacy of the stonework that he admires so much ('lapidary' is a word more commonly used to describe the carving on jewellery and precious stones rather than on buildings), and he can get those tasty polysyllables into his writing. (Say 'marmoreal' to yourself quietly, wrap it around your tongue a bit. Feels rather good, doesn't it? Better than plain old 'marble', isn't it?) There are many occasions in his book where Byron has to use bursts of words like 'cupola' and 'Romanesque' and 'buttress' because the language of architecture has its own specific and technical vocabulary. It's not really because he wants to sound impressive – we would think it ridiculous of him to talk about 'props' rather than 'buttresses' just because 'props' is a plainer, Anglo-Saxon word. Like any writer worth his salt, Byron selects words with care and precision in order that they perform the particular tasks he wants them to perform; he doesn't indulge in etymological snobbery. He would not try to impress us with something horrendous like 'Having made my valedictions, I disembarked from my equine conveyance with instantaneous alacrity and permabulated over my circuitous route.' What Byron does is say goodbye, hop off his horse, and wander off down a twisting path.

Latinate vocabulary can make your English sound impressive or knowledgeable, if that's what you want. I might describe my teaching of two students as 'providing an ongoing tutorial-based learning situation.' It might get me promoted to management (where they talk like that), but my students would quite rightly respond by calling me a pompous prat. When you read a piece of prose, you have to decide whether a writer is justified in using elaborate Latinate diction or not.

Beware of condemning a writer whose only crime is to have a vocabulary wider than your own, but don't hesitate to deflate polysyllabically inflated and pretentious nonsense.

Discotheques untouched by time

As an Englishman does not travel to see Englishmen, I retired to my room.

Laurence Sterne: A Sentimental Journey (1768)

Travel books rather worry literary critics because they are so difficult to classify. The best travel books seem almost to make a point of defying definition by leaping over categories; books like Bruce Chatwin's *In Patagonia* or Jonathan Raban's *Coasting* are wonderful mixtures of memoir, romance, essay, guide-book, history, survival manual, novel and much else. It is a point often made, but worth making again here, that the very best travel books are more about 'journeys of the mind' than they are about physical movement. For this among other reasons, travel writing can be a deeply subversive literary genre, because it urges you to abandon the idea that your society and its values are 'normal'. It is a challenge to conformity and obedience because it brings home the fact that the way you have been taught to live, the way you are expected to live, is merely one out of innumerable possibilities. (And travel itself is subversive. That old arch-Conservative, the Duke of Wellington, objected to railways on the grounds that they would 'encourage the working classes to move needlessly about', thus getting ideas above their station – if you'll pardon the expression.) But the vehicle for these journeys of the mind is still words, and if they are to liberate us from conventionalised views of the world, these words must themselves be provocative, original, and stimulating. Like these following words from a travel brochure, would you say?

> The sun-kissed isle of Delphos, embraced by the wine-dark Aegean Sea, is the ideal resort for all generations. Delphos is blessed with many delightful beaches on which you can stretch out in the sun and turn slowly more golden than the sands around you. The quaint and charming little fishing village of Mirkanos (only one hour away from the airport) meets all the demands of its summer visitors and yet still maintains its wholly authentic Greek atmosphere. Its three conveniently placed beaches are speckled in summer with rows of colourful umbrellas and sunbeds. The pretty harbour is still full of genuine working boats manned by friendly fisherman willing to sell you your meal for the evening – providing it's a fishy one!
>
> At night, the ethnic, sea-facing tavernas erupt with colour and gaiety, and they all have outdoor terraces offering stunning sunset views. The local nightlife boasts several delightful international bars and four lively discos where you can really let your hair down.
>
> From the picturesque harbour with its tavernas and nightclubs, the narrow pedestrianised main street leads up to the traditional village square thronged with unusual shops where friendly shopkeepers can offer you genuine souvenirs with a Greek flavour or interesting local specialities. Outside the shops and tavernas of Mirkanos town sit the

local residents surrounded on all sides by brilliant red geranium flowers
that daub colour all over the square.

    If you like, you can visit the pretty mountains in the scenic north of
the island where nature-lovers flock to photograph the stunning carpets
of delicate alpine-like flowers that embrace the lower slopes. You'll also
want to take some postcard views of the cliffs, rocks and dramatic
seabirds whilst you're there. All in all, Delphos is the perfect place
where the weary traveller can pause, relax and learn to enjoy life again.

We've all come across this kind of stuff. Its prefabricated vocabulary slots
together like bits of grey Lego and its jollity and energy are completely fake. It's an
exhausted form of prose because it has been so terribly overworked – it has been
round the Mediterranean a hundred times, desribing somewhere in Greece one
minute, somewhere in Spain the next, and then it has to do the same job in Turkey.
It's a kind of prose that is a direct bastard descendant of real travel writing such as
the Byron piece on Baalbek architecture. It uses watered-down versions of the
same stylistic mannerisms, even down to the gentle vocatives ('You'll also want to
take some postcard views ... '). This piece of prose is striving to achieve the
impossible; it's trying to 'wax lyrical' in a language which can barely crawl under its
burden of clichés ('sun-kissed isle', 'delightful beaches', 'local nightlife' etc.). Take a
close look at the words or phrases in this passage which you think are exhausted
and unoriginal and see if you can detect the purpose they are there to serve.

    The words in this passage are almost all tailored to evoke a standardised holiday
experience which is located in a sort of tourist fantasy world. (Presumably Delphos
does exist somewhere in the Mediterranean, although one has one's doubts.)
Ironically, and perhaps revealingly, tourese vocabulary of this kind abounds with
words such as 'authentic', 'ethnic', 'genuine', 'local' and 'specialities'. It's almost as
if the writer is, at some uneasy depth of his soul, aware that people enjoy travel
partly because it offers some degree of freedom and cultural difference, even
though his job is to make the place sound exactly like everywhere else. It is
because the function of the words in this piece is to *market*, rather than to
describe, that they suffer from such terminal semantic decay. (What do words such
as 'sun-kissed', 'delightful', 'stunning', 'lively', 'scenic' actually mean?)

    It is very easy to write prose like this precisely because it is prefabricated, instant
and packaged. (And to that extent, perhaps, it is perfect for the job, because it
stylistically resembles the holiday it is trying to sell.) A good travel writer uses
words that have the opposite effect to tourese: words that defamiliarise, that
stimulate, that intrigue; words that describe, rather than camouflage. ('Charming
little fishing village' – what, with 'four lively discos'?) Maybe Delphos is a fine place
to go, and maybe it is a good place to 'let your hair down' (whatever that's code
for); but we shouldn't have to endure this kind of verbal oil slick before we get
there.

    Time for something better. Here's an extract from a book by John Hillaby, who
spent several months walking from the southern end of England up to the
northern tip of Scotland. Here he is in the West Country:

    The locals sat round chatting, spitting into the fire, speaking slowly,
but with such a heavy burr that, heard from a distance, it might have
been a foreign language punctuated with only a few familiar words. It

sounds rather Russian. That curious *zh* consonant that you normally hear in pleasure and leisure is used at the beginning of such words as 'zsheep' and 'zshearing'. The letter *f* frequently becomes a *v*. 'Varmer Brown's got vorrty zsheep,' they say, and the *r*'s in the middle of certain 'wurrds' buzz like bandsaws. It all sounds very pleasant.

Here, as in other isolated pubs in the West Country, the landlady mothered the company, entering into their affairs with easy familiarity. Nobody seemed surprised when an old man who had some difficulty in bending down said it was about time she cut his toe-nails again. Another with a bad cough was given a couple of asprins and told to take them that night with a glass of hot milk.

Although they knew very well what I was up to, nobody asked me where I came from or where I was going. But they all said 'Good night' as they dutifully filed out at half past ten and one, in an unexpected burst of confidence, added that if I tried to cross the moor the next day he reckoned I'd go right in up to my arse.

He was wrong. I got a bit wet. I couldn't avoid it. The moor had soaked up a good deal of snow melt. It rained too, but not for long. A shepherd plodding along with a new-born lamb under each arm nodded and said it looked 'a bit mousy-like'. That sounded good. Better by far than black or leaden. I looked up at the towering clouds and decided that with a bit of imagination they might be described as oyster-coloured or dove-grey. In time there was even a glint of silver here and there ...

... Acting on ... advice to spend some time in the strange company of the Hurlers, a famous ring of stones above the village of Minion, I trudged up an obscure track wondering, as I so often did, why on earth the authority responsible for these mighty monuments doesn't do something about even trying to explain what they are.

The Hurlers look like the abandoned ring of a travelling circus: flattened turf bounded by large stones, the mute witnesses of whatever happened there long ago. Like all primitive things, the impression is great and simple. There are, in fact, three circles, two of them marked by granite uprights, the third by stones that have collapsed. They are about forty paces in diameter. As usual, Christian tradition says the uprights are men transformed to stone for the abominable practice of playing the Cornish game of hurling on the Sabbath.

For me the wonder of the stone circles has been enormously enhanced by recent theories that they were not designed merely for ceremonial parades. There are good reasons for believing that they are examples of Bronze Age geometry, a record in stone of oustanding achievements in mathematics. Many of the circles can be regarded as calendars, as the predictors of future eclipses. The men who built them sought to capture time, for the return of time and the season for special ceremonies must have been for them the only safe prophecy, showing order and symmetry in Nature.

John Hillaby: Journey through Britain

Now try answering these questions:

1 How are the 'locals' here depicted differently from the locals in the Delphos travel brochure?

2 Hillaby's words are not of the prefabricated kind found in tourese. Choose five words or phrases from the extract and suggest why they are well chosen and what sort of work they are doing in their contexts. (If you are feeling idle, you could look at five from this list: 'mothered', 'dutifully', 'burst of confidence', 'arse', 'abandoned ring of a travelling circus', 'mute witnesses', 'abominable practice'.)

3 Look at the paragraph beginning 'He was wrong.' What signs are there here that Hillaby is all too aware of the fact that good travel writing involves avoiding prefabricated diction?

4 Why is some of the vocabulary in the last two paragraphs rather more Latinate than the language of the previous paragraphs? (Look at words like 'enhanced', 'ceremonial', 'geometry', 'mathematics', 'predictors', 'eclipse', 'ceremonies', 'prophecy', 'symmetry'.) Are these words used appropriately here, and if so, why?

Finally in this section, and just in case you may have got the impression that writers tend to relish Latinate words more than Anglo-Saxon ones, here's another piece by Robert Byron, in which he has a lot of fun with mud:

> It is a mud plain, so flat that a single heron, reposing on one leg beside some rare trickle of water in a ditch, looks as tall as a wireless aerial. From this plain rise villages of mud and cities of mud. The rivers flow with liquid mud. The air is composed of mud refined into a gas. The people are mud-coloured; they wear mud-coloured clothes, and their national hat is nothing more than a formalised mud-pie. Baghdad is the capital one would expect of this divinely favoured land. It lurks in a mud fog; when the temperature drops below 110, the residents complain of the chill and get out their furs. For only one thing is it now justly famous: a kind of boil which takes nine months to heal, and leaves a scar.

> *Robert Byron: The Road to Oxiana*

Sounds like a nice place to visit.

The Eskimoes have a word for it

One obvious reason why travel writers tend to be word enthusiasts is because they transport themselves to foreign cultures where the relationship between the verbal signs made by the locals and what you understand by those signs becomes a rather urgent matter, especially if you happen to be hungry, thirsty or lost.

We've pointed out before that travel writers tend to be quick to recognise that all human languages and thought-processes are culturally determined and relative (or 'elastic'). Language and thought are products of society and its structures; they are not just things 'out there'. Here's John Hillaby again, this time writing about the inadequacies of our word 'snow' compared to the rich complexities of the term in Canadian Indian and Eskimo languages.

> Eskimoes and Indians, for instance, have their own words for at least six kinds of snow which correspond to different physical conditions, such as a sudden freeze or melt or the impact of sustained blizzards. Written down phonetically, there is *Khali* for feathery snow on trees, *Appi* for snow on the ground, with *Pukkak* the layer below into which small animals burrow. *Sikoktoack* is that hard crusty stuff, which is like walking on puff-pastry. Under extreme conditions it can immobilize animals as effectively as an electric fence. But between the layers of *Appi* and *Pukkak* there lies an intimate kingdom beneath the snow, only recently explored. The air there is always moist and warm and still. It is protected from the wildest of trans-polar winds and permeated by a pale blue light.
>
> There throughout the winter in a labyrinth of little corridors live hosts of animals including mice, voles and shrews and hares and, as they are obliged to build ventilator shafts to the upper air, there sniffs the fox who, unlike the weasel, cannot crawl into the corridors, but can jump up and down in an often successful effort to break through the roof of that frozen underworld.
>
> *John Hillaby: Journey Through Love*

Hillaby recognises how languages different from our own conceptualise the world differently from the way that our language does. The Eskimoes slot the world into different categories from the ones that we use, but when we read about their language (and, more so, if we could speak it) we are allowed to see the world differently from the way we are conditioned to. We can escape what the poet Robert Graves calls the 'web' of our own language and the structures it imposes on our minds when we describe what is 'out there'. Bruce Chatwin, in his book about Patagonia, describes how the South American Yaghans had a language that was similarly rich, unique and puzzling:

> The Yaghans had a dramatic verb to capture every twitch of the muscles, every possible action of nature or man. The verb *iya* means 'to moor your canoe to a streamer of kelp'; *okon* 'to sleep in a floating canoe' (and quite different from sleeping in a hut or with your wife); *ukomona* 'to hurl your spear into a shoal of fish without aiming for a particular one'; *wejna* 'to be loose or easily moved as a broken bone or the blade of a knife' – 'to wander about, or roam, as a homeless or lost child' – 'to be attached yet loose, as an eye or bone in its socket' – 'to swing, move or travel' – or simply 'to exist, to be'.
>
> *Bruce Chatwin: In Patagonia*

Like Hillaby, Chatwin is suggesting that these odd verbal and written signs, these words, do more than just permit us to communicate with each other; they are the tools with which we think, and they very largely determine how we function as human beings.

The last extract in this chapter is from Peter Fleming, and he is writing about travel writing. He begins by criticising what he calls the 'Nullah' school of travel writing, but then finds that he himself cannot altogether avoid it.

From my youth up I have lost no opportunity of mocking what may be called the Nullah (or Ravine) School of Literature. Whenever an author thrusts his way through the *zareba*, or flings himself down behind the *boma*, or breasts the slope of a *kopje*, or scans the undulating surface of the *chapada*, he loses my confidence. When he says that he sat down to an appetizing dish of *tumbo*, or what should he see at that moment but a magnificent *conka*, I feel that he is (*a*) taking advantage of me and (*b*) making a fool of himself. I resent being peppered with these outlandish italics. They make me feel uninitiated, and they make him seem pretentious. Sometimes he has the grace to explain what he is talking about: as in the sentence 'The *bajja* (or hut) was full of *ghoils* – young unmarried women – who, while cooking the *do*, a kind of native cake, uttered low crooning cries of "*O Kwait*", which can be freely translated as "Welcome, Red-faced One. Life is very frequently disappointing, is it not?"' But this does not improve matters much, for the best prose is not so cumbered with asides, and the poor man's muse moves stiffly in the uniform of an interpreter.

I have always regarded the larding of one's pages with foreign words as an affectation no less deplorable than the plastering of one's luggage with foreign labels. I swore that if ever I was misguided enough to write a book of my travels, my italics would be all my own; my saga would be void of *nullahs*. But now I find that this self-denial is not altogether possible ...

First of all, there are the words like *bataloa* and *rapadura* and *mutum*, which denote things unknown outside Brazil, and which it is therefore impossible to translate. ... Secondly, there are the words of which a literal translation is for one reason or another inadequate. The word sandbank, for instance, gives you a very niggardly idea of what a *praia* is, and the word *plage*, which conveys an image nearer the truth, has unsuitable associations. Similarly, an *urubú* is a far more scurvy and less spectacular a creature than the popular conception of a vulture. Thirdly, there are a few words which can be translated perfectly well, but which we, in conversation, never did translate: words like *jacaré* and *arara*. We never said 'There's an alligator', or 'There's a macaw', but – I suppose because of the presence of our men – always used the native words. So it is easier and more natural, when writing of these things, to give them the names under which they live in my memory.

Peter Fleming: Brazilian Adventure

1 Explain in your own words why Fleming was originally against the use of foreign words in his own books.

2 Why did he change his mind? Which of the reasons he gives do you find the most convincing, and why?

A checklist

These questions are by way of a summary of the ground we have covered in this chapter, and they may be useful to you as a means of investigating diction in any prose passage which you are asked to look at in some detail.

1 What are the different purposes (or the single purpose) of the piece of writing that you are reading? Do you feel that the writer of the piece has chosen his or her words in order to produce some quite specific meaning? If so, pick out words or phrases which seem to you to demonstrate this clearly.

2 Do the individual words of the piece simply inform the reader, or do they also suggest ideas, evoke sensations, or whatever? How and why do they do this? Are you being manipulated? (Are they attempting to make you lust for a package holiday, or vote for a political party?)

3 What sorts of associations do the writer's words suggest? What are their 'spheres of significance'? Are these associated meanings the conventional, culturally-conditioned ones, or are they unique to the writer?

4 Is the writer's diction primarily 'Anglo-Saxon', or is it peppered with 'Latinate' words? If there are lots of noticeable Latinisms in the piece, why are there? Are they there in the interests of precision, or are they there merely to impress? How can you tell? Might there be some quite different reason for their being there?

5 Does the language of the passage strike you as fresh and memorable, or as tired and 'off the peg'? How high is the cliché count?

6 If you are lucky enough to be reading a piece of travel writing, what sorts of experience, attitudes, feelings, about a place is the writer trying to convey? Or is the journey very much an internal one?

7 Does the travel writer take up a superior attitude towards his surroundings (human as well as geographical) or is the writer more interested in exploring different cultures, ready to change his or her (and your) mind about what counts as being 'normal'? Do the writer's words strain to convey difference?

8 Is the writer more interested in sensual or in intellectual experience? Does he or she try to make an experience concrete, or try to persuade or educate the reader in some way? Did your attitudes undergo any sort of change as a result of reading what the writer has to say? In what way?

Finally, here is a short list of travel books that we have enjoyed reading. If you feel like an hour or two of serious escapism, you could do worse than take up one of the following:

Patrick Leigh-Fermor: *A Time of Gifts*
Robert Byron: *The Road to Oxiana*
Martha Gelhorn: *Travels with Myself and Another*
Bruce Chatwin: *In Patagonia*
Peter Fleming: *Brazilian Adventure*
Dervla Murphy: *Full Tilt*
John Hillaby: *Journey Through Britain; Journey Through Love*
Eric Newby: *A Short Walk in the Hindu Kush; Slowly down the Ganges*
Jonathan Raban: *Arabia through the Looking Glass; Old Glory; Coasting*
Paul Theroux: *The Great Railway Bazaar*
Ella Maillart: *Forbidden Journey*

5
Peasants, Pastorals and Sentences

I'm sure it is perfectly ghastly having no money at all... but it must be a comfort to know that Mr. Wordsworth considers you a morally superior being...

Artificial naturalness

This chapter is about a rather odd subject: peasants. Or, if you like, farm labourers, rustics and simple country folk, and what sort of people they are, and (more importantly) what sort of people we think they are, and why we think that's what they are.

There is a traditional mental package of assumptions (you may subscribe to it) about country dwellers; its contents are something like this:

1 Simple country folk (for the sake of brevity hereafter referred to as 'peasants') live in places which are far enough away from the evils and corruptions of city life to ensure that they remain essentially good and uncorrupted.

2 Peasants are innocent, simple and childlike (and therefore open and honest) whereas city folk are sinful, complicated and more adult (and therefore more devious and dishonest).

3 Peasants live in natural surroundings, and this natural environment has a moral effect on them which makes them ethically superior to city dwellers.

4 Peasants are unambitious, content, and free from material desires. They also have a very healthy diet. Their bread is invariably brown and wholesome and keeps their bowels in good fettle.

5 Peasants are instinctively more aware of the deeper mysteries of human life – notably those of sexuality, procreation, birth and death. City people lead shallow and trivial lives by comparison and have completely lost touch with these elementary truths concerning the human condition.

6 Peasants speak in non-standard English, which makes them difficult to understand, but fascinating. Their culture is essentially pagan and obsessed with the seasons and fertility. It usually manifests itself in bizarre activities which are somehow both spontaneous and traditional, such as dancing about with hankies and large sticks, making patchwork quilts and carving huge wooden spoons with holes in them. They also like to put green stuff and flowers in unexpected places at various times of the year. They talk to animals and have a deep reverence for their surroundings.

7 Peasants are a good and proper subject for novelists and poets to write about. They are worthy of our admiration, and we should, if possible, try to emulate them, for reasons 1 to 6.

What we have here is a myth. By *myth* we do not mean 'something that isn't true'. We are using the word in a rather more strict sense to indicate a set of ideas or values that have a social and psychological importance; ideas or values that we cling to at some level despite all evidence that they are obviously highly suspect. The ideas sketched above are the products of certain cultural changes in attitude and belief which took place some two centuries ago. These changes are often referred to as the Romantic Revolution, and they still influence the ways we see the world and the people in it. Whether those ideas about peasants are true or not is very debatable. They would be very hard to test scientifically. (How would you go about measuring awareness or corruption or contentment, for a start?) Nevertheless, a great deal of English literature written over the past two centuries has been influenced by Romantic ideas which often involve the polarising of opposing ideas: the Country versus the Town, the Child versus the Adult, the Innocent versus the Experienced, and so on. The belief that the countryside is a place of peaceful harmony and moral superiority is a myth as old as the garden of Eden itself. Human beings have always entertained some doubts about that relatively recent enterprise called 'civilisation', and have habitually taken a nostalgic look back towards an imaginary, rural, Golden Age where life was always slower, simpler, kinder and less confusing. One of the earliest literary forms that this fantasy takes is known as the **pastoral**.

The pastoral began with Classical writers such as Hesiod and Virgil, became popular in sixteenth century Italy, and – because Italy was then the source of all trendy ideas – shortly afterwards came to dominate much of English poetry written by aristocratic young men (and a few professional poets). The pastoral was a highly artificial literary game played by rich and sophisticated people of both sexes who fancifully imagined themselves to be eternally youthful shepherds and shepherdesses flirting and frolicking about in an idealised and tame rural theme park. In pastoral poetry it is always summer; time is frozen, the 'players' compose 'songs' (poems) for each other's delight, no-one ever gets angry, and it doesn't rain. Such pretty escapist nonsense also produced the literary tradition of the **anti-pastoral**, in which other poets wittily mock the artificiality and impossibility of such dreams. Here are famous examples of both these literary genres:

The Passionate Shepherd to His Love

Come live with me and be my love,
And we will all the pleasures prove
That valleys, groves, hills and fields,
Woods, or steepy mountain yields.

And we will sit upon the rocks,
Seeing the shepherds feed their flocks,
By shallow rivers to whose falls
Melodious birds sing madrigals.

And I will make thee beds of roses
And a thousand fragrant posies,
A cap of flowers, and a kirtle
Embroidered all with leaves of myrtle;

A gown made of the finest wool
Which from our pretty lambs we pull;
Fair lined slippers for the cold,
With buckles of the purest gold;

A belt of straw and ivy buds,
With coral clasps and amber studs:
And if these pleasures may thee move,
Come live with me, and be my love.

The shepherds' swains shall dance and sing
For thy delight each May morning:
If these delights thy mind may move,
Come live with me and be my love.

Christopher Marlowe (1564-1593)

Notes
'prove' means try or taste
a 'kirtle' is a gown
'swains' are boys

The Nymph's Reply to the Shepherd

If all the world and love were young,
And truth in every shepherd's tongue,
These pretty pleasures might me move
To live with thee and be thy love.

But Time drives flocks from field to fold
When rivers rage and rocks grow cold,
And Philomel becometh dumb;
The rest complains of cares to come.

The flowers do fade, and wanton fields
To wayward winter reckoning yields;
A honey tongue, a heart of gall,
is fancy's spring, but sorrow's fall.

Thy gowns, thy shoes, thy beds of roses,
Thy cap, thy kirtle, and thy posies
Soon break, soon wither, soon forgotten –
In folly ripe, in season rotten.

Thy belt of straw and ivy buds,
Thy coral clasps and amber studs,
All these in me no means can move
To come to thee and be thy love.

But could youth last and love still breed,
Had joys no date nor age no need,
Then these delights my mind might move
To live with thee and be thy love.

Sir Walter Raleigh (1552-1618)

Notes

'Philomel' is a fanciful, Classical name for the nightingale.

There is perhaps a thread of double-entendre in the third stanza of the second poem. 'Wanton' means abundant, but also means undisciplined and promiscuous. 'Wayward' means unexpected or unwelcome and 'reckoning' is judgment or come-uppance, but also the period of a pregnancy. 'Fall' is ambiguous, too: it means autumn but also disgrace – as in 'fallen woman'.

Have another look at these two poems and then try the following questions:

1 What sort of 'nature' do the lovers in Marlowe's poem inhabit?

2 What are the two major criticisms that Raleigh's Nymph makes of the ardent proposals of Marlowe's 'Passionate Shepherd'?

3 Is Raleigh's poem more 'realistic'? If so, in what way?

Presumably, ordinary people who actually lived in the countryside in sixteenth-century England knew only too well that their existence was often hard, cold, wet and muddy, and they would have found the whole notion of pastoral poetry puzzling or downright nonsensical. To be fair to the poets and courtiers who wrote the stuff, they too realised that the whole business was a game: even the anti-pastoral only mocks a literary convention, it doesn't in any way attempt to provide an authentic picture of rural life. Because most villagers and agricultural workers were denied the opportunity to learn to read and write, there are very few convincing first-hand accounts of country life from this period; those few peasants who did manage to read and write poetry were rare, and generally regarded as freaks.

In the following seventeenth and eighteenth centuries, educated people (with some few exceptions) liked their nature to be tame and cultivated, to be seen from a prosperous, safe and privileged distance as scenic or picturesque. (This tradition lingers on; as tourists we pile out of our cars and coaches to 'look at the view'.)

Towards the end of the eighteenth century, however, a major change of attitude towards the countryside and the people who live in it began to take place. The best way to be introduced to these changes is to read a couple of extracts from a long and remarkable poem by William Wordsworth called *The Prelude* (written between 1799 and 1805). In this poem Wordsworth explores and analyses the events in his life that helped form his imagination and influenced his work. Some of these events were of major historical importance, notably the French Revolution; others were personal and sometimes seemingly trivial, yet of equal psychological significance to Wordsworth as a poet. *The Prelude* is by no means an easy poem to read, but it's crucial to any good understanding of the ways in which nature is depicted in literature; it put forward very new visions of the natural world, a world which Wordsworth saw as being implacably opposed to the artificial world of the city. In *The Prelude*, nature is not a decorative, escapist fantasy; it is a moral force. This first extract is a description of a London fairground, which becomes the 'epitome' of the city as a whole and the lives of the people who live there:

> All moveables of wonder, from all parts,
> Are here – Albinos, painted Indians, Dwarfs,
> The Horse of knowledge, and the learned Pig,
> The Stone-eater, the man that swallows fire,
> Giants, Ventriloquists, the Invisible Girl,
> The Bust that speaks and moves its goggling eyes,
> The Wax-work, Clock-work, all the marvellous craft
> Of modern Merlins, Wild Beasts, Puppet-shows,
> All out-o'-the-way, far-fetched, perverted things,
> All freaks of nature, all Promethean thoughts
> Of man, his dullness, madness, and their feats
> All jumbled up together, to compose
> A Parliament of Monsters. Tents and Booths
> Meanwhile, as if the whole were one vast mill,
> Are vomiting, receiving on all sides,
> Men, women, three-years' children, Babes in arms.
>
> Oh, blank confusion! true epitome
> Of what the mighty City is herself,
> To thousands upon thousands of her sons,

> Living amid the same perpetual whirl
> Of trivial objects, melted and reduced
> To one identity, by differences
> That have no law, no meaning, and no ends –
> Oppression, under which even highest minds
> Must labour, whence the strongest are not free.

William Wordsworth

Obviously, Wordsworth does not see the city as a place of civilised life. It is the very opposite, a pandemonium, a gathering of demons. Of course, it is the picture in his head that we are dealing with here, not the objective reality which is 'out there'. London may well have been a hellish place, and no doubt Wordsworth's beloved Lake District was a good deal calmer. But consider – where would you rather be: in the middle of a stinking fairground mob, or tending a flock of claggy-rumped sheep on some desolate Cumbrian moor? In other words, there's nothing intrinsically 'good' about either place; yet such is the vigour of Wordsworth's language and the force of his vision that many people were, and are still, persuaded that the city is an evil place, and that the country is the natural home of 'goodness'. Even more importantly (as far as this chapter is concerned, anyway), Wordsworth changed the way that educated readers looked at rustics. Or perhaps it might be more accurate to say that he made country-dwellers visible, when previously they were no more worthy of attention than the animals they tended. Here is Wordsworth describing a childhood encounter with a shepherd. He is not, you will notice, the kind of shepherd likely to sit about on rocks enticing nymphs:

> When up the lonely brooks on rainy days
> Angling I went, or trod the trackless hills
> By mists bewildered, suddenly mine eyes
> Have glanced upon him distant a few steps,
> In size a giant, stalking through thick fog,
> His sheep like Greenland bears; or, as he stepped
> Beyond the boundary line of some hill-shadow,
> His form hath flashed upon me, glorified
> By the deep radiance of the setting sun:
> Or him have I descried in distant sky,
> A solitary object and sublime,
> Above all height! like an aerial cross
> Stationed alone upon a spiry rock
> Of the Chartreuse, for worship. Thus was man
> Ennobled outwardly before my sight,
> And thus my heart was early introduced
> To an unconscious love and reverence
> Of human nature; hence the human form
> To me became an index of delight,
> Of grace and honour, power and worthiness.

William Wordsworth

1 Look again at some of the key words in this extract: 'bewildered', 'suddenly', 'giant', 'stalking', 'flashed', 'glorified', 'radiance', 'sublime', 'worship'. What kind of 'seeing' is Wordsworth engaging in here?

2 Is Wordsworth's shepherd more 'authentic' than the shepherd in Marlowe's pastoral poem?

3 Wordsworth seems to be saying that childhood experiences such as this one later crystallised into a philosophy about Mankind. Can you say in your own words what that philosophy seems to have been?

What should now be clear from studying these two extracts is that Wordsworth promoted some quite startling ideas about the differences between those who lived in cities and those who lived in the country. On the whole, he implies that rural folk are both more impressive and morally superior. Part of the reason for this has to do with his belief that the landscape of his own childhood was not merely a passive environment, but acted as a sort of moral guardian or guide. By implication, we are led to believe that people who are closer to the natural world are 'better' people. It is not an ethical philosophy that will bear much scrutiny, but it is close to the myth of the peasant that we outlined at the beginning of this chapter.

Wordsworth's shepherd is really just as literary as any to be found in the pastoral tradition, but in a rather different way. He is an elemental figure, rather frightening as he is seen by the young boy, looming out of the Lakeland mists – and subsequently elevated to symbolic status by the older Wordsworth who wrote *The Prelude*. In justice to Wordsworth, it has to be said that not all his poems promote peasant folk to such glorious and emblematic stature. Elsewhere he admires them for more down-to-earth reasons, like their stoicism in the face of horrible hardship. He had no illusions about the realities of life for ordinary rural workers and their families. Nevertheless, his deep admiration for country people has had a profound effect on English literature, and upon the way we see rural life. We still retain some semblance of a Romantic idea of the country and those who live there. For most people, the words 'country', 'countryside' and 'rural' are part of a complex of words and concepts which includes 'healthiness', 'goodness', 'simplicity' and 'cleanliness'. These associations are no less powerful for being at least partly unconscious, as advertisers and designers of food packaging well know. And the myth persists, despite the whiff of the battery farm from behind the hedge, the streams of belly-up fish, and the blue glow of the telly lighting up the windows of thatched cottages.

Intermission: sentences

You've now had to swallow a number of ideas about what is natural and what is artificial. Before we go on to some twentieth-century writing about 'peasants', we are going to deal with something technical and specific: the sentence.

So far in this book, you've been asked to look carefully at words and the wide variety of different things that writers can do with them. One obvious thing that we all do with words, whether we are speaking them or writing them, is put them into sentences. My typewriter is very old and crotchety, but it still has a functioning key with a dot on it, so that I can finish off this large (and still growing) group of words by plonking a full stop at the end of it and making a (wait for it) sentence. This sentence here is a **simple** sentence. A simple sentence is one which consists of just one main clause. This sentence, on the other hand, because it contains not just a main clause but also subclauses, (which make it longer, of course) is a **complex** sentence. The main clause is 'This sentence ... is a complex sentence.' The other bits are subclauses. Generally speaking, simple sentences describe simple facts or observations or actions, whereas complex sentences can contain a more complicated chain of ideas or information or shades of meaning. Complex sentences work you harder. It is often the job of subclauses to interact with, or qualify, the main clause. For example, look at the way a simple sentence like 'I believe war is wrong' can be manipulated into something far more subtle and plastic and devious by subclauses:

> I believe war is wrong, unless you are directly defending your country or its possessions from outside attack, or your government has agreed to help another friendly country in the event of it being attacked.

Remember, though, that the words 'simple' and 'complex', when applied to sentences, are grammatical terms which refer to the *form* of sentences. They have nothing to do with the *content* of sentences or the nature of the ideas they contain. Look at the following two sentences: which one is simple and which is complex?

A Deconstruction is an epistemological nightmare.

B I went down the Quay club with Michelle last night because she was depressed about splitting up with her boyfriend and I wanted to cheer her up.

> Now back to the country, but elsewhere.

The dung of the soul

The next piece we're going to look at is by William Faulkner, who lived in Mississippi, one of the states of the 'Deep South' of the United States. The South was, and to a considerable extent still is, a separate country within the Union. Faulkner wrote about several different groups of Southerners, including the rich plantation owners and black slaves; he also wrote about a rather less well known but large group of people sometimes called 'poor whites' or, more aggressively, 'white trash'. The fictional speaker in this passage, Cora Tull, is from this class of people. Look at the sentences Faulkner puts into her mouth as she speaks to us:

> So I saved out the eggs and baked yesterday. The cakes turned out right well. We depend a lot on our chickens. They are good layers, what few we have left after the possums and such. Snakes, too, in the summer. A snake will break up a hen-house quicker than anything. So after they were going to cost so much more than Mr Tull thought, and after I promised that the difference in the number of eggs would make it up, I had to be more careful than ever because it was on my say-so we took them. We could have stocked cheaper chickens, but I gave my promise as Miss Lawington said when she advised me to get a good breed, because Mr Tull himself admits that a good breed of cows or hogs pays in the long run. So when we lost so many of them we couldn't afford to use the eggs ourselves, because I could not have had Mr Tull chide me when it was on my say-so we took them. So when Miss Lawington told me about the cakes I thought that I could bake them

and earn enough at one time to increase the net value of the flock the equivalent of two head. And that by saving the eggs out one at a time, even the eggs wouldn't be costing anything. And that week they laid so well that I not only saved out enough eggs above what we had engaged to sell, to bake the cakes with, I had saved enough so that the flour and the sugar and the stove wood would not be costing anything. So I baked yesterday, more careful than I ever baked in my life, and the cakes turned out right well. But when we got to town this morning Miss Lawington told me the lady had changed her mind and was not going to have the party after all.

'She ought to taken those cakes anyway,' Kate says.

William Faulkner: As I Lay Dying

1   What words or expressions tell you that this speaker is from the Southern States of the USA?

2   How many of Cora's sentences are simple?

3   Look at the sentence which begins 'So after they were going to cost … '. How does it differ in form and content from those that precede it?

4   What's odd about 'Snakes, too, in the summer.'?

5   Convention says that you must never begin a sentence with 'and'. Why does Faulkner allow Cora to break this rule?

6   On the basis of what Cora says and how she says it, what conclusions are you inclined to make about her character?

The next passage is a very famous piece of prose: some early paragraphs from D. H. Lawrence's novel *The Rainbow*. One thing that should be obvious to you straight away is that for Lawrence the life of the ordinary farmer has to do with something quite different from muddy routine and the price of eggs:

So the Brangwens came and went without any fear of necessity, working hard because of the life that was in them, not for want of the money. Neither were they thriftless. They were aware of the last halfpenny, and instinct made them not waste the peeling of their apple, for it would help feed the cattle. But heaven and earth was teeming around them, and how should this cease? They felt the rush of the sap in spring, they knew the wave which cannot halt, but every year throws forward the seed to begetting, and, falling back, leaves the young-born on the earth. They knew the intercourse between heaven and earth, sunshine drawn into the breast and bowels, the rain sucked up in the daytime, nakedness that comes under the wind in autumn, showing the birds' nests no longer worth hiding. Their life and inter-relations were such; feeling the pulse and body of the soil, that opened to their furrow for the grain, and became smooth and supple after their ploughing, and clung to their feet with a weight that pulled like desire, lying hard and unresponsive when the crops were to be shorn away. The young corn waved and was silken, and the lustre slid along the limbs of the men who saw it. They took the udder of the cows, the cows yielded milk and pulse against the hands of the men, the pulse of the blood of the teats of the cows beat into the pulse of the hands of the men. They mounted their horses, and held life between the grip of their knees, they harnessed their horses at the wagon, and, with hands on the bridle-rings, drew the heaving of the horses after their will.

In autumn the partridges whirred up, birds in flocks blew like spray across the fallow, rooks appeared on the grey, watery heavens, and flew cawing into the winter. Then the men sat by the fire in the house where the women moved about with surety, and the limbs and the body of the men were impregnated with the day, cattle and earth and vegetation and the sky, the men sat by the fire and their brains were inert, as their blood flowed heavy with the accumulation from the living day.

D. H. Lawrence: The Rainbow

Now take a cold shower and try answering these questions:

1 The farmland of the Brangwens is not a passive, picturesque landscape, but something altogether different. In what way is it different? (Have a look at all the verbs, to begin with. What do you notice about them?)

2 You could hardly fail to notice that this is a highly literary piece of writing – if by 'literary' we mean that the language is very foregrounded and attention-seeking. (Well, it pretty much takes off all its clothes and waves them in the air, doesn't it?) In places, it is almost impossible to translate into 'ordinary' language. How would you explain 'They knew the intercourse between heaven and earth, sunshine drawn into the breast and bowels ... ', for example? It's not the kind of thing you'd find in *Farmer's Weekly*. One fairly obvious thing you might have heard in this piece is the heavy and insistent prose rhythms. Take this sentence (read it aloud or 'aloud' in your head):

They took the udder of the cows, the cows yielded milk and pulse against the hands of the men, the pulse of the blood of the teats of the cows beat into the pulse of the hands of the men.

Write a sentence or two about the sound that makes, how it makes it, and suggest what it is trying to achieve.

3 One of the major linguistic peculiarities of this passage is its use of metaphor. You'd have to be very innocent – or very squeamish – to overlook the way Lawrence depicts the relationship between nature and human beings as being primarily sexual. Why do you think he does this?

4 Finally, a chance to be judgmental. Giving your reasons, which of the following words would you use to describe this passage? Powerful, rich, vivid, exciting, convincing, mystical, fanciful, overwrought, confusing, muddled, vulgar, gross, silly. (If none of these will do, suggest others.)

After that, a little light relief might be in order. This next piece might, at first glance, seem similar to what you've just read; but it isn't. It features Adam Lambsbreath, who is in charge of a horse and buggy, and he's off to pick someone up from the local railway station.

By the time the buggy reached Beershorn, which was a good seven miles from Howling, Adam had forgotten what he was going there for. The reins lay between his knotted fingers, and his face, unseeing, was lifted to the dark sky.

From the stubborn interwoven strata of his subconscious, thought seeped up into his dim conscious; not as an integral part of that consciousness, but more as an impalpable emanation, a crepuscular addition, from the unsleeping life in the restless trees and fields surrounding him. The country for miles, under the blanket of the dark which brought no peace, was in its annual tortured ferment of spring growth; worm jarred with worm and seed with seed. Frond leapt on root and hare on hare. Beetle and finch-fly were not spared. The trout-sperm in the muddy hollow under Nettle Flitch Weir were agitated, and well they might be. The long screams of the hunting owls tore across the night, scarlet lines on black. In the pauses, every ten minutes, they mated. It seemed chaotic, but it was more methodically arranged than you might think. But Adam's deafness and blindness came from within, as well as without; earthly calm seeped up from his unconscious and met descending calm in his conscious. Twice the buggy was pulled out of hedges by a passing farm hand, and once narrowly shaved the vicar, driving home from tea at the Hall.

'Where are you, my birdling?' Adam's blind lips asked the unanswering darkness and the loutish shapes of the unbudded trees. 'Did I cowdle thee as a mommet for this?'

He knew that Elfine was out on the Downs, striding on her unsteady colt's legs towards the Hall and the bright, sardonic hands of Richard Hawk-Monitor. Adam's mind played uneasily, in bewildered pain, with the vision of his nursling between those casual fingers ...

But the buggy reached Beershorn at last, and safely: there was only one road, and that led to the station.

Adam pulled Viper up on his haunches just as the great gelding was about to canter through the entrance to the booking-hall, and knotted the reins on the rennet-post near the horse-trough.

Then animation fell from him, a sucked straw. His body sank into the immemorial posture of a man thought-whelmed. He was a tree-trunk; a toad on a stone; a pie-thatched owl on a bough. Humanity left him abruptly.

Stella Gibbons: Cold Comfort Farm

Note: Stella Gibbons' novel was published in 1932, seventeen years after *The Rainbow*.

1 What is the essential purpose of this piece of writing, do you think?

2 It is apparent, we would have thought, that this passage is a disrespectful response to the passage from Lawrence. What mannerisms of Lawrence's prose style (as demonstrated in the previous passage) is Stella Gibbons mimicking in a cheeky way? In other words, what is she parodying?

3 What are the beliefs and attitudes in the Lawrence piece that Gibbons is

satirising? Why, do you think, does she want to mock these ideas? What might she think is wrong with them?

4　Have another look at the last paragraph and compare it with the last sentence of the Lawrence passage. How is Gibbons poking fun at the literary tradition of the peasant as an elemental force?

5　What are the different sorts of comic effects that Gibbons gets out of the following groups of words?

'Frond leapt on root and hare on hare'

'and well they might be'

'every ten minutes'

'it was more methodically arranged than you might think'

'the bright, sardonic hands of Richard Hawk-Monitor'

By now you may possibly be feeling a bit confused and somewhat twitchy. So far we've looked at a number of versions of nature and country life, and we seem to be left without anything clear or consistent to cling to. One thing is certain, though, and that is that anyone brought up on a diet of standard 'Eng. Lit.' texts – Wordsworth, Thomas Hardy, D. H. Lawrence, say – would find it difficult, if not impossible, to have a clear and uncontaminated picture in his or her head of what rural life was, or is, actually like. What most of us do have in our heads is a strange amalgam of cultural and literary 'constructs' – or myths – which have a long and complicated history. You've spent much of this chapter looking at them. If you are British, or worse, English, your thoughts about the subject are almost inevitably imprisoned within a powerful set of assumptions about what nature is like and how those who live 'in' it or 'close to' it are different from the rest of us. Our beliefs about where we live constitute a rich mental soup of emotions and attitudes, and its ingredients may include escapism, idealism, nostalgia – and, now and again, the odd dash of fact. Merchandisers are only too aware of both the confusion and the strength of our ideas about nature, and are adept at tapping into them by making spurious claims about 'natural' or 'organic' products, and by decorating food packages with pictures of plough-horses and olde mills. Perhaps too it is the force of the rural myth that causes so many office-workers to tuck into Ploughman's Lunches in city pubs and to dress up as Morris Dancers at the weekends. (The only genuine ploughman – tractor-driver, that is – that I know usually has deep-fried crispy pancakes for his lunch; and I never met a farm worker who would be seen dead prancing about with bells on his trousers waving a hankie at other men.)

The last extract in this chapter also takes a less than starry-eyed view of the rural myth. Before we look at it, though, let's deal with a few more technical terms which you may find useful when writing about the way that writers use sentences.

Three styles of sentence

As well as classifying sentences and their clauses grammatically (as being simple or complex) we can also classify them *stylistically*: as **loose**, **periodic**, or **balanced** sentences.

Loose sentences are those which begin with a main clause and then add on subclauses which are there, as you would expect, to provide extra information or to qualify the main clause. That was one. The one earlier about taking Michelle down the Quay club was another, and you've read lots more during the past few pages. Loose sentences are the obvious 'commonsense' way of stringing clauses together. Wordsworth uses a huge one at the beginning of that description of the London fairground. It begins with 'All moveables of wonder, from all parts, are here ... ', and then he piles on subclause after subclause, adding more and more detail, for another twelve lines. We tend naturally to speak in loose sentences: we make our main point first and then add to it as we go along – perhaps because we don't know how the sentence will end when we start to speak. For this reason a writer may well use loose sentences to give his readers the impression of spontaneity and vernacular immediacy. One easy way to identify a loose sentence is to put a full stop after any of its subclauses; if it still makes sense, the odds are that it's a loose sentence.

The **periodic** sentence is almost a mirror-image of the loose sentence, because in this case the main clause comes at the end. Periodic sentences tend to sound less 'natural' to the ear. They are often employed as a rhetorical technique – that is, a technique which is designed to persuade or manipulate us in some way. As listeners, we are obliged to listen to a periodic sentence all the way through, because it won't make any sense until we get to the end and the main clause. Here's an example:

> If the Prime Minister had taken the time to visit some of our local hospitals himself (*first subclause*), if he had sat down and talked to some of our nurses about their feelings (*second subclause*), or, better still, if he had used the National Health Service himself when he needed treatment (*third subclause*), then I might be more willing to listen to what he has to say (*main clause*).

Most politicians (and quite a few vicars and schoolteachers, too) can speak like this for hours, effortlessly. The 'three subclauses followed by a main clause' periodic sentence is an old public speaker's trick. You might notice that it sounds better than it reads. This is why writers treat the periodic sentence with caution, as a rule. If you are forced to wade through subclause after subclause, if you have to wait for the real information to come up, and if you start to forget what was at the beginning of the sentence (see what we mean?), then the periodic sentence will evoke tedium or bafflement. If you're clever enough, the periodic sentence can be used for comic effects, especially if the long-awaited main clause turns out to be ironic or anti-climactic. In short, the periodic sentence is a device, and what it can do depends upon the ingenuity of the writer. The easy way to spot a periodic sentence is to recognise that for it to make sense, the full stop can only come right at the end.

A majority of sentences, we're glad to say, do not fit neatly into either the loose or the periodic category, and are a kind of hybrid of both. Look back at the extract from Faulkner's *As I Lay Dying*, and you'll see what we mean.

Balanced sentences are also a kind of rhetorical device, and also unnatural to the ear. They are often used to impress, to suggest 'wisdom' or 'polish', because they contain two contrasting or 'balanced' elements. Like this:

> The city dweller knows lots of things; the peasant knows one big thing.

You can even (if you're Oscar Wilde) 'balance' three ideas:

> Children begin by loving their parents; after a time they judge them; rarely, if ever, do they forgive them.

The above information may come in handy in a moment, because we are about to get thrown out of a pub with Howard Jacobson.

Out on your ear

There is an aspect of the rural myth that we have not yet touched on: something called 'English Village Life'. The phrase is a code: it serves to conjure up a whole mass of sentimental nonsense about thatched cottages and blacksmiths and friendly gossip and mellow old churches and sweet peas in the garden and good-natured darts matches in the local. Some of this stuff has been beamed at us by novelists (much less so nowadays), but it has numerous non-literary sources – tourist brochures, calendars, television advertisements and suchlike. 'The Village' often serves as a symbol for England to outsiders and tourists, but has also infiltrated the subconsciousnesses of those of us who live here. Vital to the myth of English Village Life is that great institution The Pub. The Village Pub doesn't have video games, and it probably doesn't have a jukebox either. It has never heard of Chicken Kiev or Black Forest Gateau. In the Village Pub, ruminant locals sit around the fire exchanging folk-wisdoms about the harvest or sheep-tupping (whatever that is). And, of course, no-one ever gets legless or abusive.

This next character hasn't had much luck in searching for this mythical establishment. He is the narrator of a novel called *Peeping Tom*, by Howard Jacobson. He doesn't seem to have much luck with pubs at all, in fact, but he gives Jacobson the opportunity to have a lot of fun with the English sentence:

> These days, if it's a rumbustious evening you're looking for – a drunken sing-song extending well into closing time, a noisy altercation in a brutish tongue, a spot of social danger, what's called local colour – The Jolly Wreckers is your place. Then, when I first arrived in the village and stood disconcerted – my rose flush coming and going – in the picturesque harbour, a mere yard or two from the point of Camilla's gutting-knife, The Spattered Sofa was the pub to go to. And in between times The Sour Grape and The Tight Fist have alternately enjoyed and forfeited favour. Whose turn it will be next there's no knowing. That will depend on the usual village pub imponderables: the social habits of new arrivals, the death of old loyal drinkers, the state of the landlords' marriages, the supercession of real by ever realer ale, and above all on the operation of that system of expulsions and rustications known in Castle Boterel as the Ban. Scarcely a night goes by down here, scarcely a night has gone by since I moved here all those years ago, without someone being Banned from some bar somewhere in the village. Essentially the Ban is internecine – to be used by locals on locals. When they invented it there were only locals; and no one has a better grasp than they of its original needfulness. But as the autochthonous population has become watered down by Londoners and Midlanders (and a solitary Jew) so the Ban has become popularized and even – dare

I say? – vulgarized. No landlord not actually born in Castle Boterel or thereabouts can hope to remove someone from his bar with the wild spite, the inexplicable explosion of pique of the true-born native – centuries of neglect, isolation, damp and bad diet are needed for that – but what man, let him be howsoever dedicated to the principle of hospitality, does not need to turf someone out on his arse sometimes? And since the Ban is there, it is a kind of profligacy not to apply it. I swear that I have seen the friendliest of foreign visitors, the most genially anglophile of Germans, sent packing from a pub with instructions not to return for anything up to the life of the current European Parliament as a consequence of some infinitisimal confusion of currency or mispronunciation of a flavour of potato crisps. I myself was once Banned from the bar of The Crushed Emmet for asking the landlord if Camilla had been in before me. 'I'm not having outsiders squabbling in my pub,' he told me. 'You're Banned.' 'How long for?' I asked him. I knew better, by then, than to argue. 'Life,' he told me.

Howard Jacobson: Peeping Tom

1 The extract begins with a periodic sentence. Can you find others?

2 Choose one of the periodic sentences you have found. In your head or on paper reorganise it into a loose sentence (with the main clause at the beginning). What difference have you made to the sense and the effect of the original, periodic sentence?

3 There is some wonderfully odd syntax (sentence structure) in this passage, some of it used to convey a sort of 'buttonholing' intimacy with the reader. Pick out two examples of strange sentence structure, say how they are strange, and suggest reasons for Howard Jacobson writing them that way.

4 What strikes you as peculiar or interesting about Jacobson's diction – the way he mixes together very different kinds of words?

5 There are several institutions and beliefs under attack in this passage. What are they, and how are they mocked?

6 What general attitude does this narrator have towards 'English Village Life', do you think? Provide some evidence from the text for your ideas.

... and into the fields

The last extract in this chapter is from a book by John Berger called *Pig Earth*. It's a book which refuses to be pigeon-holed; it's part autobiography, part sociological essay, part fiction, and much more besides. Some time ago, Berger quit England to go and live among the *paysans* of the French Alps. In the first part of this passage, he is describing the realities of agricultural labour as they seem to him on a hot summer's day. In the second part, he reflects upon the similarities and the differences between his French neighbours and himself.

One afternoon this summer I was haymaking in a field which was too steep for the horse and wagon; we had to fork all the hay down to the bottom of the field where the ground flattened out. It was about four o'clock, though by the sun it was only two. The weather was heavy, and on the steep slope it was easy to slip on the very dry stubble which was like straw. I was working in a vest and wearing heavy boots so as to be able to get a better foothold. The farmer had gone down to the farm below to fetch the horse. The mother was raking near the top of the field where we had already forked the hay. I was climbing halfway up to push another forkload down to the bottom. For the hundredth time since we began, I stopped, held the wooden fork in one hand and with the other wiped the sweat off my face with a drenched, dust-filled handkerchief. My sweat tends to run into my eyes and make them smart so much that I can hardly see. It would be better if I wore a hat like all the haymakers of my age do, but I've not acquired the habit. Perhaps next year I will buy one. That afternoon after a month's haymaking, we were bringing in the hay from the last field; it wasn't worth buying a hat for that year. I stood there wiping my face. The air was absolutely still and the sun was heating the slope like a grill. Forking hay, lifting it, turning it, can be like playing, but on that heavy, treacherous, wasp-filled afternoon forking the hay was like trying to carry a split sack. I cursed the heat. The heat was no longer a condition, it had become a punishment. And I cursed the punisher. I cursed the slope and the work which still had to be done. If I could have struck the sun and its heat I would have done so. I looked down on the tiles of the farmhouse below and I swore at the sky. Half an hour later, long before we had got the hay in, it began to rain and thunder. And then I cursed the rain, even though welcoming its freshness.

My anger that afternoon joined me to the field, the slope, the hay. At other times my relationship to the place and the people who live here is less simple. I am not a peasant. I am a writer; my writing is both a link and a barrier ...

My writing about peasants separates me from them and brings me closer to them. I am not, however, only a writer. I am also the father of a small child, a pair of working hands when needed, the subject of stories, a guest, a host. How then do our lives compare with those of the peasant families among whom we live? Perhaps two lists will give some indication.

In Common	*Not in Common*
Childbirth/bringing up a child.	Mother tongue.
Experience of basic manual work.	Economic prospects.
Readiness to exchange services.	Landed patrimony.
Household standards of comfort/discomfort.	Lifetime in one place.
Participation in village ceremonies: funerals, weddings, etc.	Degree of physical endurance.
Weather/seasons.	Kinship connections.
A respect accorded to work.	

We do not live apart and we share many practices with those around us. Nevertheless the two lists are unequal. We remain strangers who have chosen to live here. We are exempt from those necessities which have determined most lives in the village. To be able to choose or select was already a privilege. Yet the way we chose to live and work within the life of the community, and not in seclusion, immediately revealed, also, a disadvantage, even a lack of privilege in local terms. This disadvantage was our relative ignorance, both practical and social. Everyone from schoolchildren to grandparents knew more than we did about certain aspects of life here. Everyone was in a position, if she or he chose, to be our teacher, to offer us information, aid, protection. And many did.

John Berger: Pig Earth

1 Why, do you think, is the language in these passages less foregrounded and more transparent than the language in the extract from Howard Jacobson's novel?

2 Why might Berger have felt the need to describe one particular afternoon's work in such detail?

3 Which of the entries in the In Common list do you think might be the more important in terms of 'belonging' to the community? And which, in the other list, might be the most likely to prevent his family's integration? Explain why you chose these entries.

4 What are your views about Berger's decision to leave his relatively comfortable and sophisticated lift in England and settle for a much harder, poorer life in the French countryside? Does the 'peasant life' appeal to you?

5 Of all the passages you have read in this chapter, which have you found the most interesting, and why?

A checklist

The following are questions that this chapter has raised in one form or another. You may find them useful when you are asked to discuss or criticise prose.

1 Does the writer use prose rhythms to convey actions or emotions or attitudes? If so, how are these rhythms created? Are they successful?

2 What sort of sentences are you reading: simple, complex, loose, periodic, balanced? All sorts? How does the syntax – the positioning of the main clause and the subclauses – affect the way meaning is created?

3 Are there sentences that strike you as being particularly odd in some way? What's odd about them? The diction? The syntax? Does their oddness mean that they are somehow more significant than other sentences?

4 Is the language of the piece 'transparent', or is it 'opaque'? Is it highly metaphorical or is it literal? If it is predominantly of one sort or another, why might this be so? Are there subjects that demand one kind of writing? Is it the case, for

example, that 'documentary', informative writing needs to be transparent rather than opaque?

5 Is the writer addressing you directly, or is he or she speaking 'through' a character? If the latter, what is there about the way in which that character speaks that tells you things about that character's personality?

6 If the passage you are reading is comic, what makes it so? The characters and incidents being described, or the way that the writer describes them? Is it possible to separate these two things? Are there certain kinds of sentence or syntax which are inherently comic, or which lend themselves to comedy more than other kinds of sentence and syntax?

7 Is the writing interesting? Or is it dull? What is it about the writing that grabs you or bores you to death? If you don't enjoy it, is it the writer's fault, or is the truth of the matter that there are things you simply don't want to read about? If you think that the writing isn't good, how would you do better?

6

Metaphor 1: Holy Kitchens and Drunken Pilots

The next clutch of chapters deals with the subject of metaphor. We're going to be a bit technical, a bit analytical, and even a bit historical. The danger is that we might lose sight of the fact that metaphor is a very basic yet magical linguistic device. So before we start looking into what metaphor is and how it works, we should look at some of the things it can do.

This chapter is, for the most part, a selection of pieces of writing which (with one exception) use metaphor in ways which we hope you'll find entertaining and interesting. For the time being, let's define metaphor as a figure of speech which brings together two different things and creates some kind of similarity between them. It is quite normal, for example, to compare an angry person to a kettle: 'he was boiling with rage'.

Metaphor is often the only way we can think and speak about abstract things which we cannot experience with our physical senses. Take, for instance, the familiar concept 'school', or 'college'. Is 'school' the building itself, or the teachers, or the teachers and the students? Is it the relentless daily process of transferring knowledge, or is it the name you give to the sum total of all those moments of pain and boredom and discovery and success? Metaphor can be a short cut through the complication of saying what such an abstract concept means to you. Have a look at this list of choices:

school or college is
> a prison
> a giant anthill
> a grey filing cabinet with many drawers
> a hurdle race
> a large family with its own rules and language

Which of these comparisons seems to you the most appropriate? Why does it? (And if they are all way off beam, what is your suggestion?) If you did find one of these comparisons valid, then obviously you detected similarities between it and school. At the same time, though, you will have 'filtered out' some of the obvious differences between the two things. We can all recognise what the similarities are between an anthill and a busy school, but when we see that comparison we filter out a great deal of what we know about ants; in other words, we don't actually see students as having six legs and antennae. What we mean is that students at school are like ants in that they ...

Here's another list to choose from:

knowledge is
> a vast, mysterious and dusty library with mazes of shelves, staffed and
> guarded by uniformed attendants
> a totally bald, swollen human head covered in strange bumps and ridges
> a huge and forbidding tree with innumerable branches, and each of its
> millions and millions of leaves is printed with a single word
> a large container of coloured liquid, from which emerge numerous
> coloured tubes, all labelled differently, each with a tap at the end
> a darkened room in which sits a small TV monitor chattering away to itself
> and filling its screen with colourful charts and diagrams

Again, which of those analogies made the most sense to you, or had the most impact on you, and why? (And again, can you do better?)

Here's another:

childhood is
> a large open field in the mountains full of flowers and butterflies
> a small room in which there is a loudspeaker softly issuing orders which make
> only partial sense
> a doll's house in which every single article is labelled with a name written in
> lower case letters
> a cardboard box containing old clothes, a few broken toys and some dog-
> eared reading books

Most of you are less distant from your childhood than the writers of this book are. Your relative closeness to it will no doubt affect the way you choose metaphors to describe it. Invent two metaphors of your own which convey your feelings about childhood more accurately and effectively than ours do.

Now that you have done a bit of preliminary metaphorical thinking, let's go on to look at a few short passages of prose. Generally it is true that prose is less densely metaphorical than poetry, because prose usually needs to have 'transparent' passages which give the reader information about things and actions and so forth. In prose, therefore, metaphors tend to be more isolated and distinct, which makes them a little easier to pick out and analyse. Still, we don't want to get bogged down in huge and mapless categories like 'prose' and 'poetry' just yet. Here's a brief extract from a short story about life 'below stairs':

> And, indeed, is there not something holy about a great kitchen?
> Those vaults of soot-darkened stone far above me, where the hams and
> strings of onions and bunches of dried herbs dangle, looking somewhat
> like the regimental banners that unfurl above the aisles of old churches.
> The cool, echoing flags scrubbed spotless twice a day by votive persons
> on their knees. The scoured gleam of row upon row of metal vessels
> dangling from hooks or reposing on their shelves till needed with the
> air of so many chalices waiting for the sacrament of food. And the range
> like an altar, yes, an altar, before which my mother bowed in perpetual
> homage, a fringe of sweat upon her upper lip and fire glowing in her
> cheeks.

> *Angela Carter: The Kitchen Child*

1 **What signs are there in the passage that Angela Carter wants to get her metaphor across forcefully and suggest that she isn't in dead earnest about it?**

2 **The very fact that a kitchen is not, really, very much like a church is what makes the metaphor surprising and amusing. Yet metaphor is meant, supposedly, to compare things that are somehow similar. Why is the difference between a kitchen and a church important to the effect that Angela Carter is trying to produce?**

The extract from *The Kitchen Child* establishes a metaphor (kitchen as church) and then goes on to elaborate it in different ways. For obvious reasons, this technique is known as **extended metaphor.** This next paragraph uses a somewhat similar device, but instead of elaborating on a single metaphor, it uses a series of metaphors which have the same source.

> Out of the station, through gradually thinning fog-banks, away from
> London. Lentil, saffron, fawn were left behind. A grubby jaeger shroud
> lay over the first suburbs; but then the woollen day clarified, and
> hoardings, factory buildings, the canal with its barges, the white-boled
> orchards, the cattle and willows and flat green fields loomed secretively,
> enclosed within a transparency like drenched indigo muslin. The sky's
> amorphous material began to quilt, then to split, to shred away; here

and there a ghost of blue breathed in the vaporous upper rifts, and the air stood flushed with a luminous essence, a soft indirect suffusion from the yet undeclared sun. It would be fine. My favourite weather.

Rosamond Lehmann: The Weather in the Streets

These are the impressions of a young woman called Olivia Curtis. She hasn't been awake long. She has been jerked out of sleep by a 'phone call telling her that her father is seriously ill, and she has caught the first available train out of London to her family's home town. The London she is leaving is under a dense fog. Does this information affect the way you feel about all those 'fabric' metaphors? Apart from the weather and the landscape, what else might these metaphors be describing?

Extended metaphors – when someone like Angela Carter uses them – can often be comic, but they can be relentless and oppressive, too, especially when they produce crude and obvious allegories. My old headmaster had a nasty little book full of that kind of stuff. It was called something like *Talks for Growing Boys*. We would sit in dull Monday-morning rows listening to stirring tales from 'the rugger field of life', and being exhorted to grab 'the ball of hope' and race through 'the goalposts of achievement'. I forget what the showers were meant to stand for.

My headmaster was not quite old enough to have been invented by Charles Dickens, but he had many Dickensian characteristics. One of Dickens' redeeming features is his profound dislike of schoolmasters, and here he is using metaphor to flay a particularly repellent member of the species:

> The scene was a plain, bare, monotonous vault of a schoolroom, and the speaker's square forefinger emphasised his observations by underscoring every sentence with a line on the schoolmaster's sleeve. The emphasis was helped by the speaker's square wall of a forehead, which had his eyebrows for its base, while his eyes found commodious cellerage in two dark caves, overshadowed by the wall. The emphasis was helped by the speaker's mouth, which was wide, thin, and hard set. The emphasis was helped by the speaker's voice, which was inflexible, dry, and dictatorial. The emphasis was helped by the speaker's hair, which bristled on the skirts of his bald head, a plantation of firs to keep the wind from its shining surface, all covered with knobs, like the crust of a plum pie, as if the head had scarcely warehouse-room for the hard facts stored inside. The speaker's obstinate carriage, square coat, square legs, square shoulders – nay, his very neckcloth, trained to take him by the throat with an unaccomodating grasp, like a stubborn fact, as it was – all helped the emphasis.

> 'In this life, we want nothing but Facts, sir; nothing but Facts!' The speaker, and the schoolmaster, and the third grown person present, all backed a little, and swept with their eyes the inclined plane of little vessels then and there arranged in order, ready to have imperial gallons of facts poured into them until they were full to the brim.

Charles Dickens: Hard Times

1 To what things is this pedagogue compared, and how do these comparisons influence our feelings towards him?

2 What is the educational 'philosophy' that lies behind the metaphor of children as 'little vessels'? Is it one that appeals to you? If not, why not? Do you see it as your teacher's job to 'pour'?

Dickens' satirical attack in that passage is obvious enough; what is perhaps less obvious is one of the ways that Dickens uses metaphor to make this attack. We mean the way that he so often likens animate things to inanimate things, and vice versa. Take that extraordinary 'neckcloth', for example: it begins as an inanimate thing, a scarf, turns into something like a ferocious dog, 'trained to take him by the throat', and then becomes an abstraction, a 'stubborn fact'.

This next piece uses metaphor in a rather less forceful and obvious way. It's from F. Scott Fitzgerald's *The Great Gatsby*. The narrator of the novel, Nick Carraway, is describing his encounter with two young and rich women:

> We walked through a high hallway into a bright rosy-coloured space, fragilely bound into the house by french windows at either end. The windows were ajar and gleaming white against the fresh grass outside that seemed to grow a little way into the house. A breeze blew through the room, blew curtains in at one end and out at the other like pale flags, twisting them up toward the frosted wedding cake of the ceiling, and then rippled over the wine-coloured rug, making a shadow on it as the wind does on the sea.
>
> The only completely stationary object in the room was an enormous couch on which two young women were buoyed up as though upon an anchored balloon. They were both in white, and their dresses were rippling and fluttering as if they had just been blown back in after a short trip around the house. I must have stood for a few moments listening to the whip and snap of the curtains and the groan of a picture on the wall. Then there was a boom as Tom Buchanan shut the rear windows and the caught wind died out about the room, and the curtains and the rugs and the two young women ballooned slowly to the floor.

F. Scott Fitzgerald: The Great Gatsby

1 What do you consider to be the 'key' words in that first paragraph, and what do they tell you about Carraway's impressions of the house?

2 The second paragraph contains a 'hidden' metaphor. The two women look as if they had been 'blown back' after a 'short flight'. What are they being compared to? How might this underlying metaphor affect our attitudes towards these two characters? Why might Fitzgerald want to keep this metaphor understated (as compared to, say, the very foregrounded metaphors in the passage by Dickens)?

It might be worth saying at this stage that an abundance of inventive and vivid metaphors does not necessarily make for good writing. Metaphors are by no means compulsory, and in fact there are writers who have treated them as if they are contaminated, writers who strive for the utmost literalness and transparency.

Probably the best-known of such writers is Ernest Hemingway. The next passage is from his rigorously unembroidered, autobiographical account of what it was like to be a young writer in Paris between the two World Wars. It's a rather famous piece, much read, and partly responsible for the presence in Paris each summer of hundreds of young American backpackers and would-be writers.

> The fireplace drew well in the room and it was warm and pleasant to work. I brought mandarines and roasted chestnuts to the room in paper packets and peeled and ate the small tangerine-like oranges and threw their skins and spat their seeds in the fire when I ate them and the roasted chestnuts when I was hungry. I was always hungry with the walking and the cold and the working. Up in the room I had a bottle of kirsch that we had brought back from the mountains and I took a drink of kirsch when I would get towards the end of a story or towards the end of the day's work. When I was through working for the day I put away the notebook, or the paper, in the drawer of the table and put any mandarines that were left in my pocket. They would freeze if they were left in the room at night.
>
> It was wonderful to walk down the long flights of stairs knowing that I'd had good luck working. I always worked until I had something done and I always stopped when I knew what was going to happen next. That way I could be sure of going on the next day. But sometimes when I was starting a new story and I could not get it going, I would sit in front of the fire and squeeze the peel of the little oranges into the edge of the flame and watch the sputter of blue that they made. I would stand and look out over the roofs of Paris and think, 'Do not worry. You have always written before and you will write now. All you have to do is write one true sentence. Write the truest sentence that you know.' So finally I would write one true sentence, and go on from there.

Ernest Hemingway: A Moveable Feast

This sort of 'transparent' prose is much harder to write convincingly than it might seem. (If you doubt us, try it.) It would certainly be a mistake to think of Hemingway's prose as simple. Try thinking about these questions:

1 **What do you notice about the sound and the pace of the sentences in this passage?**

2 **What do you think Hemingway means by the rather odd phrase 'one true sentence'?**

3 **Do you feel that Hemingway is right or wrong to imply that metaphorical language is somehow 'ornamental', or, worse, that it obstructs the truth? Do you associate 'transparent' language with truthfulness? Do you think that metaphorical language gets between the reality and the reader? How does it?**

Actually, Hemingway was a lot less doctrinaire about the art of writing than we may have suggested. He did, of course, use metaphor and he used it well, if sparingly. In case you are on the verge of heading off for truth and fame and a

Parisian attic, it might be good moment to point out just how artful that 'plain' Hemingway style is. There is a temptation – and Hemingway exploited it – to believe that unadorned, non-metaphorical language is more 'natural', more honest, than figurative language. But leaving metaphors out of your writing doesn't make it natural. The opposite is more likely to be true. What seems striking (to us, anyway) about Hemingway's 'plain' sentences is just how stylised they are, the way they are built out of carefully-timed repetitions, the way their rhythms are manipulated. The overall effect – that of an honest man carefully picking his way through the treacherous swamps of language, guided only by the star of his own integrity – is a product of deliberate artistry. In fact, the Hemingway Style is one of the more immediately recognisable styles of writing, and parodying it has always been a popular game. You could have a go yourself: 'It was good, the going to college, the walking and the catching the bus and the weight of the big books and I would do this every day until I got it right ... '

None of this alters the fact that if you are interested in writers and the art of writing then *A Moveable Feast* is a most enjoyable (and gossipy and scurrilous) read.

Good writers seem to know instinctively when to be figurative and when to be literal; so, finally, two contrasting pieces by Peter Fleming, who is best known for his travel books. The first passage describes a Brazilian crowd and its response to a loudspeaker, the second a rather shambolic boat launching.

> In Ribeirão there happened one of those tiny, casual incidents from which one gets – or imagines one gets – an insight into one aspect of a people's character. I was sitting on a high chair outside the hotel, having my shoes shined. A hundred yards away, at the corner of the square, a loud-speaker was blaring propaganda from Sao Paulo to the assembled citizens. One after another, all the oldest tricks of rhetoric came blundering through the air over the heads of the crowd, creaking in their flight like swans. At last the speech came to an applauded end. There was a pause filled only by those terrifying asthmatic crackles which rend the ether for some reason which I can never remember. Then the National Anthem began, flooding the square with its deafening and pretentious strains. Instantly the crowd removed their hats and stood as if magically pollarded by that blast of sound. From their chairs in cafes and outside shops, from the seats in the public garden, men and women rose to their feet and stood respectfully erect. My bootblack excused himself and faced the music. A very small negro boy with a bundle of newspapers under his arm whipped off his cap, clapped it between his knees, and stood saluting with the arm thus freed. His eyes were very solemn, his body very stiff; only his jaws moved, completing with an air of ritual the consumption of a sweet. The policeman on point duty was saluting too, dapper and motionless, while the four streets controlled by that now patriotically rigid arm were slowly choked by traffic. The moment was an impressive one.

'Pilot!' we shouted. 'Vai embora! We're off! Come here, pilot. Come here at once!'

The pilot began to sing.

He was drunk: not ordinarily, but magnificently. Few people can ever have been so drunk. We clambered up the bank and laid hold of him and marched him down to the boat. He fell out of the boat. We got him into the boat. He fell out of the boat. We got him back into the boat, and this time he threw himself overboard and lay face downwards in the shallows, groping vaguely for a pair of dark glasses which had fallen off his nose. We saved him, against his will, from drowning, and made ready to push off.

The ladies on the bank waved. Casimiro and the Caraja came forward and bade us an affectionate farewell, in the attractive Brazilian formula which includes a request – usually all too pertinent – that you will pardon the faults they have committed in your service. (One of us had given the Caraja a white vest and a pair of navy blue bathing drawers. No longer naked, he looked – with his long, disordered hair, his rather horse-like face, and his proud, half-sheepish expression – exactly like the victor of a women's cross-country race in a News Reel.)

The ladies waved again. Our men replied with a valedictory broadside of innuendo. The pilot sang. We put our shoulders to the gunwale. The boat stirred, slid down the shingle. The parrot squawked. We scrambled in. The ponderous oars flashed. The boat began to move. Her bows headed once more for the Amazon. We were off.

The pilot fell overboard again.

Peter Fleming: Brazilian Adventure

Note: 'pollarded' in the first passage is a word normally applied to those rather sad and alien-looking trees, often willows, which have had their branches lopped off close to the trunk, leaving bulbous stumps.

1 What do the metaphors in the first extract reveal about Fleming's attitude towards political speeches and ritual occasions? Do you think we are to take that last sentence at face value, or not?

2 Why, do you think, is Fleming's language so metaphorical in the first of of these two passages and almost wholly literal in the second?

3 What is the cumulative effect of those short crisp sentences at the end of the second piece?

4 Which of the two extracts do you prefer? (You are allowed to say that this is a daft question, but you have to say why.)

7
Metaphor 2: All at Sea

Worms

The poet makes silk dresses out of worms.

Wallace Stevens

An American, describing the experience of looking into an apparently straightforward matter and finding it full of unpleasant complexities, might use the expression 'opening a can of worms'. This elegant phrase (itself a metaphor) is nicely appropriate to investigating metaphor as a subject: something apparently specific and technical quickly reveals itself as a confusing mass of intertwining and slithery issues in which the head of one thing turns out to be the tail of another.

Deceptively innocent questions like 'What is metaphor?' and 'How does metaphor work?' suddenly become far deeper ones like 'What is language and what is its relationship to reality?' We find that metaphor, which, we may have thought, was merely a trick or device used by writers for special effects, is the subject of much debate and hefty books by critics, philosophers and anthropologists. Why is this?

Deep water

Reality is a cliché from which we escape by metaphor.

Wallace Stevens

Let's begin by risking a few definitions. Metaphor comes down to us from the Greek word 'metaphora' which means 'carrying over' or 'transference'. In speech and writing metaphor is a device in which one thing is expressed or characterised by giving it the qualities or characteristics of another thing. For example, we might say of a naïve person that she is 'a bit green'. She is naïve, therefore immature, therefore 'unripe', therefore like a green fruit. We are transferring to one thing (she) the characteristics of something else (an unripened apple).

Metaphor is a basic element in figurative language. Figurative language is language which does not mean what it says. Our naïve person is not actually green. A disturbing complex of problems is not really a can of worms. Issues do not have heads and tails.

If there is figurative language, then there ought also to be plain language: language, that is, which does mean what it says and only what it says, and which is made of words which do not have meanings borrowed or transferred from elsewhere. But is there?

Plain, or 'ordinary', speech contains a multitude of metaphors: the neck of a bottle, the roof of the mouth, the mouth of a river. Because they are so familiar we no longer notice the transference involved in their use. We call them 'dead metaphors'. Presumably, though, in the far dim past some person made the imaginative connection between the narrow part of a flask or bottle and his or her own neck. (And in so far as this was an imaginative connection between two dissimilar things, it was a 'poetic' insight which then passed into everyday speech. 'Language is fossil poetry' said the American philosopher Emerson.)

If we go a little deeper into 'ordinary' speech we find that it is not only these 'dead' metaphors that involve a transference from one area of life to another. Words which are apparently plain or abstract turn out to be metaphorical also. The word 'explore', for example, is the English translation of the Latin word meaning to pour out (like water). The word 'depend' means to hang from. Even the word 'plain' (as in 'plain language') comes from the Latin for flat (and 'explain' means to spread out flat, like a map). Since language has no physical substance, it cannot be literally flat, any more than it can be bumpy. In this usage, plain has had its meaning transferred from our observation of the physical world. 'Plain' is a metaphor.

Another possible definition, then: language is the means by which we make connections between the different things in the world around us, and between these things and ourselves. Which is to say, language is what we use to invent reality.

And a problem: is there a plain language which we can use to discuss figurative language?

This definition, and this problem, could lead us into deep water. And that's where we find those critics and philosophers and anthropologists splashing about arguing amongst themselves as to which of them has the safest bit of wreckage to cling to; we should return to more solid ground.

Those last two sentences, by the way, are another (rather strained) example of extended metaphor.

The Ground (and the Vehicle and the Tenor)

Poetry is a renovation of experience.

Wallace Stevens

Since a metaphor transfers characteristics from one thing to another, two things are obvious: first, that more than one thing is involved, and second, that the user of the metaphor sees a resemblance between them. In a simile, which is perhaps the most straightforward form of metaphor, these things are openly stated by the use of words such as 'like' or 'as' or 'as if'. Here is a simile from common speech: 'His face was as white as a sheet.' Three elements are being specified:

1 the thing being characterised, his face;
2 the thing being used to characterise it, a sheet;
3 the nature of the resemblance, whiteness.

There are technical terms we might use for these three elements. They are:

1 the **tenor**, which is the thing being characterised;
2 the **vehicle**, the thing being used to characterise it;
3 the **ground**, the basis of the resemblance.

Please note that tenor, vehicle and ground are terms coined by I. A. Richards some sixty years ago. As you might expect, other critics have since quarrelled with these terms and suggested different ones. We use them here for the following reasons: they are good enough; they have become more or less traditional, which means that if you choose to read other books about metaphor you are almost certain to come across them and at least you will know what they mean; and they are rather odd words, which may make them easier to remember. We are not suggesting that you need to use them when you are writing about poetry and prose, but they are quite useful when you are discussing metaphor in isolation, as we are now.

Here is a simile from uncommon speech (it is from a sonnet by Shakespeare):

> Like as the waves make towards the pebbled shore,
> So do our minutes hasten to their end.

It is a simile because two things are stated to be 'like' each other. The sense of the lines is that 'our minutes (our time, our brief lives) hasten to their end' (death) like waves make towards the shore. It differs from our previous simile in two ways: the vehicle (waves) comes before the tenor (our minutes) and the ground is not openly stated. Shakespeare leaves it to the reader to work out the ground, to work out why our lives are like waves. It's not that difficult, of course: our lives are like waves because although each is discernible from the other they all end up 'breaking' in death. Like the tides, life and death are universal and inevitable processes. There is a similarity between the regularity of minutes and the regularity of waves. 'Hasten' suggests that we move towards the end more swiftly than we might choose.

The important difference between the two similes is that whereas 'His face was as white as a sheet' does it all for us, Shakespeare's involves us in the process of making the connection. We need to use our imaginations a little bit in order to understand. We need to look into the metaphor. In a small way, we are 'renovating our experience' by looking at our lives in a way that differs somewhat from the usual way.

Dissimiles

Why is a raven like a writing desk?

The Mad Hatter, in Alice in Wonderland

Perhaps you might like to take a break at this point and play a game. Here are two lists of things, randomly arranged:

A	B
idea	birdcage
money	ship
poem	fist
sleep	crocodile
school	umbrella
television	garden
love affair	empty bottle
exam	desert island
hospital	ashtray
politician	game of cards

The object of the game is to invent your own similes by taking any word from column A as the tenor and any word from column B as the vehicle. Your similes can be as obscure or silly or serious as you like, but you must indicate the ground of the comparison, as in, for example, 'like a garden, a love affair needs weeding.' You may make the words singular or plural, and, if you wish, insert adjectives: bright idea, black umbrella, or whatever.

Fastness and speed

Because it states the things being compared (e.g. face and sheet, lives and waves), a simile is an open, or overt comparison. Other kinds of metaphor – most metaphors, in fact – do not name all the elements in a comparison and are therefore covert. And, of course, they are shorter. A metaphor is often a single word. This is the case with many dead metaphors. We do not say 'the vertical support of a table like a leg', we simply say 'the table-leg'. In this instance, no imaginative, connective process is necessary. (But it would be a different matter, wouldn't it, if you came across the phrase 'the varicose legs of antique tables', which would revive the idea of table-legs and human legs being alike.)

One way we might approach (or even evaluate) metaphors, then, is to consider to what extent they involve us in the connective process, to what extent they trigger our imaginations. This is not to say that to be good a metaphor needs to be far-fetched or wonderfully inventive. Here is a metaphor from Andrew Marvell's *To his Coy Mistress*:

> And yonder all before us lie
> Deserts of vast Eternity.

We are given the tenor (Eternity) and the vehicle (Deserts), and the ground is partly stated (vastness). It is left to the reader to supply the other common characteristics of eternity and deserts: emptiness, inhospitability, formlessness, and so on. (What they all add up to, of course, is death.) The fact that these associations are fairly obvious does not detract from the force of the metaphor. Their obviousness, their appropriateness, means we experience them quickly; so quickly, in fact, that we experience them almost unconsciously. Marvell 'gets us there' fast.

How 'fast' would you say these two metaphors are?

> i look where stealing needles of foam
> in the last light
> thread the creeping shores

> *e. e. cummings*

> The mountain sat upon the plain
> In his tremendous chair,
> His observation omnifold,
> His inquest everywhere.

> *Emily Dickinson*

Metaphor as concentration, metaphor as expansion

So far, we have suggested three things that metaphor is or can be: that it is a transfer of meaning from one thing to another; that it is a 'trigger' for imaginative activity; and that it may be a way of looking at or even ordering the world around us. Now we want to suggest two further functions of metaphor – functions that are directly related to the practice of writing, that make metaphor a supremely useful device to the writer. We have already hinted at the first of these when we said that Marvell's 'Deserts of vast Eternity' was a 'fast' metaphor. We could put it slightly differently and say that the word 'Deserts' is a concentration of meaning, because it brings with it those associated concepts like emptiness and inhospitability, and so forth. Marvell's phrase means 'the infinite nothingness of death'; but 'Deserts of vast Eternity' is far, far better, not only because it is more vivid or concrete, but also because it is more concentrated, more economical, more efficient. 'Deserts' comes with a wider range of associations than 'infinite nothingness' does.

As we said in Chapter 4 when we were talking about words like 'travel' and 'ramble', most words have an 'aura' of what are sometimes called 'radiated meanings'. These two terms encourage us to see words as operating within spheres of significance, as shown in the diagram opposite..

Perhaps we could see what the poet tries to do with metaphor as an attempt to reverse the direction of these arrows: to draw in (or concentrate) these radiated meanings into his poem. Or perhaps we could say it this way: the special skill of the poet is the ability to find the word within the sphere which carries with it the other meanings in the sphere.

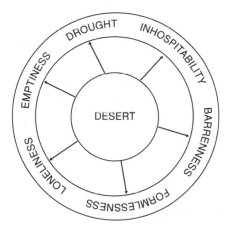

A digression (but one worth thinking about)

It may have occurred to you that the aura of 'desert' (for example) could have numerous other 'radii'. One could include any or all of the following: sand, Bedouin, cactus, dune, mirage, oasis, palm tree, scorpion, camel, rat, island, and so on and so on. Yet we know that these perfectly acceptable associations of 'desert' are not involved in the phrase 'Deserts of vast Eternity'. But how do we know? What is the 'filter' that prevents these things getting into the poem? Given that most of us have imaginations that function in a pretty haphazard way, we must suppose that the filter is put there by the poet, not by us. How does a poet do this? What does he write that tells us to exclude some of the possible associations of a word and include others?

Metaphor is a means of expansion because it increases enormously the vocabulary that a writer can use. Here are the opening lines of another sonnet by Shakespeare:

> When I to the sessions of sweet silent thought
> Summon up the remembrance of things past

Reduced to a banal level, this means 'When I think about the past'. Thus the word 'sessions' could have the general meaning of periods of time spent doing something, as in 'a drinking session'. But in close proximity to the word 'summon' it becomes more specific. Both words have a judicial connotation. 'Sessions' here is a legal proceeding, as in 'Petty Sessions', 'Quarter Sessions'. This meaning of the word has two effects. First, it alters our perception of the phrase 'sweet silent thought', which takes on a rather ironic aspect – it becomes a magistrate sitting in judgement rather than a pleasant and peaceful abstraction. It comes to mean 'judge' as opposed to 'nostalgia'. Second, and more important, it is a 'key' which gives Shakespeare access to a whole new vocabulary which is normally quite unrelated to remembering. This is the vocabulary, the aura, of the word 'Court': judge, jury, wrongdoing, justice, sentence, and so forth. Having keyed into this vocabulary, Shakespeare can, if he wishes, deploy it throughout the sonnet to express whatever feelings he has about the past. It increases his options. (But the judgemental implication in the first two lines lets us know in advance that he is not going to be dealing in cosy retrospection.)

This technique of using metaphor as a way of breaking into vocabularies not obviously related to the subject is one which Shakespeare uses frequently, not only in the sonnets but in his plays, too. In *Romeo and Juliet*, for example, when Juliet's mother is trying to sell her daughter the idea of marrying Count Paris, she advises her daughter to:

> Read o'er the volume of young Paris' face
> And find delight writ there with Beauty's pen ...

And she goes on to elaborate the initial book (volume) metaphor into Paris' pages and margins and suchlike. He is, she says, an 'unbound lover who only lacks a cover'. (Since 'cover' is also the horse-breeder's term for what stallions do to mares in stud farms, the speech has a nicely vulgar undercurrent of sexual innuendo.)

The importance of being different

We have been saying, in various ways, that metaphor is a means of establishing a meaningful relationship between two things, and we have spoken rather loosely about 'similarity' and 'resemblance'. We should say, to end with, that the difference between the two elements (vehicle and tenor) of a metaphor is at least as important as the similarity. If the two components of a metaphor – let's call them simply A and B – are already similar in our everyday way of looking at things, then that metaphor will not give us the enjoyable surprise of seeing something (A) in a new way (as being somehow like B). It will not achieve one of the most important functions of metaphor, which is to defamiliarise commonplace experience. For example, to describe a lawn as 'a green carpet' is very feeble, because those two things are at least as similar as they are dissimilar. It's a comparison we expect. On the other hand, there's this, the beautiful metaphor which opens a poem by Dylan Thomas:

> The force that through the green fuse drives the flower
> Drives my green age ...

If you think that 'fuse' here means the little gizmo inside an electrical plug, you're going to miss the point. Thomas' fuse is a sort of string or cord of combustible stuff; when you light the end of it, the flame hisses along the fuse and sets off the explosive charge at the other end. Thus the 'green fuse' is the flower's stalk, and the 'force' explodes as a flower at the end of it (the petals being seen as flames). The point is that a fuse isn't really like a flower stem at all; the 'resemblance' exists because Thomas persuades us to see it. And as well as getting across this visual likeness, the metaphor does something else: it suggests that the force – Nature – is destructive (explosive) as well as creative. The metaphor releases ideas which disappear if you replace the word 'fuse' with 'stalk'. These ideas can only exist if we are persuaded to see the similarity between two things while at the same time knowing that they are dissimilar. An interesting paradox.

It's time to apply the ideas raised in this chapter to some real writing. A hospital, which is (we like to think) a sterile place, may seem an unlikely place for poets to find the breeding-ground of metaphor; but then surprise is one of the more interesting things that metaphor has to offer.

The New Hospital

It might be a space ship
invented for nothing
but the longest journey
to a different world:

luxuriant flowerbeds
of brilliant dials
keep a constant spring
with electrical bees.

Even the lavatories
create a myth of peace –
porcelain pelicans
repeat to infinity,

glittering mermaids sit
side-saddle on basins,
and each urinal calmly
sucks its own peppermint.

A foetus in free fall
drifts through formaldehyde
forever, as if it was
the slow golden bubble

in a spirit level.
It knows neither illness
nor the painful pull
of gravity, the force

in tartan dressing gowns
and slippers like orphans
the patients cannot leave.
But, before they arrive,

death seems old-fashioned,
a drowsiness and a dream
of children duelling
with flintlock bananas ...

Craig Raine

1 What are

‘electrical bees’ (line 8)
‘porcelain pelicans’ (line 11)
‘glittering mermaids’ (line 13)
the ‘peppermint’ (line 16)?

2 Why is it important that the hospital is new, rather than old?

3 Take any two of the metaphors in this poem and say what their grounds are. In what ways are these metaphors 'appropriate'? How quickly do you 'get' them?

4 Is there a difference between the way metaphor works in lines 9 to 16 and the way it works in lines 17 to 21?

5 The syntax of lines 24 to 27 is rather peculiar. Are there more ways than one to read these lines? (Try putting in brackets and commas until you get what seems to you a satisfactory meaning. Then take them out and try it another way.)

6 What words would you use to describe the way Raine looks at things?

After Visiting Hours

Like gulls they are still calling —
I'll come again Tuesday. Our Dad
Sends his love. They diminish, are gone.
Their world has received them,

As our world confirms us. Their debris
Is tidied into vases, lockers, minds.
We become pulses; mouthpieces
Of thermometers and bowels.

The trolley's rattle dispatches
The last lover. Now we can relax
Into illness, and reliably abstracted
Nurses will straighten our sheets,

Reorganise our symptoms. Outside,
Darkness descends like an eyelid.
It rains on our nearest and dearest
In car-parks, at bus-stops.

Now the bed-bound rehearse
Their repertoire of movements,
The dressing-gowned shuffle, clutching
Their glass bodies.

Now siren voices whisper
From headphones, and vagrant
Doctors appear, wreathed in stethoscopes
Like South Sea dancers.

All's well, all's quiet as the great
Ark noses her way into night,
Caulked, battened, blessed for her trip,
And behind, the gulls crying.

U. A. Fanthorpe

1 The words 'we', 'us', and 'our' are used several times; how does this affect the way you read the poem?

2 There are three similes in this poem. What are they? How do they 'work'? (It may help if you think about the ground of each one.)

3 How do the following verbs operate as metaphors: 'confirms' (line 5); 'is tidied' (line 6); 'reorganise' (line 13); 'rehearse' (line 17)?

4 Three sentences begin with the word 'Now'. Why, and to what effect?

5 Gulls begin the poem. They also end it. How have they changed?

6 Look up the word 'ark' in a big dictionary. Which meanings might apply in this poem?

7 What do you find similar and dissimilar in the way that Craig Raine and Ursula Fanthorpe use metaphorical language? Do their views of hospital have something in common? How do they differ?

CENTRAL INTAKE HOSPITAL

Admittance Sheet   *Friday, August 15th, 1969*

Name...   Unknown
Sex...   Male
Age...   Unknown
Address...   Unknown

General remarks
... At midnight the police found Patient wandering on the Embankment near Waterloo Bridge. They took him into the station thinking he was drunk or drugged. They describe him as Rambling, Confused and Amenable. Brought him to us at 3 a.m. by ambulance. During admittance Patient attempted several times to lie down on the desk. He seemed to think it was a boat or a raft. Police are checking ports, ships, etc. Patient was well-dressed but had not changed his clothes for some time. He did not seem very hungry or thirsty. He was wearing trousers and a sweater, but he had no papers or wallet or money or marks of identity. Police think he was robbed. He is an educated man. He was given two Libriums but did not sleep. He was talking loudly. Patient was moved into the small Observation ward as he was disturbing the other patients.

NIGHT NURSE 6 *a.m.*

Patient has been awake all day, rambling, hallucinated, animated. Two Librium three-hourly. Police no information. Clothes sent for tracing, but unlikely to yield results: chainstore sweater and shirt and underclothes. Trousers Italian. Patient still under the impression that he is on some sort of voyage. Police say possibly an amateur or a yachtsman.

DOCTOR Y. 6 *p.m.*

I need a wind. A good strong wind. The air is stagnant. The current must be pounding along at a fair rate. Yes, but I can't feel it. Where's my compass? *That* went days ago, don't you remember? I need a wind, a good strong wind. I'll whistle for one. I would whistle for one if I had paid the piper. A wind from the East, hard on to my back, yes. Perhaps I am still too near the shore? But who knows, I might have drifted back again inshore. Oh no, no, I'll try rowing. The oars are gone, don't you remember, they went days ago. No, you must be nearer landfall than you think. The Cape Verde Islands were to starboard – when? Last week. Last *when*? That was no weak, that was my wife. The sea is saltier here than close inshore. A salt, salt sea, the brine coming flecked off the horse's jaws to mine. On my face, thick crusts of salt. I can taste it. Tears, saltwater. I can taste salt from the sea. From the desert. The deserted sea. Sea horses. Dunes. The wind flicks sand from the crest of the dunes, spins off the curl of waves. Sand moves and sways and masses itself into waves, but slower. Slow. The eye that would measure the pace of sand horses, as I watch the rolling gallop of sea horses would be an eye indeed. Aye Aye. I. I could catch a horse, perhaps and ride it, but for me a sea horse, no horse of sand, since my time is man-time and it is God for deserts. Some ride dolphins. Plenty have testified. I may leave my sinking raft and cling to the neck of a sea horse, all the way to Jamaica and poor Charlie's Nancy, or, if the current swings me south at last, to the coast where the white bird is waiting.

Doris Lessing: Briefing for a Descent into Hell

1 Here we have three 'voices'. In just a few words, describe how they differ.

2 What is the metaphor that the patient's 'monologue' is built on? Can you say what its tenor and vehicle and ground are?

3 There is something ironic about the police checking ports, ships etc., and supposing the patient might be a yachtsman. Why is this ironic, exactly?

4 Doris Lessing has set herself a problem: she has to make the patient's words rambling and incoherent, but we, her readers, must be able to follow them somehow. What linguistic devices has she used to achieve this double purpose? Do you think she succeeds?

8

Metaphor 3: Up the River

'I beg your pardon,' said the Mole, pulling himself together with an effort. 'You must think me very rude; but all this is so new to me. So – this is – a River!'

'*The* River,' corrected the Rat.

'And you really live by the river? What a jolly life!'

'By it and with it and on it and in it,' said the Rat. 'It's brother and sister to me, and aunts, and company, and food and drink, and (naturally) washing. It's my world, and I don't want any other. What it hasn't got is not worth having, and what it doesn't know is not worth knowing.' ...

'But isn't it a bit dull at times?' said the Mole.

Kenneth Grahame: The Wind in the Willows

Symbols

At the end of the last chapter Doris Lessing used the sea as an 'existential metaphor' – a metaphor, that is, for life or death. The river is a similarly timeless and universal existential metaphor. Before you read the following two pieces of writing, you should think about or discuss why this is. You might consider the historical and cultural relationships between rivers and people; the way there is a two-way traffic of language between rivers and people (rivers have heads and mouths; the proverb says 'still waters run deep'; we have our 'sources' of inspiration or metaphor or whatever). What are the qualities that rivers possess that make them appropriate metaphors for human life?

If you pursue these lines of thought you are almost certain to come up with the word 'symbol'. Since the two pieces that follow have symbolic elements, this seems a suitable place to try to define this word.

Symbolism differs from metaphor generally in that symbols need not have – and usually do not have – any resemblance, physical or otherwise, with the things they 'mean' or 'stand for'. The simple reason for this, of course, is that symbols frequently represent ideas or beliefs or philosophies or identities: abstract things, in other words, which do not have a physical reality. Symbols of this sort include the wheel (representing fate or destiny), the star of David (Judaism), the cross (Christianity), the hour-glass (Time).

There is a distinction to be made between public symbolism and private symbolism. Public symbols, like those just mentioned, are drawn from religion or mythology, or they are traditional in literature (the rose as a symbol of beauty, for instance). Private symbols, as you might imagine, are developed by individual writers or groups of writers in their work. Such symbols will be understood only if the writer indicates in some way what they stand for, or if we, as readers, are already familiar with the writer's use of such images. William Blake, W. B. Yeats and T. S. Eliot are perhaps the best-known of writers who use systems of private symbolism. (Just to make matters a little more complicated, these writers also use public symbols in private ways; they give their own meanings to traditional images.)

Some symbols are, so to speak, more symbolic than others. Some symbols are unambiguous, others less so. The white dove, for example, automatically indicates peace. Likewise, if you came across a raven perched on a skull it would have to mean death. On the other hand, if in a poem or a novel you encountered a tower rising out of a desolate landscape you might reasonably suspect that it was symbolic – but of what? Security, perhaps? Or pride, or civilisation, or solitude? The symbol would be ambiguous; its meaning would depend upon its context – the language used to describe it, the events or feelings the writer associates with it, the content of the poem or novel as a whole. The river is another such ambiguous or complex symbol. The river that fascinated Jonathan Raban as a child was the Mississippi. It was, however, an imaginary Mississippi, conjured up by the stories of Mark Twain; Raban lived in Norfolk:

> The only river I knew was hardly more than a brook. It spilled
> through a tumbledown mill at the bottom of our road, opened into a
> little trouty pool, then ran on through watermeadows over gravelled
> shallows into Fakenham, where it slowed and deepened, gathering
> strength for the long drift across muddy flatlands to Norwich and the
> North Sea. All through my Huckleberry Finn summer, I came down to

the mill to fish for roach and dace, and if I concentrated really hard, I could see the Mississippi there. First I had to think it twice as wide, then multiply by two, then two again … the rooftops of Fakenham went under. I sank roads, farms, church spires, the old German prisoner-of-war camp, Mr. Banham's flour mill. I flooded Norfolk; silvering the landscape like a mirror, leaving just an island here, a dead tree there, to break this lonely, enchanted monotony of water. It was a heady, intensely private vision. I hugged the idea of the huge river to myself. I exulted in the freedom and solitude of being afloat on it in my imagination.

Jonathan Raban: Old Glory

Thirty years later, Jonathan Raban decided to set this private vision against the reality of the river. In an aluminium boat with an outboard motor, he travelled the length of the Mississippi southwards from Minnesota to the Gulf of Mexico. In this next extract we find him about a quarter of the way down.

I had meant to sleep in, to spend at least one more day in Savanna, but when I awoke at nine there wasn't a leaf moving in the maple tree outside my window. It was too good a travelling day to lose. I had seen from the charts that there was a huge pool above the lock and dam at Clinton, just a little way downstream. I was scared of facing it in any measurable wind at all; it was a lake seven miles long and four miles wide, without a single marked island to give cover and the channel running clean through its middle. I packed my bags in a hurry, keeping one eye on the leaves to make sure that they weren't beginning to stir.

10   The river was safely dead in the sun. Every flourish and excursion of the current was marked as a neat crease on its top. I was sad to leave Savanna; even the old satirist at the gas dock was unpredictably friendly.

"I hear you was out last night treeing coon. How many you get?"

"Just one, and a skunk. I thought you'd have smelled it on me."

He laughed. "Yeah. Maybe I did."

Perhaps, at last, I'd lost my urban taint. I slid past Sabula on the current, dodged the wakes of a couple of upstream tows, rounded a long string of green islands, and entered the pool above Clinton. The chart

20   just called it "Big Slough". This seemed a strange falling-down on the creative job of naming sloughs. Either they were christened after people or they had memorable names which expressed their shape, or what lay in them, or what grew on their islands: Snag, Hubble, Soupbone, Hickory, Crooked, Dead Man's … No-one, apparently, had found anything to say about Big Slough except that it was big, and its bigness had rendered every other feature irrelevant.

On this windless morning, the water of Big Slough looked as viscous as thick machine oil. It was blackened by the decomposing forest which lay under it. Miles of it were so shallow that the stump fields on either

30   side of the channel were exposed right down to their spreading roots. Wedded to their own immobile reflections, the stumps, in their hundreds of thousands, made arabesque patterns of flattened hexagons.

Away across the slough there was the rigid outline of a man in a punt, fishing for his image, and the image casting back. Not a sound, not a ripple, fractured the great, empty symmetry of the place. With the motor killed, I was part of it: doubled in water, I was as lifeless a component of the scheme as a carboniferous stump.

If only one could make the notion of freedom into a tangible object, I thought, it would look like Big Slough – a huge, curved, reflective
40 vacancy. No sea could quite attain this greasy calm, or communicate the essential place of dead things, rottenness, torpidity in the vision. Big Slough could.

In my old, city life there hadn't been a day when I didn't sweat at the sheer fiddle of the thing: the rows, makings-up, the telephone ringing, or failing to ring; the brown envelopes with windows; the jumpy claustrophobia of just surviving as one small valve in the elaborate and hazardous circuit of ordinary society. If only .. if only .. and at the end of the sentence there was always somewhere the word free, a careless stand-in for a careless notion of benign emptiness. But Big Slough
50 really looked free, and for all its peat-brown beauty, it made me shudder. Floating on it felt like being dead, and I reckoned there was a lesson to be learned from that sensation.

Freedom, though, would never be so conveniently marked with such a regular, winding trail of buoys. Red and black, red and black, their roulette colours lead out past the stumps, away from the enormous weir and into the chamber of Lock 13. For the first time in my trip, I saw a Mississippi lock as a safe, contained place; it felt just the right size, and it was good to be inching down the wall with Big Slough behind me.

Jonathan Raban: Old Glory

Notes
'treeing coon': the American pastime of hunting racoon at night with dogs and torches. The unfortunate racoons try to escape by climbing trees.
'tow': enormous rafts of lashed-together barges pushed (not towed, in fact) by flat-fronted three-storey-high tugs.

The following questions apply to the second passage:

1 What do the first two paragraphs (down to 'friendly') tell you about the writer's experience of the river so far? What do you get from the sentence 'The river was safely dead in the sun'?

2 What does the writer mean by 'my urban taint' (line 17)? How does this phrase relate to his conversation with the old satirist? And what does 'at last' tell you?

3 Look up the word 'slough' in a fairly large dictionary (The Shorter Oxford English Dictionary, for example). Which of its meanings might be relevant to this passage?

4 What strikes you about the fifth paragraph (beginning 'On this windless morning') as a piece of descriptive 'Nature' writing?

5 Pick out the key words in the fifth paragraph which most strongly convey the 'feel' of Big Slough. Is there a word or idea that connects them all?

6 How is the word 'reflective' used in line 39?

7 The sentence that begins 'In my old, city life ... ' connects back with an earlier phrase. Which?

8 The word 'careless' is used twice in lines 48-49. Does it have the same meaning each time?

9 Apart from the colour association, why, do you think, does Raban use the word 'roulette' in connection with marker buoys (line 55)?

10 Pick out two metaphors from this passage and say why they are, in your opinion, effective (or not).

Refer to both extracts to answer these questions:

11 What, briefly, is 'the lesson to be learned' (line 52 of the second extract)?

12 Are there things in these passages that encourage us to see the river as symbolic in some way?

In the following poem, the rivers are – at first glance, anyway – rather more modest affairs than the Mississippi:

Rising Damp

"A river can sometimes be diverted, but it is a very hard thing to lose it altogether."
J. G. Head: paper read to the Auctioneer's Institute in 1907

At our feet they lie low,
The little fervent underground
Rivers of London.

Effra, Graveney, Falcon, Quaggy,
Wandle, Welbrook, Tyburn, Fleet

Whose names are disfigured, frayed, effaced.

These are the Magogs that chewed the clay
To the basin that London nestles in.
These are the currents that chiselled the city,
That washed the clothes and turned the mills,
Where children drank and salmon swan
And wells were holy.

They have gone under.
Boxed, like the magician's assistant.
Buried alive in the earth.
Forgotten, like the dead.

They return spectrally after heavy rain,
Confounding surburban gardens. They infiltrate
20 Chronic bronchitis statistics. A silken
Slur haunts dwellings by shrouded
Watercourses, and is taken
For the footing of the dead.

Being of our world, they will return
25 (Westbourne, caged at Sloane Square,
Will jack from his box),
Will deluge cellars, detonate manholes,
Plant effluent in our faces,
Sink the city.

30 *Effra, Graveney, Falcon, Quaggy,*
Wandle, Walbrook, Tyburn, Fleet

It is the other rivers that lie
Lower, that touch us only in dreams
That never surface. We feel their tug
35 As a dowser's rod bends to the source below

Phlegethon, Acheron, Lethe, Styx.

U. A. Fanthorpe

Notes

'Magogs' (line 8): giants. In ancient British legend Gogmagog was the last of a race of monstrous giants to be defeated by King Brute (or Brutus). In another version of the myth, the giant becomes two – Gog and Magog – who were captured and brought in chains to London where they became porters at the Royal palace. In the poetry of William Blake, Gog and Magog are two strong demons compelled to subdue their master, Satan.

Phlegethon, *Acheron*, *Lethe* and *Styx* are the four rivers of Hades (the Underworld, Hell) in Classical mythology. Styx is the river across which the souls of the dead are ferried; the waters of Lethe cause those who drink them to lose all memory of their past lives; Acheron is the river of woe; Phlegethon is the river whose waters are fire.

1 A number of words and phrases in this poem are deliberately ambiguous. Some manage to be both literal and metaphorical at the same time. Using a dictionary if necessary, consider the meaning of the following: 'lie low' (line 2); 'fervent' (line 3); 'confounding' (line 19); 'slur' (line 21); 'shrouded' (line 21); and 'footing' (line 23).

2 Look at those words again. How does the context of each one affect its meaning?

3 Another name for Hades is *Dis*. Is there a pun (a play on words) in line 7?

4 The three six-line stanzas (i.e. lines 8 to 13; 18 to 23; 24 to 29) describe in turn what the rivers once did, what they do now, and what they will do in the future. For each stanza, write a few sentences on

(a) the character of the rivers

(b) the way the sound and form of the stanza is used to convey the character of the rivers.

Consider the sounds of individual words and phrases, punctuation, and the rhythm of the lines. (You should read them aloud, or at least 'aloud in your head'.)

5 What strikes you about lines 14-17 as compared with the lines immediately before and after them?

6 What is the meaning – or meanings – of 'source' in line 35?

7 What is the point of the quotation at the head of the poem?

8 Finally, how are the rivers – buried and mythical – used in this poem? Do you think they are symbolic? Of what?

9
Metaphor 4:
Wholes in the Ground

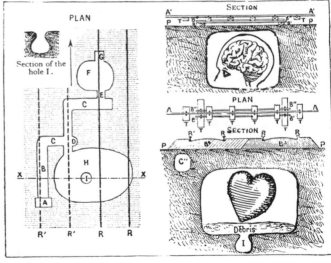

AN OLD SUBTERR~~XXXXXX~~ ~~XX~~FUGE.

In this chapter we are going to do three things. We are going to look at different attitudes to metaphor; we'll try examining closely a 'complex' metaphor; and to end with we'll offer a checklist of questions that you might find useful to ask yourself about metaphorical language. But let's begin with a satirical piece by Thomas Carper.

The Resident Poet

*The quiet tones of his poems only lay a delicate skin over the
abyss he has seen too well.*
    From a book review.

The Resident Poet walked along a path
Across the campus. He was bleary-eyed
From last night's reading, and its aftermath,
And feeling, well, like hell when he espied,
As only poets do, a hole being dug
(Some steam pipes for the dorm had sprung a leak)
Right in his way. "A metaphor," he smug-
Ly thought, "for all the quintessential bleak-
Nesses of our existence." Looking in
The shallow trench – it would become "abyss" –
He made his notes (as Susan's delicate skin
Nudged him in recollection, with her kiss
Beginning morning, once her youthful arm
Had reached past his to shut off the alarm).

Thomas Carper

Think about – or, better still, write down answers to – these questions:

1 This poem is written in a particular conventional form. Do you happen to know what this form is called?

2 What is Thomas Carper suggesting about the way poems 'happen'? Do you think he may be right?

3 Why do holes in the ground always seem to be associated metaphorically with miserable ideas? Can you imagine some way in which holes in the ground could be used as a metaphor for something happy?

4 With the previous question in mind, do you consider the Resident Poet's notion of the trench being a metaphor for 'the quintessential bleaknesses of our existence' to be a) original b) profound c) banal d) silly?

5 What do you notice about the endings of lines 7 and 8? Can you make any connection between the way these lines end and what the Poet is doing?

6 How are we meant to take 'As only poets do' (line 5)?

7 Who might Susan be? (There is a clue in line 3.)

8 Do you think that the Resident Poet is honest? What evidence is there in the poem for (or against) his existence being 'quintessentially bleak'?

9 What do you think of the metaphor used in the book review? What does it mean? And what does Carper achieve by quoting it?

10 What is Thomas Carper mocking, exactly?

Now we have to go on a brief historical excursion.

Greeks and Romantics

Traditionally, there are two ways of looking at metaphor, and they are often referred to as the Classical view and the Romantic (or even Post-Romantic) view. They represent very different sets of ideas, not only about what metaphor is but also about what poetry should do and how it should be read. That's why they're worth knowing about. Please be aware that because we want to summarise these views as briefly as possible, we have to simplify and generalise outrageously.

The Classical view

It's Classical because it originates in the writings of the Ancient Greek and Roman writers and philosophers; in the writings of the Greek philosopher Aristotle, in particular. You will be tempted to conclude from this that we are talking about ideas that belong in the far and murky past, but this is not so. These elderly ideas have had a remarkably long and active life. They had a powerful effect upon literature up to and into the nineteenth century, and as a way of looking at language they are still worth thinking about.

Aristotle had strong views on language, and at the heart of these views is the concept of clarity. Language, he argued, should be plain and transparent. This is because language is a uniquely human gift which enables us to understand and make sense of the world around us. Language should be transparent because we need to look 'through' it at real things. Language which draws attention to itself rather than to the things it is meant to indicate is potentially dangerous because it 'gets in the way' – it handicaps understanding. Figurative language, metaphorical language, is, of course, language which draws attention to itself, and Aristotle was not altogether happy with it. He saw it as a departure from ordinary language, a deviant use of language. (This attitude lives on in our phrase 'poetic licence', which contains the idea that poetic language inevitably deviates from the truth.) As we all know, deviants need to be kept under control; accordingly, Aristotle and later Classical writers busied themselves developing and refining rules for governing the use of metaphorical language. The key to these rules is the concept of **decorum**, which means being 'appropriate, proper, seemly'. Here, very simply put, are the Classical rules for metaphor:

metaphor should	**metaphor should not**
be used sparingly	interrupt the narrative or the development of the theme
be decorative and/or illustrative	be lewd or ugly
be 'signalled' or overt (e.g. by being clearly announced as being a simile)	be covert (i.e. presented as as if it were 'plain' language)
be in itself 'ennobling' or 'elevating' or 'charming' or 'beautiful'	be far-fetched or strange
be fitting (i.e. appropriate to the tone or the theme or the subject)	bring together two things that are incongruous

Put at its simplest, the Classical view of metaphor is that it is an 'extra', something added to plain language. Aristotle called it 'the seasoning of the meat'. The Roman writer Quintillian called it 'the supreme ornament' of style. Metaphor is a 'special effect'; it is for decorating ordinary language to make it more striking or beautiful or memorable. Or it can be used to illustrate an idea, conveying something new by comparing it with something familiar, or expressing something abstract by comparing it with something concrete. But the overriding consideration is that, however it is used, it must be in the service of clarity.

Now while you, as a modern reader, are almost certain to find the very idea of rules for poets alien or irritating, it is more than likely that these Classical criteria (the 'shoulds' and 'should nots' above) for the use of metaphor still have some hold over you. Look at them again: which could you say you completely reject? Or accept? Most student groups contain the odd lurking Aristotelian who will be a 'message-hunter', who will cling to the notion that poets use figurative language to decorate or disguise what they are 'really' saying. Isn't this attitude a rude descendant of the Classical concept of the 'decorative' metaphor? And don't we all, in moments of weakness, resent coming across 'difficult' or 'obscure' metaphors because they 'get in the way'?

One last question before we jump two thousand years: what, do you suppose, would Aristotle have thought of Craig Raine's *The New Hospital* (page 85) or Ursula Fanthorpe's *Rising Damp* (page 93)?

The Romantic or Post-Romantic View

The Classical view of poetic language – that it was a special language which differed from 'natural' language – persisted for a very long time. Here's the poet Thomas Gray, writing in 1742:

> The language of the age is never the language of poetry ... Our poetry has a language peculiar to itself; to which everyone that has written has added something by enriching it with foreign idioms and derivatives ...

(The idea that language can be 'enriched' by adding 'derivatives' sounds rather odd to a modern ear.)

The net result of this kind of thinking was that generations of English poets wrote in a language that was highly artificial and stylised, and jam-packed with Classical references to gods and goddesses and nymphs and whatnot. We call this language Poetic Diction; if you'd like a taste of it, get hold of an anthology and look up Gray's *The Progress of Poesy*. You'll probably not understand a word of it, but never mind.

The first real challenge to this pseudo-Classical poetic language came at the end of the eighteenth century, with what we now call the Romantic Revolution, and in particular with the work of the two poets William Wordsworth and Samuel Taylor Coleridge.

Wordsworth flatly rejected the basic Classical premise. There is, he insisted, no special language that is peculiar to poetry. There is no fundamental distinction to be made between the language of poetry and ordinary speech. A poet, he said, should be 'a man speaking to men' in 'language really used by men'. (Let's be charitable and assume he meant by women too.) The language of poetry should be democratic, not elitist. What's more, there is no essential difference between the languages of prose and verse. No matter what form the writer uses, his task is to express his 'vision' and his 'passion' in language which is 'alive with metaphors.'

These ideas saw the light of day in 1798, when Wordsworth and Coleridge published a book of poems called *Lyrical Ballads*. The critics slated it.

In 1817 Coleridge published his *Biographia Literaria*, which contains a wealth of ideas and opinions, some contradictory, some confusing, many pinched from earlier writers. For the purposes of this chapter we'll limit ourselves to looking at one of his key words: **imagination**.

The word 'imagination' has lost a good deal of its force during the hundred and fifty-odd years that separate us from Coleridge. In common speech today, 'imagination' means simply invention or inventiveness. A fond mother will say that her son has 'a vivid imagination' to indicate that he is a pathological little liar. But for Coleridge, the imagination (which he would write with a capital *I*) was not only a creative faculty (producing images) but was also, just as importantly, a kind of inner vision. You should understand the word as having the meanings of insight ('seeing into') and perception ('seeing through'), as well as invention.

Coleridge describes the imagination as **synthetic**. Forget the modern associations of the word – 'imitation' or 'fake' – Coleridge means that the imagination synthesises, and to synthesise is to make a new, single thing out of different materials. It involves not just assembling things, as a chair might be assembled out of various bits of wood, but transforming things, as, for example, sand and lead oxide are transformed by heat into glass. In a similar way, says Coleridge, the poet's imagination should transform different things into a new unity, and this unity is the poem. This synthesising, transforming process in which things (seen or experienced) are made into a new unity is metaphorical language, because metaphor is the device which brings together and 'fuses' different things. This is the heart of the difference between the Classical and the Romantic views of metaphor. The Classical view is that metaphor illustrates or decorates an idea. The Romantic view is that metaphor *is* the idea. We could set out these opposing views like this:

the Classical metaphor	the Romantic metaphor
is decorative	is intrinsic
is incidental	is essential
illustrates thought	expresses thought
should be drawn from and appeal to universal human understanding	comes from and appeals to the individual imagination

It should be obvious from these 'lists' that they add up to very different views of metaphor and very different ideas about what poetry should do, where it comes from, and the poet's relationship with the reader. For one thing, Classical poetry in Ancient Greece and Rome was public: it was recited to listeners, and therefore it was desirable that its language could be 'taken in' at a single hearing. Coleridge, on the other hand, was writing at a time when the usual medium for poetry was the printed book. For him, therefore, the communication between poet and reader was individual and personal, rather than public: the poet addressed himself to a single reader on a one-to-one basis. The obvious advantages that printed verse has over spoken verse are that it can be read as fast or as slowly as the reader wishes, it can be read several times, and it can be taken bit by bit – the reader doesn't have to remember the whole thing in order to see its overall shape and the way it develops. This means that the writer can make certain demands upon the reader – for example, by using complex metaphorical language, which is in turn a demand upon the reader's imagination. It is not the poet's primary task, said Coleridge, to use language to achieve the greatest clarity (which was the Aristotelian view). The poet's job is to affect directly the reader's imagination. A poet is a good poet only to the extent that he or she activates and energises that imagination. Reading a poem should be an imaginative event or journey:

> The reader should be carried forward, not merely or chiefly by the mechanical impulse of curiosity, or by a restless desire to arrive at a final solution; but by the pleasurable activity of the mind excited by the attractions of the journey itself.

For Coleridge, the absolute, the ideal, achievement of a poem is that in some way (and he could come up with only the word 'magical' to describe this process) it enables the reader to experience or re-enact the workings of the poet's imagination when he was creating the poem. Speaking of a passage by Shakespeare, Coleridge says 'You feel him to be a poet, inasmuch as he has made you one.'

Now, all this may stike you as fanciful or hopelessly idealistic, and perhaps it is; but, if you are an A-level Literature student, Coleridge's ideas directly affect you, and in two ways:

1 The idea that a poem is a shared imaginative experience – that it is, so to speak, a joint production of the poet's imagination and the reader's – means that in writing about a poem you are (or should be) writing about yourself. If you are good at it, you'll be writing about *your* responses to the poem, you'll be describing what *your* imagination is up to. That is what Coleridge thought literary criticism should be, and that is what A-Level examiners like to see too.

2 If a poet's greatness consists in his or her power to activate and involve the reader's imagination, then, says Coleridge, Shakespeare is the best there is. Coleridge was the first English poet to idolise (and that is not too strong a word) Shakespeare. There is the belief, still, that you cannot properly study English Literature without studying the Man from Stratford; and that is largely thanks to Coleridge. We're sure you are all duly grateful.

Single, double and complex vision

In Chapter 7, you may remember, we talked about the different elements of metaphor – tenor, vehicle and ground – and said that a transference takes place between vehicle and tenor. The trouble with that is (and it's a problem that haunts you whenever you try to write about metaphor) that the very act of writing 'vehicle and tenor' makes them seem separate, or at least separable, entities. But metaphor, at its best, doesn't work like that. The elements of a metaphor are – or can be – an interaction; and this interaction can produce a third, new, idea. One of the 'magical' (to use Coleridge's word) powers of metaphor is that it can defy the laws of arithmetic by making one plus one equal three. We'll use the word 'image' for this third thing, this product of metaphor, even though image suggests something visual and not all metaphors appeal to the mind's eye.

Imagine a photograph of a man's face. Now imagine a transparency of a wolf's face laid over it. Your eye has three choices: it can look through the wolf's face at the man's face; it can stop at the wolf's face; or it can see both at once, the composite image wolf-man. This image may trigger certain ideas in your mind: the Werewolf, that popular star of horror movies and fairy tales; the concept of the 'wolfishness' of Man, his violent and predatory nature; a vision of man stripped of his civilising mask ... and so on. It will also, probably, evoke certain feelings: revulsion, perhaps, or fear, or (if you are more than usually cynical) amusement. Whatever your reaction, the point is that the double-vision composite image wolf-man is different from, and more than, either wolf or man or wolf and man; it is wolf as man, man as wolf. Not A and B, but A as B: a synthesis.

Metaphorical language often strives for this double-vision effect and for the resultant image which is more complex than the sum of its component parts. The American poet Ezra Pound said that 'An image is that which presents an intellectual and emotional complex in an instant of time', which suggests that we register or take in the complexities of imagery quickly or perhaps even unconsciously; maybe so, but in practice (and certainly in A-Level essays) these complexities of meaning and association may take a little teasing out.

Of course, not all metaphors achieve, or try to achieve, the kind of intellectual and emotional complexity that Pound speaks of. Metaphors that have a 'Classical' role, that serve to decorate or illustrate, are unlikely to achieve it. But because we live in a 'Post-Romantic' era rather than a 'Neo-Classical' era, we tend to value complex, image-producing metaphorical language more highly. This does not mean that only modern writers have dealt in this kind of language. Shakespeare did it – which is one of the main reasons Coleridge thought so highly of him.

We are going to try now to prise apart (as sensitively as possible, of course) one of these complex metaphors. It's from a poem you have already read. It is the last four lines of U. A. Fanthorpe's *After Visiting Hours* (which in its complete form is on page 86):

> All's well, all's quiet as the great
> Ark noses her way into night,
> Caulked, battened, blessed for her trip,
> And behind, the gulls crying.

This ark, you may remember, is a metaphor for a hospital. The gulls are – or were, at the beginning of the poem – visitors to patients. We'll set out the components of this metaphor, along with the more obvious associations of each, some of their 'radiated meanings':

tenor	ground	vehicle
hospital	a device for saving life	ark
treatment		voyage
cure		security
life		survival
death		Flood

Clearly, there are parallels, or connections, between the words in the tenor column and those in the vehicle column. Now we'll try to represent graphically the network of connections between the terms of the metaphor and the words of the stanza:

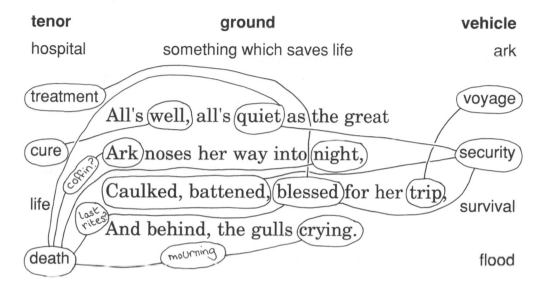

These lines of interaction are, so to speak, the web that binds together the components of the metaphor – hospital and ark – into the single complex image of hospital-as-ark. Many of the connections are ambiguous. 'Trip', for instance, clearly links with the life-saving voyage of the ark, but it is a trip into night, which suggests death. 'Quiet' means peaceful, but it might be 'quiet as the grave'. Despite the strong associations between ark and survival, several of these lines connect to death; so perhaps at one level the poem's meaning is ironic – that both hospital and ark are only temporary refuges from the 'Flood' which is death. And as well as all this, there is the surreal visual image of a hospital moving like a great ship through night-time suburbia.

These four lines of Ursula Fanthorpe's poem help us to make a couple of points:

1 If a metaphor does achieve the double-vision or complex vision effect that we have been discussing, then it cannot be taken at face value. Complexity in an image almost always involves ambiguity – for the simple reason that the image will mean more than one thing.

2 Complex images can alter our understanding of the poem as a whole. They can take it in a new direction, they can affect the way we have interpreted the poem so far. When Fanthorpe springs her ark image on us in the very last stanza of her poem, we revise – or ought to revise – our understanding of the gulls in the first line, the rain that falls on the outside world, and the general air of preparation that pervades the poem. When that ark pops up, it doesn't just illustrate or decorate the general idea of 'hospital', it changes the way we've understood the hospital and what's gone on inside and outside it.

A metaphor checklist

If you find yourself lost in the forests of metaphor, one way out is to ask yourself questions. The following list of leading questions may help you. It is also a way of summing up what we have said in our chapters about metaphor. Where questions are followed by numbers in brackets, these refer to pages where these questions have been discussed or examples given.

Is the metaphor overt, or is it covert?

Is it a simile (80) or is it suggested by a single word?

Is it 'foregrounded' in some way?

If so, then how? Does it, for example, have a line to itself? Does it use words that are incongruous in the poem, or very unusual words? Does it come at the end of a poem unexpectedly?

Are all three elements of the metaphor stated?

If not, how much of its meaning do you have to supply? Is it a 'fast' or a 'slow' metaphor? (82)

Is it an 'expansive' metaphor? (83)

Does it enable the poet to key into other kinds of vocabulary?

Is the metaphor illustrative or decorative?

Does it strike you as being 'incidental'? Is its purpose to describe more vividly? Does it meet some of the requirements of the 'Classical' metaphor? (100)

Do you know what all the words in the metaphor mean?

How many of a word's possible meanings is the writer exploiting? Even quite familiar words may have unfamiliar meanings which the poet is making use of. (94)

Is the dissimilarity between the terms of the metaphor as striking – or even more striking – than the similarity?

Is the metaphor a symbol, or does it have symbolic qualities? (90)

Does it fulfil any of the requirements of the 'Romantic' metaphor? (100)

Does it create (or 'synthesise') a new idea?

Does the metaphor achieve, or try to achieve, double or complex vision? (101)

Does it create a new image, of 'A as B'? If so, what does this image convey to you? Does it cause you to re-think the poem? (103)

How successful do you think the metaphor is in achieving
    vividness?
    clarity?
    economy?
    emotional force?
    a new way of looking at things?

10

The Angel and the Private Eye

Once upon a time ...

This chapter is about the ways writers of fiction use different narrative techniques in order to produce different effects upon you when you're reading, in order to persuade you to interpret and understand what you are reading in different ways. The subject of 'narrative method' should be of interest to any would-be novelist or critic because it involves the actual working practices of individual writers and the sorts of decisions that they have to make before they tell a story. Just as poems are made of formal patterns as well as being kinds of information, so narratives are formal arrangements of their material.

'Telling stories' involves a whole series of decisions and choices, some of which may be your own, some of which may be forced upon you by the kind of story you are telling, the attitude you have towards your material, the sort of relationship that you to desire to establish with your readers (or listeners), and the different reactions you want from them.

Unusual for a Monday

Let's imagine that we want to tell a story about an unexpected visitor to a classroom. There are probably hundreds of different ways in which this event can be told, but here are six 'standard' narrative approaches. We'll begin with the 'buttonholing-the-reader-in-order-to-get-a-hearing' approach and go on from there:

1   What do you know, dear reader, of angels: those pretty but sexless beings adorned with golden tresses of hair and feathered wings that peep over the shoulder and drag at heel? They live in Victorian engravings and Mediaeval Bibles, but no one seems to see them very often in our drab and unimaginative century. You must believe in them though, because, if you do not, then this story will remain as words on the page and become neither pictures in your mind nor feelings in your heart.

2   Mr Peet stood at the front of the class and opened his own dull brown copy of a school edition of Chaucer's *The Merchant's Tale*. His students, with considerable reluctance, found their dull brown books. Outside, the wind was blowing furiously against the side of the nissen hut classroom and slamming rain against the rusty metal windows and the corrugated asbestos roof. Not so far away, at the eastern edge of the Atlantic Ocean, huge, grey and magnificent waves were rolling towards the Cornish coast and keeping fishermen indoors. The lesson dragged on. "'To doon hir ful plesance ... ' Now, who can translate that for us all? Higgens?' The students all giggled; they knew this quote was probably rude, and that Higgens never did his homework, and so didn't know what they all knew: that this was one of Chaucer's 'earthy' bits, and so good for a laugh. Then Peet noticed something in the corner of the room. Nothing precise at first, just a sort of gilt presence. There was something over there that had been transparent and was slowly becoming opaque, standing quietly by the wall near the classroom door. It was a kind of golden cloud, an outline of something, as yet undefined. Could it be that he was, at last, going mad?

3   There's something weird happening, thinks Alex as she sits pretending to be utterly fascinated by the lecture Peet is providing for her on the fourteenth century English Church's attitudes towards women. There's definitely a strange sound behind her, very faint, like a thin angry mosquito whine, combined with a sort of irregular low breathing sound. The light in the classroom as a whole is slowly changing, getting brighter. Even Peet notices.

4   I'm not a very imaginative person really. You know what I mean; I like to escape with a novel now and again, and I definitely enjoy a good horror video, but this, well this was different. It was a very ordinary sort of day, raining (as always), and it was Monday, so that meant Chaucer. Pretty boring stuff on the whole, apart from the rude bits. Well, anyway, something happened on that day which I suppose I can only call a supernatural occurrence. (Sorry about the long words!) There was something in the corner of the classroom, that's all. The lesson was dragging on as usual, and then there was something. I'm sorry that I

can't be clearer than that. Something just 'arrived' into the room. I know this sounds crazy, and I've already told you that I'm a very unimaginative kind of person, but, well, it appeared to me like one of those hologram things and it looked just like, well, an angel. It had wings, very tall thin ones sort of folded up, made of feathers, and the whole thing was a sort of golden colour. You could see the door through it at first and then slowly it became more solid and so, clearer. And you know, the strangest thing was that it had an incredibly wrinkled old face. You always imagine angels as being in their twenties or something ... Well, you do, don't you?

5   Doesn't it rain in this county? Sometimes you think you'd better start building youself an ark, forty cubits by sixteen cubits. It'd have to be big. Wood? Glass fibre these days probably. Couldn't really take all the animals – too many. Why did Noah allow mosquitoes and wasps on board anyway? Odd. That sounds like a mosquito – thin faint whine they make. No. Can't be. Wrong time of the year. Where do they go in Autumn? Hide under the carpets? Hibernate? Die? Emigrate south then, as swallow food? Hotter climates. Flotillas of them in the air, heading for Africa. Armadas for Africa. How do they know south? Compasses in their heads somehow. Hang on. There's that noise again. It's in the room. Here. Not in my head. What? Has anyone else noticed yet? I'll wait until someone else says something. Old man with wings on his back? Covered in gold leaf? How do they do that?

6   Angel 473 here. Beam me back up please. Someone's made a cock-up again. I thought He said that we weren't to be manifested in front of mortals any more. It frightens them. I haven't done this sort of thing since the Old Testament days. I seem to be in some kind of prison. Most of the prisoners are young, and have to wear tight breeches made of thick blue cloth, some of it very faded. There's a time malfunction here. The Chief Warder and the prisoners are all wearing twentieth century clothing, and yet the Chief Warder is reading out fourteenth century stuff. I'm no good with this sort of confusion. They know that up there. It's their fault. I put in for retirement last week. I've done my four thousand years, haven't I?

It's a rather silly story, granted, but it will do to demonstrate that there is a range of different narrative methods available to anyone to wants to write fiction. The kind of narrative technique that writers choose will usually depend on two things: the kind of fiction they want to produce, and the relationship they seek to establish between themselves and the reader. It's a very practical business, and something you will have to think about if you're contemplating being a writer.

Look back at passages 1, 2 and 3. They are all written in the third person (the characters are all referred to as he, she, they, or by name). This is a very common narrative method, and writers like it because 'third person narrative' fits rather well with the 'omniscient' point of view (with which the author gives himself godlike powers.) The narrator of passage 2, for example, can travel miles in an instant (' ... at the eastern edge of the Atlantic Ocean, huge, grey and magnificent waves were rolling towards the Cornish coast ... '); or get inside characters' heads and listen to what they are thinking. An omniscient narrator can also be very 'visible' and intrusive, as in passage 1, which uses the old 'Dear Reader' approach, addressing the reader directly. This cosy style of narrative was quite commonplace among certain eighteenth century novelists, who, for various reasons, wanted to establish a relationship with the reader in order to comment upon their fictional characters and the events that befell them. It is probably because this particular narrative technique goes back such a long way that it now seems old-fashioned or maybe artificial. (However, this kind of narrative device has had a revival in recent years.) The most interesting and odd thing about it, though, is this: that the 'narrator' who 'speaks' to us from the page isn't really the actual author of the piece. Look at passage 1 again: no real, flesh-and-blood author would speak like that – it's an assumed voice, a pretence. In other words, the old codger whose voice we hear is himself a fictitious character, every bit as fictitious as the characters he describes. In this instance, the narrator is not the writer, he's one of the cast. (Critics call him the author's persona.) The classic example of this kind of narrating persona is the 'Author' of Henry Fielding's *Tom Jones* (published in 1749). This person frequently interrupts the story to comment, to explain or to apologise to the reader for bits we might find offensive or far-fetched. But although this polite intruder calls himself The Author, he's not Henry Fielding. (There's more about this tricky Narrating Persona business in our chapter on irony.)

Most modern novelists consider that this 'buttonholing', Dear Reader approach to narrative is awkward and rather patronising: they feel that their readers should be able to interpret and evaluate what they are reading without the assistance (or interference) of a 'visible' or foregrounded narrator. But the absence of a guide, or visible narrator, does not mean that the reader is freed from the author's control. All novelists are in the manipulation game, especially those who assume the godlike powers of the omniscient narrator. Writers who remain 'invisible' in their novels are being just as manipulative as the eighteenth century writers – Fielding, say, or Laurence Sterne – who use visible narrators; it's just that they're doing it in a more subtle and indirect way.

Most omniscient narrators confine themselves to the past tense: 'Mr Peet stood at the front of the class and opened his dull brown copy ... ' It is perfectly possible, though, for a writer to use the present tense instead, as in passage 3: 'The light in the classroom as a whole is slowly changing ... ' The use of the present tense makes the events seem more 'present' (obviously enough): we, the readers, are 'in' the book at the same time as the characters, so that, in a sense, we share their experiences in a more direct way; the illusion is that we witness events, rather than being informed about them retrospectively – it's a 'live' recording, so to speak. Quite a few novelists also go in for switching unobtrusively from one tense to another so as to achieve dramatic effects or changes of viewpoint. To write a whole novel in the present tense is quite a different matter. A novel written totally in the present tense can become tiresomely urgent, like someone thrusting his face right up to yours at a party in order to tell you about himself. Nevertheless, some writers have written novels in this way, and it can be an effective device for conveying what they see as the empty, relentless, humdrum routine of modern life:

> Mr Bleek wakes up and goes to the office. He feeds his number into the security lock by the main door and begins his day. He climbs the stairs. The lift is out of order. He sits down at his desk and switches on his PC; it glows greenly at him. He stares greenly back.

Quite apart from the power and the freedom it gives the writer, a novelist's omniscience has certain psychological effects upon the reader. To put it simply, it's reassuring; it gives the reader some sort of security. In the company of an omniscient narrator, we can feel assured that, no matter how mysterious and chaotic his world and its inhabitants might at first appear to be, he knows what to make of them. He will explain and clarify, and perhaps finally give the whole business some kind of completeness and meaning that we can grasp and which will resolve our confusion. In earlier, more optimistic times, writers often seemed to believe that real life was like that: that as human beings progressed towards greater knowledge and wisdom, we would eventually be able to make sense of the world and live more securely in it, that the Great Novelist in the sky would reveal all, in the end. Most modern writers cannot bring themselves to subscribe to this optimism, and many of us see ourselves as living not in a world of ever-increasing clarity, but in a quarrelsome global village surrounded by a threatening darkness. This being so, an increasing number of modern writers seem to feel that it would be misleading – or downright dishonest – to pretend that a single human being, who happens to be a writer, can adopt an omniscient, explanatory role. Instead, the way they write and the way they structure their novels suggest that there can only be partial, subjective glimpses of the world: clues, not satisfying solutions.

Writers who feel this way are often attracted to a more limited narrative viewpoint: that of the fictional narrator taking part in the events of the plot. This is, after all, the narrative method most of us employ when talking about ourselves – although we describe what happens to us personally, rather than employ a fictitious character to do it for us. (This is not quite so clear-cut as it might appear, however. Most of us, let's admit it, tend to 'embroider' or dramatise the stories we tell about our past experiences, or edit out bits that are embarrassing. When we do this, we are, in a small way, fictionalising; and thus the 'I' that stars in these stories is at least partly fictitious.) This is commonly known as 'first person narrative', and passage 4 is written in this way: 'I'm not a very imaginative kind of person ... ' The disadvantages of this narrative technique should be clear enough: if you are a fictional character *and* the narrator, both participating in and commenting upon the events that take place, then you cannot plausibly leap into the minds of the other characters; and as a physical being you are confined to the normal restrictions of time and space. You cannot, for example, fly out of that classroom to observe the waves rolling in on the Cornish coast. The first person narrative method looks, at first, to be impossibly inflexible, especially if compared to the omniscient narrative that we have been discussing. But part of the joy of writing in the first person lies in the demands it makes upon the writer's ingenuity. There are all sorts of tricks a writer can use to get round the limitations it might seem to impose – and without resorting to crude devices like telepathy and time machines. But let's look first at the advantages of first person narration. These are fairly subtle.

The garrulous narrator of passage 4 demonstrates some of the strengths of having the story-teller as a participant in the story. Here is a character whom the novelist can explore and develop in great depth – but without seeming to. His personality and his experiences can be portrayed not from the outside but by the character himself, 'from the inside'. The writer can exploit the possibilities of his narrator's vernacular speaking voice, and he can create the illusion of greater immediacy and dramatic impact by telling the story through someone who is actually 'there'. A fictional narrator like this can be a liar, a fool, or mad; he can have an axe to grind or a bee in his bonnet. In such cases, the reader has lots of scope to question or disbelieve or interpret the narrator's version of events. In other words, the reader gets to participate more actively in the working out of the novel. But as we said, this is a fairly subtle business. Let's imagine that the narrator of passage 4 has something strange about him – let's imagine that he is an escapee from an institution for the criminally insane passing himself off as a student (maybe there's one in your class), and that what he tells us is not, therefore, strictly true. How would we get to know that he is a lunatic and how would we re-assess what he says? In other words, if the narrator is unreliable or partial or dishonest, and we re-interpret his words from a more 'superior' point of view, where does this superior perception of what is actually going on come from? Do we bring it with us, sort of 'ready-made', when we begin the novel? Or is it something that the author secretly conveys? If all we have to go on is what this dodgy narrator tells us, how is it that we can somehow learn to doubt him? One thing worth remembering is that we can learn as much from what is not said as we can from what is.

But, yes, as a narrative technique, the first person is limiting. So how do writers get out of the trap of being restricted to only one consciousness? One of the most famous of all American novels is Scott Fitzgerald's *The Great Gatsby*, which is told in the first person by one of its characters, Nick Carraway. The book is full of ingenious techniques that enable Fitzgerald's narrator to travel in time and space and get inside the heads of the other characters. Carraway doesn't have to be telepathic, just a good listener. Most of the people he meets are either unhappy or drunk (or both) and consequently feel the need to confide in him, which they very frequently do. His readiness to listen means that we readers can also, via Carraway, 'listen in' and find out from others about incidents that he himself could not possibly have witnessed. We get inside the heads of other characters because, whenever Nick is around, they blurt out their innermost feelings and desires, and reveal their opinions of the other characters in the novel. Sometimes Fitzgerald sidesteps the problems of first person narrative by using the breathtakingly simple and fraudulent device of conjecture. Here is Nick Carraway describing the unknowable thoughts of a man (Gatsby) who, for reasons of plot (he is just about to be murdered), has to be alone:

> He must have looked up at an unfamiliar sky through frightening leaves and shivered as he found what a grotesque thing a rose is and how raw the sunlight was upon the scarcely created grass.

> *F. Scott Fitzgerald: The Great Gatsby*

Just look at what an immense amount of work the words 'He must have' do in that sentence, and what an outrageous cheat it is. You have to be good to get away with that sort of thing: in this case, the startling adjectives 'frightening', 'grotesque', 'raw' and 'scarcely created' deflect our attention from the trick that Fitzgerald is playing on us – which is, of course, that Nick Carraway could not have known what Gatsby was feeling.

Passage 5 (have another look) is an example of a narrative technique which is often called 'stream of consciousness'. This kind of narrative attempts to mimic the constant and random thoughts that rush through our minds during our waking (and maybe sleeping) hours. It is a very twentieth-century narrative method. There is some doubt about who first 'invented' it, although a novelist called Dorothy

Richardson was probably the first to explore its potential. Most literary people would direct you to better-known writers like James Joyce, Virginia Woolf and William Faulkner for examples of this style of writing. What stream of consciousness narrative suggests is that the human mind is constantly busy with a kind of associative chatter which is almost incoherent to anyone other than the thinker. And this means that stream of consciousness narrative is very far 'in there', very subjective and partial: it is at the other end of the scale from the omniscient point of view. The advantages of the technique are that the writer can create an absorbing intimacy between the reader and a character's innermost thoughts and obsessions, and we readers (if we are so inclined) can have some fun 'ordering' and making connections between what are apparently disorderly thoughts and images. The disadvantage is that for the reader it is such wretchedly hard work, and very few of us have the stamina to struggle through more than a page or two of this sort of jumbly stuff – which is why only about six people have ever read James Joyce's *Finnegan's Wake*, even though thousands claim to have done so.

Passage 6 gives us the panicky thoughts of the angel himself (or herself – the gender of angels is never too easy to determine). Like passages 4 and 5 it is an 'interior monologue'; but unlike the stream of consciousness 'garble' of passage 5 it consists of more or less coherent sentences – it is silent speech, rather than a transcript of disorderly thought-processes. And it differs from passage 4 because it is written from what is sometimes called the 'Martian' viewpoint. A good many writers now and in the past have got mileage and amusement out of this technique. It involves using a narrator who is an alien or outsider, and who therefore misunderstands and misinterprets everything around him – often in a bewildered and comic way. It isn't necessary to have your narrator an alien or an angel, either: in a novel called *Other People*, Martin Amis shows us the world through the eyes of a woman who has lost her memory, and she describes everyday objects and activities in a bizarre, uncomprehending way. We read passage 6 confident in our superior knowledge that colleges are not really prisons, that wearing denim is not compulsory, that students are not prisoners and that teachers are not warders. Because this divine visitor is from outside our culture, he misinterprets what is, to us, obvious. Consequently, the Martian narrative is rich in irony: it enables a writer to exploit comically the gap between what the narrator thinks he sees and what we know he is 'really' seeing. But, as is usually the case with irony, the effects of this can be quite subtle. At first, the reader is presented with little puzzles, or riddles – what are these blue cloth breeches? – and so forth. But then the Martian view starts to challenge our complacent view of our own world – interpretations that seem naïve or ignorant become satirical. Perhaps our educational system does 'imprison' the minds of those who are 'confined' within it. Perhaps students are rigidly conformist in their choice of clothes (there's no shortage of fashion victims in my college). And perhaps the way we do things, and the way our society is organised and controlled is not natural or inevitable at all. In challenging our comfortable or lazy assumptions, the Martian viewpoint can be the most subversive narrative technique of all.

So much for our Angel in the Classroom story. We have not, of course, covered all the available narrative techniques – and if we tried to do so we'd be here all day. We should, though, say a word or two about one ancient and important literary form, the epistolary novel: the novel, that is, which is written in the form of letters exchanged between its characters. One of the first great eighteenth century novelists, Samuel Richardson, used this technique in a number of his works. As with the first person narrative, the epistolary narrator is limited by place and time, and the reader is confined to being in one head at a time. But a fictional correspondent can write many different letters to several different characters, and in this way reveal a variety of relationships; and such letters will, of course, undergo modulations of tone and language depending on to whom they are addressed. The furtive reading of other people's letters is something many of us enjoy but few of us would admit to; reading an epistolary novel is a guilt-free way of indulging in this less than admirable desire to snoop. This may be one reason why this long-established narrative method remains popular, as the more recent success of Alice Walker's *The Color Purple* demonstrates.

Write your own story

The best way to investigate the possibilities of different kinds of narrative technique is for you to try them for yourself. Have a go at it. Here are six basic plot situations. Choose one and then write at least four paragraphs, each one using a different narrative approach, until you complete the plot-line of your story.

1 An old man or woman reminisces about the past.

2 A child witnesses a murder.

3 A student returns home to find that his/her furniture can talk.

4 A ventriloquist tries to claim Unemployment Benefit for his/her dummy.

5 A crazed poet tries to assassinate the star of a soap-opera.

6 Three astronauts discover that their on-board computer is disobeying them.

Feel free to adopt, adapt or ignore the six kinds of narrative used in our tale of the angel. When you have written your story, ask yourself which of the narrative techniques you used felt the most comfortable to you, and with which one you consider you were the most successful. (The chances are that they will be one and the same, but they may not be). Then ask yourself why this particular approach worked best. Was it because it just came naturally to you, or was it because something about the nature of the story demanded that kind of technique? Or were there other more subtle reasons?

The private eye

We're going to look next at two particular species of narrative fiction – detective stories and crime novels.

For a short while, one of the writers of this book worked as a mobile librarian, squeezing a vanload of culture through the lanes of deepest Devon, providing the locals with, sometimes, the works of Jane Austen and Joseph Conrad, but more often – much more often – with bales of what is often called 'genre fiction'. Genre fiction is written to a specific kind of formula or pattern, and its subdivisions can be quite extensive and precise. It wouldn't do to offer the inhabitants of Cheriton Fitzpaine Romances: they would want Hospital Romances, while the more bloodthirsty populace of Sampford Peverell would demand War Romances.

Genre novels are usually classified by subject: the Western, Science Fiction, Horror, Occult, and – most popular of all – Detective Stories and Crime Fiction. It's probably best to start by making a few distinctions between detective fiction and crime fiction. Most readers of detective stories are interested primarily in playing the 'whodunnit' game, to discover whether it really was the butler who knocked off Mrs Bumbleby-Scott, and to find this out before the detective does. A variation on the whodunnit is the howdunnit, where it is the method of the murder, rather than the identity which is the issue. Conventionally, the identity, motives and method of the criminal are revealed in an often tiresome exposition towards the end of the story. Like all games, detective fiction has to obey certain rules. The writer must provide his readers with clues, the culprit's methods must seem more or less plausible, the detective cannot employ supernatural powers to snare the killer, and so on. In that sense, detective novels cannot disregard the rules of physical reality in the way that fairy stories, say, can; yet the way they are constructed and the way they operate are just as much bound by genre convention. The characters in detective stories are frequently as melodramatically two-dimensional as those who populate fairy stories, and in both these kinds of story-telling it is the plot that is of greatest importance. A detective story which delved into the complexities of the criminal mind, or which explored the the more mysterious areas of human relationships would cease to be a 'real' detective story as far as traditional readers are concerned, and would be returned very grumpily to the mobile library.

Writers of detective fiction are an orthodox bunch when it comes to narrative method. They tend to choose either the omniscient third person narrator (who, of necessity, has to spend much of his time withholding information from the reader) or, just as commonly, the first person narrator – often the detective himself or a close acquaintance (like Holmes' good friend Dr Watson). First person narrative works very well in this genre, because it allows the writer to disguise the story as an autobiographical reminiscence or 'case study'. The originators of detective fiction include some famous names: Edgar Allen Poe (*The Murders in the Rue Morgue*), Charles Dickens (*The Mystery of Edwin Drood*), Wilkie Collins (*The Moonstone*) and, of course, Sherlock Holmes' creator, Conan Doyle. The Golden Age of English detective fiction was probably the 1920s and 30s, when writers such as Dorothy Sayers, Agatha Christie, John Dickinson Carr and Ellery Queen provided their readers with hundreds of ingenious fictional puzzles to solve.

Classic English detective fiction tends to be populated by middle-class characters living relatively prosperous lives in a society which is both stable and highly stratified. Crime is a very real threat to the status quo, the stability and security of this social world. Villains are frequently subversive in that they can imitate the dress, speech and behaviour of those they prey upon; the detective (often an amateur and often an upper-class gent) is therefore in the business of apprehending these bounders so that social order can be restored. (This is, after all, what the word 'order' means in the phrase 'law and order'.)

Here's a fairly typical and relatively modern example of the detective genre. These are the opening paragraphs of a short story. Questions follow.

> In a first-floor office in Hatton Garden two men sat at separate tables, silent, almost motionless, each one staring fixedly in front of him – doing nothing. In one corner of the room a small but very modern safe had been let into the wall; it now stood open, as did the four drawers at the bottom of it; the thoughts of the two occupants of the room were concentrated upon that safe, and for the last twenty minutes, after a

spate of furious argument, they had not spoken to one another. Apart from the distant rumble of Holborn traffic the ticking of the clock alone broke the silence.

Except for a similarity of well-made, sombre clothing, and certain unmistakable racial characteristics, the two men were utterly unlike each other; the elder was short, fat, and grey; the younger, tall, thin and black; they were, in fact, unrelated, but for nearly thirty years they had been intimate friends – until today.

Footsteps sounded on the stairs, a knock; a small boy ushered in a young man in a dark blue suit carrying a bowler hat.

'Detective-Inspector Poole, New Scotland Yard,' said the new-comer. 'You're Levi, Berg and Phillips, gentlemen? I'm instucted that you asked for an officer to be sent round?'

Instantly the two partners burst into a torrent of speech, stopped, and glared at one another. Inspector Poole recognised the situation at a glance.

'Perhaps it would be more convenient if I took your statements separately, gentlemen,' he said.

After a moment's struggle to control his raging suspicions the thin Mr Berg retired and the stout Mr Levi burst into his tale.

'We are diamond merchants,' he said. 'We have been in partnership, Aaron Berg and I, for thirty years. For the last fifteen we have had another partner, George Phillips, who brought capital into the business when things were bad – in the war, when Aaron, who is a German, was interned. Phillips brought his young brother into the business too, a few years ago, but not as a partner – as a clerk.'

'He is here now – your partner, Mr Phillips?' asked Poole.

'He and his brother have gone away for the Easter holidays; they went last night.'

'Leaving you and Mr Berg in charge?'

'Yes; we do not need a holiday at Easter; we are not Christians.'

Mr Levi spoke with quiet dignity; the detective felt an unreasonable inclination to blush.

'In the ordinary course of business,' continued Mr Levi, 'we keep in that safe diamonds, cut and uncut, to a value of from five thousand to twenty thousand pounds at a time. Lately we have been negotiating a big sale and we have had some fine uncut stones of unusual value. When we locked the safe last night there were in it stones to the value of more than 30,000 pounds. This afternoon there are .. none.'

The old man's flabby jowl quivered with emotion.

'You say the safe was locked last night, sir; who locked it?'

With a gesture of his pudgy hand, Mr Levi indicated that he would explain everything – in his own way.

'The safe has three keys, two of which open the door and one which opens the drawers – in which the diamonds are kept; the body of the safe only holds ledgers and important papers. Berg and Phillips each have key of the door, I alone have the key of the drawers – but I have not a key of the door. Once the drawers and safe have been locked, the diamonds can only be reached if both Berg and I or Phillips and I are present. The keys never leave our possession; we never give them to anyone else to open the safe or the drawers; the holder of the key, alone operates it. That is the only way to be safe.'

The Detective, his eyes on the empty safe, reflected that even this system did not appear to be infallible.

Henry Wade: The Three Keys

1   What sort of narrative technique is this, and why might it be an appropriate one for this story?

2   How does the first paragraph try to grab the reader's attention? (You might consider the syntax and the rhythm of that first sentence, as well as the way those small details signal particular kinds of relevant information.)

3   Characterisation in detective fiction tends be relatively uncomplicated. What sort of information are we given about the three characters here, and how are we provided with it?

The Jewish diamond merchants seem to come very close, at times, to being 'racial stereotypes'. What is racial stereotyping, and how would it be likely to affect our reading of this story?

4   From the sentence beginning 'We are diamond merchants ... ', our interest is focussed not on the characters or the relationships between them, but on a totally different matter: what?

5   The function of this writer's prose is, on the whole, to be transparent and to be an efficient conveyor of information. What is interesting about the sentence which begins 'Except for ... ' and the paragraph beginning with 'The safe has three keys ... '?

6   What would you suggest is the ultimate purpose of this story?

A greyer area

The social world of the crime novel tends to be rather different to that of the detective novel. This next extract should make the distinction clear enough.

I have a client named Teddy Franklin. Teddy Franklin is a car thief. He is thirty-two years old, and he is one of the best car thieves on the Eastern seaboard. Cadillac Ted is so good that he is able to support himself as a car thief. He has been arrested repeatedly, which is how he made my acquaintance, but he has never done time. That is because I am so good. It is also because Teddy is so good.

Teddy is as cute as a shithouse rat. He is an expert. He never leaves any prints. He never does anything in the presence of unreliable people who might turn out to be witnesses for the prosecution. He does not become attached to any of the cars he steals, but unloads them within an hour or so of the instant that he steals them. If you have a car with a kill switch cutting out the ignition, and Teddy wants your car, he will have it started within thirty seconds of the time that he spots your car. If you have a car with a hidden burglar alarm, Teddy will have that alarm disabled before it has even gone off. If you have a crook lock, a steel bar immobilising the steering wheel and brake, he will remove it inside a minute – I do not know how Teddy does this, but Teddy assures me that he does do it, and I'm sure he does have some professional secrets. The only device that Teddy admits to be sufficient to defeat him is the invention that shuts off the gas and the ignition and seals the hood shut so that Teddy cannot get at the wires and jump them.

'I dunno,' Teddy said, 'I don't think I can beat that one. Short of taking a torch to it, I don't think I can do it. I tried a couple of times, just for the hell of it. Didn't even have an order for that particular car, but I saw the sticker that said it had one of those things, and sure enough it worked. 'Course when the owner got back, he wasn't goin' nowhere in it neither, which is something, because if I need a torch to get into it, so does the guy who's got a right to get into it. I imagine the only way you could take one of those things is if you backed the wrecker up to it and towed the damned thing off to some place where you could work on it.'

George V. Higgins: Kennedy for the Defense

Clearly, we are more than a million miles from the polite drawing-rooms of English detective fiction with their decanters of poisoned sherry on the sideboard. This 'hard-boiled' prose style owes a lot to the founding fathers of American crime fiction, namely Dashiell Hammet, James M. Cain and Raymond Chandler. The first two wrote their best-known novels in the 1930s, Chandler mostly in the 40s and 50s. George V. Higgins has written several novels which continue this great tradition. Try reading that short piece again and answering the following questions:

1 **The narrator of this novel (Kennedy) is a lawyer, not a detective. How does this affect his attitude towards criminals and criminal behaviour? Where do his sympathies lie? What words or phrases in the passage provide you with clues?**

2 **What kind of relationship is Kennedy establishing with the reader in the first paragraph?**

3 **Why, do you suppose, does Higgins make his narrator begin his sentences with similar patterns of words in the second paragraph?**

4 **What are the advantages of using this kind of narrative technique over the omniscient narrator method? What are the bonuses that Higgins gets by using a first person narrator here?**

The language of this extract is not standard British English, and the moral values displayed by the lawyer-narrator are distinctly not those that you would find in that comfortable and assured world so ably defended by the detective heroes of earlier English novels. The social world of the American crime novel has morals and values that are a gritty grey in colour, and it is a world which the narrator often distrusts or despises. In American cities the streets are mean and the cops are not people from whom you would ask directions or the time of day.

The first person narrative is obviously crucial in this passage because it's a fast, no-messing-about way of getting across the personality and the attitudes of the central character who is also the narrator. The no-nonsense style reflects the nature of the man. The vocabulary is aggressively vernacular, the tone is forceful and the language is almost totally literal (look at the effect of that one startling simile). But it is worth noting how, for all its energetic rhythms, the language is highly stylised, which should suggest to us that the world of the crime novel is just as artificial as that of the traditional detective novel, even though the criminals do shoot and stab rather than resort to more elaborate forms of homicide involving obscure poisons. The modern crime novel does not usually set the reader puzzles to solve (a Higgins story is as likely to begin with the capture of a murderer). But, if you think about it, all readers and writers of fiction are involved in a 'game' because there is always some kind of understanding about what the rules and conventions are. When we declare that a novel is 'good' we are perhaps saying that the novelist has 'won' (won us over, won our admiration). It's an important part of being a good critical reader to understand the rules and conventions of the game, and how different kinds (or genres) of fiction will have different sets of rules. (We do not expect from science fiction the same 'logic', for example, that we expect from detective fiction.)

The private I

It would be wrong to think that the 'rules and conventions' of a particular genre are a self-imposed handicap for the writer. Quite the opposite is true: they are a means to an end. They allow the writer to give a recognisable shape to a story. The conventions of the detective, crime or spy novel can also be a means to an end for writers whose aims and intentions differ from or transcend those usually associated with the genre. Authors whom we like to think of as 'serious' writers (Joseph Conrad and Graham Greene, for examples) have adopted the manners of the spy novel for their own ends. One reason for this is that the detective, the private eye and the spy easily lend themselves to symbolic interpretation. They are all observers, they are all concerned with finding The Truth, they try to penetrate and make sense of the mystery and confusion of the world. And many, or most, of us feel the need to do this with regard to our own lives at some time or another. One of the great attractions and pleasures of the detective story is that when the hero 'cracks the case' it reassures us that it is possible to solve the mysteries of life. In fact, it is even reassuring if the hero fails, because if the Ace Investigator cannot make sense of it all, then it's not so depressing if we can't either. Another possible reason why 'serious' writers are attracted to detectives and spies is that such characters resemble writers in certain ways. Writers and detectives are both in the business of observing and investigating and looking for clues as to the reasons behind human behaviour; and both are inclined to see themselves as outsiders. The private eye is perhaps a natural alter ego for a writer.

With these possibilities in mind, we'll end this chapter with a brief look at some passages from a novel by the American writer Paul Auster, who has employed some of the conventions of the crime and detective story for his own rather peculiar but fascinating purposes. Auster's book *The New York Trilogy* features private eyes who are employed by often anonymous clients; and often their job is to watch apparently innocent people. Here is what Quinn, one of Auster's protagonists, thinks about private eye novels and the kind of desperate searching for meanings that distinguishes both the sleuth and the writer:

What he liked about these books was their sense of plenitude and economy. In the good mystery there is nothing wasted, no sentence, no word that is not significant. And even if it is not significant, it has the potential to be so – which amounts to the same thing. The world of the book comes to life, seething with possibilities, with secrets and contradictions. Since everything seen or said, even the slightest, most trivial thing, can bear a connection to the outcome of the story, nothing must be overlooked. Everything becomes essence; the center of the book shifts with each event that propels it forward. The center, then, is everywhere, and no circumference can be drawn until the book has come to its end.

The detective is the one who looks, who listens, who moves through this morass of objects and events in search of the thought, the idea, that will pull all these things together and make sense of them. In effect, the writer and the detective are interchangeable. The reader sees the world through the detective's eye, experiencing the proliferation of its details as if for the first time. He has become awake to the things around him, as if they might speak to him, as if, because of the attentiveness he now brings to them, they might begin to carry a meaning other than the simple fact of their existence. Private eye. The term held a triple meaning for Quinn. Not only was it the letter 'i', standing for 'investigator', it was 'I' in the upper case, the tiny life-bud buried in the body of the breathing self. At the same time, it was also the physical eye of the writer, the eye of the man who looks out from himself into the world and demands that the world reveal itself to him.

Paul Auster: The New York Trilogy

Quinn is clearly in trouble here, as is anyone who starts to lose sight of the distinction between life and fiction. It is true that in detective fiction it is often the indiscriminate close observation of tiny details that solves mysteries. But as human beings we cannot survive that way – we have to be discriminating in the way we see things. If everything around us was constantly signalling information to us, we would quickly be unable to see anything at all, and drown in confusion. Quinn, who seems to want to be an all-seeing, all-knowing eye, is heading for trouble, maybe for madness. He is called out on a case to meet a Mr Stillman, and as soon as he enters Stillman's apartment Auster again takes up the theme of seeing and perception:

As he crossed the threshold and entered the apartment, he could feel himself going blank, as if his brain had suddenly shut off. He had wanted to take in the details of what he was seeing, but the task was somehow beyond him at that moment. The apartment loomed up around him as a kind of blur. He realized that it was large, perhaps five or six rooms, and that it was richly furnished, with numerous art objects, silver ashtrays, and elaborately framed pictures on the walls. But that was all. No more than a general impression – even though he was there, looking at those things with his own eyes.

Paul Auster: The New York Trilogy

We spend most of our lives, probably, forming such 'general impressions' of the world; it's one of the great survival processes we are equipped to perform, and no-one could possibly do otherwise in, say, a supermarket or a library. This is, quite naturally, what Quinn does when he goes into Stillman's apartment. What is unusual is Quinn's dismay when he does it; he wants more: he wants to do what he thinks a detective in a detective novel should do, which is take in everything in detail. He's beginning to think that he may not be up to the part that his creator has lumbered him with. But if Quinn thinks he might be having an identity crisis, it's nothing compared with the one that the mysterious Stillman is going through. The meeting between Quinn and Stillman is highly ironic: here we have a private eye who is none too sure that he is one, confronted by someone who doesn't seem sure that he exists at all:

> Everything about Peter Stillman was white. White shirt, open at the neck; white pants, white shoes, white socks. Against the pallor of his skin, the flaxen thinness of his hair, the effect was almost transparent, as though one could see through to the blue veins behind the skin of his face. This blue was almost the same as the blue of his eyes: a milky blue that seemed to dissolve into a mixture of sky and clouds. Quinn could not imagine himself addressing a word to this person. It was as though Stillman's presence was a command to be silent.
>
> Stillman settled slowly into his chair and at last turned his attention to Quinn. As their eyes met, Quinn suddenly felt that Stillman had become invisible. He could see him sitting in the chair across from him, but at the same time it felt as though he was not there. It occurred to Quinn that perhaps Stillman was blind. But no, that did not seem possible. The man was looking at him, even studying him, and if recognition did not flicker across his face, it still held something more than a blank stare. Quinn did not know what to do. He sat there dumbly in his seat, looking back at Stillman. A long time passed.
>
> 'No questions, please,' the young man said at last. 'Yes. No. Thank you.' He paused for a moment. 'I am Peter Stillman. I say this of my own free will. Yes. That is not my real name. No. Of course, my mind is not all it should be. But nothing can be done about that. No. About that. No, no. Not anymore.
>
> 'You sit there and think: who is this person talking to me? What are these words coming from his mouth? I will tell you. Or else I will not tell you. My mind is not all it should be. I say this of my own free will. But I will try. Yes and no. I will try to tell you, even if my mind makes it hard. Thank you.
>
> 'My name is Peter Stillman. Perhaps you have heard of me, but more than likely not. No matter. That is not my real name. My real name I cannot remember. Excuse me. Not that it makes a difference. That is to say, anymore.
>
> 'This is what is called speaking. I believe that is the term. When words come out, fly into the air, live for a moment and die. Strange, is it not? I myself have no opinion. No and no again. But still, there are words you will need to have. There are many of them. Many millions I think. Perhaps only three or four. Excuse me. But I am doing well

today. So much better than usual. If I can give you the words you need to have, it will be a great victory. Thank you. Thank you a million times over.

'Long ago there was mother and father. I remember none of that. They say: mother died. Who they are I cannot say. Excuse me. But that is what they say.

'No mother then. Ha ha. Such is my laughter now, my belly burst of mumbo jumbo. Ha ha ha. Big father said: it makes no difference. To me. That is to say, to him. Big father of the big muscles and the boom, boom, boom. No questions now, please.

'I say what they say because I know nothing. I am only poor Peter Stillman, the boy who can't remember. Boo hoo. Willy nilly. Nincompoop. Excuse me. They say, they say. But what does poor little Peter say? Nothing, nothing. Anymore.

'There was this. Dark. Very dark. As dark as very dark. They say: that was the room. As if I could talk about it. The dark, I mean. Thank you.

'Dark, dark. They say for nine years. Not even a window. Poor Peter Stillman.'

Paul Auster: The New York Trilogy

As in all classic detective stories, we are here presented with a puzzle; but this time the puzzle is a matter of who? rather than whodunnit? The mystery that Quinn is confronting here is a really big one: what is a human being? As Peter Stillman's rather allegorical name implies, he seems to have all the outward appearances of a member of the human race, but he seems to be seriously lacking in some of the qualifications you need to be a full member. Answering the following questions may help you to decide whether or not Stillman is still a man:

1 What is the significance of the colour of Stillman's clothing and the colour of his eyes?

2 What are the social skills that Stillman seems to lack?

3 Stillman's language is, of course, most peculiar. But what is different about it compared to normal human language?

4 Stillman has a rather 'Martian' view of the nature of words and language. What is it?

5 Play the detective for a moment: is there anything significant about Stillman's last few remarks? Are there clues there that might explain something?

6 Stillman repeatedly refers to free will, memory and opinion – saying that he has the first but not the other two. Do you believe him, on either count? Why, do you think, does he harp on these things? How are they relevant to our concept of human identity?

The last part of that last question gets us into deep waters, and nobody could reasonably expect you to come up with a complete answer. Philosophers and writers seem to agree that there isn't one. Yet these things – free will, memory and opinion (or judgement) do seem to be essential components in the 'package' we call human identity. If Stillman lacks them, does that mean he is not 'one of us'? And where does Quinn go from here? You'll have to read *The New York Trilogy* to find out.

One of the things that Paul Auster's books imply – and one of the things that we have been getting at in this chapter – is that the way we see things is the same thing as the way we understand things. 'See' and 'understand' are sometimes synonymous, if you 'see' what we mean. And seeing is not a passive receiving of objective images: we make choices about what we see, and in so doing impose meanings on the world. In choosing a particular narrative technique, a writer is choosing a position, and in so doing is imposing a certain view or version of the world on us, the readers. Which is to say that narrative is much more than just a way of telling a story.

11
Women and Rhyme

MALE
PALE
STALE
SNAIL
TRAIL
FAIL

Poetic injustice

You might think it odd, or even outrageous, to find a book like this one devoting a section to 'Women Poets'. After all, most of us would think it very odd to find a similar section called 'Men Poets' in its place. Why we would find this odd is a perceptual and political matter. Women writers still have to battle against prejudices and traditions which put misleading labels (like ours?) on their work, or which state or imply that there are certain topics which women 'specialise' in writing about. Most of us have grown up in a society which encourages the view, for example, that women write best about relationships, and men about science. As free-thinking individuals, determined to take nothing for granted, it's your job to think about and challenge such assumptions.

After much discussion and argument, the authors of this book have decided to devote a section to women poets. This might, in its small way, encourage the very same lazy and prejudiced habits of masculine thought that frequently place women's writing on the margins, in specialist ghettoes. On the other hand, there are feminist publishing houses (like Virago and The Women's Press) that make a point of producing and commissioning work written almost exclusively by women. You should think about whether grouping writers together in this way has either a positive or negative effect on the way that people (of both sexes) picture women poets and then evaluate their work. If you are at least aware of the sorts of problems that such an act of classification brings in its wake, then perhaps that is a good thing in itself. Furthermore, most of us are lazy and don't like to think very long or hard, and for that reason we often like to cope with the complexities of the world and its inhabitants by relying on stereotypes. We cling to an inward mental picture of what a Frenchman is like, for example. (Dodgy moustache, striped sweater, garlic breath, totally selfish in not speaking the English language.) We do the same with 'The Poet': long hair, wears tweeds or flowing cloak, strides over hills and talks to birds and trees, and rarely gets arrested for so doing. The same is doubly true of 'The Woman Poet'. In her introduction to *The Bloodaxe Anthology of Contemporary Women Poets*, Jeni Couzyn states her belief that there are three such powerful stereotypes often present in the minds of readers of women's poetry: 'Mrs Dedication', 'Miss Eccentric Spinster', and 'Mad Girl'. The ideal woman poet, in other words, has to be either the emotional slave of one powerful man, a tweedy recluse, or a suicidal manic depressive, or all three. If we are to read and respond to women's poetry with open hearts and minds, we have to disregard these stereotypes and do something rather hard: think for ourselves.

It gets worse though. When we read and try to understand poetry written by women, we do so as members of a society that puts filters or blinkers in our heads. We are all still encouraged to believe that women have specific, traditional roles to perform in our society, centering especially on the institutions of marriage and child-rearing. This may mean that some women have had to adopt various poses or masks (like that of 'eccentric spinster', for example) in order to be given the right to be themselves and to exist as independent human beings and writers.

These are some of the questions that we have tried to raise. We think that they are worth thinking about:

1 **Do you think that grouping women writers together in anthologies or textbooks is useful or harmful? Shouldn't women writers be treated simply as writers?**

2 **Is it important to know the gender of the writer whose work you are reading?**

3 **Do you think that there are any subjects that women are uniquely qualified to talk or write about because they possess more knowledge or expertise than men about those subjects? What might such subjects be? Would that disqualify men from writing about them?**

4 Are there, or should there be, any distinctions to be made between feminist writers and women writers? Are feminist writers just more critical of their society and its attitudes towards, and expectations of, women? Or does it go deeper than that?

Rhymes and regulations

Whether or not it is 'ideologically correct', in this chapter we are going to look exclusively at poems written by women. Doing so, we are going to concentrate on rhyme and the different ways it can be used, and the various effects it can achieve.

The first poem is by Marilyn Hacker. It is written in a poetic form called villanelle, a form that has to obey certain rules. If you want to play the villanelle game, these are the rules you have to follow:

1 The poem must contain five stanzas of three lines each (these are often called 'tercets') and then one final four-line stanza (or 'quatrain') – making a total of nineteen lines in all.

2 The first and third lines of the first tercet must recur alternately as the last line of the following stanzas, and also form a final rhyming couplet at the end of the poem.

It sounds complicated, doesn't it? It's easier to demonstrate than to explain:

Villanelle: Late Summer

I love you and it makes me rather dull
when everyone is voluble and gay.
The conversation hits a certain lull.

I moon, rattled as china in a bull-
shop, wanting to go, wanting to stay.
I love you and it makes me rather dull.

You might think I had cotton in my skull.
And why is one in Staithes and not in Hay?
The conversation hits a certain lull.

You took a fretful, unoriginal
and unrelaxing friend on holiday.
I love you and it makes me rather dull.

A sheepish sky, with puffs of yellow wool,
watches the tide interrogate the bay.
The conversation hits a certain lull.

And I am grimly silent, swollen full
of unsaid things. I certainly can't say
'I love you.' And it makes me rather dull.
The conversation hits a certain lull.

Marilyn Hacker

As you can see, Marilyn Hacker obeys all the rules with great expertise. It's a challenging formal discipline, one that most poets avoid, although in fact it is this challenge itself that attracts poets who attempt it. (Wendy Cope once said that it was 'the desire to show off a bit' that persuaded her to write a villanelle.) One of the problems posed by the form is obvious enough: the prescribed repetition of the same two lines looks, on the surface, to be a recipe for tediousness. Part of the 'game' is to ensure that the meaning of these repeated words changes in subtle ways through the poem. You can do this by turning statements into questions, for example, or by using different punctuation to change the meaning from that which the words had in the first tercet (as in the penultimate line of Hacker's poem). Read the poem again and try the following questions:

1 What sort of social world, or class, would you say the speaker in this poem belongs to? What are the linguistic clues that might provide an answer?

2 What is the speaker's attitude to the event at which she finds herself? ('Herself?' Is the speaker necessarily a woman?)

3 What preconceived ideas do you already have about poems that describe falling in love? Does this poem fulfil your expectations or not?

4 What does the speaker reveal about her lover, herself and their relationship? Does 'you' always refer to the same person?

5 The villanelle is well known as a poetic form employed during the late Middle Ages by aristocratic young men to express their romantic feelings. Does this remote piece of literary scholarship affect the way you understand the poem?

6 End-rhyme can have all sorts of different effects – for example, it can make the reader pause very slightly, it can give a sense of 'finality' to a line, it can surprise. What effects do the rhymes have at the end of these tercets and at the end of the quatrain?

7 How has Hacker used the rigid formal tradition of the villanelle in an interesting and amusing way?

Before we leave this poem, another quick look at the fifth tercet. We all know that the sky cannot be literally 'sheepish' – in the sense of 'foolishly reticent', that the sky cannot 'watch', and that tides don't 'interrogate'. This is metaphorical language being used in a particular way. We human beings tend to project human qualities onto the non-human world in a very unscientific way, especially when we are more than usually prey to our emotions. This attributing of human personality and qualities to non-human things is known as **personification** or **anthropomorphisation**. When feelings are attributed to the natural world (as in 'sheepish sky', for instance) critics sometimes refer to this device as **pathetic fallacy**. This is a phrase coined by the Victorian writer Ruskin. If you find it a bit odd, it may be because the modern commonplace use of the word 'pathetic' has come to mean 'ineffectual', or 'sad' or 'useless'. For Ruskin, the word simply meant 'having to do with feeling'.

In effect, what this means is that we frequently, or perhaps even normally, see the things around us in a way that reflects our mood. Or, to put it another way, we impose our feelings on the things around us. We rarely sit in the world passively receiving information. We are constantly projecting meaning and feeling onto the world: we create what we see. The sea floods into a bay: it seems to be 'interrogating'. I feel 'soft in the head': I see clouds as 'puffs of yellow wool'. Hacker's last tercet provides us with some information about the view, but tells us more about the state of mind of the person observing it.

The next poem, *By the Boat House, Oxford*, also employs rhyme, but in a very different way. This poem is in three quatrains, and in each one there are two rhymes; but it is only in the last quatrain that the rhyme is 'close' ('hairs'/'impairs'). Elsewhere the poet, Anne Stevenson, uses half-rhyme (also called near-rhyme or para-rhyme or slant-rhyme). Some of you may be familiar with the poems of Wilfred Owen, who used this technique in several of his poems. (There is an example in Chapter 14; also in that chapter is more technical stuff about rhyme.)

Rhyme is a most peculiar business. Our need to invent and listen to rhyme would seem to have deep and primitive origins. We frequently use it to teach children language. It is a game played with sounds that are similar, and the effects it can achieve are very variable and often very subtle. One effect that rhyme can have upon us is to make us feel more secure, perhaps because it forces language into a recognisable shape and pattern. It can also help us to remember – it is reassuring because it is useful. (It can have less desirable effects, too: rhyme may convince us that we are reading poetry when we are reading prose with rhymes in it, or it may even lead us into believing that poetry *has* to rhyme.) Rhyme is also a game played with sounds that are somewhat dissimilar – with half-rhymes, in other words. If 'close' or 'full' rhyme is somehow reassuringly predictable, then half-rhyme should be less so. And perhaps there is something about the sound of half-rhymes which creates a feeling of incompleteness, or unease, or disorder. Bearing these things in mind, read Anne Stevenson's poem:

By the Boat House, Oxford

They belong here in their own quenched country.
I had forgotten nice women could be so nice,
smiling beside large sons on the makeshift quay
frail, behind pale faces and hurt eyes.

Their husbands are plainly superior, with them, without them.
Their boys wear privilege like a clear inheritance, easily.
(Now a swan's neck couples with its own reflection,
making in the water a perfect 3.)

The punts seem resigned to an unexciting mooring.
But the women? It's hard to tell. Do their fine grey hairs
and filament lips approve or disdain the loving
that living alone, or else lonely in pairs, impairs?

Anne Stevenson

Here are some questions that may help you understand the poem and the way it works more fully:

1 **The people referred to in the poem are probably of a similar social class**

to those in the previous poem by Marilyn Hacker. But in this poem the relation between them and the speaker seems different. How is it different – how close or detached is the 'I' of this poem to the 'nice women'?

2 To whom does 'They', in the first line, refer?

3 What are the ambiguities and suggestions in the following words?

'belong', 'quenched' (line 1)

'large' (line 3)

'behind' (line 4)

'plainly' (line 5)

'wear' (line 6)

'mooring' (line 9)

4 Why, do you think, does Stevenson repeat the word 'nice' in line 2? When a writer repeats a word like this so blatantly, what does it do to the word's conventional meaning? What meanings does the word have or conceal in this poem?

5 The sudden digression into the swan's reflection must, presumably, be related to the poem's theme. First, what is that theme? And second, how does the swan connect with it? (It might help to tease out the ambiguities in 'couples', 'reflections', and 'perfect'.) Why does the poet write '3' and not 'three' here? Does it help to know that swans have a reputation for being relentlessly monogamous?

6 What do you notice about the way that the last quatrain is put together? How does its syntax differ from earlier lines?

7 In what way, or ways, could 'fine grey hairs' and 'filament lips' express approval or disdain?

Now have a go at the following questions, which are about the poem's rhymes specifically:

1 Look at the pairs of words that are linked together by rhyme (even if it is only half-rhyme). Do they comment or reflect upon each other in any way? Do they seem to you somehow to belong together? Or do they seem strained or uneasy?

2 In the last two lines there are three pairs of words that approximately rhyme: 'loving'/'living', 'alone'/'lonely' and 'pairs'/'impairs'. How do the words in each of these rhymes relate to each other?

3 The apparent clumsiness of having two rhymes for 'hairs' ('pairs' and 'impairs') might be there for a purpose. Have you any idea what this might be?

4 Why would Anne Stevenson want to avoid that reassuring sense of 'completeness' or 'polish' that full rhyme can have?

One small item of incidental information before we move on: sometimes you may come across the terms **masculine rhyme** and **feminine rhyme**. Masculine rhyme is the 'full' rhyme of single-syllable words (e.g. make/take); feminine rhyme is the pairing of words with more than one syllable (e.g. Mabel/table). The traditional view is that masculine rhymes are 'complete', 'strong' and 'forceful', while feminine rhymes are 'weak', 'hesitant' and 'often comic'. Enough said. (Perhaps you might prefer the alternative terms **single** and **double** rhyme.)

A rhyme checklist

In your reading of poetry, you will certainly find poets using rhyme in hundreds of different ways in addition to the ones we have looked at in this chapter. (Half-rhyme, for example, can be used merely to 'stitch' a poem together, rather than for any more ambitious purpose such as 'creating unease'.) The following checklist of questions may be useful to you when you are considering the use of rhyme in a particular poem.

1 Does the poem that you are reading merely rhyme, or does it use rhyme to achieve certain specific effects?

2 Does the rhyme help provide some kind of formal organisation to the poem? (The villanelle is an extreme version of this.) If so, where and how does it do it?

3 Does the rhyme take some form of special or specified pattern (like that in quatrains, couplets, tercets or sonnets)? If so, is the patterning effortless and 'natural', or do you detect signs of strain or awkwardness? (Look at the syntax of the individual sentences, for one thing.)

4 Does the rhyme seem to you to be integral to the poem and its structure, or does it seem to be superficial embroidery?

5 Are the rhymes deliberately obtrusive, or are they restrained and discreet? Or a mixture of both? Are there reasons for this?

6 What sounds do the rhymes make in your head? Pleasant? Unpleasant? Harsh? Lyrical? Do these sounds suggest anything in themselves, such as finality, harmony, humour?

7 Do the rhyming words link or contrast in some way? Does the meaning of one word influence the way you interpret the other word or words that rhyme with it? Do they 'comment' on each other?

It's worth remembering that although you may find rhyme difficult and artificial to use, many poets do not. W. H. Auden, for instance, seems to be able to make rhymes as naturally and as effortlessly as most of us can make our lungs take in air. Don't assume that because a poet has decided to write a sonnet he or she has to torture language and syntax in order to wrap it around a predetermined rhyme-scheme. Good poets don't work this way. It is often said that the best sonnets are poems that you read and enjoy, only later realising, with surprise and pleasure, that you have been reading something written to a form which has rules laid down perhaps nine centuries ago.

Woman incognito

One of the things that men like to think about women is that they are obsessed by clothes. The last poem in this chapter is about what a woman wears – but it has precious little to do with glamour or fashion. Try writing a critical piece on it, applying to it the questions about rhyme that we listed above.

The Oxfam Coat

I do not wear this coat to be admired,
not even to be seen;
it is for seeing from.
I am a walking look-out post, attired

in mist and dead-leaf coloured camouflage –
a watcher's hide, a property
avisible as poverty,
as inconspicuous as middle-age.

It must have needed thirty years, at least,
to reach this natural state
and yet remain an artefact
that keeps me warm. To ditch it would be a waste.

It cost me twenty pence. Good Harris cloth,
springy as heather turf:
it has outworn the striding farmer's wife
its cut suggests. Her scarecrow bones are earth.

It has outworn its power to startle birds
and has become a rough
looking-glass fibre stuff
chameleon, reflecting wintry woods.

That matted sheep – potential bale of wool
on knitting-needle legs –
sees me as sheep. Those twigs
sense me as bark-skinned tree if I stand still.

Obliterated by this patina
I travel incognito. Outline blurs.
Brown dyes revert to lichen, bracken, furze;
I register on no man's retina.

Anna Adams

Women in love

The poems that we have been reading in this chapter are very different in tone and in form, but they all set out to challenge and perhaps subvert certain questionable habits of thought and attitude that many of us have towards being in love and middle-class marriage. It is this kind of examination of conventional attitudes that energises the work of many contemporary women poets. Currently, the inter-relationship that exists between women, women writers and their society is extremely complicated, and it is way beyond the scope of this book – and, probably, beyond the ability of its writers – to look into its depths. Nevertheless, we feel that it is part of your job, as literature students, to ask questions about these issues and to look carefully and critically at the way writers use language to challenge or enforce social assumptions. If you are a hard-headed kind of character, and you are disinclined to bother yourself about 'ideological' issues, then perhaps you should remember this: that students with open minds usually get higher marks in A-Level Literature examinations.

12
Rhyme Games

Here are two exercises which involve playing around with rhymes.

Have a look at these four lists of rhyming words:

A	B	C	D
aided	light	sublime	though
faded	fight	quicklime	show
jaded	tight	berhyme	glow
raided	night	beslime	slow
bladed	kite	enzyme	blow
gladed	trite	mistime	flow
braided	slight	begrime	stow
shaded	right	sometime	grow
waded	spite	lifetime	crow
traded	might	daytime	snow

The first exercise is this: write a short poem consisting of two four-line stanzas (quatrains). **Don't** decide in advance what the subject of your poem is. Choose two words from each of the above lists – A, B, C and D. Use these words as the rhymes in your poem. You can, of course, mix and match these rhymes in any order you wish. You could, for example, arrange them like this:

> first stanza: ABBA
> second stanza: CDDC

or

> first stanza: BCBC
> second stanza: ADAD

Let the meaning(s) of the rhyming words, and the way they affect each other, guide you to the subject of the poem.

The second exercise is this: take one word from each of **two** of the lists. Now think of two half-rhymes (or near-rhymes, if you prefer that term) for each one. Like, for instance, *faded/forehead/ordered* or *night/nought/trait*. You now have six words. Use these as the rhymes in a six-line poem arranged in two three-line stanzas (tercets). Your rhyme-scheme could be

> first stanza: ABA
> second stanza: BAB

or

> first stanza: CCD
> second stanza: DDC

Again, let the meanings of the rhyming words lead you to the subject of the poem.

The point of both these exercises is to allow yourself to be controlled by words, rather than trying to control the words.

13
Form 1: Disguises

MR. WALTER PATER

MR. DYLAN THOMAS

The next few chapters of this book will concentrate on form and structure, and will deal with poetry, mostly. This means that we will be struggling with specific questions like these:

Why do some poems wander about all over the page while others march down the page in tidy little blocks?

Why do some lines rhyme and others not?

Why do poets sometimes leave half a phrase dangling at the end of a line so that it doesn't make sense until you've read the next line?

Why does a line end when it does?

And these questions lead us to wider ones, such as:

What is rhythm in poetry, and has it got anything to do with rhythm in music?
Why is sound important to poetry, even when we read it to ourselves, silently?
What comes first, the form or the words that fit it?
Why would poets choose to write in a traditional form (such as the sonnet or the villanelle) which has 'rules and regulations' when they are free to write in any way they like?

And beyond these questions there are deeper mysteries, such as:

Why is a poem a poem? Why isn't it just prose set out differently on the page?
Is there some difference between the way we read poetry and the way we read prose? Do we have different expectations when we read poetry and prose?

Let us begin with a game. Playing it, you may discover that you already know the answers to some of these questions. The passages that follow are either

a) poetry

b) prose

c) poetry disguised as prose

d) prose disguised as poetry.

The idea is, of course, that you decide which is what and then write out the passages you think have been tampered with in what you think might be their proper form (they haven't *all* been interfered with). It's important to be aware of and clear about *why* you decide which is what, and it's important that when you are rewriting a passage you are conscious of why you are doing it the way you are doing it. You should be asking yourself 'What is there in this passage that tells me it should be written like *this* and not like *that*?' (You can take liberties with punctuation, because we have.)

When you've finished, you can compare your versions with the originals and draw your own conclusions. You might decide, for example, that your versions are improvements. You'll find the originals on page 285 of this book. There's no point in cheating, because we are not awarding prizes to the first readers to send us the correct answers on a postcard.

We'll start with an easy one:

A There was an old lady from Kent whose tastes were exceedingly bent; with a rug on her back (so's to look like a yak) she lived with a goat in a tent.

B Herring gulls heckling down to the harbour where the fishermen spit and prop the morning up and eye the fishy sea smooth to the sea's end as it lulls in blue. Green and gold money, tobacco, tinned salmon, hats with feathers, pots of fish-paste, warmth for the winter-to-be, weave and leap in it rich and slippery in the flash and shapes of fishes through the cold sea-streets. But with blue lazy eyes the fishermen gaze at that milkmaid whispering water with no ruck or ripple as though it blew great guns and serpents and typhooned the town.

C Officious monitors pushed them
Into a hundred symmetrical rows –
Dark-haired, dark-suited men alternating
With rows of brides all wearing
Identical
White
Flouncy
Dresses.

They seemed surprisingly
Uncurious about each other;
There were no side-
Long glances through
White veils: all eyes
Were fixed upon
The red-carpeted stage
Where

Mr Moon and his wife
Stood (looking
More royal than religious)
In ankle-length
White and gold
Gowns
And matching
Crowns.

D A touch of cold in the Autumn night. I walked abroad, and saw the
ruddy moon leap over a hedge like a red-faced farmer. I did not stop
to speak, but nodded, and round about were the wistful stars with
white faces like town children.

E It's my lunch hour, so I go
for a walk among the hum-coloured
cabs. First, down the sidewalk
where labourers feed their dirt
glistening torsoes sandwiches
and Coca-Cola, with yellow helmets
on. They protect them from falling
bricks, I guess. Then onto the
avenue where skirts are flipping
above heels and blow up over
grates. The sun is hot, but the
cabs stir up the air. I look
at bargains in wristwatches. There
are cats playing in sawdust.

F She is older than the rocks among which she sits; like the vampire
she has been dead many times, and learned the secrets of the grave;

and has been a diver in deep seas, and keeps their fallen day about her; and trafficked for strange webs with Eastern merchants: and, as Leda, was the mother of Helen of Troy, and as Saint Anne, the mother of Mary; and all this has been to her but as the sound of lyres and flutes.

G   When the sun falls behind the sumac thicket, the wild yellow daisies in diffuse evening shade lose their rigorous attention and, half wild with loss, turn any way the wind does and lift their petals up to float off their stems and go.

H   I was a Flower of the Mountain
        Yes
        When I put the rose in my hair
        Like the Andalusian girls used

        Or shall I wear red
        Yes
        And how he kissed me under
        The Moorish wall and I thought Well

        As well him as any other
        And then I asked him with my eyes
        To ask again
        Yes

        And then he asked me
        Would I
        Yes
        To say yes my Mountain Flower

        And I put my arms around him
        Yes
        And drew him down to me so
        He could feel my breasts all perfume

        Yes and his heart
        Was going like mad and yes
        I said yes I will
        Yes

I   The house is so quiet now. The vacuum cleaner sulks in the corner closet, its bag limp as a stopped lung, its mouth grinning into the floor, maybe at my slovenly life, my dog-dead youth.
    I've lived this way long enough, but when my old woman died her soul went into that vacuum cleaner, and I can't bear to see the bag swell like a belly, eating the dust and the woollen mice, and begin to howl because there is old filth everywhere she used to crawl, in the corner and under the stair. I know now how life is cheap as dirt; and still the hungry, angry heart hangs on and howls, biting at air.

14

Form 2: Rhythm

The ear inside your head

We'll go straight to the basics:

1 Poems are organised words.

2 Words are sounds.

3 Therefore poems are organisations of sound.

This gives us our three basic problems, which are:

1 Words are sounds, yes, but they are also these things – black marks, or signs, on a page, which are silent. For most of us, most of our experience of poetry comes in the form of reading, not listening.

2 It is difficult to talk about the sounds that language makes. It is easy enough to make general, descriptive comments about sound, and usually they rely upon analogy, upon comparing one sound to another: 'He had a voice like nails being prised from a coffin', or 'Turkish is a language that sounds like a fridge being defrosted at high speed'. But this kind of comment (which is highly subjective) is not very useful when we have to discuss the sound of, say, a line in a particular poem. Take these lines from two poems about the whale:

> Where great whales come sailing by,
> Sail and sail, with unshut eye,
> Round the world for ever and aye
>
> This the black sea-brute bulling through wave-wrack,
> Ancient as ocean's shifting hills, who in sea-toils
> Travelling, who furrowing the salt acres
> Heavily, his wake hoary behind him ...

It's obvious, we hope, that these two extracts are very different in sound. They are organised very differently in terms of line-length, rhyme and rhythm. But what words do we use to discuss the sound of these words?

3 Words are not 'pure' sounds, like musical notes or chords. They also have meanings – they indicate things in the world around us. It's very difficult simply to enjoy the nice sound of words like 'sludge' or 'pneumonia' without our enjoyment being interfered with by their meanings. Given that a poem is a highly-organised word-structure, can we expect there to be a meaningful relationship between the sound of words and the meaning of words?

We'll start with the first of these three problems. It may be that in your school or college there is a wonderful reader of verse. Or you may get to hear recordings of a honey-tongued actor reading some of the poems you study. But in any event, the fact is that you are going to spend much more time reading verse to yourself than you spend listening to verse being read. This means you are going to have to develop a sort of controlled schizophrenia: you need to be reader and listener simultaneously. What you need is a third ear – a critical, impartial ear – inside your head; an ear that can detect whether your reading is good or bad.

Growing a third ear is a tricky business, and you won't succeed unless you accept from the start that a poem is an artifice. To state the obvious (again) a poem is a deliberate and conscious arrangement of words which will differ in a number of ways from 'normal' or 'natural' use of language. We think, speak and apparently dream in prose. The vast majority of what we read is in prose. Consequently, we think of prose as natural, and we all have an understandable tendency to read poetry as if it were prose. It is not easy to overcome this tendency. It takes a conscious effort. It's worth making that effort, though, because it is one way of avoiding what we might call the Form/Content Trap. A great many (most, probably) of our students have fallen into this trap at one time or another. The trap depends, basically, upon a misconception which goes something like this: this poet has something to say (i.e. the Content of his poem) which he could have said in natural language (i.e. prose); but because he has chosen to say it in a poem which has four stanzas and a rhyme-scheme and a regular rhythmic pattern (i.e. Form) he is forced to bend and twist and pervert his natural language to make it fit.

People who fall into the Form/Content Trap see an inevitable conflict between what a poet says and how the poet says it. They tend to say things like 'The poet is forced to use the old-fashioned word "aye" instead of "ever" because it rhymes with "eye"' or 'The poet joins the words "sea" and "toils" together in order that they fit the rhythm'; or (more sophisticated, this) 'The meaning of the poem is obscure, partly because the poet is very inflexible with his use of rhyme.'

What lies behind comments like this is a certain frustration, an irritation caused by the poet's refusal to write 'naturally'. The ultimately daft comment of this sort – and it keeps popping up – is 'The use of language in this poem is very artificial', which is like complaining that a painting of an apple doesn't taste very nice, or that a singer has to say words in a funny way so as to make them fit the music.

If your internal ear is going to be at all sensitive, you might as well make a simple, primitive assumption about the form (the sound-arrangement) of any poem you read. This assumption is that the poet *chose* that form as a means of expression, and not as a hindrance to it. Very often, in fact, poets have said that the form, the overall sound, of a poem comes before the words themselves. It's a case of the structure making the words possible, rather than the words being forced into the structure:

> One useful way of considering the structure of a passage is to regard it as a means of making it possible for forms of language used in it to have more meaning than they would otherwise have; the structure is a solution to the problems involved in getting a particular thing said.

> *Winifred Nowottny: The Language Poets Use*

So a poem is an artifice, and the ear inside your head needs to be alert to (and tolerant of!) the way poetic language may be organised differently to ordinary language. The next problem is: how do you write about what the inner ear hears?

Because it is difficult to write about sound, it is understandable that students often take refuge in vagueness, hedging their bets with comments like 'the opening lines are very smooth', 'the rhythm changes in line 4' and 'there is a hard feel to the second stanza'. While such vagueness is understandable, it's not really desirable. To avoid it, you need, in addition to a good inner ear, a small vocabulary of technical terms. As we said in Chapter 1, technical terms are useful in that they save time. They also save you the embarrassment of having to warble on in an imprecise way about something for which there is a more precise term. Allow us, though, to repeat the warning about technical terms, which is that splattering them about in an attempt to sound impressive is unwise; the result will tend to sound like jargon, and nobody likes it. In the following pages we will try to define and demonstrate some technical terms which we hope you will find useful. But just before that, here's some advice which may help you cultivate that ear inside your head.

When you are reading to yourself, treat yourself to your best voice. Take some trouble over pronunciation, and try to avoid that slurring of vowels and blunting of consonants in which we all indulge in everyday speech. (Please note: we do not mean trying to sound posh – we're talking about *clarity*.) Slow down from your normal reading speed. Give the words a chance to work. Respect the different pauses indicated by full stops, commas, semi-colons, etc. If you are not sure how a word should be pronounced, don't be too embarrassed to go and find someone who is.

Experiment. Read a poem several times and play about with it a bit. Try shifting and varying the 'weights' of the stresses (emphases) in a line until it sounds 'right' to your ear. Likewise with pace: different lines may want to be read at different speeds. Are there words that slow you down? Are there sequences of sound that hurry you along?

Congratulate yourself when you read a poem well.

Rhythm methods

There are two basic questions about rhythm:

What is it?
What is it for?

To all intents and purposes, there are two forms of organised sound – music and speech. (For now, for the sake of argument, we'll treat writing as a form of speech.) In both forms, rhythm is essentially a matter of repetition: sounds, or sequences of sounds, are repeated in some sort of pattern. In both music and speech there are very many different ways of creating rhythm, very many different kinds of rhythm, and many degrees of immediacy of rhythm. Reggae is not necessarily more rhythmic than, say, a Mozart concerto, but its rhythms are more immediate, more 'foregrounded'. These lines

> Water, water, everywhere,
> And all the boards did shrink;
> Water, water, everywhere,
> Nor any drop to drink.

> *Coleridge: The Rime of the Ancient Mariner*

have a heavy, foregrounded rhythm, but it is not 'more' rhythmic than this, which uses repetition in a less insistent way:

> And lonely as it is that loneliness
> Will be more lonely ere it will be less –
> A blanker whiteness of benighted snow
> With no expression, nothing to express.

> *Robert Frost: Desert Places*

What rhythm does is give unity, or coherence, to what might otherwise be a series of unrelated sounds. A piece of music might possibly consist of a passage of singing followed by a saxophone playing against synthesiser chords followed by a duet between a kazoo and a ukelele – but if all of these sounds are played to a more or less consistent rhythm we get a sense of listening to a single piece of music. Without pushing the analogy between music and speech too far, we could say that rhythm in poetry does a similar thing: it's the stitching which holds the fabric of a poem together.

In practice, in the act of reading or listening, rhythm creates **expectancy**. If the rhythm in the first three lines of a four-line stanza goes like this:

```
DOM de   DOM de   DOM de   DOM
de DOM   de DOM   de DOM
DOM de   DOM de   DOM de   DOM
```

we can't help expecting the fourth line to be

```
de DOM   de DOM   de DOM.
```

Expectation can be either **fulfilled** (what you expect to happen does happen) or **defeated** (it doesn't). It's worth thinking about what our reactions are likely to be in each case. If our expectancy is fullfilled, if that fourth line does indeed turn out to be de DOM de DOM de DOM, we are likely to feel that something has been completed, or 'rounded off'. We are in a sense satisfied. (But if the rhythm went on in the same way for another 133 stanzas we would be satisfied half to death, would we not?) But what if our expectancy is defeated? Defeated expectancy is, in fact, a device used very widely and variously by poets, especially by those who work with regular rhythms. Its effects can vary enormously, but we can risk two generalisations: first, that when it happens it attracts our attention (in the way that the abnormal or surprising always does); second, that the stronger and more predictable the rhythm in a poem, the greater the impact of defeated expectancy will be. In extreme cases, defeated expectancy could cause a poem to fall apart in a ludicrous manner; for example, if instead of that expected de DOM de DOM de DOM the stanza did this:

> Water, water, everywhere,
> And all the boards did shrink;
> Water, water, everywhere,
> And there wasn't a drop of drink to be had anywhere on the boat.

It can be comic without being slapstick. Here are three lines describing a bride:

> Her lips were red, and one was thin,
> Compar'd to that was next her chin
> (Some bee had stung it newly.)

The poet is pretending to be discreet. He tucks away the remark about the unfortunate bee-sting inside brackets so that it appears to be an incidental and not very important thing, as if to say 'Oh, and she had a bee-sting, by the way'. But in fact he draws our attention to it by an unexpected 'ruffling' of the rhythm at 'stung it newly'. If we put some de DOMs in it becomes more obvious:

```
Her lips  were red and one  was thin
de DOM   de DOM de DOM de  DOM

Compar'd  to  that  was next her chin
de  DOM de DOM de  DOM de DOM

(Some bee  had stung  it    newly)
 de   DOM de DOM DOM DOMde
```

(We guess that by now you'll have realised that these DOMs and des correspond to **syllables**.)

Defeated expectancy – unexpected switches in rhythm – need not be comic at all. Let's go back to the becalmed and thirsty Ancient Mariner and see what happens in the next stanza:

> Water, water, everywhere,
> And all the boards did shrink;
> Water water, everywhere,
> Nor any drop to drink.
>
> The very deep did rot: O Christ!
> That ever this should be!
> Yea, slimy things did crawl with legs
> Upon the slimy sea.

The first thing to notice is that in this second stanza the rhythm is the reverse of what it is in the preceding one:

The ve   ry deep did rot
de DOM de DOM de DOM

This is a quicker rhythm than the rhythm of 'Water, water, everywhere' (there are no commas, for one thing) but it only hurries us along to a pause – a heavy pause, signalled by a colon. This is a 'dramatic pause' which 'sets us up' for the loud, double-beat exclamation 'O Christ!' The effect of rhythmic variation here is to dramatise, to give additional force to the Mariner's cry of horror at what he sees.

Defeated expectancy (and other more subtle forms of rhythmic variation) can be used for comic effects, for dramatic effects, for ironic effects, and for a hundred and one other effects, and there doesn't seem much point in subjecting you to loads of examples at this stage. We'll need to return to the subject anyway, when we look at something called **metre**.

You may have noticed that in the short passages we have quoted so far there are several different kinds of repetition. They are:

the 'pulse', the repetition of beats or emphases in a line (those de DOMs and DOM des).

the use of lines which have the same number of beats

the repetition of words: 'Water, water'; 'lonely ... lonely'

the repetition of whole lines: 'Water, water, everywhere'

the repetition of sounds at the beginnings of words: 'drop ... drink'; 'blanker ... benighted'; 'slimy ... sea'

the repetition of sounds at the ends of words (end-rhyme): 'shrink ... drink'; 'be less ... express'; 'thin ... chin'

What all this means, clearly, is that the poets who wrote these passages wanted, for some reason, to have their rhythms heard quite distinctly. Rhythm is foregrounded in these extracts. But rhythm in poetry is just as often a more subdued affair, operating at a level where we are only just aware of it. What's more, it is not necessary for poets to use all of those repetition techniques – or any of them – to create rhythm. Quite simple, minimal devices will do. Here, for instance, are the first few lines of a poem by the eighteenth-century poet Christopher Smart. It's about his cat, Jeoffrey:

> For I will consider my cat, Jeoffrey.
> For he is the servant of the Living God, duly and daily serving him.
> For at the first glance of the glory of God in the East he worships in his way.
> For this is done by wreathing his body seven times round with elegant quickness.
> For then he leaps up to catch the musk, which is the blessing of God upon his prayer.
> For he rolls upon prank to work it in.
> For having done duty and received blessing he begins to consider himself.
> For this performs in ten degrees.
> For first he looks upon his forepaws to see if they are clean.
> For secondly he kicks up behind to clear away there.
> For thirdly he works it upon stretch with the forepaws extended.
> For fourthly he sharpens his paws by wood.
> For fifthly he washes himself.
> For sixthly he rolls upon wash.
> For seventhly he fleas himself, that he may not be interrupted upon the beat.
> For eighthly he rubs himself against a post.
> For ninthly he looks up for his instructions.
> For tenthly he goes in quest of food.

Christopher Smart

This has a conspicuous absence of the rhythmic devices employed in the passages we have looked at so far. The lines do not have a regular 'pulse', and they vary considerably in length. They do not rhyme. The only repetitions that set up expectancy are the consistent use of the word 'For' at the beginning of each line, the simple device of counting from one to ten, and the placing, more often than not, of the main verb immediately after the first two words in each line ('For fourthly he sharpens ... For fifthly he washes' and so on.) The fabric of this poem is held together by very few simple stitches. But it works. (At least, *we* think it does.)

Before we get down to some technical stuff, there is one other form of rhythmic repetition we think we should mention. It is to be found in both prose and poetry, and is easier to demonstrate than to explain. Unfortunately, the only name for this technique that seems to fit is **syntactical parallelism**. This is actually far less dreadful and more simple than it sounds. Syntax, as we've said before somewhere, is the various ways that sentences can be constructed. Syntactical parallelism, therefore, is a way of setting up rhythm by using a sequence of sentences that are constructed in the same way. One reason for the frequency of this technique in English writing is that it is used in the Bible (the Authorised Version of 1611, not one of the Janet and John versions of recent years). The Bible has always been a source book for writers (including Christopher Smart). Here's part of a particularly famous passage from that part of the Bible called Ecclesiastes:

The wind goeth toward the south, and turneth into the north; it whirleth about continually, and the wind returneth again according to its circuits. All the rivers run into the sea, yet the sea is not full; unto the place whence the rivers come, thither they return again. All things are full of labour; man cannot utter it; the eye is not satisfied with seeing, nor the ear filled with hearing. The thing that hath been, is that which shall be; and that which is done is that which shall be done; and there is no new thing under the sun.

The very pronounced rhythm of these lines is achieved by the simple syntactical device whereby each sentence consists of four clauses separated by three punctuated pauses, like this:

All the rivers run into the sea,	yet the sea is not full;	unto the place whence the rivers come,	thither they return again.
All things are full of labour;	man cannot utter it;	the eye is not satisfied with seeing,	nor the ear filled with hearing.

Put very crudely, what the writer of these lines is saying is that despite all the ceaseless activity of things and men, nothing changes profoundly. There is nothing new under the sun; everything returns to what it was. The way these sentences repeat each other in form seems to echo, or enact, the idea of things returning to what they were.

The Ecclesiastes passage is very consistent in the way that it balances one similarly-structured sentence against another, and for this reason the rhythm in the piece is strong – i.e. foregrounded and predictable. The strength of rhythms set up by syntactical parallelism (or 'sentence-balancing', if you like) varies according to how closely the syntax of each sentence matches the syntax of the other sentences in a passage. And, of course, the more that sentences deviate from one syntactical pattern, the fainter the rhythm will become.

It is time now to turn to particular kinds of rhythm, how they are created and what they are created from, so let's recapitulate very quickly what we have said so far. Rhythm is patterned repetition. There are multitudes of different patterns, and numerous things that can be repeated: beats, or emphasised syllables in a line;, words; individual sounds; sentence structures, and so on. Attention-seeking 'rhythmic events' are usually the result of the expected, predictable pattern being disturbed in some way. Rhythm's basic job is to give coherence, or shape, to a poem's language.

Kevin's bike and Wordsworth's Daffodils

We said earlier that poetic language is organised differently to 'ordinary' language. This is true, but if poets are to make themselves understood they can only manipulate the natural rhythms of ordinary speech. They cannot change or re-order them altogether. But what, you may ask, do we mean by 'the natural rhythms of ordinary speech'?

English, unlike some other languages, depends largely for its meaning on the varying emphasis, or stress, that we put on parts of words (syllables). Both words and sentences depend upon stress-variation. For example, in the words 'swallow bacon sandwiches' we stress the first syllable of each word: SWALlow BAcon SANDwiches. We would sound daft if we said swalLOW baCON sandWICHes. In the simple sentence 'I want to go', the meaning changes according to where we put the stress:

<u>I</u> want to go (rather than anyone else)

I <u>want</u> to go (I do, really)

I want to <u>go</u> (I don't want to stay)

This business of stress is quite complicated, actually, because we are capable of voicing quite subtle shades of emphasis to achieve quite subtle shades of meaning. What's more, we've been doing it since we first learned to talk, and to be conscious of it is at least as difficult as being conscious of what our legs are doing when we walk or what our lungs are doing when we breathe. But this subtlety of stress-variation is one of the first things the inner ear needs to be able to hear.

The patterns of stress position and variation are what we mean by 'the natural rhythms of ordinary speech', and by common consent (with just a few poets dissenting) there are limits to the liberties we can take with them.

At this point we need some sort of method for marking the position of stresses in words and lines. From now on we'll use the following marks to indicate (very crudely) differently stressed syllables:

/ indicates a strongly stressed syllable

˘ indicates a lightly stressed or unstressed syllable

We frequently speak in a more or less regular rhythm without being particularly aware of it. Here's an ordinary sentence:

I had a go on Kevin's bike and smashed it up against a bus.

Its natural stresses go like this:

˘ / ˘ / ˘ / ˘ / ˘ / ˘ / ˘ / ˘ /
I had a go on Kevin's bike and smashed it up against a bus.

As you can see, it follows a regular sequence of light, heavy, light, heavy stresses. And it divides into eight similar units:

˘ / | ˘ / | ˘ / | ˘ / | ˘ / | ˘ / | ˘ / | ˘ /
I had | a go | on Kev | in's bike | and smashed | it up | against | a bus.

We could even arrange it into two equal lines of four units each, like this:

˘ / | ˘ / | ˘ / | ˘ /
I had | a go | on Kev | in's bike

˘ / | ˘ / | ˘ / | ˘ /
and smashed | it up | against | a bus

This doesn't sound much like poetry, maybe, but it happens to have almost exactly the same rhythm as two of the most famous lines in English literature:

I wan | der'd lone | ly as | a cloud

That floats | on high | o'er vales | and hills

The fact that The Tragedy of Kevin's Bike (a piece of colloquial speech) and the opening lines of Wordsworth's *The Daffodils* happen to be rhythmically near-identical illustrates a couple of important points.

First, no matter how complex or 'artificial' a poem's form may seem, its basic structural device – the ordering and variation of stresses – is taken from ordinary speech as used by you and me. Second, a poem is an artifice, and so we accept that poets manipulate language in certain ways. But there are limits to the extent that a poet can interfere with natural speech rhythms. We can allow Wordsworth to shorten (elide) 'over' into 'o'er'; but if he were to try to overturn the stress-order of part of a line, like this, say:

I wanDER'D loneLY as ...

or like this:

ON high O'ER vales AND hills ...

we would refuse, or simply be unable, to read it that way.

Perhaps you may be objecting to some of this. You might reasonably say 'Hang on – if I were actually to say "I had a go on Kevin's bike and smashed it up against a bus" I wouldn't say it in that regular, rhythmical de DOM de DOM way. I wouldn't put the same stress on "I" and "smashed", for a start.' True; and what's more, Wordsworth's poem would start to sound exceedingly silly if we read it in that evened-out sort of a way. What we did with both pieces was simplify and exaggerate their rhythms. In a sensible reading of a poem, rhythm is more subdued. It operates as what W. B. Yeats called 'a ghostly voice'. A poem is not a collection of rhythmic units any more than a body is merely a skeleton (although poems without rhythms and bodies without skeletons tend to be a bit limp). And, of course, very few poems plod along to one unvarying rhythm – that would be too boring. In poems that do have an underlying rhythm of some sort, the deviations from that rhythm, and the variations in it, are at least as important as the rhythm itself. But, obviously, you are not going to spot these deviations and variations unless you have already 'got' the rhythm. Therefore one of the things that the ear inside your head should be able to do is crank up the rhythm, so to speak, by simplifying and over-emphasising it. You should also be able to crank it down again so that you are not deafened to other levels of sound.

What all this amounts to is that your inner ear should make you hear consciously what you already hear unconsciously. Although in our everyday lives we are largely unaware of it, most of us have an innate feel for the rhythmical organisation of language. For instance, if you played the 'disguises' game in the previous chapter, you will (we trust) have realised that the first passage

There was an old lady from Kent whose tastes were exceedingly bent; with a rug on her back (so's to look like a yak) she lived with a goat in a tent

is really a limerick:

> There was an old lady from Kent
> Whose tastes were exceedingly bent;
> With a rug on her back
> (So's to look like a yak)
> She lived with a goat in a tent.

If you twigged it, you no doubt noticed that the line-endings are indicated by two rhymes: 'Kent'/'bent'/'tent' and 'back'/'yak'. But you almost certainly heard – possibly even before you spotted the rhymes – that the piece has a pattern of two kinds of rhythmic unit, and they dictate, even more effectively than the rhymes, the form:

There was | an old la | dy from Kent

Whose tastes | were exceed | ingly bent;

With a rug | on her back

(So's to look | like a yak)

She lived | with a goat | in a tent.

A caution

Without admitting it, we have begun to talk about **metrics**, and before we go any further we should issue a sort of health warning. What follows could cause headaches. We are going to talk about something called **metre**, things called **feet** and something called **scansion**; and the fact is that these things are not generally taught in schools and colleges these days. The reason for this is that many people – teachers included – consider these topics difficult or boring or out of date or off-putting. We have a lot of sympathy with this view. Neither of us enjoyed learning these things either, and perhaps we would have been no worse off if we hadn't. The problem is, however, that that the vast majority of English poetry (poetry written in the English language, we mean) is, in fact, metrical. Almost all poetry written between about 1350 and 1900 – more than five centuries' worth – is metrical, and so is much that has been written since. (Bear with us – we'll explain what metrical poetry is in a moment.) It seems to us that writing about or discussing metrical verse (as written by Shakespeare, say) without any grasp of how metre works is rather like ... well, perhaps like riding Kevin's Honda without any idea of how it works: possible – just – but not really sensible. In spite of that, it is perfectly possible to get a pass in A-Level Literature without knowing a thing about metre. Most people do. To this extent, what follows is optional, and this may reassure those of you who find it off-putting. Actually, the next few pages are not all that difficult (compared with astro-physics or the Chinese alphabet, anyway). We suggest you just hold your nose and plunge in.

Metrics and metrical verse

'Metre' means measure. Metrical verse, therefore, is verse which can be 'measured'.

What this means is that in a metrical poem the lines consist of a number of rhythmical units which can be counted. Kevin's Bike, Wordsworth's *The Daffodils* and the limerick are all metrical.

In the line 'The time has come, the Walrus said' there are four of these rhythmic units:

$$\breve{\text{The}} \ \acute{\text{time}} \ | \ \breve{\text{has}} \ \acute{\text{come}}, \ | \ \breve{\text{the}} \ \acute{\text{Wal}} \ | \ \breve{\text{rus}} \ \acute{\text{said}}$$

and in the line that follows it there are three:

$$\breve{\text{To}} \ \acute{\text{talk}} \ | \ \breve{\text{of}} \ \acute{\text{man}} \ | \ \breve{\text{y}} \ \acute{\text{things}}$$

These rhythmic units are called **feet**. A foot nearly always has one stressed syllable and one or more unstressed or lightly stressed syllables. Feet differ one from another according to how many syllables they have and where the stress comes. You will not be particularly surprised to learn that each kind of foot has its own peculiar name. They sound like creatures in some weird academic zoo:

the **iamb** is an unstressed syllable followed by a stressed one:

$$\breve{\text{to}} \ \acute{\text{be}} \ | \ \breve{\text{or}} \ \acute{\text{not}} \ | \ \breve{\text{to}} \ \acute{\text{be}}$$

the **trochee** is the iamb in reverse:

$$\acute{\text{stop}} \ \breve{\text{it}} \ | \ \acute{\text{Da}} \breve{\text{vid}}$$

the **anapest** has two unstressed syllables followed by a stressed:

$$\breve{\text{de}} \ \breve{\text{com}} \ \acute{\text{pose}} \ | \ \breve{\text{in}} \ \breve{\text{the}} \ \acute{\text{ground}}$$

the **dactyl** is the reverse of the anapest:

$$\acute{\text{pa}} \breve{\text{ra}} \ \breve{\text{chute}} \ | \ \acute{\text{grace}} \breve{\text{ful}} \breve{\text{ly}}$$

Iambic and trochaic feet are called **double measures** (because they have two syllables); anapestic and dactylic feet are called **triple measures** (because they have three). It may all sound crazy, but you can't deny it's logical.

In metrical verse, lines have a certain number of these feet. Such lines also have names. They will not sound particularly odd if you have done some maths:

a two foot line is a dimeter
a three foot line is a trimeter
a four foot line is a tetrameter
a five foot line is a pentameter
a six foot line is a hexameter
a seven foot line is a septameter

Most metrical lines in English have three or four or five feet. By putting together the kind of foot used and the number of feet used, you get what is called a **metrical description** of a line. For example, in the following two lines the first is an anapestic trimeter and the second is an anapestic dimeter:

˘ ˘ / | ˘ ˘ / | ˘ ˘ /
I have come | to the bord | ers of sleep

˘ ˘ / | ˘ ˘ /
The unfath | omable deep

This line is an iambic pentameter:

˘ / | ˘ / | ˘ / | ˘ / | ˘ /
The bree | zy call | of in | cense-breath | ing dawn

For deeply interesting and mysterious reasons (which we shall not get lost in here) iambic pentameter is by far the most common metre in English poetry. There is probably a computerised American academic somewhere who has worked out what percentage of metrical English verse is in iambic pentameter. We'd guess that his VDU would show a figure of between seventy-five and ninety per cent. Iambic rhythms seem to be more 'natural' to an English speaker. It seems that it is more natural for us to go de DOM (iambic) than DOM de (trochaic). Trochees seem to interfere with language more than iambs do; they seem more 'pushy' and intrusive. (Police cars wail trochaically.) For whatever reason, it is likely that if you come across a line of verse which has ten syllables, that line is an iambic pentameter. And perhaps because iambic pentameters are so common, poets tend to use them very flexibly – by adding a syllable on here and there, for instance.

This business of working out metrical patterns in feet is called **scansion** or **scanning**. Scansion can get dizzyingly complicated, and the deeper you go into it the more wonderful and bizarre the terminology becomes. It is probably not very useful to lumber your head with too much of it. If you should happen to find the subject fascinating and you want to investigate further, then your teacher can point you towards books that contain more detailed information. For our purposes, we wish to deal with only one more area of scansion.

As we said earlier, any poem that sticks rigidly to one prevailing metrical pattern will inevitably be very tedious, and in almost all metrical verse there will be a good deal of variation within the prevailing metre. These variations (which are a form of defeated expectancy, something we discussed earlier) are often called **metrical substitutions**. Some metrical substitutions are more common than others, and you could learn to recognise them. The two most frequently employed are:

1 swopping one foot in a line for a different kind of foot

2 cutting a foot short

It's worth noting that these substitutions occur most often at the beginnings or ends of lines. Why? Well, if you are a poet working in either iambic measure (˘ /) or anapestic measure (˘ ˘ /) then the first syllable of each line will be 'weak' – that is, unstressed. And if you are using trochaic (/ ˘) or dactylic (/ ˘˘) measure, then the last syllable of each line will be weak. But you might want – for any number of possible reasons – to begin or end a line with a strong beat rather than a weak one. For example, on Shakespeare's tomb in Stratford there's this little iambic verse:

> Good Friend, for Jesu's sake forbear
> To dig the dust enclosed here.
> Blest be the man who spares these stones
> And curst be he who moves my bones.

Assuming that Shakespeare wrote this himself (and it's hard to imagine him leaving the job to someone else) he clearly wanted an arresting, direct address opening ('I'm talking to *you*'), so he substitutes a double-stress foot for the first iamb:

$$\acute{G}o\acute{o}d\ fri\acute{e}nd,\ \Big|\ f\breve{o}r\ J\acute{e}\ \Big|\ s\breve{u}'s\ s\acute{a}ke\ \Big|\ f\breve{o}rb\acute{e}ar$$

This replacing of an iamb with a double-stress foot is in fact so common that this double-foot stress has its own name; it's called a **spondee**. What this little trick does is draw extra attention to the words where it takes place; which is what metrical variations almost always do.

Now let's look at the second common form of metrical substitution: cutting a foot short. (The technical term for this is **catalexis**.) This usually happens to feet that end with an unstressed syllable (trochees and dactyls). Here is a very well-known example – the opening of William Blake's *The Tiger*:

> Tiger! Tiger! burning bright
> In the forests of the night

The first line scans like this:

$$\acute{T\imath}g\breve{e}r!\ \Big|\ \acute{T\imath}g\breve{e}r!\ \Big|\ b\acute{u}rn\breve{i}ng\ \Big|\ br\acute{i}ght$$

It is a sequence of four trochees (a trochaic tetrameter, in other words) with the last unstressed syllable missing. In fact, *most* trochaic lines have this final syllable snipped off. The reasons for this, and the effects of it, will vary from poem to poem, but perhaps we can risk one generalisation. This has to do with rhyme. In English, true rhyme depends upon matching stressed syllables, not unstressed ones. Thus 'looking' and 'hooking' rhyme, whereas 'standing' and 'walking' do not, even though all four words end in *ing*. Likewise with 'ration' and 'passion', which rhyme, and 'station' and 'fission', which do not. If, therefore, you want to end a line with a strong true rhyme, a stressed syllable is what's called for. In *The Tiger*, this rhyme is important because it is one of the ways Blake sets up a very strong four-beat rhythm, almost like an hypnotic chant, with which he 'conjures up' the vision of the tiger. The strength of this beat is reinforced by the repetition of 'Tiger' and the repetition of the *b* sound in 'burning bright'. If the 'missing' syllable of the last trochee were put back:

> Tiger! Tiger! burning brightly

the line loses an awful lot of punch and goes limp at the end. Not only that, but it poses a very tricky problem as far as rhyme is concerned. What can rhyme with 'brightly'? 'Nightly', perhaps:

> Tiger! Tiger! burning brightly
> In the forests, lit up nightly ...

Or 'slightly'?

> Tiger! Tiger! burning brightly
> In the forests, scorching slightly ...

Clearly there's a danger of getting silly here. But perhaps there is something about the metre itself, not just the rhymes, which is inherently comic or silly. Is it possible that two lines of intact trochaic tetrameter would inevitably sound funny, no matter what the words were? After all, even verses in which silliness would be more acceptable – such as nursery rhymes – generally have that last syllable lopped off:

> Twinkle, twinkle, little star ...

Perhaps there are certain rhythms and certain forms which we can never take quite seriously. Could you write a serious or passionate or even tragic limerick, for example? But this raises the question of whether certain forms have meanings or associations of their own, regardless of subject matter, and we are getting ahead of ourselves.

Summary

In the past few pages we have thrown at you several odd technical terms, so perhaps we should summarise briefly before going on.

Metrical verse is verse which is made up of repeated rhythmic units called feet. It is therefore regular (up to a point). These feet can be identified by the number of syllables they contain and the position of the stressed syllable. The type of foot used and the number of feet used together give a metrical description of a line. In almost all metrical verse, the variations in and deviations from the prevailing rhythm are at least as important as that rhythm itself. These variations are called metrical substitutions and have the obvious function of preventing unbearable monotony, but also direct our attention to the significance of the words where they occur.

Stress-verse

Stress-verse differs from metrical verse in that only the stressed syllables are counted, and the unstressed ones can vary in number and position. Most stress-verse (which is also known as strong-stress metres) has four stresses, or beats, to a line. These beats are usually given extra emphasis by the use of alliteration (the repetition of sounds at the beginnings of neighbouring words). To give you the general idea, here's the opening line of Langland's *The Vision of Piers Plowman*, which was written sometime between 1350 and 1400:

> In summer season, when soft was the sun

In this line there are four alliterated stresses: 'summer', 'season', 'soft' and 'sun'. It's more usual for only the first three beats to be alliterated, as in the fourth line of *Piers Plowman* which tells how he

> Went wide in this world, wonders to hear

('Went' is an unstressed syllable here.) As well as this pattern of alliterative stresses, stress-verse is characterised by a strong pause, called a **caesura**, which divides the line into two parts. In each of the two lines just quoted, the caesura is indicated by a comma. (In scansion, you represent the caesura with a colon.) English stress-verse is much older than English metrical verse. It goes back a very long way. It was the native verse here centuries before the Normans turned up at Hastings. It is a Saxon (German) and Scandinavian verse form, and was the usual metre of Old English and Middle English poetry; it was not until the late fourteenth century that Chaucer made continental (i.e. French-Italian) metrical verse generally popular.

You could say that stress-verse is Northern (Teutonic) while metrical verse is Southern (Latin).

As the English language moved from Anglo-Saxon towards modern Anglo-French English, stress-verse declined in usage. Or perhaps it would be truer to say that it was absorbed into metrical verse, because metrical verse is, in a sense, a smoothing-out or regularising of stress-verse. That opening line of *Piers the Ploughman* is after all very nearly metrical: you could scan it as two iambs and two anapests:

$$\breve{\;}/\;|\;\breve{\;}/\;|\;\breve{\;}\;\breve{\;}/\;|\;\breve{\;}\;\breve{\;}/$$

In sum | mer sea | son when soft | was the sun

In modern times, a few poets have experimented with stress-verse; Gerard Manley Hopkins and Coleridge in the nineteenth century, notably. But it is only in our century that it has had anything resembling a revival. When, eighty-odd years ago, the pioneers of free verse (about which more later) broke away from metrical verse, they saw stress-verse as one of the alternatives. Ezra Pound, for example, wrote a version of the Anglo-Saxon poem *The Sea-farer*. Later, W. H. Auden wrote a number of stress-verse pieces. Among contemporary poets, Ted Hughes is one who uses the form. At the beginning of this chapter, if you remember, we quoted lines from two different poems about whales. If we look at them again now, perhaps you will see that the essential difference is that the first (written in the 1840s) is metrical while the second (written in the 1950s) is a form of stress-verse.

> Where great whales come sailing by,
> Sail and sail with unshut eye
> Round the world for ever and aye.

> This is the black sea-brute bulling through wave-wrack,
> ancient as Ocean's shifting hills; who in sea-toils
> travelling, who furrowing the salt acres
> heavily, his wake hoary behind him

The first line of the first piece scans like this:

$$\breve{\;}/\;|\;/\;\breve{\;}\;|\;/\breve{\;}\;|\;/$$

Where great | whales come | sailing | by

Can you scan the rest of it? And can you locate the stresses and sound repetitions in the second piece?

To end with, try these two questions about the two pieces:

1 How would you describe the way they differ in sound?

2 How do these differences in sound – especially rhythm – convey different ideas about whales?

15
Form 3: Sound Effects

metre

onomatopoeia

consonance

alliteration

rhyme

XANADU

We're sure that it has already occurred to you that to describe the rhythm in a line of poetry is not at all the same thing as describing the *sound* of that line. A metrical description of a line of verse is a very crude shorthand for its rhythmical organisation; it does not and cannot take account of all sorts of other things which affect the way the line 'moves' – things such as the length of syllables, the 'roundness' or 'sharpness' of vowel sounds (compare *groan* and *grin*) or the 'hardness' or 'softness' of different consonants (compare *skittle* with *dribble*). Metrical description cannot tell us very much about intonation (the various ways that a word can be pronounced so as to slightly change its meaning or significance). It is also fairly obvious that two lines of poetry will not sound alike because they are both iambic pentameters – for the simple reason that those two lines will consist of different words. They would not sound the same if they consisted of the same words in a different order. If you say 'These two lines are both iambic pentameters', you are saying what they have in common (which may in itself be a useful comment) but you are not saying anything about what distinguishes them one from another, nor are you saying anything about the contribution that sound makes to the meaning of either line. Rhythm is important to form because it is the overall way in which sound is organised; but we also need some way of talking about particular sounds and groups of sound. This is what this chapter is about. But first we have to dispose of a red herring.

The music of poetry

This red herring is 'the music of poetry'. If you read books of criticism, or reviews, or (even worse) lots of A-Level essays, you will sooner or later come across loose talk about the 'music' of such-and-such a poet's work or the 'musicality' of so-and-so's prose. You might even find lines of poetry annotated with musical notes – which will not mean a thing to you, of course, if (like us) you do not know how to read music. We simply wish to warn you here against the temptation to waffle on about the 'musical qualities' of poetry. (We exclude from this poetry which is specifically written to be musical, like song lyrics, and verse intended to be accompanied by music.)

It is true that because speech and music are both forms of organised sound we use some words to apply to both: rhythm, pitch, intonation, phrasing, sometimes even counterpoint and harmony. It is also true that poets usually pay close attention to the sound of words, and to that extent might be said to 'compose' in a way similar to musical composition. But the parallels between music and speech are limited, because musical sound is pure abstraction. Music can suggest or evoke feelings and 'meanings', but words *have* meanings, and you can't get away from them. (Even when we read nonsense verse, we can't help trying to attach meanings to meaningless words.) Music is wonderful stuff because we can be moved or excited by it without needing to know 'what it's about'. It's hard to imagine being moved by a poem without knowing what it's about. For this reason it is often very misleading to apply musical terminology to poetry. But at the same time it's true that in poetry and (less commonly) in prose, sound is often organised so as somehow to affect the meaning of the words. Alexander Pope's famous dictum is 'The sound must seem an echo to the sense'. Those lines at the end of the last chapter, about the whale 'bulling' through the sea are trying to do that; those strongly-stressed and alliterated *b*s might suggest the action of the whale shoving along through the waves.

Well, it's a fairly straightforward business when the sound of a poem somehow reflects its subject. The problem we have to cope with arises when this *doesn't* happen: when sound is clearly being manipulated by the poet, but there is no apparent connection between the sound and the sense of the lines. And of course this connection, this 'echo' cannot always happen, because while there is a considerable number of words which do have sound which echoes their meaning, the fact is that most do not. It may be that poets would always prefer to use words which 'sound like what they mean', but if they want to make sense they can't.

So, let's imagine you have in front of you a poem in which sound is obviously important, because you can hear that it's been very deliberately arranged. But there's apparently no connection between that sound-arrangement and what the poem's about. What can you say about it? What can you write about it?

If you were to ask a poet why he or she had arranged a certain line this way as opposed to that way, there's a good chance the answer would be something like 'Well, I just liked the sound of it'. Once you start talking about pleasurable sound, everything becomes very subjective; it's like talking about music. And that's when you might be tempted to start wittering on about 'melodious vowels' and 'arpeggios of sharp consonants' and truck like that. You mustn't, though. The only good advice, probably, is this: if you are aware that a poet is 'composing' sound in a poem, and you can see *how* but not *why*, then say so or say nothing. Don't waffle.

Conveniently, there are technical terms for several linguistic sound-effects, and they may help you to avoid sounding vague when writing about the way words are 'composed'.

A short glossary of sound effects

Most of the sound-arrangements which have names are forms of repetition. They are forms of rhyme, which is the repetition of similar sounds. We discussed rhyme in Chapters 11 and 14, and some of what follows is recapitulation.

End-rhyme is what most people recognise as rhyme: the repetition of sounds at the ends of lines.

Internal rhyme is (equally obviously) rhyme that occurs within a line. Sometimes, though, the term is used more loosely, to mean rhymes occurring within different lines throughout a stanza.

A **rhyme-scheme** is the pattern of end-rhyme in a poem. The easiest (and traditional) way of indicating a rhyme-scheme is to give a letter of the alphabet to the lines that share a rhyme.

The following stanza from Edwin Muir's *The Child Dying* has a rhyme-scheme AABCCB (end-rhymes); there is an internal rhyme ('grace'/'face') in line 4:

1	It's said some memory will remain	A
2	In the other place, grass in the rain,	A
3	Light on the land, sun on the sea,	B
4	A flitting grace, a phantom face,	C
5	But the world is out. There is no place	C
6	Where it and its ghost can ever be.	B

These lines also demonstrate other kinds of sound-repetition:

Alliteration is the recurrence of the first sound in words that are adjacent or neighbouring, as in 'said some', 'flitting ... phantom'. Line 3 has alliterations where the beats fall – 'Light on the land, sun on the sea' – and thus resembles stress-verse. Alliteration is sometimes misunderstood as being the repetition of first letters, not sounds. But *hotel* and *heirlooms* and *knee* and *kick*, for example, are not alliterative.
Alliteration is one of the most foregrounding of sound-effects. It is both striking and memorable – which is why it is so loved by advertisers and by the sleazy tabloids: Mad Monster Minces Mum-in-law, etc.

Consonance is, strictly speaking, the recurrence of consonants but with a change in the vowels that separate them; as in *tighter* and *tauter*, *people* and *purple*, *drag* and *drug*. But consonance is frequently used in a more general way as a term for the repetition of consonant sounds throughout a line or passage, as in, from the Muir stanza, 'so<u>me</u> <u>me</u>mory will re<u>m</u>ain'.

Assonance is to vowels what consonance is to consonan<u>ts</u>: the recurrence of vowel sounds through a passage. Muir doesn't use this technique in the above stanza, so here's an example from a sonnet by Shakespeare:

'A liquid prisoner pent in walls of glass'

(which also employs consonance – on *l* – and alliteration.) You need a good ear for assonance, because vowels are rubbery creatures. They vary in pronunciation much more than consonants do. The five English vowels produce, in their different combinations and contexts, scores of different sounds. This makes assonance a very flexible and useful device for poets, who will happily use approximate assonances.

The rhymes in the Muir stanza are all true rhymes (otherwise known as full or perfect rhymes). But English happens to be rich in **near rhymes**. The poet best-known for his use of near rhyme is Wilfred Owen. In these few lines from his poem *Strange Meeting* he rhymes words like 'escaped' and 'scooped' and 'groaned' and 'groined':

> It seemed that out of battle I escaped
> Down some profound dull tunnel, long since scooped
> Through granites which titanic wars had groined.
> Yet also there encumbered sleepers groaned
> Too fast in thought or death to be bestirred.
> Then, as I probed them, one sprang up, and stared
> With piteous recognition in fixed eyes,
> Lifting distressful hands as if to bless.
>
> *Wilfred Owen*

In this next extract, near rhyme is even less tight, a fainter echo:

> A baron of the sea, the great tropic
> swordfish, spreadeagled on the thirsty deck
> where sailors killed him, in the bright Pacific
>
> Yielded to the sharp enquiring blade
> the eye which guided him and found his prey
> in the dim place where he was lord.
>
> *Keith Douglas: The Marvel*

The obvious advantage of near rhyme is that it gives the poet more choice. There may be only a handful of words that truly rhyme with 'brain', but perhaps ten dozen that nearly rhyme. The danger in near rhyme consists in the interesting paradox that while it is less 'obvious' than true rhyme, it is often more noticeable. Which is to say that when we find words at the ends of lines that sound almost (but not quite) alike, the difference is as noticeable as the similarity; and this can work against a writer if his or her intention is to subdue or understate the rhyme.

The last of our sound-effects is everybody's favourite: **onomatopoeia**. Unlike the terms we have defined so far, onomatopoeia is not a form of repetition. It is the technical word for 'sound echoing sense'. The danger of this word is that students are often so pleased that they've learned to spell it correctly that they slip it into essays at the slightest provocation. Onomatopoeia is also a very seductive idea if we try to imagine the origins of language. It seems reasonable, on the face of it, to imagine that in some distant innocent past, when our ancestors lived in caves, nipping out now and then to club a mammoth to death, they communicated with each other by making noises that imitated the sound of whatever it was they wished to indicate. One of our Neanderthal great-grandfathers comes in hissing away like mad to warn his colleagues of the presence of a snake; and, as the aeons pass, this hissing sound becomes the snake-shaped letter *s* which features in snake, serpent, asp ... Well, perhaps. And perhaps not. The problem with onomatopoeia is that it is very difficult to separate the actual sound of a word from the associations of that word's meaning. Is the word 'soft' soft? Is the word 'pillow' soft, or do we only hear it as soft because pillows are soft? The fact is that only a small fraction of English words are truly onomatopoeic. If a line of verse, or a phrase, seems onomatopoeic, it is likely to be because the poet made it seem so rather than because the words themselves are. There is a well-known demonstration of this, almost always quoted in books that deal with the subject. The last two lines of Tennyson's *Come Down, O Maid* have been cited time and time again to demonstrate the skilful use of onomatopoeia:

> The moan of doves in immemorial elms,
> And murmuring of innumerable bees.

The convential wisdom used to be that all these *m*s and *n*s and *l*s and long rounded vowels conjured up, onomatopoeically, the sound of a hot peaceful afternoon. But then an American critic called John Crowe Ransom naughtily pointed out that if you change only two consonants in the last line the peaceful afternoon disappears and we get what sounds like a rural slaughterhouse:

> The moan of doves in immemorial elms
> And the murdering of innumerable beeves.

Onomatopoeia is very subjective. The rhythm of a line of poetry might suggest to one reader a herd of wildebeest galloping across an African plain, while another reader might hear a heap of dishes falling off the draining board. There is a strong temptation to hear what we want or expect to hear. So how can you be reasonably confident that the comments you make about onomatopoeia are useful or relevant? Well, the first point to take on board is that for a word to be truly onomatopoeic it must signify something which is itself a sound or which makes a sound. The words 'crackle', 'buzz', 'cuckoo' are words of this sort. A word cannot be truly onomatopoeic if it signifies something which is abstract or normally silent. The second point is a little more shifty, but much more relevant to reading: words may have latent onomatopoeic qualities which will only emerge if the meaning of the words release them. It is part of the poet's craft to trick us into hearing the thing or things being described. In other words, there has to be something in the poem which tells us what to hear. This is easier to demonstrate than to explain. Let's take the sound *s* or *ss*. This is frequently used 'onomatopoeically' to suggest the sound of wind blowing over or through things – perhaps because we make the sound by expelling air through a narrow gap formed by teeth and tongue. In this sense, the first line of Wilfred Owen's *Exposure* is onomatopoeic: 'Our brains ache, in the merciless iced east winds that knive us', but these *s* sounds are 'windy' because we have the word 'winds' there to tell us so. Shakespeare's line 'When to the sessions of sweet silent thought' has the same *s* sounds, but they do not conjure up any idea of 'windiness' because wind is irrelevant to the line's meaning.

A word of caution, then: be sparing in your use of the word 'onomatopoeia', even if you can write it without moving your lips. Onomatopoeia is a fortunate by-product of meaning; few words, and relatively few arrangements of words, have sounds which are meaningful in themselves.

The Xanadu sound

In this chapter and the preceding one, we have heaped quite a lot of theoretical and technical stuff onto you, and maybe you have found the experience less than thrilling. If you have the stamina left, you should try out what you've learned on the following short piece of verse. It's a piece that is often quoted to demonstrate the 'musical' qualities of poetry: the first lines of Coleridge's *Kubla Khan*. But before you start, here's a summary of Coleridge's own account of how the poem came into being.

In the summer of 1797, Coleridge was living in a rather remote cottage in Somerset. One day, because (he says) he was feeling unwell – he had a spot of dysentery at the time – he took an 'anodyne'. This anodyne, or medicine, was most probably laudanum, a potent little brew of opium and alcohol. Then, and not altogether surprisingly, he fell into a deep trance. While in this condition, which lasted some three hours, the whole of *Kubla Khan* – some two or three hundred lines – came to him 'without any sensation or consciousness of effort'. When he came round, he seized his pen and set about getting this vision down on paper. There then occurred the most famous interruption in the history of literature (with the possible exception of Shakespeare's theatre burning to the ground halfway through *Henry the Eighth*): this was the arrival of 'the man from Porlock'. Whoever this visitor was, he kept Coleridge away from his desk for an hour or more; and when the poet returned to his work, he was dismayed to discover that the poem had evaporated from his mind 'with the exception of some eight or ten scattered lines and images'. And that is why we have only a 54-line 'fragment' of the original visionary poem. Here are the first five of those lines:

> In Xanadu did Kubla Khan
> A stately pleasure-dome decree:
> Where Alph, the sacred river, ran
> Through caverns measureless to man
> Down to a sunless sea.

For the time being, let's avoid the word 'musical' and simply say that it should be obvious that sound is important in this piece. (If this is not obvious to you, you could try reading it again and applying the reading techniques we suggested on page 139.)

You should write the lines out on a large sheet of paper so that you can make marks all over it.

First, work out the metre, marking where the feet divide. The first line is like this:

$$\breve{\text{In}} \; \acute{\text{Xan}} \;\Big|\; \breve{\text{a}}\acute{\text{du}} \;\Big|\; \breve{\text{did}} \; \text{Ku}\acute{} \;\Big|\; \text{bla}\breve{} \; \acute{\text{Khan}}$$

When you've done this 'scanning', you should realise that the verse has a very strong 'beat'. Perhaps you might imagine Coleridge sitting at the mixing desk in a recording studio. He's got the rhythm tracks and now he has to mix in other sounds to stop that rhythm being too heavy and monotonous. How does he do this?

Look for changes in the rhythm, those metrical substitutions (there are two of them).

Where do you need to make pauses in the reading? Are some pauses longer than others?

Write and read out the lines as if they were prose. Where are the 'natural' pauses and stresses? Do they coincide with the metre?

Write out the vowels in the first line. What do you notice about the pattern they make?

What sort of rhymes are there? Write out the rhyme-scheme.

Look for and mark (maybe you should use different coloured pens) all these features: consonance, assonance, alliteration, internal rhyme.

By the time you've marked all these things, your paper should look like it's been danced on by a crazed centipede dipped in ink. And you should now try to say something about how all these different sound-effects affect the underlying rhythm of the piece.

But the big question is: so what? What is all this sound-arranging *for*, and what does it have to do with the meaning? And what *does* it all mean? We're going to leave you to sort that out. But here are some leading questions which may help you:

1 Do you believe Coleridge when he says he 'composed' this amazingly complex little piece when he was completely stoned?

2 Who was Kubla Khan, and how might he have had an indirect effect on Coleridge's imagination (and his bowels)?

3 What is 'Inspiration', and why might poets be attracted to the idea?

4 What do you think 'Alph (as in *alph*abet) the sacred river' might be?

16
Form 4: Free Verse

This is the one we all have trouble with.

Let's begin with a cautious definition: free verse is non-metrical verse. Which means that it is not organised like the verse-forms we have discussed so far. It is not necessarily built with repeated rhythmic units; it does not necessarily rhyme in any schematic way. Free verse is often written in lines of varying length, and these lines sometimes do and sometimes don't begin with a capital letter. Free verse may be organised into regular stanzas; there again it may not. In fact, it is very difficult to say what free verse is – one has to sneak up on a definition by hiding behind negatives. What *is* known about free verse is that it can inspire a kind of panic in some readers, and for all we know you may be one of them. The feeling is: if this stuff doesn't conform to any rules, how are we supposed to deal with it? When we conducted our survey (see Chapter 1), several people said that they found it much more difficult to deal with 'wobbly' poems than with 'regular' poems.

Before we go any further, we should just make sure we know what kind of thing we are talking about. Some of the free verse poems that you have already encountered in this book are:

Billy Collins' *Books* (right at the beginning)
Craig Raine's *The New Hospital* (page 85)
U. A. Fanthorpe's *After Visiting Hours* (page 86) and *Rising Damp* (page 93)
all the poems (except the limerick) in Chapter 13

Have a look at them again. What might strike you about them is that they are all very unalike in form, whether or not they have anything otherwise in common. So the first point is this: that we cannot make easy generalisations about free verse forms. We have to take each poem as it comes.

'Free verse' is a literal translation of the French phrase *vers libre*. Free verse – as an idea or theory – is originally French. Nobody seems quite sure which French poet first produced *vers libre*, but in 1910 two French poets published a little book called *Notes sur la Technique Poétique*. It was the kind of book that shouts. The two poets announced a revolution, no less. The age of the Tyranny Of The Metre was over. They declared, among other things, that people who dogmatically defended 'regular versification' were 'either blind or stupid'. A new age of freedom had begun, in which 'we can dance without the big bass drum, and sing without the metronome'. This may well sound a bit over-excited, but it's necessary to realise that this was by way of being a political statement as well as a literary one: for the *vers libre* poets, metrical verse was conventional and bourgeois and therefore conservative and dishonest; whereas free verse was novel, individual, disrespectful and liberating.

Although French metrics differ considerably from English metrics (because, for one thing, the French language does not employ syllable-stress in the way that the English language does) the *vers libre* revolution was taken up enthusiastically by a number of English and American writers (many of whom were slumming it in Paris during the 1910s and 1920s). Free verse was seen as a way out of the 'decadent, stuffy, enfeebled' poetry of late Victorian and Edwardian England, the kind of thing being churned out by mild-mannered clergymen in rural rectories. While there had been innovators in the nineteenth century – Gerard Manley Hopkins, Edgar Allan Poe, Robert Browning, for examples – they had experimented with form but without stepping out of the mainstream of metrical verse. The idea of chucking out metre altogether was genuinely radical and exciting. Here, for instance is a convert to free verse called D. H. Lawrence, a man you can always rely on to get excited:

... in free verse we look for the insurgent naked throb of the instant moment ... free verse has its own nature ... it is neither star nor pearl, but instantaneous, like plasm. It has no goal in either eternity. It has no finish. It has no satisfying stability, satisfying those who like the immutable. None of this. It is the instant, the quick; the very jetting of all will-be and has-been. The utterance is like a spasm, naked contact with all influences at once. It does not want to get anywhere. It just takes place.

D. H. Lawrence: New Poems

Gosh. Or perhaps Gush. As usual whenever Lawrence gets excited, everything turns into some sort of exploding cosmic sexuality – but behind all this naked throbbing and jetting and so forth there are a couple of ideas about free verse that we should think about. First and foremost there is the half-baked but popular idea that a poet who writes in traditional, metrical verse-forms somehow restricts or cripples his or her imagination or 'vision'. Traditional verse-forms (so this argument goes) are public – that is, understood and accepted by the public. A poet who wants to say something personal or immediate or intense will be forced into dishonesty and compromise if he or she has to 'put on' a public voice, i.e. write in conventional metrical verse. What this argument implies (and it's clear enough from Lawrence's language, with all its cosmic terminology) is that free verse allows the poet to deal with the Big Subjects: the Soul, Man's relationship with Nature, the Spirit: the things that Lawrence likes to call 'the quick of the Universe'. And in turn this implies a new role for the poet. In turning away from traditional verse, the poet turns away from the general public; he refuses to adopt a 'public voice', and because he rejects familiar, comfortable verse-forms he will be understood by fewer (but more aware) people. The Lawrentian poet becomes something other than an entertainer; he becomes the poet as priest, the poet as mystic, crying out in the Philistine wilderness.

Fortunately, very few modern poets have taken so inflated and megalomaniac a view of themselves and their trade. Poetry would be a very dreary business if they did.

The second idea (more relevant to our present concern with form) which we can disentangle from Lawrence's rhetoric is this: the world is a constantly-changing place, a shifting thing, not only in its organisms but in its values, too; life is change, only dead things are constant; and somehow poetry should reflect this. Traditional verse-forms (says Lawrence) cannot depict an ever-changing organic world because they are static, fixed, 'immutable', finished. We cling to traditional kinds of poetry because we are afraid of change; we like them because they have a 'finality which we find so satisfying because we are so frightened'. Free verse, on the other hand, according to Lawrence, enables and encourages the poet to depict the great natural flux. Because the poet is freed from the tiresome business of conforming to metre and rhyme and stanza and whatever, his work can be 'natural', can be 'spontaneous and flexible as flame'. Free verse is the poetry of the 'immediate present' and in the immediate present 'there is no perfection, no consummation, nothing finished'. Free verse does not want to 'get anywhere'. It 'just happens'.

This is a very attractive (and dramatic) view of modern poetry. Unfortunately, there's not a grain of truth in it. Lawrence has provided us with the two great fallacies about free verse, and it will be useful to dispose of them before they interfere with any attempt we make to see what free verse does do. These two fallacies are that free verse is somehow 'spontaneous' (more spontaneous than traditional verse, anyway); and that it is somehow 'natural'. Let's look at these two ideas in turn.

Poetry does not 'just happen'. Poetry happens because people called poets sit down and write poems. The desire to do so, and the decision to do so, may be spontaneous; but the actual writing is deliberate and sometimes painstaking and lengthy. And – to state the blindingly obvious – when poets write, they are thinking about how to do it, which means looking not only for the right words, but also for the form in which those words will work best. They have no choice but to do so, because formless writing – the kind of thing that you might get if you sat a drunken orang-utan at a typewriter – is meaningless writing. And since it doesn't say anywhere that modern poets *have* to write in a particular form, it follows that modern poets who choose to write metrical verse do so because it suits them; metrical verse allows them to find a way of saying what they have to say. For such poets, writing free verse would not be in the least spontaneous.

Poetry, free verse or not, can never be natural. Lawrence said that he wanted his poems to be 'like flowers'. W. H. Auden (who had a good deal of respect for Lawrence) said that:

> Lawrence draws a false analogy between the process of artistic creation and the organic growth of living creatures ... An artist who ignores the difference between natural growth and human construction will produce the exact opposite of what he intends. He hopes to produce something which will seem as natural as a flower, but the qualities of the natural are exactly what his product will lack. A natural object never appears unfinished; if it is an inorganic object like a stone it is what it has to be; if an organic object like a flower, what it has to be at this moment. But a similar effect – of being what it has to be – can only be achieved in a work of art by much thought, labour and care. The gesture of a ballet dancer, for example, only looks natural when, through long practice, its execution has become 'second nature' to him.

> *W. H. Auden: The Dyer's Hand*

The key phrase in there is 'being what it has to be'. Auden is suggesting that a free verse poem should somehow persuade us that it comes in the form it does because no other form would be right. This points us towards an essential difference in the ways we approach traditional forms on the one hand, and free verse on the other.

Imagine you have in front of you a traditional, metrical poem: a sonnet by someone called Stalin, let's say. There are some fairly standard questions you could ask yourself about its form:

How successful is it as a sonnet?
Or (to put the same question another way): How does Stalin use the conventions of the sonnet form to get his meaning across?
How much flexibility does Stalin find within the sonnet form? Does he bend the 'rules' in any way, and why?

If you happen to know a bit about sonnets, you could ask:
What kind of sonnet is it?

And you could make comparisons:
How does it resemble or differ from Wordsworth's sonnet on a similar theme?
How does this differ from other sonnets by Stalin?

Now imagine you are looking at a free verse poem by someone we'll call Trotsky. It has no prevailing metre, it doesn't rhyme, the lines are all sorts of different lengths, it is divided into unequal stanzas, and it has a really unhelpful title – something like *Poem 27*. What do you do? Well, you'd be entitled to panic for a minute or three; but eventually, we hope, you'd realise that the questions you find yourself asking tend to begin with *why* rather than *how*. Something like this perhaps:

Why, after three long opening lines, does the fourth line consist of a single three-syllable word?
Why does the poem divide where it does?
Why is the second short section in almost regular metres?
Why are there so many hard consonants in the last stanza?

And so on. All these whys add up to a single question: why has Trotsky written the poem in this form and not in some other form?

In the case of the traditionalist Stalin, asking why he chose the sonnet form is more or less irrelevant. Perhaps he just likes sonnets. Perhaps he doesn't know how to write anything else. The important question is: what does he do with the sonnet form? How does he use it? But the free versifier Trotsky has not selected a form – he has built one of his own devising. So in this case, as in the case of any free verse poem, the question is: why is this form better suited to the poet's intentions than any other form he could have devised? This is by far the harder of the two questions, we admit. In a moment we'll apply it to two real poems and see where we get. But before that we should say something about language, because we wouldn't want you to think that free verse is only a matter of form. It is not simply metrical verse without the metrics.

We said earlier that free verse was originally a reaction, a revolution, against conventional, 'safe' Victorian and Edwardian poetry. (At least, that was how the free verse pioneers saw it.) It wasn't just metrical form that had to go; lots of other lumber had to be cleared out of the attic as well: stuff like sentimentality and 'sweetness', clichés, merely pleasant 'musical' sound effects, elaborate decoration, convoluted sentences. Literary upheavals like this do not take place in a vacuum. There were political, social and cultural dimensions to the free verse 'revolution' which it would be dishonest to ignore even in a short chapter like this one.

It is easy to oversimplify the relationship between literary movements and social movements. Actually, the question of how writers respond to their times is a complicated one. Yet it is no coincidence that a period of tremendous innovation in literature (involving, most famously, Ezra Pound, T. S. Eliot and James Joyce) was also a period of other kinds of upheaval. Between 1900 and 1920 the world – as Europeans saw it – changed. No one thing changed it, of course; but what we generally call The Establishment (those in political power, the Church, the 'Ruling Class') found itself having to look the twentieth century squarely in the eye, and there's no doubt that it disliked what it saw. It saw itself under attack from all sides.

In Britain, there was the 'Class Struggle'. The broad mass of working people saw themselves – quite correctly – as excluded from and exploited by the political Powers That Be. One response was the formation and very swift development of the Labour Party. In 1906 socialism changed the course of mainstream politics when thirty Labour candidates won Parliamentary seats.

Women were left with their own fight to win. The Suffragette movement continued to make a most unseemly fuss; its members had to be kept in order by a combination of jeers, imprisonment and physical humiliation. Eventually, in 1928, Britain did become technically democratic when (almost) everyone over the age of twenty-one was given the right to vote.

If in Britain the natives were restless, they were decidedly on the rampage elsewhere. The long-simmering revolution in Russia finally boiled over in 1917, presenting western Europe with the nightmare vision of Bolshevik Red Hordes poised to engulf the world (an hallucination still popular, especially in America). At the same time Britain was losing its grip on what was – and still is – its greatest-ever fantasy: the Empire. Ireland, the colony closest to home, was in an almost permanent state of armed revolt. And in the midst of all this, of course, there was the World War of 1914 to 1918 in which hundreds of thousands of people, commanded by criminally incompetent generals, died defending political institutions in which they had no say and values they did not share.

Even at a safe distance from the smell of blood, the Establishment found itself menaced by Dark Forces. The authority and the values of the established church (the Church of England) were being undermined by grass-roots, lower-class, 'low church' movements such as Methodism at a time when the church was still struggling to come to terms with (or, if possible, resist) the teachings of the great heretic Charles Darwin – according to whom we were not created in God's image in Chapter 1 of Genesis after all, but are instead a species of sophisticated ape. (In 1925 American schoolteachers were still being prosecuted for teaching Evolution theory.) The First World War had taught a great many people that God was not on Our Side (nor Theirs, either). And of course there was the horrible spectre of millions of armed Red atheists on the horizon.

As if Darwinism, Marxism and universal carnage were not enough to bring traditional beliefs into question, over in Vienna Sigmund Freud was coming to the conclusion that even the normal human mind is a dark and mysterious beast over which decency and 'civilised values' have only intermittent control.

To this rich stew of political and philosophical issues we should add one relevant item of demographical data. By 1910, eighty per cent of the population of England and Wales lived in towns or cities or suburbs. During the previous forty or so years, agriculture (in terms of the numbers actively involved in it) had declined rapidly. In short, by the beginning of this century, most people led urban, not rural, lives.

Any generalisation drawn from such an historical complex must inevitably be more or less trite; but it seems reasonable to say that what all these things added up to was a sense of disintegration, of things falling apart – either because they had been smashed or because they had decayed. The old values and institutions of Imperial Victorian England began to look tired and irrelevant. They certainly didn't seem worth dying for, and the patriotic slogan *Dulce et decorum est pro patria mori* ('It is lovely and honourable to die for your country') left a bitter taste in the mouth after 1918. Here's Ezra Pound:

> Died some, pro patria,
> non 'dulce' non 'et decor' ....
> walked eye-deep in hell
> believing in old men's lies, then unbelieving
> came home, home to a lie,
> home to many deceits,
> home to old lies and new infamy;
> usury age-old and age-thick
> and liars in public places.
>
> Daring as never before, wastage as never before.

Young blood and high blood,
fair cheeks, and fine bodies;

fortitude as never before

frankness as never before,
disillusions as never told in the old days,
hysterias, trench confessions,
laughter out of dead bellies.

There died a myriad,
And of the best, among them,
For an old bitch gone in the teeth,
For a botched civilisation,

Charm, smiling at the good mouth,
Quick eyes gone under earth's lid,

For two gross of broken statues,
For a few thousand battered books.

Ezra Pound: E.P. Ode pour l'élection de Son Sépulchre

If civilisation is 'an old bitch gone in the teeth' or just a heap of 'broken statues' and 'battered books', and if both political and spiritual values are in decay, it is absurd (said Pound and his fellow writers) to go on writing and reading traditional and 'comfortable' verse as if nothing were happening. Why, if they were living in an unstable, urban world, should writers feel obliged to carry on wittering nostalgically about pastoral England? Why feel constrained to write about what poets were 'supposed' to write about – summer twilight on the green hills, moonlight on the sea, nightingales and suchlike? And why, if the world was difficult to understand, should poetry be easy? If the world was rather nasty, why should poetry be nice?

T. S. Eliot's first collection of poems, *Prufrock and Other Observations*. appeared in 1917. The first poem in the book, *The Love Song of J. Alfred Prufrock*, begins

Let us go then, you and I,
When the evening is spread out against the sky
Like a patient etherised upon a table;
Let us go, through certain half-deserted streets,
The muttering retreats
Of restless nights in one-night cheap hotels
And saw-dust restaurants with oyster-shells:
Streets that follow like a tedious argument
Of insidious intent
To lead you to an overwhelming question ....
Oh, do not ask, 'What is it?' Let us go and make our visit.

T. S. Eliot: The Love Song of J. Alfred Prufrock

Prufrock is a long poem, and should be read in its entirety to be appreciated fully, but this short extract gives a taste of what is to come. The reader is accosted by a strange, twitchy, evasive sort of chap and dragged off through the sordid backstreets of a nameless city towards an unspecified destination. Overhead, the evening sky is 'Like a patient etherised upon a table' – a weird, surrealistic image. And what is this 'overwhelming question' that Prufrock wishes to avoid?

Living at the end of the twentieth century, you are probably used to poems which contain 'sordid' or surrealistic images, and which do not offer you any reassurance or certainty. To appreciate how peculiar – and shocking – Eliot's early work was, you have to make an imaginary leap back in time and be someone whose idea of what poetry is comes from reading late Victorian verse like this:

> In summertime on Bredon
> The bells they sound so clear;
> Round both the shires they ring them
> In steeples far and near,
> A happy noise to hear
>
> *A. E. Housman*

or perhaps this:

> The sleep-flower sways in the wheat its head,
> Heavy with dreams, as that with bread:
> The goodly grain and the sun-flush'd sleeper
> The reaper reaps, and Time the reaper.
>
> *Francis Thompson*

This is the kind of thing that Pound dismissed as 'blurry, messy, sentimentalistic, mannerish.' And which, by contrast, made Eliot's work so disturbing a challenge to accepted notions of poetry.

So the early free verse poets were not in favour of cosy pastoral, or of easy 'melodic' verse, or of traditional metrical verse-forms, or of 'acceptability'. What were they in favour of?

Some sort of answer is provided by a group of American and English poets who called themselves Imagists. Early in his chequered career, Pound was a leading light in this group. Other members were (for a while) Amy Lowell, William Carlos Williams and D. H. Lawrence. T. E. Hulme (whose poem *Autumn* appears in disguise in Chapter 13, passage D) was a founder member; he was killed in the First World War. We ought to say a word or three about the Imagists because although they were a loose-knit, quarrelsome and short-lived group they have had a considerable influence on modern English and American poetry. In his *Glossary of Literary Terms*, Professor Abrams says quite simply that Imagism 'proved to be the beginning of modern poetry'. In 1913 Pound published a 'manifesto' for Imagism called *A Few Don'ts by an Imagiste*. It insisted that writers should strive for clarity, for freshness, for excellence, for skill. It condemned sloppiness and 'vague abstractions'. Here are a few extracts from it:

> It is better to produce one image in a lifetime than to produce voluminous works.

Use no superfluous word, no adjective, which does not reveal something.

Go in fear of abstractions. Don't retell in mediocre verse what has already been done in good prose. Don't think any intelligent person is going to be deceived when you try to shirk all the difficulties of the unspeakably difficult art of good prose by chopping your composition into line lengths.

Don't suppose the art of poetry is any simpler than the art of music, or that you can please the expert before you have spent at least as much effort on the art of verse as the average piano teacher spends on the art of music.

Use either no ornament or good ornament.

Ezra Pound: A Few Don'ts by an Imagiste

It is not easy to base a theory or 'school' of poetry on a list of don'ts: 'Fine, Ezra, but what *are* we supposed to do?' Perhaps for this reason the Imagist poets soon went off on their different – if perhaps parallel – paths. But the basic principle of Imagism, implied in the 'manifesto', survives as a criterion in both writing and reading modern poetry. That principle is **concentration**. One of the things that we still tend to respect – or even expect – in poetry is the ability to convey meaningful, complex images in language that is concentrated, fresh, vivid and controlled. We tend to disrespect poetry that is woozy, padded-out, half in love with its own voice and half-drunk on its own music.

This Imagist desire to get across what Amy Lowell called 'hard, clear and concentrated images' has obvious implications for poetic form. Concentration implies reduction, a process of stripping-down, of cutting. Imagist verse is usually short, terse stuff; words that are not doing something are pruned out. There is no room for syllables that are there just to carry a metre, nor for words or phrases that elaborate or decorate an idea; metaphor should work instantly, not accumulatively.

(Robert Frost, the American poet, was in England from 1912 to 1915. Although he was not an Imagist himself – nor a free-verse man, for that matter – he knew Ezra Pound and a number of Imagists. One day Pound invited Frost to a meeting of the Imagist poets. 'What do you do at these meetings?' asked Frost. Pound said 'We rewrite each others poems.' 'Why?' asked Frost. 'To squeeze the water out of them,' said Pound.)

When the Imagists turned their backs on nineteenth century English verse they found themselves, naturally, looking in new directions for stimulation. As far as form is concerned, the most interesting Imagist 'discovery' was Japanese poetry. Classical Japanese verse-forms are extremely disciplined, and based on syllable count. The *tanka*, for example, has thirty-one syllables (and no more and no less) arranged in five lines: five, then seven, then five, then seven, then another seven syllables. The *haiku* has exactly seventeen syllables arranged in three lines. The haiku in particular, within this very tight form, seeks to present a small, clear fragment of the poet's experience in the form of a single image. Here are translations of two haiku by Matsuo Basho (1644-1694):

> Clouds now and then
> Giving men relief
> From moon-viewing

You say one word
And lips are chilled
By autumn's wind.

Matsuo Basho

Formal discipline was not the only characteristic of Japanese verse which appealed to the Imagists. Its wonderful oddness, its 'otherness' also made it attractive. It was something that ordinary people would not understand, something they would find alien. (It has now become quite commonplace for those who reject decadent Western values to turn their faces to the East in search of profundity. The floral rebels of the 1960s, for example, enthusiastically took up Zen Buddhism and suchlike, and backpacked off to India to sit at the feet of gurus, where they contracted hepatitis.)

It's time we applied some of these ideas about form, language and image to actual verse. What follows is a comparison of two poems written quite close together in time, but worlds apart in form. The first is a traditional, metrical piece by George William Russell, who wrote under the pseudonym 'A. E.' It was written in about 1904.

When the breath of twilight blows to flame the misty skies,
All its vapourous sapphire, violet glow and silver gleam,
With their magic flood me through the gateway of the eyes;
I am one with the twilight's dream.

When the trees and skies and fields are one in dusky mood,
Every heart of man is rapt within the mother's breast:
Full of peace and sleep and dreams in the vast quietude,
I am one with their hearts at rest.

From our immemorial joys of hearth and home and love
Stray'd away along the margin of the unknown tide,
All its reach of soundless calm can thrill me far above
Word or touch from lips beside.

Aye, and deep and deep and deeper let me drink and draw
From the olden fountain more than light or peace or dream,
Such primeval being as o'erfills the heart with awe,
Growing one with its silent stream.

George William Russell ('A.E.')

The odd thing about this poem is that is doesn't actually mean anything at all. It's full of lovely relaxing wallowy sound, but it dosn't seem to add up to anything. One can hardly fail to notice the insistent rhythm (predominantly trochaic heptameter – seven feet – to be technical); and there is a great deal of use of 'musical' sound-effects. The line 'Aye, and deep and deep and deeper let me drink and draw' is so heavy with alliteration and assonance and undulating rhythm that it is hard to get to the end of it without falling asleep. This poem is a kind of verbal muzak; reading it is like lapsing into a drunken stupor while having a warm bath (which may have been the effect Russell intended). Despite its conventional form, this poem strikes us as being remarkably obscure. The shorter closing lines of each stanza suggest that it is about some kind of merging, or being 'one with' various things; perhaps the prevailing vagueness and softness of the poem is meant to suggest a merging or melting of some sort. What the poet finally dissolves into is a 'silent stream', but what this silent stream is depends upon what that 'olden fountain' is two lines previously. The poem is called *By the Margin of the Great Deep*. Roughly translated, this means 'On the Beach'. Possibly this may help you make sense of it.

The next piece is free verse; it's from *An Aquarium* by Amy Lowell.

> Streaks of green and yellow iridescence,
> Silver shiftings,
> Rings veering out of rings,
> Silver – gold –
> Grey-green opaqueness sliding down,
> With sharp white bubbles
> Shooting and dancing,
> Flinging quickly outward.
> Nosing the bubbles,
> Swallowing them,
> Fish.

Amy Lowell

What is noticeable about this is that despite having been written only a dozen or so years later than the Russell poem it seems so strikingly modern by comparison. This is as much a result of what Lowell leaves out as it is of what she puts in. She uses some of the same poetic devices as Russell – alliteration (especially of *s* and *sh* sounds), repetition within lines ('rings veering out of rings') and across lines ('silver and green'), and assonance ('streaks of green'). But whereas Russell lays them on with a trowel Lowell uses them very precisely and systematically. This is because in her poem these sounds do a lot of work. Simultaneously

• they give the poem its form. Because Lowell doesn't build her lines from repeated rhythmic units (metre), the poem has to get its shape from patterns of sound. In particular, the suffix *ing* (which appears in seven of the eleven lines) is one of the 'stitches' that give the piece its continuity. The echoing of *s* and *sh* is another.

• they provide contrast as well as continuity; for instance where the smooth, rounded sound of 'Grey-green opaqueness sliding down' takes us into the much sharper and busier sound of 'With sharp white bubbles'.

• they are mimetic – that is, the sounds of words imitate the things and movements those words signify. The two lines (5 and 6) just quoted are the clearest example. The repetition in 'Rings veering out of rings' imitates the repetitive movement of ripples moving outward on a water surface. And throughout the poem there is that 'watery' sound of *s* and *sh*.

Amy Lowell's poem is turning out to be a little more complex than it seems at first glance, because as well as these formal arrangements of sound there is a kind of visual correspondence between the form of the poem and what the poem is about. We do not mean that the poem looks like a fish tank. It's a shade more subtle than that. What happens is that as our eyes move down the lines of the verse, they also move down the aquarium. We start at the top with the effects of the light on the surface of the water ('iridescence/Silver-shiftings'), go through the ripples ('rings'), down through the 'Grey-green opaqueness' of the water, past the aerator pumping out 'sharp white bubbles' and, eventually, at the bottom of the tank, come to the fish. And at the same time as our eyes track down through the poem and the tank, our hearing makes the same movement, because all those wet *s* and *sh* sounds finally condense down into the ultimate syllable: 'Fish'.

All these synchronised formal schemes make *An Aquarium* an excellent example of a poem 'being what it has to be', in Auden's phrase. It has the form it has because no other form would do. To put the point very crudely, the poem couldn't work the way it does if the fish were at the top. Compared with Lowell's very deliberate, purposeful use of sound patterns, Russell's use of similar effects is both extravagant and merely decorative. It is (in a phrase of Shakespeare's) 'full of sound and fury, signifying nothing', or (in a phrase of my Granny's) 'all mouth and no trousers'.

Despite its ingenuity, Lowell's poem is not pretentious. Russell slips in certain 'trigger' words – 'magic', 'heart', 'deep', 'awe' – as a cheap device to persuade us that he is writing about something profound. Lowell's poem has none of these 'philosophical' trappings. Her intention is to present a single (but not necessarily simple) image with as much coherence and clarity as possible. This image may have some deeper meaning; it may have a different meaning for each different reader; but it doesn't have a big sign saying 'This Is Meaningful' attached to it. The poem is concerned with seeing things in a certain way, not in drawing conclusions or inviting interpretations.

Now let us turn to another free verse poem which appears to have a 'difficult' form. It's by e. e. cummings, and was published in 1950.

> i'm
> asking
> you dear to
> what else could a
> no but it doesn't
> of course but you don't seem
> to realise i can't make
> it clearer war just isn't what
> we imagine but please for god's O
> what the hell yes it's true that was
> me but that me isn't me
> can't you see now no not
> any christ but you
> must understand
> why because
> i am
> dead

e. e. cummings

At a first reading, two things are fairly obvious: first, the poem doesn't 'make sense' in a conventional way, and second, it has a distinctive triangular shape. What is the connection between these two things?

The poem doesn't make sense (apparently) because half of it is missing. The speaker's words are fragments of sentences because he is continually interrupted by someone we can't 'hear' – a woman, presumably. Her half of the dialogue is missing. Reading the poem is like being in a room with someone who is talking on the telephone. Written out in a more conventional way, his half of the dialogue might be scripted like this:

> I'm asking you, dear, to ...
> What else could a ...
> No, but it doesn't ...
> Of course! But you don't seem to realise ...
> I can't make it clearer. War just isn't what we imagine ...
> But ...
> Please! For God's ...
> O, what the hell ...
> Yes, it's true, that was me, but that me isn't me ...
> Can't you see now?
> No not any ...
> Christ!
> But you must understand ...
> Why?
> Because I am dead.

Writing it out like this destroys much of the poem's meaning (as we shall try to demonstrate in a moment) but it does at least show that, for all its weird appearance, the poem is actually written in ordinary conversational English.

We have here a man who is struggling to explain himself to someone who is giving him a hard time. The situation, at first, could be one of many: the husband who is not going to be home in time for dinner, the boyfriend who has broken a date. Until, that is, we get to 'war' in line 8. Even then, the conversation could have a mundane explanation: a soldier trying to explain to his wife or lover that he can't get home on leave, perhaps. Then we come to 'that was/me but that me isn't me', at which point we should suspect that he is attempting to explain the effect that war has had on him. At the last line we realise that this effect has been extreme. The poem is therefore ironic – this man trying to make his excuses is in fact trying to explain how he could have been so inconsiderate as to go off and get himself killed.

When we overhear one side of a telephone conversation, we can't help trying to supply the other; we try to imagine what's being said at the other end of the line. Likewise with the cummings poem: consciously or not, we try to provide the other half of the dialogue, try to imagine the woman's voice. This voice also changes as the poem progresses. At the beginning, we can hardly help hearing a complaining, nagging voice: 'Why can't you get home on time? Why can't someone else do it?' But it turns out that the man on the other end of the line is 'late' in a sense quite different to 'unpunctual', and by the time we get to the end of the poem we have to revise our first impressions of the woman's voice. It's not irritation that she's feeling, it's pain; she isn't nagging, she's grieving.

What is there about the form of the poem that fits this interpretation? You may have noticed that each line down to line 9 ('we imagine but please for god's O') is one syllable longer than the line before. Line 1 has one syllable, line 2 has two syllables, and so on. After line 9 the lines shrink back one syllable at a time. We can see the resulting shape as an arrow, pointing to something. We can also see it as the visible half (also the audible half) of a rectangle. This half is what 'he' says. The invisible and inaudible half is what 'she' says. Like this:

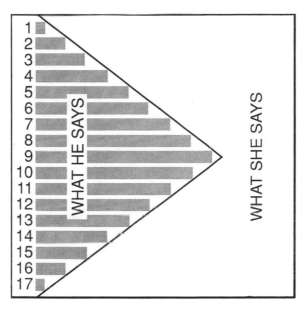

Looked at in this way, each line can be seen as advancing inch by inch, or syllable by syllable, into her space, as he 'pushes back' her interruptions, as he gets nearer to finishing a sentence, nearer to 'getting across'. It is a kind of visual pun: he is trying to get a word in edgeways, or maybe 'get through' like the voices from 'the other side' at a seance. But by the end of line 9 the voice has run out of energy or willpower, and in subsequent lines subsides syllable by syllable into the final silence of 'dead'.

There is a visual, typographical joke (if joke is the right word) in the poem if we see its shape as an arrow. Then, the tip, or point, of the arrow is the end of line 9. 'O what the hell' is an exasperated cry; but the enjambment of the phrase – the way it is cut off by the line-ending – leaves the 'O' isolated; and it becomes a nought, a zero. The form of the poem says: when it comes to the point, there is nothing; nothing I can say to you, nothing the dead can explain to the living.

Now let's look at the poem from one more angle. Turn the page around so that the poem is lying on its side, with the O at the highest point. Now the line-endings form a 'graph' of the 'sound-level' of the poem. The voice rises in intensity, and maybe in pitch, from the quiet, apologetic 'i'm/asking/you dear to' towards a peak at 'please for god's O' and then falls back and down to the resigned, almost inaudible 'i am/dead'.

This poem by cummings is an instance of form carrying a large proportion of the overall meaning. The systematic lengthening and shortening of lines interrupts the proper syntax of phrases that are already fragmentary, and gives the voice its jerky, frustrated character. The form is also an enactment of what is happening in the poem. The appearance of the lines on the page enacts the idea of trying to get across the barrier that separates the dead from the living. The futility of the effort is also enacted, when, at the furthest point of the words' advance, they come to nothing – that 'O' at the end of line 9. Again, a poem 'being what it has to be'; these effects are lost if the form is altered. In the form of 'naturalistic' dialogue (as on page 172) these words do not mean the same things at all. We tried to show a similar enactment in the lines by Amy Lowell a page or two back. In that poem the downward movement of the viewer's gaze is imitated by sound and lineation. In the cummings piece, the function of form is far more conspicuous – because, obviously, the appearance of the poem smacks you in the eye. We ought to say here that cummings is something of a special case. Relatively few poets have found it worthwhile trying to achieve this degree of correspondence between the visible form of a poem and the language of the poem. In many of his poems, cummings dismantles and rearranges words into strange new formations which move around and down the page, almost as if he were using paint, rather than language, as a medium. As a result, his poems can often appear to be audio-visual puzzles, or cryptograms; they have effects on the page which are almost impossible to reproduce by speaking them. We used the cummings poem to demonstrate as straightforwardly as possible the way that form can operate as meaning, and perhaps we were cheating a little bit to use a piece in which form is a visual metaphor for the events in the poem. (Incidentally, you may have noticed that there are no metaphors at all in the language.) But if cummings is unusual, it is in the degree to which he uses typographical effects and peculiar layout to enact the substance of his works. Even with more conventional poetry, it is worth thinking about its appearance, the way it occupies its space on a page. After all, there are no laws which dictate how short or long a poet should make his lines, or which dictate how many lines should be grouped together into stanzas. These are matters over which the poet has freedom of choice, and it seems reasonable to assume that a poem's lines vary in length and grouping according to what the poet wants those lines to do. Therefore it is always worth looking at the right-hand edge of a poem, and at the spaces between the lines; these may be signals as to what is going on within the lines themselves.

Now we'll try to summarise very briefly what we've said about free verse in this chapter.

Free verse was originally a reaction against traditional metrical verse and a reaction to a complex of political and cultural circumstances. 'Public' or popular Victorian and Edwardian poetry, in terms of both form and content, seemed to the early free-versifiers to uphold ideas and values (like naïve patriotism and nostalgia) which were obsolete and dishonest. The early free verse poets set out deliberately to alienate, or at least upset, readers with orthodox habits and expectations. Poets have seen this as part of their job ever since.

Free verse asserts the right of the poet to freedom of choice in subject matter, language and form. Now we take this for granted. (Well, almost, and until recently; you couldn't expect to find this book in the school library if we included poems or prose which 'promoted' homosexuality, for example. Perish the thought, of course.)

Free verse is free *in* form, not free of form. Formless poetry is a contradiction in terms.

A poet writing in free verse has to be at least as attentive to form as a poet writing in a traditional form. There are more choices to make.

A poem in free verse should leave us with the feeling that it is 'what it has to be', that it is in the form it comes in because that is the form it *should* come in.

Words need forms to create their meaning. Sometimes forms can convey their own meanings in addition to the literal meanings of the words.

Robert Frost, a very good poet who preferred to work in traditional verse-forms, once said that writing free verse was like playing tennis without the net. In our humble opinion, he was wrong – it is more like performing on the trapeze without the net.

Finally, one small observation that may be quite meaningless: while we were gathering material for this book, we found a surprising number of contemporary poets – contemporary women poets in particular – working with traditional, highly disciplined verse-forms such as the villanelle and the sonnet. Why might this be, do you suppose?

THE PYTHON DIDN'T LIKE FREE VERSE

17
Fish, Wolves and Cats: Exercises

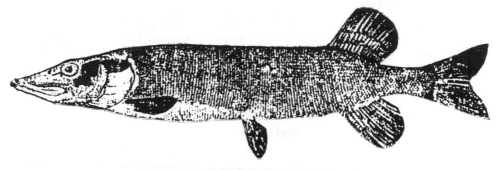

Fig. 27. *Esox lucius*, Pike.

Fig. Pike.

1 This is an exercise in concentration and condensation – characteristics of some of the poetry we discussed in the previous chapter.

Passage A is a naturalist's observation:

> What is extraordinary about pike when they are young is that they are perfect reproductions of what they are like when they are adults: they don't go through any intermediate stages at all. They are green and gold in colour, these colours alternating in a series of irregular stripes. Even more extraordinary, they are programmed to hunt and kill as soon as they emerge from the egg form. Disturbingly, they also seem to grin malevolently, as if they were sadistic in some way. They've been like this for a long time, of course. On summer days they look as if they are dancing on the surface of the water: just as the flies are.

Passage B is the first four lines of Ted Hughes' poem, *Pike*:

> Pike, three inches long, perfect
> Pike in all parts, green tigering the gold.
> Killers from the egg: the malevolent aged grin.
> They dance on the surface among the flies.

Ted Hughes

Passage C is a familiar story:

In the wood, the trees are covered in a white frost which makes them look crystalline and strangely still. The grass crunches beneath your feet. You can see your breath. The very old sound of wolves howling to each other scares you; you are eager to get to the cottage where you know there is a big log fire waiting. And a strong wooden door.

Suddenly, in a clearing ahead of you, you see a strange young man. He is dressed like a courtier – scarlet, gold embroidery, lace – beneath a wonderful fur coat and hat. There is something slightly odd about the cut of the coat – almost as if it had a tail growing out of the back. The young man is very handsome, and although you are fascinated by his appearance you are slightly disturbed by his eyebrows, which are bushy and which meet in the middle.

Passage D is for you to provide. Write a response to Passage C in verse. The only limitations are these: two stanzas only, each of only four lines.

2 This too is a comparison exercise, but of a rather different sort. These two short poems are by American poets who use form in unusual ways. The second is by e. e. cummings, one of whose poems we discussed in the last chapter. The first is by William Carlos Williams:

> As the cat
> climbed over
> the top of
>
> the jamcloset
> first the right
> forefoot
>
> carefully
> then the hind
> stepped down
>
> into the pit of
> the empty
> flowerpot

William Carlos Williams

(im)c-a-t(mo)
b,i;l:e

FallleA
ps!fl
OattumblI

sh?dr
IftwhirlF
(Ul) (lY)
& & &

away wanders: exact
ly;as if
not
hing had, ever happ
ene
D

e. e. cummings

Write a short piece discussing the way these two poets use form to 'capture' a cat. Do you think that one poem is more successful than the other? If so, which, and why?

The clue word for this exercise is *enactment*.

18

How Claire Does It: The Drafting Process

LITERATURE BEING REELED OFF AND SLICED INTO EXAMINATION PAPERS

This is a nuts-and-bolts chapter about putting an essay, or 'critical appreciation', together.

The complicated act of writing about a poem is a process consisting of different stages of reading, thinking and writing, all of which culminate in the 'product' known as 'the critical essay'. There is no one universal and ideal way of performing this task – which is fortunate, because if there were there would be less room for individualism and eccentricity. Many of the mental activities involved in writing about literature are private and instinctive and therefore mysterious. Others, however, are more obvious, practical and describable, and it is these that we are dealing with here.

Working on the principle that it is usually more helpful to listen to those who do a job, rather than to those who merely write textbooks about it, we asked a sixth-form student – one whose essays consistently obtained fairly high marks – to describe how she set about writing a critical essay. We asked Claire to write on two poems and compare them; what follows is the transcript of an interview with her, in which she describes her responses and her planning techniques.

Here are the two poems. To get the most out of this chapter, you should read them carefully and then write down your own brief notes describing your first impressions of them before you read on to what Claire has to say.

The Cool Web

Children are dumb to say how hot the day is,
How hot the scent is of the summer rose,
How dreadful the black wastes of the evening sky,
How dreadful the tall soldiers drumming by.

5   But we have speech, to chill the angry day,
And speech, to dull the rose's cruel scent.
We spell away the overhanging night,
We spell away the soldiers and the fright.

There's a cool web of language winds us in,
10   Retreat from too much joy or too much fear:
We grow sea-green at last and coldly die
In brininess and volubility.

But if we let our tongues lose self-possession,
Throwing off language and its watery clasp
15   Before our death, instead of when death comes,
Facing the wide glare of the children's day,
Facing the rose, the dark sky and the drums,
We shall go mad no doubt and die that way.

Robert Graves

Words

Out of us all
That make rhymes,
Will you choose
Sometimes –
5   As the winds use
A crack in a wall
Or a drain,
Their joy or their pain
To whistle through –
10   Choose me,
You English words?

I know you:
You are light as dreams,

Tough as oak,
15 Precious as gold,
As poppies and corn,
Or an old cloak:
Sweet as our birds
To the ear,
20 As the burnet rose
In the heat
Of Midsummer:
Strange as the races
Of dead and unborn:
25 Strange and sweet
Equally,
And familiar,
To the eye,
As the dearest faces
30 That a man knows,
And as lost homes are:
But though older far
Than oldest yew, –
As our hills are, old, –
35 Worn new
Again and again;
Young as our streams
After rain:
And as dear
40 As the earth which you prove
That we love.

Make me content
With some sweetness
From Wales
45 Whose nightingales
Have no wings, –
From Wiltshire and Kent
And Herefordshire,
And the villages there, –
50 From the names, and the things
No less.

Let me sometimes dance
With you,
Or climb
55 Or stand perchance
In ecstasy,
Fixed and free
In a rhyme,
As poets do.

Edward Thomas

Claire's method

CLAIRE: What I do first (obviously) is read both poems through fairly quickly so that I've got some idea of what they are about, you know, the content. Reading these two poems, I can see straightaway that both of them are about words and language – although there are a lot of things I'll have to puzzle out and ask questions about. We've always been told that there isn't a 'right' answer to questions like this, and that you get marks for asking intelligent questions, as well as for coming up with stunning insights. I seem to get quite a lot of marks for asking questions and expressing doubts, if you see what I mean. I wouldn't overdo it, though.

Anyway, I didn't like the look of that Thomas poem – it seemed anarchic and weird – all those short lines – although the meaning of the poem seems simple enough: 'I love the English language!' The Graves poem seems harder, the language more opaque, maybe even symbolic – those soldiers symbolise war, I should think. I'm also not sure whether Graves is for language or against it, which is a bit odd, really: I mean it's language that makes us human, after all. No language, no society. Funny sort of thing for a poet to say ... bit like a butcher saying meat is murder. Ironic, maybe.

Anyway, once I've done that 'first impression' reading, and let a few ideas wander around in my head, I read both poems again, this time more carefully, underlining what I feel are the key words and images, and I sometimes put boxes or whatever around what I feel are the really central ideas or arguments of the poem. Then I ask a lot of questions, sort of interrogate the poem ... At the same time, I try to discover what the poems' 'arguments' are: I don't want to get bogged down in 'line by line' details at this stage – especially with two poems to write about. (I wonder what the poets themselves would feel about this sort of thing anyway – compare and contrast my poem with someone else's?) So, this mess which follows is what I end up with after about twenty minutes. It makes sense to me, believe it or not. I scribble underlinings, questions, arrows and all sorts of stuff all over the poems, and finish by writing down a very brief plan of what I think my essay will look like, at the bottom of the paper. These essay notes are usually a bit longer than those here, but then these are just two or three key ideas. My annotations are shown on the next two pages.

I used to work out the rough plan of my essay in much more detail, and I used to write out a first rough draft of the whole essay. I don't do that any more. I haven't got the time, and anyway I've got a lot more confidence now, after the best part of two years at it ... that's going to sound cocky, I suppose, but there you are ... I've been told that the 'really good' students write about both poems simultaneously, but I just can't do that – I have to get them clear in my mind first, each one separately, before I can start doing the comparing bit right at the end. But I do try to spend some time on the comparison in the last quarter or thereabouts of the essay.

why cool?

*language like
a web?
– how?
– why?*

*contrast with
cool web*

The (Cool)(Web)

*unable to
speak?* — Children are dumb to say how **hot** the day is, *a*

repetition X How **hot** the scent is of the summer rose, *a*

X How **dreadful** the black wastes of the evening sky, *b*

X How **dreadful** the tall soldiers drumming by. *b*

ie. adults But (we) have speech, to (chill) the angry day, — *the cool web
doom?*

And speech, to (dull) the rose's cruel scent. / *dull*

*spell
= write correctly* X We spell away the (overhanging) night, *a* *= make less
intense*

*= use magic
(of language?)* X We spell away the soldiers and the fright, *a* *= make boring*

why is night frightening? *of what? war?*

There's a [cool web of language] winds us in, — *trapped by
language?*

*fear
yes, but joy??* Retreat from too much joy or too much fear:

*latinate words
(why?)
= saltiness and
talkativeness* We grow sea-green at last and coldly die *a* *drowning?!*

In brininess and volubility. *a*

But if we let our tongues lose self-possession, *sinister –
dragging us down*

Throwing off language and its watery clasp —

Before our death, instead of when death comes, *ie. the dead
don't talk!*

X Facing the wide glare of the children's day, *b*

X Facing the rose, the dark sky and the drums, *a*

We shall go mad no doubt and die that way. *b*

*not wholly
certain*

*finality of the
rhyme*

4 'paragraphs'/sections:
① children's dumbness
② adults' power of speech
*③ the cost of being able to use
language?*
*④ if we were ever to
'throw off' language
we'd go mad and die –why?*

Not a sonnet!
*18 lines
rhyme but not
regular*

*People are language users – see
world only through language*

*ambivalence
towards
language?*

Words [poets?]

Out of us all
That make rhymes,
Will you choose
Sometimes – [digression – odd syntax]
As the winds use
A crack in a wall
Or a drain,
Their joy or their pain
To whistle through – [wind = inspiration]
Choose me, [words choose poets]
You English words? [more provincial, localised]

I know you:
You are light as dreams,
Tough as oak,
Precious as gold,
As poppies and corn,
Or an old cloak: [how precious?]
Sweet as our birds
To the ear,
As the burnet rose
In the heat
Of Midsummer: [words given sensuous qualities, tangible]
Strange as the races
Of dead and unborn: [odd idea]
Strange and sweet
Equally, [strange/familiar old/new]
And familiar,
To the eye,
As the dearest faces
That a man knows, [like old friends]
And as lost homes are:
But though older far
Than oldest yew, – [stress on 'old']
As our hills are, old, –
Worn new
Again and again;
Young as our streams
After rain: [natural elements]
And as dear
As the earth which you prove
That we love.

Make me content
With some sweetness
From Wales
Whose nightingales—[poets?]
Have no wings, –
From Wiltshire and Kent
And Herefordshire, [mouthful!]
And the villages there, – [pastoral]
From the names, and the things
No less.

Let me sometimes dance
With you,
Or climb ×
Or stand perchance
In ecstasy, ×
Fixed and free ×
In a rhyme,
As poets do. [poetry can be both patterned rhyming and free verse]

[is this free verse or rhyme? (or both?)]

[celebration of English language. – lyrical outpouring, not as difficult as the Graves]

[① words 'choose' poets
② qualities of English words
③ prayer? to English language for poetic gifts?]

Anyway, here's what my 'essay plan' looked like:

1 Intro on both poems – both about words and language

How similar/different?

Different attitudes to language

NB Very different in Form! Graves more dense and concentrated, Thomas a bit insubstantial (??) Impressionistic (??)

2 Cool Web: Children's non-verbal view of the world versus adult's view caught in web of language.

Simple language and syntax at the beginning (NB but also ambiguous, e.g. "dumb" and "spell"). End-stopped lines.

Words become more complicated (latinate) eg. line 12

Adults and words: the drowning metaphor

War poetry and propaganda (Graves fought in 1st World War; compare to Rupert Brooke?)

RHYTHMS

Conclusion? Or straight on?

3 Words: Form the obvious issue. Free verse or what? It rhymes, but irregularly. NB 'Fixed and free' at end of poem – is it a poem about poetry?

Why are the lines so short? To make the words seem stronger? Does it work?

Pastoral stuff: trees, flowers, hills etc. Slushy?

NB Romantic idea of poetry: words choose the poet, not vice versa. Wind = INSPIRATION? (line 4)

4 Comparison: Language falsifies/betrays (Graves) versus celebration of language (Thomas)

5 Preference: Graves!! Why?

And here's the final essay. I'd have liked to have changed it around a bit, and to have written more at the end, and there are a couple of obvious things that I missed out. (Well, they're obvious now!) But, well, you have to know when to quit, and I thought that three hours' work was enough.

> Both these poems are concerned with the use of words and language, but The Cool Web appears to be claiming that language acts as a restriction upon the emotions and maybe even upon the perceptions, whereas Words is an enthusiastic celebration of the joys of language and the fulfilment it brings – especially through the medium of poetry.

Throughout <u>The Cool Web</u> there are very powerful images of blinding hot days, roses, forbidding night skies and marching soldiers. These (probably) symbolic images are viewed first from a child's viewpoint – untainted by the intricacies of 'cool' adult language which mutes and deadens the 'hot' and sharp perceptions and feelings: 'There's a cool web of language winds us in, Retreat from too much joy or too much fear'.

The words used to describe the perceptions of children are simple and uncomplicated, as well as repetitious ('hot', 'dreadful'). These lines have a simple, insistent rhythm, but at the same time they have a slightly uncertain rhyme pattern – at times forming compact, end-stopped rhyming couplets yet at other points ending with uneasy and jarring half rhymes (is/rose). The effect of these simple rhythms and uncertain rhymes is (it seems to me) to give the lines a sort of child-like feel, just a touch like a nursery-rhyme. In addition, there are several internal half-rhymes or assonances within the second stanza (chill/dull, for example) which are meant, perhaps, to call attention to the ambiguity of the word 'spell' – a word that can mean 'magical formula' as well as 'forming words out of letters'.

As the oppressive nature of language closes in on the adult mind, the poem's diction becomes more latinate: 'We grow sea-green at last and coldly die In brininess and volubility'.

The complicated diction of this line reflects its meaning: as the individual becomes more engulfed in words, so this obscures the actual realities of the world that words are supposed to be describing: the words themselves become more complex and weaker; the forceful images of the soldier and the rose are replaced by misty references to drowning in a sea of words that hold you under.

Robert Graves' intentions are finally and forcefully stated in the last stanza. This stanza is noticeably different from the preceding ones. It contains six lines, not four, and the diction is obviously more complex, at first sight. This final stanza is a contemplation of what might happen if the chains placed upon us by language were loosened. This loss of the control that words have over us is perhaps only acceptable at the point of death, and if allowed before death would result in insanity because no adult could cope with the world as a 'dumb' child would experience it:

' ... if we let our tongues lose self-possession,
Throwing off language and its watery clasp ...

Facing the wide glare of the children's day ...
We shall go mad no doubt and die that way.'

The repetition of 'facing' ('Facing the wide glare ... Facing the dark sky and the drums') implies that the adult who does reject language would be engaged in a distinct turning away from passivity and 'blindness' – to see the true nature of the world without the restrictive web of language. This may have something to do with Graves' experience in the First World War. (During the earlier stages of the war, the British Government, and even a few poets such as Rupert Brooke, did attempt to smooth over the horrors and destruction by disguising them in elaborate metaphors and 'heroic' language, thus 'cooling' the raw facts and emotions of the war.)

Graves' listing of the recurrent images (the rose, the dark sky, the drums) returns the reader to the beginning of the poem, so that one can compare the self-persuasion and (false) linguistic security of the adult with the child's straightforward and overwhelming experience of the world. Ultimately, Graves seems to be saying that to view life in its true, frightening essence is still preferable to the muted and safer version produced by the 'web' of adult language. The subject matter of the poem is cleverly reflected in its style, and this makes it an impressive and forceful piece of writing.

Words is a far less substantial and simpler poem, which makes it rather more accessible. While the subject matter of the poem concerns Thomas' views and his own particular usage of the English language, it is, compared to Graves' ambiguous poem, a straightforward celebration of the joys of speech. Initially, the short lines and the long uneven stanzas cause the actual words to be more isolated and thus noticeable in themselves – and this is done in a rather clever way. Yet the meanings of the words in Words don't have the weight that they have in The Cool Web. Words resounds with constant references to a rather Georgian, idyllic, maybe even sentimental view of the English countryside:

'You are light as dreams,
Tough as oak,
Precious as gold,
As poppies and corn'.

The diction of the poem is freshly and surprisingly simple and plain, although the images that it conjures up are quite rich and evocative (gold, oak, poppies). Thus the poem shows us, in quite a subtle way, the imaginative power that individual words can have upon us.

The rhyme-patterns are strangely distorted and irregular – on close inspection one can see that the rhyme-patterns are present for only short spans of time and then disintegrate into half-rhymes and completely isolated phrases, which means, again, that certain individual words are accentuated.

At the same time as proclaiming the natural wonders of English words, Thomas also seems to be questioning his right to use them, and is attempting to ascertain, by the way he writes the poem, whether or not he is worthy of them. He also seems to be a full-blown Romantic: he believes in poetic inspiration (language is like the wind, breathing into him). Words choose the poet, not the poet the words:

'Will you …
Choose me,
You English words?'

The entire poem is essentially a list of similes and analogies, in which words are compared to an idealised kind of very English pastoral beauty. Thomas obviously revels in both words and countryside, in stark contrast to Graves in The Cool Web.

Both poets appear to be asserting, in their different ways, that the poet has important things to say about language. Graves insists that the poet's aim must be to show the potentially false and deceptive nature of language, whilst

Thomas claims, very lyrically, that poetry is almost the epitome of beauty. Thomas talks about 'dancing' with words, of standing in 'ecstasy' with them, being both 'fixed and free'. 'Fixed and free' could be a fair description of the poem, as well as a summary of its meaning: Thomas' poem is written in a kind of anarchic semi-rhyming free verse – the poem is itself a defier of categories, really.

<u>Words</u> is a fundamental declaration of joy in the English language, and its simple diction effectively conveys the natural power of words over us and, more dramatically, over Thomas himself. This power is exemplified in a number of different ways. For instance, he clearly delights in the onomatopoeia in lines like

'A crack in the wall
Or a drain
Their joy or their pain
To whistle through ... '

And while Thomas does seem to suggest here that words can transmit pain as well as pleasure, this power is itself glorious, and of little importance when compared to the wonder and evocative powers of individual words. Graves seems to believe that more pain than pleasure is caused by words (is he, a poet, being ironic?) and that language is a potential hindrance to our 'innocent' perceptions of the surrounding world. (Language can, for example, create a false myth of an idyllic, 'Georgian' English countryside.) Perhaps because Graves' poem is so thought-provoking and because its form is so nicely matched to its subject-matter, his is the poem I prefer. It is the better poem.

Well, that's the essay. I was quite pleased with it at the time – I was in a good mood and the poems were interesting, so I was writing quite well that day. (I don't always). Re-reading the essay four weeks on, there are some things I'd like to change. I now think that knowing a bit about Georgian and First World War poetry was of some help in understanding these poems, but not that much. Although I wish I'd known that Thomas was killed in the war – there's an irony in that, somehow ... There are one or two places where the essay is a bit vague, and I was clearly running out of steam towards the end – I didn't really like the Thomas poem all that much and I couldn't really be bothered with it – you can tell that I was struggling, can't you? I'd rather have written a longer piece on the Graves poem, which I really did like. I'd have liked to say something about the use of iambic pentameter in the Graves poem, and about the connotations of the word 'web'. I'd like to have said more about the repetitions in that one. And I should have said more about that poetic inspiration business in the Thomas poem, something about the idea that poets make 'old' words 'new' ... Still, I'm fairly happy with it on the whole. It only took about three hours from start to finish, and it got a decent mark. What more can I say? I know that there are students here who are better and loads more perceptive than I am, but the fact is that I can usually keep up with them by being a bit more methodical than they are. There are some that are worse, too. I was absolutely dreadful when I started writing this kind of essay. It's mostly a question of practice, I think.

That's Claire's account of how she sets about writing a 'critical appreciation'. Apart from omitting a few 'ums' and 'ers' it's a more or less unedited transcript of what she said. She's the kind of student who likes to think for herself; for that reason she might have got a lot out of the last chapter of this book, which is very largely about the 'cool web' of language.

Let us just extract a few points that emerge from Claire's approach:

A literary critical essay never arrives in your head in a complete, edited form. Writing is a daunting process of constant self-criticism and dissatisfaction. Four weeks on, Claire is still re-thinking and criticising parts of her essay. But she's not too self-critical: she's prepared to pat herself on the back when she thinks she's earned the right to do so. It's important to do that. She also knows when to stop writing on one point and to go on to something else. Constant and obsessive rewriting becomes totally counter-productive and soul-destroying and bad for your morale.

Claire is at least as methodical as she is inspired. The two are not mutually exclusive. Here is a brief summary of her method:

1 Read the poem(s) all the way through before you pick up your pen. In this way you get an 'overview' of what you're being asked to write about, and you can pace your work accordingly. (This is especially important if you are writing to a time limit.)

2 Take some time to annotate the poem with what teachers sometimes refer to as 'marginalia' (underlinings, notes and reminders in the margin, and so on). Don't just stare at the poems and hope that words will 'choose' you; read and examine and attack the poem's meanings actively.

3 Produce a quick rough plan or guide for your essay – it helps stop you wandering about the texts in a vague and disconnected manner. (Claire might have written a better and tighter comparison of the two poems at the end of her essay if she'd made a more detailed sketch of her thoughts earlier on.) It's probably better to write about a poem by tracing its 'argument' – the way its ideas develop – rather than to jump about all over the place; but beware of getting bogged down in the line-by-line approach of the Running Commentary Heresy. (See Chapter 3.) Claire does follow the ideas through the Graves poem, but she doesn't lose sight of the wood of the poem by spending too much time looking at its individual trees. Because she has an overview she can detect patterns – she sees how final lines of a poem can refer back to the opening lines, and so forth.

Try to get lots of practice at writing critical essays. Don't wait to be set the task. Get into the habit of reading a poem as if you were going to be asked to write about it, even though you may not be. In other words, read like a writer. Claire admits that her early efforts were pretty dire, and indeed they were, even though she was always clearly an intelligent person. After almost two years of pretty hard work she now does write very well: this is something like her twentieth Unseen exercise. Her essay is especially confident and skilled in the way that she writes about the form and the content of a poem simultaneously, or, in other words, she always tries to relate what the poet says to how the poet says it.

The next time you are asked to write a critical essay or appreciation, try (or adapt) the Claire method and see if it works for you.

19
An A to Z of Irony

SATIRE is a sort of GLASS, wherein beholders generally discover everybody's face but their own.

~ Jonathan Swift.

Of all the slithery topics we have tried to grip in this book, irony is probably the fastest to slip through the fingers. Trying to come up with a good working definition of the word is a lost cause. Dr Johnson had a stab at it and missed: irony, he said, is 'a mode of speech in which the meaning is contrary to the words'. The Shorter Oxford English Dictionary offers a definition which is a long-winded version of Johnson: 'A figure of speech in which the intended meaning is the opposite of that expressed by the words used; usually taking the form of sarcasm or ridicule in which laudatory expressions are used to imply condemnation or contempt.' Neither of these definitions seems to have much relevance to the following uses of the word found in my newspaper:

Ironically, the protests against the book have resulted in a huge increase in its sales.

In the light of these policies it is ironic, to say the least, that the Prime Minister claims to represent 'Green' interests.

... and so it was a nice irony that the winning goal came as a result of the failure of the Spurs' off-side trap.

These quotations are more useful than either Johnson's or Oxford's definition. They demonstrate that the writer's way of looking at things differs from the way that the people he or she is writing about look at these things. The protesters against the book would not see its increased sales as ironic but as very regrettable; the Prime Minister would not see his position as ironic but (inevitably) as completely justified; the Spurs' defence would be too busy being sick as parrots to appreciate any 'nice irony'. And there is a third, equally important point to be made about these three extracts: that in each case the writer assumes that readers will see the irony of the situation even if those whom he or she is writing about do not. In other words, the writer assumes a shared point of view with the reader.

The three press extracts announce an ironic attitude by using forms of the word itself. In literature the presence of irony is not usually signalled so clearly – it is up to us readers to detect it. Furthermore, in each of those little pieces the writer is not using language ironically, but pointing to situations that seem ironic. So let's distinguish first between **situational irony** and **verbal irony**.

A newspaper recently reported a mishap in the American mid-west. One hundred and fifty people had to flee from a fair when a barbecue set fire to the marquee. The fair was being held to raise funds for the local fire brigade.

We find that among events merely casual, those are the most wonderful and striking which seem to imply design: as when, for instance, the statue of Mytis at Argos killed the very man who had murdered Mytis by falling down upon him as he was surveying it; events of this kind not having the appearance of an accident.

Aristotle: Poetics

We assume there's no need to labour the point as to how and why those events are ironic, but perhaps one thing should be said: that the perceiving of situational ironies involves a certain detachment. Neither the people escaping from the marquee inferno nor Aristotle's flattened assassin could be expected to see their situations as ironic; only an observer could. This detachment is not necessarily an emotional detachment. If we smile at the newspaper report it's not (we hope) because we are uncaring about fire victims, and there's no reason to suppose that Aristotle was indifferent towards the man crushed to death. The detachment is perceptual – an ability to see, from a non-involved point of view, the relationship between disparate things. It is often said, though, that the use of irony in writing is 'cold', that it implies an absence of compassion or feeling. Whether it is or not is a judgment perhaps best postponed until the end of this chapter.

The newspaper reporter and Aristotle 'found' their situational ironies, but of course writers can and do create situational ironies for their own purposes. At the end of Melville's *Moby Dick*, for instance, Ishmael saves himself from drowning by clinging to a floating coffin. In theatre, situational irony is a traditional and common device and is generally called **dramatic irony**. Dramatic irony depends upon the audience knowing something that the play's characters do not know. Shakespeare was fond of the device: in *Measure for Measure* a low-life character called Lucio, in conversation with a friar, slanders the Duke of Vienna – not knowing (as the audience does) that the friar is the Duke in disguise. In Tom Stoppard's *Rosencrantz and Guildenstern are Dead* the title characters do not know what the audience knows: that they are characters in a play called *Hamlet* and that they come to a sticky end. When Rosencrantz and Guildenstern discuss what's going on and what's best to do, their dialogue is ironic because we (the audience) know that no matter what they decide, they have no control over their fate – they are stuck in someone else's play.

Our concern in this chapter, however, is with verbal irony and some of the often quite complicated and subtle things it can achieve. And because it can be complicated and subtle and immensely varied in its effects, any attempt to divide irony up into handy types or categories is doomed from the start. There are one or two ironic techniques that are recognisable and which have names, and we'll offer examples of those later; but before we do that let's go back for a moment to those definitions of irony with which we opened this chapter: Dr Johnson's and the Oxford Dictionary's. Both contain the idea that when irony is involved the true meaning of the words is opposite (or 'contrary') to the apparent meaning. Actually, this is true only when irony is relatively simple. To put it another way, the simpler irony is, the more likely it is to involve opposite or contrary meanings. For example, the simplest, crudest form of irony is **sarcasm**:

In this instance, everybody involved (including the victim) is aware that what is meant is more or less exactly the opposite of what is said. 'Pretty' really means 'ugly'. In literature, pure sarcasm is comparatively rare (outside of character dialogue, that is). And that means that in literature ironic language is unlikely to mean the simple opposite of what it says. We think that it would be more useful for you to think in terms of there being a discrepancy, a gap, between what is said and what you, as a reader, are meant to understand. And as a critical reader your task will be to understand what that discrepancy is and what it is for. If that seems somewhat difficult and abstract, consider that in our everyday lives we rarely mean what we say. In ordinary conversation, much of what we say is latent rather than stated. The meaning of what we say is conveyed to a great extent by physical position or gesture ('body language') and – most effectively – by tone of voice. For example, if someone spills their coffee down your shirt and walks off without apologising, you might say 'Charming', but the way you say it will indicate something quite different. These things allow us to 'read the subtitles' below what is being said to us, to fill in the gap between what is actually said and what is meant. Critics often tell us that irony functions as a 'tone of voice' – the problem being, of course, that words on a page are inaudible. Nevertheless, it is important to learn to 'hear' a writer's tone of voice because that is what will reveal his or her attitude (both towards the subject matter and the reader) and irony is, fundamentally, an attitude – a way of looking at things.

The following collection of bits and pieces are all ironic in differing ways. They are not connected or ordered in any thematic way. We've chosen them simply because we hope you'll find them enjoyable.

A   Oh, life is a glorious cycle of song,
    A medley of extemporanea;
    And love is a thing that can never go wrong,
    And I am Marie of Roumania.

Dorothy Parker

Here irony takes the form of language subverting itself. Since we know that Dorothy Parker is Dorothy Parker and not Marie of Roumania (whoever she was) the last statement is not true. By implication the preceding statements are likewise untrue. The absurd rhyme of 'extemporanea' and 'Roumania' suggests that all those assertions are ridiculous. Another way of looking at it might be this: that anyone who says she is Marie of Roumania and isn't, is mad; and you'd have to be mad to believe all that stuff about life and love.

A favourite technique of ironists is **incongruity**. In Neil Bennet's drawing overleaf, the incongruity is between the sweet old Granny and the fearsome bigotry of her views. There is a further incongruity – which is what makes the joke work – between the words and what she's using them for. She's embroidering a sampler, one of those usually pious or cosy needlework messages ('Bless This House', 'There's No Place Like Home' – that sort of thing) which are framed and hung on the parlour wall.

B

C   "After the success of the Firearms Amnesty," said Convenor Graham
Watt of Clackmannon District Council, "we thought the time had come
to stiffen up on our approach to dogs and dog-fouling. Therefore we
provided a one-off low-cost hand-in-your-dog-and-have-it-killed-gratis
facility, along with the hand-over-your-gun-pattern. Basically, it was
designed for dog-lovers who can prove hardship."

Poor Mr Watt. There can be no doubt that he is a humane and sensitive person –
he could hardly have been elected to his high office if he were not – but he has
unfortunately made himself vulnerable to mild ridicule by his excessive use of the
Bureaucratic Hyphen. (The purpose of the Bureaucratic Hyphen is to make a
ramshackle collection of words look as if they have been seriously considered and
assembled by an official committee.) There is some incongruity involved in this
passage: the way, for instance, that the pretentious word 'gratis' is yoked to the
exceedingly blunt phrase 'have-it-killed'. But the basic irony in this passage exists as
a discrepancy between what Mr Watt meant to say and what he (reportedly) did
say. Clearly he has the public interest at heart: no-one particularly likes dog
excrement, after all; and it can be rather expensive having your slack-bowelled pet
put down by a vet. Regrettably, however, his words came out in such a way as to
make him sound like a cold-blooded dog-slaying bureaucrat. (These hyphens are
infectious.)

Let us imagine for a moment that Mr Watt is, really, a cold-blooded dog-slaying
bureaucrat. In which case his words would not be merely ill-chosen, they would be
unconsciously honest; they would give him away. Then we would have an example
of **self-revealing irony**.

Self-revealing irony is, fairly obviously, what's at work when a character 'inadvertently' reveals certain facts or aspects of his or her personality or attitudes which he or she would rather not be noticed. Here are two examples:

D March 16th

A gentleman friend and I were dining at the Ritz last evening and he said that if I took a pencil and a paper and put down all my thoughts it would make a book. This almost made me smile as what it would really make would be a whole row of encyclopediacs. I mean I seem to be thinking practically all the time. I mean it is my favourite recreation and sometimes I sit for hours and do not seem to do anything else but think. So this gentleman said a girl with brains ought to do something else with them besides think. And he said he ought to know brains
10 when he sees them, because he is in the senate and he spends quite a great deal of time in Washington, dc, and when he comes into contract with brains he always notices it. So it might have all blown over but this morning he sent me a book. And so when my maid brought it to me, I said to her, 'Well, Lulu, here is another book and we have not read half the ones we have got yet.' But when I opened it and saw that it was all a blank I remembered what my gentleman aquaintance said, and so then I realised that it was a diary. So here I am writing a book instead of reading one.

But now it is the 16th of March and of course it is to late to begin
20 with January, but it does not matter as my gentleman friend, Mr Eisman, was in town practically all of January and February, and when he is in town one day seems to be practically the same as the next day.

I mean Mr Eisman is in the wholesale button profession in Chicago and he is the gentleman who is known practically all over Chicago as Gus Eisman the Button King. And he is the gentleman who is interested in educating me, so of course he is always coming down to New York to see how my brains have improved since the last time. But when Mr Eisman is in New York we always seem to do the same thing and if I wrote down one day in my diary, all I would have to do would be
30 to put quotation marks for all other days. I mean we always seem to have dinner at the Colony and see a show and go to the Trocadero and then Mr Eisman shows me to my apartment. So of course when a gentleman is interested in educating a girl, he likes to stay and talk about the topics of the day until quite late, so I am quite fatigued the next day and I do not really get up until it is time to dress for dinner at the Colony.

It would be strange if I turned out to be an authoress. I mean at my home near Little Rock, Arkansas, my family all wanted me to do something about my music. Because all my friends said I had talent
40 and they all kept after me about practising. But some way I never seemed to care so much about practising. I mean I could not simply sit for hours and hours at a time practising just for the sake of a career. So one day I got quite tempermental and threw the old mandolin clear across the room and I have never really touched it since. But writing is different because you do not have to learn or practise and it is more

tempermental because practise seems to take all the temperment out of me. So now I almost really have to smile because I have just noticed that I have written clear across two pages onto March 18th, so this will do for today and tomorrow. And it just shows how tempermental I am when I get started.

Anita Loos: Gentlemen Prefer Blondes

1 Select two sentences that tell you more about this speaker than she thinks they do (or something different from what she thinks they do) and say what it is that they reveal about her and her life. Incidentally, is it just the speaker who is being mocked in this passage?

2 The sentence that begins 'So this gentleman said ... ', and the sentence that follows it (lines 8 to 12) are capable of a number of ironic interpretations. How many can you detect? What is ironic about the misspelling in line 11?

E   In my temporary office on the Island I read through Head Nurse Herbie Flamm's report on Eric Cannon.
        "It is necessary to report that Patient Eric Cannon is a trouble maker. There haven't been many patients in my lifetime that I would have to label that, but this is one. Cannon is a consciously evil trouble maker. He is disturbing the other patients. Although I have always kept this one of the quietest [sic] wards on the island, since he has been here it is noisy and a mess. Patients who haven't said a word in years now can't shut up. Patients that have stood always in the same corner

10   now play pitch and catch with chairs. Many of the patients are now singing and laughing. This disturbs the patients who want peace and quiet to get better. Someone keeps destroying the television set. I think Mr. Cannon is schizophrenic. Sometimes he wanders around the ward nice and quiet like he was in a dreamworld and other times he sneaks around like a snake, hissing at me and the patients like he was the boss of the ward and not me.
        Unfortunately he has followers. Many patients are now refusing sedation. Some do not go to the machine shop for factory therapy. Two patients confined to wheelchairs have pretended to walk. Patients are

20   showing disrespect for the hospital food. When one man was ill to his stomach, another patient began eating the vomit, claiming it tasted much better that way. We do not have enough maximum security rooms on the ward. Also patients who are refusing or not swallowing their sedation will not stop singing and laughing when we politely ask. Disrespect is everywhere. I have sometimes had the feeling on the ward that I do not exist. I mean to say no one pays attention any more. My attendants are often tempted to treat the patients with physical force but I remind them of the Hypocratic Oath. Patients will not stay in their beds at night. Talking with each other is going on. Meetings I

30   think. They whisper. I do not know if there is a rule against this, but I recommend that a rule is made. Whispering is worse than singing.
        We have sent several of his followers to ward W [the violent ward]

but patient Cannon is tricky. He never does anything himself. I think
he is spreading illegal drugs on the ward but none have ever been
found. He never does anything and everything is happening.

I have this to report. It is serious. On September 10, at 2.30 p.m. in
the Main Room right in front of the destroyed and lifeless television set,
a large group of patients began hugging each other. They had a circle
with their arms around each other and they were humming or moaning
40   and kept getting closer and humming and swaying or pulsating like a
giant jellyfish or human heart and they were all men. They did this and
attendant R. Smith attempted to break them up but their circle was
very strong. I attempted to break their circle also as gently as I could
but as I was so endeavouring the circle suddenly opened and two men
physically clamped me with their arms and hands and I was drawn
against my total will into the horrible circle. It was disgusting beyond
my ability to say.
The patients showed no respect but continued their illegal hugging
until four attendants from ward T plus R. Smith rescued me by
50   breaking up the circle as gently as they could, unfortunately
accidentally breaking my arm (the lower tibia minor, I believe).

This event is typical of the poor conditions which have developed on
our ward since patient Cannon came. He was in the circle but since
there were eight, Dr. Vener said we couldn't send them all to ward W.
Hugging is also not technically against the rules which again shows the
need for more thinking.

The boy never talks to me. But I hear. Among the patients I have
friends. They say he is against mental hospitals. You should know that.
They say he is the ringleader of all the trouble. That he is trying to
60   make all the patients happy and not pay attention to us. They say he
says that patients ought to take over the hospital. That he says even if
he leaves them he will come back. These patients, my friends, say this.

Because of the facts what I have written I must respectfully
recommend to you:

(1) that all sedation be given by needle to prevent patients from
falsely swallowing their tranquilisers and remaining active and noisy
during the day.

(2) that all illegal drugs should be strictly forbidden

(3) that strict rules be developed and enforced regarding singing,
70   laughing, whispering and hugging.

(4) that a special iron mesh cage be developed to protect the
television set and that its cord go directly from the set which is ten feet
off the floor to the ceiling to protect the wire from those who would deny
the television set to those who want to watch it. This is freedom of
speech. The iron mesh must form about inch wide squares, thick
enough to prevent flying objects from entering and smashing the screen
but letting people still see the screen although with a waffle-griddle
effect. The TV must go on.

(5) Most important. That patient Eric Cannon be transferred
80   someplace else."

Head Nurse Flamm sent this report to myself, Dr. Vener, Dr. Mann, Chief Supervisor Hennings, State Mental Hospital Director Alfred Coles, Mayor John Lindsay and Governor Nelson Rockefeller.

Luke Rhinehart: The Dice Man

1 What are Herbie Flamm's true attitudes towards mental patients? What is it that tells you what they are?

2 Herbie's grasp of grammar and syntax is not all it could be. Does this mean that Luke Rhinehart is cruelly mocking someone who is not very bright? Or are Herbie's linguistic quirks an ironic way of revealing his attitudes? Apply these questions to Herbie's recommendation number 4. Generally, what indications are there that Herbie's grasp on sanity is not much stronger than those he is in charge of?

3 In the paragraph beginning 'The boy never talks to me', Herbie's description of Eric Cannon hints at a comparison with a rather more well-known 'ringleader': who?

4 How does this passage explore and subvert conventional notions of 'madness' and mental hospitals?

In each of the last two extracts there is, clearly, a discrepancy between what the speaker tells us and what is really going on. This leaves room for the reader to indulge in some sceptical speculation. What, exactly, is involved in Mr Gus Eisman's 'educational' methods? Is Herbie Flamm any saner than his patients?

When a text invites us to treat it with suspicion, we are usually in the presence of an **unreliable narrator**. The Unreliable Narrator is a device that goes back a very long way – in English literature at least as far as Chaucer, whose pilgrim narrator of *The Canterbury Tales* is one such. Gus's girlfriend and Herbie Flamm are all Unreliable Narrators. All novels and stories which are told in the first person are to some extent unreliable narratives because they are told by someone who is involved in the action and who is therefore not impartial or objective. (You may remember that we discussed some of these issues in the earlier chapter on narrative techniques.) This is true of non-ironic works as well as ironic ones, but in ironic works there are usually clues (not necessarily as transparent or comic as in the last two passages) which serve to throw suspicion upon the story-teller. This gets us to an important point about irony: because you cannot take ironic writing at face value, you are automatically involved in interpreting it; and this means that you are actively engaged in creating the meaning of the text rather than passively accepting it.

A rather extreme version of unreliable narrative is something which has come to be called (confusingly, perhaps, but never mind) **Romantic irony**. This involves the narrating character revealing himself not 'inadvertently' but quite openly and deliberately – usually by addressing the reader directly. What this kind of narrator reveals is that he is well aware that he is telling a story, that telling stories is a peculiar and tricky business, and that he really ought to explain to and consult with the reader about the problems involved and the best way to proceed. The classic work of Romantic Irony is Laurence Sterne's *The Life and Opinions of Tristram Shandy*, written during the years 1759 to 1767. It is a spoof autobiography. It begins at the very beginning, with Tristram's conception; which is unfortunately marred by his mother asking her husband at the crucial moment whether he has remembered to wind the clock. This interruption, Tristram says, had a lasting effect on him. It might explain why he interrupts himself so frequently and digresses so madly that in the book's entire length of six hundred pages we never get beyond his earliest infancy. The book is an artfully-contrived shambles, and Tristram is continually stepping out of the pages to explain and justify his shambolic 'method' of writing. Here's a brief snippet:

F   I have dropped the curtain over this scene for a minute – to remind you of one thing, and to inform you of another. What I have to inform you comes, I admit, a little out of its due course; for it should have been told a hundred and fifty pages ago; but I foresaw then that it would come in pat hereafter, and be of more advantage here than elsewhere. Writers had needs look before them, to keep up the spirit and connection of what they have in hand.

   When these two things are done, the curtain shall be drawn up again, and my Uncle Toby, my father and Dr. Slop shall go on with their discourse without any more interruption.

Laurence Sterne: The Life and Opinions of Tristram Shandy

What Sterne does, and what Romantic Irony generally does, is draw attention, humourously, to the artifice of fiction. A text, a book, is an invented thing, not a 'slice of life'.

Romantic Irony is a technique that that has had a renewed popularity in fairly recent years. American writers such as John Barth, Robert Coover and Walker Percy have used it. Anthony Burgess and John Fowles, English novelists, have used it in different ways. (Fowles offers two different endings to his novel *The French Lieutenant's Woman*; the reader can choose.) The Italian writer Italo Calvino, in his novel *If on a Winter's Night a Traveller* (which is really a bewildering series of transformations in which one novel turns out to be part of a different novel inside another novel ...) manipulates the reader to such an extent that you end up as a character in the book: that character being The Person Who Is Reading *If on a Winter's Night a Traveller*. Here's an extract from it:

G   You have now read about thirty pages and you're becoming caught up in the story. At a certain point you remark: "This sentence sounds somehow familiar. In fact, this whole passage reads like something I've read before." Of course: there are themes that recur, the text is interwoven with these reprises, which serve to express the fluctuation of time. You are the sort of reader who is sensitive to such refinements; you are quick to catch the author's intentions and nothing escapes you. But, at the same time, you also feel a certain dismay; just when you were beginning to grow truly interested, at this very point the author feels called upon to display one of those virtuoso tricks so customary in modern writing, repeating a paragraph word for word. Did you say paragraph? Why, it's a whole page; you make the comparison, he hasn't changed even a comma. And as you continue, what develops? Nothing: the narration is repeated, identical to the pages you have read!

Wait a minute! Look at the page number. Damn! From page 32 you've gone back to page 17! What you thought was a stylistic subtlety on the author's part is simply a printer's mistake: they have inserted the same pages twice. The mistake occurred as they were binding the volume: a book is made up of sixteen-page 'signatures'; each signature is a large sheet on which sixteen pages are printed, and which is then folded over eight times; when all the signatures are bound together, it can happen that two identical signatures end up in the same copy; it's the sort of accident that occurs now and then. You leaf anxiously through the next pages to find page 33, assuming it exists; a repeated signature would be a minor inconvenience, the irreparable damage comes when the proper signature has vanished, landing in another copy where perhaps that one will be doubled and this one will be missing. In any event, you want to pick up the thread of your reading, nothing else matters to you, you had reached a point where you can't skip even one page.

Here is page 31 again, page 32 ... and then what comes next? Page 17 all over again, a third time! What kind of book did they sell you, anyway?

Italo Calvino: If on a Winter's Night a Traveller

But what is the point of all this? The first and possibly most important thing to say about Romantic Irony is that we shouldn't take it too seriously. It's a game, and if you are the kind of person who likes games and puzzles and mazes and riddles, then you are quite likely to enjoy it. (And if not, not.) Also, broadly speaking, Romantic Irony is used for comic effects, and we ought not to be too solemn about it. On the other hand, comedy can have serious aspects, as Salman Rushdie knows. One of the things that romantic ironists like Sterne and Calvino are saying is that although a novel is created, as a sequence of words, by its writer, it can 'happen', have meaning, only when a reader takes it up. The novelist is totally dependent upon your participation and involvement. (In *Tristram Shandy*, Tristram is incapable of describing the great physical charm of Widow Wadman, so he leaves a blank page so that the reader can draw her for himself.) The quality of the experience that a novel can provide depends greatly upon the quality and the degree of the reader's (your) participation. After all, it is at least as easy to read a novel badly as it is to write a novel badly. Romantic Irony is a way – as all irony is – of getting you to consider the way you are responding to what you are reading, a way of getting you to commit your imagination to the process.

The novelist who adopts the techniques of Romantic Irony seems to be saying that he is depicting only a subjective, partial, unreliable view of reality. Romantic Irony says 'Look, I'm making all this up, and I'd like you to go along with it and we'll see what we can make of it together'. It's a trick, but at least it's an honest trick.

We're getting philosophical. Let's move on. It's Spring in the country:

H   Spring advanced apace in Witney Scrotum.

Ten miles away in Keating New Town it was still winter. It always was.

But here in the village small birds sang besotted and bemused in tangled hedgerows.

Lapwings wheeled and whirled above Farmer Emburey's new-ploughed pastures.

Arctic-bound geese flew high above the sun-tossed Mendis Hills in great V-shaped straggles, and grass snakes and dry-lipped lizards sunned themselves on the sandy heathlands that skirted the vast and lonely Rumsey Downs.

And one day the first house-martin of the summer arrived in Witney Scrotum and commenced to rebuild and refurbish its nest tucked in the eaves of the roof above the lady wife's bedroom.

The Brigadier stared long and hard at it as it sat preening itself with fastidious vagueness.

'Amazing, eh, Vileness?' he said. 'The poor little brute has travelled thousands and thousands of miles to get here. He's crossed vast deserts, towering mountain ranges, storm-tossed oceans to come back here to set up home outside the lady wife's bedroom.'

He paused for a moment, and then he said:

'Bloody fool. I wouldn't.'

Peter Tinniswood: Tales of Witney Scrotum

And it's Spring in London:

I   Now was the time of year when the trees got their first fine powdering of cement dust. Some morning, unaware, he would see at their roots the tiny white clusters of discarded chicken-bones, while suspended from a low bough swayed a supermarket trolley. Soon the black stems of the railings that topped his patio would blossom with upturned gaudy magenta and silver cans, and in the patio itself might drift and float an early harbinger of the season, a pale inflated condom.

Michael Levey: Men at Work

Both the Tinniswood and the Levey passages are to some extent **parody** in that they mimic and thus subvert the clichés of descriptive nature writing (or pastoral). Peter Tinniswood does it with **bathos**. Bathos (the Greek word for depth) is the sudden and ludicrous dropping in tone from the high-flown and lyrical (all those lapwings and lizards and 'storm-tossed oceans') into the vulgar or ridiculous ('Bloody fool ... '). The effect is fairly straightforwardly comic. In the Michael Levey piece, the tone has a rather sad and regretful edge to it. The irony comes from the coupling together of the lyrical (pastoral) and the squalid (urban); basically, the technique is incongruity again. Levey writes about tin cans and other garbage *as if they were* flowers and suchlike, and by this means sets up expectations in the reader's mind which are then quickly defeated: 'tiny white clusters' of ... crocuses? No – discarded chicken bones; an 'early harbinger of the season' ... A butterfly? No, 'a pale inflated condom'.

When two incongruous things are coupled ironically together by a single word (usually a verb) we sometimes get a **zeugma** (another Greek word, this one meaning 'yolking together'). Here's a famous one:

Note: a 'watchful spirit' knows that a disaster is about to befall a 'Nymph' – that is, a shallow and flirtatious young woman of fashion – but what exactly this disaster will be the spirit does not know. Diana, by the way, is the goddess, not the princess, and her 'law' is chastity.

J   Whether the Nymph will break Diana's law,
     Or some frail china jar receive a flaw;
     Or stain her honour or her new brocade,
     Forget her prayers, or miss a masquerade;
     Or lose her heart, or necklace, at a ball ...

Alexander Pope: The Rape of the Lock

With zeugma the joke is to pretend that the discrepancy between two things does not exist. Pope is pretending that there is no discrepancy between utterly different things – or, rather, he is suggesting that this 'Nymph' sees no distinction between things so essentially different as her virginity and a china vase. The satirical point is, of course, that this girl places equal value upon these things. You might also have noticed that in these extracts zeugma works by using the same verb in a metaphorical and a literal sense:

stain	(metaphorical)	— honour
	(literal)	— new brocade
lose	(metaphorical)	— her heart
	(literal)	— necklace

As we seem to be dealing in Greek terms at the moment, here are two more. **Litotes** (pronounced 'lie-tote-ease') is an impressive word for a simple and commonplace form of irony, not far removed from sarcasm. It involves implying a strong positive statement by making a mild negative one, as in:

K The Minister is not being altogether honest.
   (meaning 'The Minister is lying through his teeth.')

L Emerging from the Hope and Anchor, she seemed not to have perfect control of her legs.
   (meaning 'She was hopelessly drunk.')

Litotes is a popular device among politicians and journalists because it is a neat way around the laws of slander and libel. You are perhaps familiar with the journalistic code which has politicians appearing to be 'tired and emotional' (i.e. drunk as skunks) and businessmen as 'fun-loving' (i.e. grossly promiscuous).

Litotes is a close relative of **meiosis**, which is more commonly and less pretentiously known as **ironic understatement**. This is one of the most widely-used ironic techniques, and so naturally its effects vary greatly. Generally speaking, it is the use of mild language to describe sensational events or powerful emotions. The reader is thus amused or surprised or shocked by the discrepancy between the tone of voice and the subject-matter, and this reaction may make us more acutely aware of the nature of the things being described. Perhaps the most famous (and nasty) use of ironic understatement is this:

M   Last week I saw a woman flayed, and you will hardly believe how much it altered her appearance for the worse.

Jonathan Swift: A Tale of a Tub

Note: Flaying involves whipping someone's body until the skin is stripped away from the flesh.

On a rather lighter note, here is a description of a suburb of Singapore in 1937. The last sentence, in particular, is a lovely ironic understatement.

N   At first glance Tanglin resembled any quiet European suburb with its winding, tree-lined streets and pleasant bungalows. There was a golf course close at hand with quite respectable greens; numerous tennis courts could be seen on the other side of sweet-smelling hedges and even a swimming pool or two. It was a peaceful and leisurely life that people led here, on the whole. Yet if you looked more closely you would see that it was a suburb ready to burst at the seams with a dreadful tropical energy. Foliage sprang up on every hand with a determination unknown to our own polite European vegetation. Dark, glistening green was smeared over everything as if with a palette knife, while in the gloom (the jungle tends to be gloomy) something sinister which had been making a noise a little while ago was now holding its breath.
    If you left your bungalow unattended for a few months while you went home on leave, very likely you would come back to find that green lariats had been thrown over every projecting part and were wrestling it to the ground, that powerful ferns were drilling their way between its bricks, or that voracious house-eating insects, which were really nothing more than sharp jaws mounted on legs, had been making meals of the woodwork. Moreover, the mosquitoes in this particular suburb were only distant cousins of the mild insects which irritate us on an English summer evening: in Tanglin you had to face the dreaded anopheles variety, each a tiny flying hypodermic syringe containing a deadly dose of malaria. And, if you managed to avoid malaria there was still another mosquito waiting in the wings, this one clad in striped football socks, ready to inject you with dengue fever. If your child fell over while playing in the garden and cut its knee, you had to make sure that no fly was allowed to settle on the wound; otherwise, within a day or two, you would find yourself picking tiny white maggots out of it with tweezers. At the same time, when parts of the suburb were still bordered by jungle, it was by no means uncommon for monkeys, snakes and suchlike to visit your garden with the idea of picking your fruit or swallowing your mice (or even your puppy if you had an appetising one). But all I mean to suggest is that, besides the usual comforts of suburban life, there were certain disadvantages, too.

J. G. Farrell: The Singapore Grip

What do you make of the phrases 'the jungle tends to be gloomy' and 'visit your garden'?

As must be fairly plain by now, the ironist frequently adopts a consciously lop-sided view of things. Sometimes this point of view rotates an extra few degrees until things appear upside-down. The result is **ironic inversion**, whereby our conventional attitudes are challenged by being inverted or reversed. Oscar Wilde and George Bernard Shaw were rather good at it.

O   Really, if the lower orders don't set us a good example, what on Earth is the use of them?

P   I hope you have not been leading a double life, pretending to be wicked and really being good all the time. That would be hypocrisy.

Oscar Wilde: The Importance of Being Earnest

Q   The reasonable man adapts himself to the world: the unreasonable one persists in trying to adapt the world to himself. Therefore all progress depends upon the unreasonable man.

George Bernard Shaw: Reason

It is a matter of personal taste as to whether or not you find the rather self-conscious cleverness of such witticisms off-putting. If you do, you are likely to be unwilling to see any interesting or serious point lurking behind the irony. Nevertheless, do you think that Wilde is in some way subverting or challenging conventional notions of class and hypocrisy, and that Shaw is doing something similar with the ideas of 'reason' and 'progress'?

There is no defineable point at which irony becomes **satire**. Irony, as we hope we have shown, can be used to all sorts of effect – to amuse, to surprise, to subvert, to shock. Satire is used to attack. But then, you can attack amusingly, or surprisingly, or subversively, or shockingly. M. H. Abrams defines satire as

the literary art of diminishing or derogating a subject by making it ridiculous and evoking towards it attitudes of amusement, contempt, scorn or indignation ... it uses laughter as a weapon.

M. H. Abrams: A Glossary of Literary Terms

Put simply, a satirist identifies something as being wrong (morally or ideologically or politically) and sets out to mock it. Alexander Pope said something to the effect that people who are ashamed of nothing else are ashamed of appearing ridiculous. Satire can come in any form – as a play, a sketch, a parody, a novel, a poem – and it can vary in strength, like curry: from the mild put-down at the korma end of the scale to out-and-out verbal savagery at the vindaloo end. It can attack general human vice as well as particular individuals. Here's a sonnet, to begin with:

R   *Ozymandias*
        I met a traveller from an antique land
        Who said: Two vast and trunkless legs of stone

Stand in the desert. Near them, in the sand,
Half sunk, a shattered visage lies, whose frown,
And wrinkled lip, and sneer of cold command,
Tell that its sculptor well those passions read
Which yet survive, stamped on these lifeless things,
The hand that mocked them, and the heart that fed:
And on the pedestal these words appear:
'My name is Ozymandias, King of Kings:
Look on my works, ye Mighty, and despair!'
Nothing else remains. Round the decay
Of that colossal wreck, boundless and bare
The lone and level sands stretch far away.

Percy Bysshe Shelley

Try these questions:

1 The irony hinges on the tenth and eleventh lines. How did Ozymandias
 intend these lines to be understood? How does Shelley intend them to be
 understood?

2 The sonnet creates a very vivid pictorial image of this ruined statue in the
 desert; why is it important that it does this?

3 What, exactly, is being satirised in this poem?

As we have said, in a number of ways, irony is a useful device for the writer
because it is essentially ambiguous. The writer can say something by seeming to say
something else, and by so doing can involve the reader in the working-out process.
For the satirist, irony brings a problem with it. Satire has a target: vice, corruption,
hypocrisy, the abuse of power, or whatever (there's plenty of choice); but irony,
which is indirect in its approach, is not always a weapon ideally suited for target-
shooting. On the other hand, you cannot, as a satirist, simply come out and say
what you mean, because the result would be merely accusation or invective or
abuse. You might, to give a far-fetched example, believe that the President of the
United States is an embezzler, a liar, an arms smuggler and an international
terrorist, and you could say so. But it wouldn't be funny, it could be easily
dismissed as mere opinion, and you might well find yourself being pursued by
American lawyers. To be satirical, you need to make people laugh – or smile at least
– by writing as if these things were true; not least because we are less likely to
dismiss things that make us laugh. (Jokes are more memorable than either facts or
opinions.)

Then there is the problem of the audience or reader. If we enjoy the work of a
satirist, it is more than likely to be because we are 'on the same side', that we share
that satirist's point of view. If you write a sonnet satirising the arrogance and
megalomania of tyrants, then you can be fairly sure that tyrants, Presidents and
Prime Ministers are the very people least likely to read it. By and large, satire is a
matter of preaching to the converted. Preaching to the converted is not a waste of
time – it helps keep up their morale – but it doesn't change the world very much.
Satirists who have brought down governments, or removed social evils, or even
made minor adjustments to prevailing attitudes, are very rare creatures. One reason

for this is that when we read satire we tend to exempt ourselves from the attack: it's always somebody else's stupidity or wickedness which is being mocked. Jonathan Swift described satire as a mirror in which we see reflected everyone's face – except our own. Satirists who attack or ridicule their own readers' attitudes are few and far between. (Swift's particular genius is that he is willing and able to do it.) All this adds up to satire being a difficult and complex art, which is probably the reason why so much of what passes for satire in magazines or on television and radio is such crude and feeble stuff.

Some of these issues – ambiguity, the shared point of view, the reader's response – are raised in this next extract. In a way, this piece is a satirical assault by a satirist upon another satirist; the tones of voice are complicated by the fact that the two are good friends. Ralph Steadman is English, a wonderful illustrator with a strong sideline in grotesque and savage political caricature. Such drawings have illustrated books by his American friend, the notorious 'Gonzo' journalist Dr. Hunter S. Thompson.

S   *The Pro-flogging View*

(Note: the following is Dr Thompson's response to a desperate letter from his friend Ralph Steadman in England, on the subject of raising children.)

Dear Ralph,

I received your tragic letter about your savage, glue-sniffing son and read it while eating breakfast at 4:30 a.m. in a Waffle House on the edge of Mobile Bay ... and I made some notes on your problem, at the time, but they are not the kind of notes that any decent man would want to send to a friend ... So I put them away until I could bring a little more concentration to bear on the matter ...

And I have come to this conclusion:

Send the crazy little bugger to Australia. We can get him a job herding sheep somewhere deep in the outback, and that will straighten him out for sure; or at least it will keep him busy.

England is the wrong place for a boy who wants to smash windows. Because he is right, of course. He should smash windows. Anybody growing up in England today without a serious urge to smash windows is probably too dumb for help.

You are reaping the whirlwind, Ralph. Where in the name of art or anything else did you see anything that said you could draw queer pictures of the Prime Minister and call her worse than a denatured pig – but your own son shouldn't want to smash windows?

We are not privy to that kind of logic, Ralph. They don't even teach it at Oxford.

My own son, thank God, is a calm and rational boy who is even now filling out his applications to Yale and Bennington and Tufts and various other Eastern, elitist schools ... and all he's cost me so far is a hellish drain of something like $10,000 a year just to keep him off the streets and away from the goddam windows ...

What do windows cost, Ralph? They were about $55 apiece when I used to smash them – even the big plate-glass kind – but they now probably cost about $300. Which is cheap, when you think on it. A wild boy with a good arm could smash about 30 plate-glass windows a year and still cost you less than $10,000 per annum.

Is that right? Are my figures correct?

Yeah. They are. If Juan smashed 30 big windows a year, I would still save $1,000.

So send the boy to me, Ralph – along with a certified cheque for $10,000 – and I'll turn him into a walking profit machine.

Indeed. Send me all those angry little limey bastards you can round up. We can do business on this score. Just whip them over here on the airbus with a $10k cheque for each one, and you can go about your filthy, destructive business with a clear conscience.

Have you ever put a brick through a big plate-glass window, Ralph? It makes a wonderful goddam noise, and the people inside run around like rats in a firestorm. It's fun, Ralph, and a bargain at any price.

What do you think we have been doing all these years? Do you think you were getting paid for your goddam silly art?

No, Ralph. You were getting paid to smash windows. And that is an art in itself. The trick is getting paid for it.

What? Hello? Are you still there, Ralph?

If your son had your instincts, he'd be shooting at the Prime Minister, instead of just smashing windows.

Are you ready for that? How are you going to feel when you wake up one of these mornings and flip on the telly at Old Loose Court just in time to catch a news bulletin about the Prime Minister getting shot through the gizzard in Piccadilly Circus ... and then some BBC hot rod comes up with exclusive pictures of the dirty freak who did it, and it turns out to be your own son?

Think about that Ralph; and don't bother me any more with your minor problems ... Just send the boy over to me; I'll soften him up with trench work until his green card runs out, and then we'll move him on to Australia. And five years from now, you'll get an invitation to a wedding at a sheep ranch in Perth ...

And so much for that, Ralph. We have our own problems to deal with. Children are like TV sets. When they start acting weird, whack them across the eyes with a big rubber basketball shoe.

How's that for wisdom?

Something wrong with it?

No, I don't think so. Today's plate-glass window is tomorrow's BBC story. Keep that in mind and you won't go wrong. Just send me the boys and the cheques ...

I think you know what I mean. It's what happens when the son of a famous English artist shows up on the telly with a burp-gun in his hand and the still-twitching body of the Prime Minister at his feet ...

The subsequent publicity will be a nightmare. But don't worry – your friends will stand behind you. I'll catch one of those Polar-Route flights out of Denver and be there eight hours after it happens. We'll have a monster news conference in the ... lobby of Brown's Hotel.

Say nothing until I get there. Don't even claim bloodlines with the boy. Say nothing. I'll talk to the press – which is, after all, my business.

Your buddy,

HST

PS. Jesus, Ralph, I think I might have misspoke myself when I said ten thousand would cover it for the murderous little bastard. No. Let's talk about thirty, Ralph. You've got a real monster on your hands. I wouldn't touch him for less than thirty.

April 12, 1986

Hunter S. Thompson: Generation of Swine

In the language of literary critics, Hunter S. Thompson is using **unstable irony**, which is to say that the ironic point of view is inconsistent, or shifting. It is not possible to say with any certainty that he doesn't mean any of this. He might mean some of it. Or even all of it. When irony is stable, the reader has some solid ground to stand on: the writer is saying X but means Y. In which case, there is some solidarity, some agreement, between writer and reader. This solidarity, the shared point of view, is less available – or not available at all – when the irony is unstable. In extreme cases, unstable irony can be 'a means to betrayal', and it is the reader who is 'betrayed': the writer gets the reader 'on his side' in order subsequently to confront or satirise that reader's own comfortable assumptions.

When a writer employs unstable irony, one or both of two things tends to happen:

1 The personality of the writer (as conveyed by language and tone of voice) seems to change from paragraph to paragraph or even from line to line, so that we are never quite sure who is speaking to us or what his or her intentions are;

2 One ironic stance is set up, which we accept as the writer's 'true' position, only to be undercut by another and different ironic stance.

Do you see these things happening in *The Pro-flogging View*?

Perhaps you might like to read the Thompson piece again, and then ponder the following mysteries:

1 The passage appears to be a letter written to Ralph Steadman on the 12th of April 1986, but it appears in a book published in 1988. It seems reasonable to suppose, therefore, that one of the following is true:

a) Thompson wrote the letter, but kept a copy for publication;

b) he retrieved the letter from Steadman with permission to print it;

c) the piece was written for publication and only pretends to be a letter.

Does your understanding of the extract (that is, the tone of voice you hear and what you take to be the writer's intention) change according to which of these options you accept?

2 Assuming that Ralph Steadman first read this as a private letter, how, do you think, did he react?

3 If you received such a letter, how would you react? How would you reply?

The final two passages in this chapter come without any comment from us. When you have read them, try answering the following questions about each one:

1 How simple is the irony?

2 What is the discrepancy between what is said and what is implied? And how obvious is this discrepancy?

3 Can you identify any of the particular ironic devices that we have illustrated in this chapter?

4 Is there a tone of voice that comes through the text? If so, what does it tell you about the writer's attitude and intention?

5 Is the irony stable or unstable?

6 Is the passage partly or wholly satirical? If you think it is, what is the target of the satire? To what extent does the author make his feelings about the subject plain?

The next extract comes from a play. Mr Mcleavy's wife has been murdered by her nurse, Fay. Mcleavy's son, Hal, and Hal's friend, Dennis, have tried to conceal the proceeds of a bank robbery in Mrs Mcleavy's coffin. But Truscott of the Yard has uncovered these evil deeds.

T   TRUSCOTT (*stoops and picks up a bundle of notes*). Would you have stood by and allowed this money to be buried in holy ground?
HAL. Yes.
TRUSCOTT. How dare you involve me in a situation for which no memo has been issued. (*He turns the notes over.*) In all my experience I've never come across a case like it. Every one of these fivers bears a portait of the Queen. It's dreadful to contemplate the issues raised. Twenty thousand tiaras and twenty thousand smiles buried alive! She's a constitutional monarch, you know. She can't answer back.
DENNIS. Will she send us a telegram?
TRUSCOTT. I'm sure she will.
He picks up another bundle and stares at it.
MCLEAVY. Well, Inspector, you've found the money and unmasked the criminals. You must do your duty and arrest them. I shall do mine and appear as witness for the prosecution.
HAL. Are you married, Inspector?
TRUSCOTT. Yes.
HAL. Does your wife never yearn for excitement?
TRUSCOTT. She did once express a wish to see the windmills and tulip fields of Holland.
HAL. With such an intelligent wife you need a larger income.
TRUSCOTT. I never said my wife was intelligent.
HAL. Then she's unintelligent? Is that it?
TRUSCOTT. My wife is a woman. Intelligence doesn't really enter into the matter.
HAL. If, as you claim, your wife is a woman, you certainly need a larger income.

TRUSCOTT *takes his pipe from his pocket and sticks it into the corner of his mouth.*

TRUSCOTT. Where is all this Jesuitical twittering leading us?

HAL. I'm about to suggest bribery.

TRUSCOTT *removes his pipe, no one speaks.*

TRUSCOTT. How much?

HAL. Twenty per cent.

TRUSCOTT. Twenty-five per cent. Or a full report of this case lands on my superior's desk in the morning.

HAL. Twenty-five it is.

TRUSCOTT (*shaking hands*). Done.

DENNIS (*to* TRUSCOTT). May I help you to replace the money in the casket?

TRUSCOTT. Thank you, lad. Most kind of you.

DENNIS *packs the money into the casket.* FAY *takes* MRS. MCLEAVY'S *clothes from the bedpan on the invalid chair and goes behind the screen.* TRUSCOTT *chews on his pipe.* HAL *and* DENNIS *take the coffin behind the screen.*

MCLEAVY. Has no one considered my feelings in all this?

TRUSCOTT. What percentage do you want?

MCLEAVY. I don't want money. I'm an honest man.

TRUSCOTT. You'll have to mend your ways then.

MCLEAVY. I shall denounce the lot of you!

TRUSCOTT. Now then, sir, be reasonable. What has just taken place is perfectly scandalous and had better go no farther than these three walls. It's not expedient for the general public to have its confidence in the police force undermined. You'd be doing the community a grave disservice by revealing the full frightening facts of this case.

MCLEAVY. What kind of talk is that? You don't make sense.

TRUSCOTT. Who does?

Joe Orton: Loot

U   The name of Lady Hypatia Smythe-Browne (now Lady Hypatia Hagg) will never be forgotten in the East End, where she did such splendid social work. Her constant cry of 'Save the children!' referred to the cruel neglect of children's eyesight involved in allowing them to play with crudely-painted toys. She quoted unanswerable statistics to prove that children allowed to look at violet and vermillion often suffered from failing eyesight in extreme old age; and it was owing to her ceaseless crusade that the pestilence of the monkey-on-a-stick was almost swept from Hoxton. The devoted worker would tramp the streets untiringly, taking away the toys from the poor children, who were often moved to tears by her kindness. Her good work was interrupted partly by a new interest in the creed of Zoroaster, and partly by a savage blow from an umbrella. It was inflicted by a dissolute Irish apple-woman, who, on returning from some orgy to her ill-kept apartment, found Lady Hypatia in the bedroom, taking down an oleograph, which, to say the least of it, could not really elevate the mind. At this, the intoxicated Celt dealt the social reformer a severe blow, adding to it an absurd accusation of theft. The Lady's exquisitely-balanced mind received a shock, and it was during a short mental illness that she married Dr. Hagg.

G. K. Chesterton: How I Found the Superman

Notes

'the creed of Zoroaster': Zoroastrianism is an ancient Persian religion based on the duality of light and dark, good and evil. This may or may not be relevant.

An oleograph is an oil-colour print, a sort of crude copy of an oil-painting.

20

How to Seduce a Member of the Opposite Sex

(if that's what you really want to do)

Of all the hundreds of critics and literary theorists and authors of textbooks who are all scribbling away, very few would claim that poetry was something useful – in the usual sense of 'getting things done'. On the whole, there's no doubt that, just like novels and films and painting and theatre and music, poetry merely serves to make life more interesting, entertaining or bearable. Poetry can be used for stirring people up and inciting violence (when it's set to stirring military music). More interestingly, it has the reputation of being able to help you seduce people you like the look of; so perhaps it has its uses after all.

Poems of seduction have a long history, and up until recent times, nearly all of them have been written by men. There are traceable historical reasons for this. The complex cultural concept of courtship (*of* women *by* men) has its origins in thirteenth-century France; it was popularised by French poets and taken up seriously by the aristocracy of England about a century later. (And we still lag behind the French in sexual matters, according to the French.) Subsequently the odd ritual of men 'courting' women has been accepted by the rest of us as the normal way for people to behave. This complicated tradition, or game, or myth, of 'falling in love' and 'seduction' has a number of components. The essential ones are these (you're bound to find them familiar):

1 When a person falls in love, it is painful, like an illness. It is accompanied by unpleasant physical symptoms. The organ most painfully afflicted is, of course, the heart.

2 Nevertheless, falling in love is an ennobling and wonderful experience about which poems are written and songs sung (incessantly).

3 Men are expected to chase women. Women are expected to pretend, at first, to be reluctant to be caught. Women who don't do this are despised by men. Women who do feign indifference to male advances subsequently find themselves placed on pedestals and adored.

What this all boils down to is that initiating an emotional and sexual relationship between two people (usually, but not always, of different genders) tends to be a traditional, complex, ritualised, artificial and altogether odd business. What is even odder is that, to a large extent, poetry must take the blame for this state of affairs – along with an obscure French queen called Eleanor of Aquitaine, who is largely responsible for popularising the whole notion of falling in love and wooing and writing poems about it. Throughout what we loosely term the Renaissance, many thousands of upper-class young (and not so young) Englishmen who fancied their chances (and themselves) wrote poems which they thought (or hoped) would have the effect of seducing young women. Here's an example, a sonnet by a fellow called Henry Constable:

> My lady's presence makes the roses red,
> Because to see her lips they blush for shame:
> The lily's leaves, for envy, pale became,
> And her white hands in them this envy bred.
> The marigold abroad her leaves doth spread,
> Because the sun's and her power is the same;
> The violet of purple colour came,
> Dyed with the blood she made my heart to shed.
> In brief, all flowers from her their virtue take:
> From her sweet breath their sweet smells do proceed.
> The living heat which her eye-beams do make
> Warmeth the ground, and quickeneth the seed.
> The rain wherewith she watereth these flowers
> Falls from mine eyes, which she dissolves in showers.

Henry Constable

1 What are the two well-worn seduction techniques that Constable is trying to use in this poem?

2 What are your feelings and opinions about the metaphors he uses to describe his 'lady'?

3 What is the effect upon the reader of all those end-stopped lines? Do you find the poem difficult to read rhythmically? If so, why?

4 Dashing off a sonnet or two was something young men of fashion were expected to be able to do in the sixteenth and seventeenth centuries – along with being able to ride a horse and fight with swords. (Nowadays it's usually driving fast cars and getting a job in the City.) Many of these sonnets were worse than Constable's, because, for one reason, they were written to a dull and worn-out set of formulae. Why, do you think, have this sonnet and its author faded into obscurity? What signs are there that this poem was written to a formula?

Here's another sonnet, this one by a less obscure poet (and perhaps a more successful seducer) called Shakespeare:

> My mistress' eyes are nothing like the sun;
> Coral is far more red than her lips' red:
> If snow be white, why then her breasts are dun;
> If hairs be wires, black wires grow on her head.
> I have seen roses damaskt, red and white,
> But no such roses see I in her cheeks;
> And in some perfumes there is more delight
> Than in the breath that from my mistress reeks.
> I love to hear her speak, yet well I know
> That music hath a far more pleasing sound;
> I grant I never saw a goddess go;
> My mistress, when she walks, walks on the ground.
> And yet, by heaven, I think my love as rare
> As any she belied with false compare.

William Shakespeare

Notes
'dun' is dull brown
'wires': sonnets conventionally described the loved one's hair as 'gold wires', 'wires' being gold thread, as used in embroidery.
'damaskt': roses of mingled pink and white colour. Damask is also a rich silk fabric.
'reeks', in Shakespeare's day, did not mean 'stinks', as it does for us; it meant something like 'exhales'.

1 Who, or rather what, is Shakespeare attacking in this sonnet?

2 How does he attack what he attacks?

3 Why is he attacking it?

4 What do you think he means by that last line?

Henry Constable was using two of the three classic seduction techniques: flattery ('flowers envy you your beauty') and pleading ('take pity on my tears'). The third technique is somewhat nastier. For it to work, its female victim needs to be convinced that her only real value lies in how physically attractive to men she is. Do you know what this technique is? Have you been on the receiving end of it yet? Have you *used* it? Here it is being employed by another Elizabethan hopeful:

Look, Delia, how w'esteem the half-blown rose,
The image of thy blush and summer's honour,
Whilst yet her tender bud doth undisclose
That full of beauty Time bestows upon her.
No sooner spreads her glory in the air,
But straight her wide-blown pomp comes to decline;
She then is scorned that late adorned the fair;
So fade the roses of those cheeks of thine.
No April can revive thy withered flowers,
Whose springing grace adorns thy glory now;
Swift speedy Time, feathered with flying hours,
Dissolves the beauty of the fairest brow.
Then do not thou such treasure waste in vain,
But love now whilst thou mayst be loved again.

Samuel Daniel

Note: 'blown' here, applied to roses, means blossomed or opened – although the Dictionary may reveal other meanings which could possibly apply.

1 As the previous two poems also suggested, the rose is a long-standing symbol for female beauty. Does this mean that Daniel is using technique number one – flattery?

2 If this poem isn't simply flattering Delia, how is it attempting to seduce her?

3 'Feathered ... flying' suggests two different metaphors. What are they? Which might be the better suited to Daniel's purpose?

4 Because most of the lines of this poem are end-stopped, the rhymes are emphasised. Why might Daniel have wanted to stress these words:

'rose'/'disclose'

'decline'/'thine'

'flowers'/'hours'?

5 What are the key words in the last two lines? What is the purpose of this couplet?

6 How would you advise someone to read this poem? Which words would you stress, where would you put pauses?

As you've doubtless now realised – or perhaps you already knew – the third traditional seduction technique, as used by Samuel Daniel, is blackmail. Expressed unpoetically, it says 'You'd better come across now, because pretty soon you'll be old and ugly and no-one will want you'. This kind of emotional blackmail is sometimes called *carpe diem* verse. (Literally, 'seize the day', or 'do it while you can'.) What are your feelings about it? Do you regard these veiled – or not so veiled – threats as a harmless game, or do you have more serious views about them? If you do happen to take a light-hearted attitude towards the seduction techniques of flattery, pleading and blackmail, how would you mark them out of ten for effectiveness?

Most A-Level students and other insightful people, we think, realise that, just like most of the things we do, our emotional and sexual behaviour is really cultural or conditioned rather than natural. Most of us (women and men) are still forced into gender roles which we find difficult to escape from. One of the effects of this is that there are, so far, very few poems of seduction written by women—because men are supposed to do the chasing. The reality is, no doubt, that seduction has always been a reciprocal business, but women have been forced to be more subtle and discreet about it. Anyone who has read or seen *Othello* soon comes to realise that it is Desdemona who seduced Othello, even though he, poor chap, thinks it was the other way about. Desdemona spent hours listening devotedly to Othello's lengthy accounts of his military campaigns (yawn) which, she says, are 'strange' and 'wondrous pitiful'. Here's part of Othello's story (as told to a group of men) of how *he* seduced *her*:

> She gave me for my pains a world of sighs;
> She swore i' faith 'twas strange, 'twas wondrous pitiful;
> She wished she had not heard it, yet she wish'd
> That heaven had made her such a man: she thanked me,
> And bade me, if I had a friend that lov'd her,
> I should but teach him how to tell my story;
> And that would woo her. Upon this hint I spake ...

William Shakespeare: Othello

Do you recognise the seduction techniques used by Desdemona? What do you think about the word – 'hint' – that Othello uses to describe them? What does this little extract tell you about Othello and his interpretation of what went on between himself and Desdemona?

On the whole, women poets who write about love and seduction do so with less pomp and bluster than most men. Here's a sad and moving piece by Christina Rossetti:

> Remember me when I am gone away,
> Gone far away into the silent land;
> When you can no more hold me by the hand,
> Nor I half turn to go yet turning stay.
> Remember me when no more day by day
> You tell of our future that you planned:
> Only remember me; you understand
> It will be late to counsel then or pray.
> Yet if you should forget me for a while
> And afterwards remember, do not grieve:
> For if the darkness and corruption leave
> Investige of the thoughts that once I had,
> Better by far you should forget and smile
> Than that you should remember and be sad.

Christina Rossetti

1 This poem is about love, rather than seduction (isn't it?), and the key word is, obviously, 'remember'. But how does this word change its significance in the sonnet's last six lines (the sestet)?

2 How would you describe the irony in line 6?

3 What do you think of the way that Rossetti depicts that great abstract called Death?

4 How would you describe the differences in tone between this sonnet and the three earlier sonnets, written by men, in this chapter?

5 In case our male readers are feeling a bit got at in this chapter, we would suggest that Christina Rossetti is not above a touch of blackmail herself; how could you argue a case against her?

Finally, another poem by a woman in love, but in a much more modern vein:

Message

Pick up the phone before it is too late
And dial my number. There's no time to spare –
Love is already turning into hate
And very soon I'll start to look elsewhere.

Good, old-fashioned men like you are rare –
You want to get to know me at a rate
That's guaranteed to drive me to despair.
Pick up the phone before it is too late.

Well, wouldn't it be nice to consummate
Our friendship while we've still got teeth and hair?
Just bear in mind that you are forty-eight
And dial my number. There's no time to spare.

Another kamikaze love affair?
No chance. This time I'll have to learn to wait
But one more day is more than I can bear –
Love is already turning into hate.

Of course, my friends say I exaggerate
And dramatize a lot. That may be fair
But it is no fun being in this state
And very soon I'll start to look elsewhere.

I know you like me but I wouldn't dare
Ring you again. Instead I'll concentrate
On sending thought-waves through the London air
And, if they reach you, please don't hesitate –
Pick up the phone.

Wendy Cope

1 What are the rather complicated attitudes of the speaker in this poem as regards the traditional rituals of 'seduction'?

2 How does Wendy Cope use and comment on some of the conventions of traditional 'poetry of seduction' (as used, for example, by Constable and Daniel)?

3 What do you think a 'kamikaze love affair' is?

4 What is the effect of all those short, blunt sentences and phrases?

5 What do you notice about the way rhyme is used in the poem? And why does the last line break the rules?

And to end with, wider questions: what are your personal views on our 'cultural norms' of sexual behaviour? Do you see them as useful rituals, as a way of initiating relationships, or do they seem to you to be repressive, male-oriented controls? Do you know of other societies or groups which arrange things differently, and do these alternatives (like, for example, chaperoning and arranged marriages) seem preferable? If our patterns of male-female behaviour were changed profoundly – if, for instance, it became the cultural norm for women to 'court' men – what difference might this make to the way that men dressed or spoke, and wrote about love? Do you find these things very difficult to imagine? If so, why?

21
Organised Violence

Sexnviolence

It is generally agreed (in this part of the world, anyway) that writers are free to discuss, depict and even provoke all sorts of human emotion: anger, joy, indignation, moral outrage, pity, religious fervour, delight, or whatever. In fact, we expect writers to deal in and with these things, and we praise them for doing it well. There are, however, two normal and universal human activities, highly emotional ones, about which there is wide disagreement. These are, of course, sex and violence. The passages in this chapter are about violence. (This may come as a disappointment to those of you more interested in the other thing.)

When these matters are discussed in the context of television, a strange thing tends to happen: the two different matters become a single entity called sexnviolence, and generally the debate is about how much sexnviolence there is and how much less there should be, and at what time of night lots of sexnviolence is all right. It is rare in such debates for sex and violence to be discussed separately;

one seldom hears Dame Whatsit or Sir Thingmejig saying they'd like more sex and less violence. What they want is less sexnviolence. It's worth asking yourself what the habitual pairing of these two things is doing to your perception of each one. (And why Dame Whatsit and Sir Thingmejig see them as being the same thing.) Where literature is concerned, the debate is less hot and the distinctions somewhat finer. The novel had its fig leaf removed as long ago as 1960, when, in an entertaining farce called The Lady Chatterley Trial, a third-rate romantic melodrama by D. H. Lawrence was acquitted of obscenity. These days, I find my grey-haired old mother calmly reading books by lady novelists in which there are lurid accounts of activities which I, as an adolescent, used to get slapped just for thinking about. However ... we were going to talk about violence.

There are, of course, plenty of best-selling writers who put oodles of violence in their blockbusters because, for some reason, it helps increase sales. The depiction of violence is more of a problem for what we call 'serious' writers, those writers who produce Literature. On the whole, serious writers are Against Violence. One of the problems that then arises is how do you write about violence in a way that is stimulating, but which does not stimulate the 'wrong' kind of response? How do you avoid, in other words, the 'pornography of violence'? You can't write an account of violence which is wrapped up in disapproving words, because then your reader will feel that he or she is being moralised at – and what's more, you will get between reader and book and jeopardise the reader's involvement with your material. Rather more subtle techniques are called for if you wish to moderate your reader's response in some way. These techniques are inevitably only the same techniques available to writers when they are dealing with any subject: diction, phrasing, characterisation, tone of voice, narrative position, and so on. And beyond all this, there is the real possibility that a writer can have only very imperfect control over the way readers respond.

The four pieces that you are about to read all deal with fairly large-scale acts of violence. They do not have much else in common. After each piece there are some textual questions; at the end there is a choice of exercises for you to tackle.

The first piece is, in a sense, the odd one out, in that it is a piece of direct reportage from a newspaper. It is hardly run-of-the-mill journalism, however. For several weeks during the spring of 1989, Peking was the centre of the world's attention. The huge expanse of Tiananmen Square was the site of a protracted and vast political demonstration, a student-led demand for greater freedom and democracy in China. It looked for just a while as though they might actually succeed. In the early hours of June 4th, however, the Chinese government finally lost its patience, or its nerve, or its mind, and sent in the troops. No-one knows, nor is likely ever to know, how many hundreds of people were killed. Michael Fathers, an English newspaper correspondent, got too close for comfort:

> It will go down in the annals of China's Communist Party as The Glorious Fourth of June when the army that was founded for the people turned on the unarmed citizens of Peking to destroy a peaceful student-led democracy movement.
> The killing around Tiananmen Square started soon after midnight. It was a different army from the unarmed one which had tried to enter the square on Friday night and failed. This one was told to kill, and the soldiers with their AK-47 automatic rifles and the armoured personnel

carriers with their machine guns opened fire indiscriminately, in the air, directly at the huge crowds, at small groups, everywhere.

Lined up in rows across The Avenue of Eternal Peace, they advanced slowly, shooting all the while, then they would halt and kneel and fire directly into the crowd. They did the same at the other end of the square by Zhengyang Gate. When both ends of the square were cleared, they switched off the lights and encircled the thousands of students who had crowded together on the Revolutionary Heroes' Monument. Dawn broke and riot police moved in with truncheons. Everyone expected the army. But no one expected such ferocity, such armour, such numbers. There were more than 100,000 soldiers.

I was at the southern end of the square at midnight, walking along the main boulevard to see the student barricades. Suddenly, out of the night, two APCs appeared from a side street and roared down the boulevard, one behind the other, smashing through the barriers. They were followed by about 3,000 soldiers who positioned themselves near the square. One APC stalled and was set on fire by the mob. I kept walking towards a barricade of buses a mile away, where four lorries with troops and two earth-moving vehicles were trapped on either side by buses and people. Then flares and tracer bullets shone from behind me and the cracks of automatic gunfire could be heard. The troops were advancing on the square. My colleague, Andrew Higgins, was behind at Qianmen Gate, the front entrance to the square. He said the troops surged past the Roast Duck restaurant and were met with a hail of bricks and stones before they opened fire. Everyone fled but then regrouped.

To the north, more gunfire could be heard. I moved up a side street heading for the Avenue of Eternal Peace, where tanks had broken through a barricade of burning buses. It was 1.30 a.m. and the start of a huge troop advance to the square. About 50 Chinese and I hid at the entrance to a tiny lane and watched them. Other people were on the roofs of the houses. The armour was followed by troop trucks, scores of lorries, interspersed with petrol tankers, lorries with mesh trailers for prisoners and some stores.

Having sucessfully walked past the soldiers as they moved to the square in the south, I decided to leave the lane and follow this other army to Tiananmen, about half a mile away. The Avenue of Eternal Peace was deserted. Cracks of gunfire mingled with explosions from two burning buses behind me. Further towards the square, on the northern side of the avenue, was New China Gate, the entrance to Zhongnanhai, the compound of China's Communist Party leaders beside the Forbidden City.

I looked behind as I walked along the pavement on the opposite side. A squad of army goons, waving pistols, electric cattle prods and batons were running towards me. They jumped me, screamed at me, pointed a pistol at my head, beat me about the legs with their batons and dragged me across to New China Gate. Several soldiers broke ranks and ran to me, punching me, kicking me with karate leaps in the back, thighs and chest. There was pure hatred in their eyes.

They pushed me down into a kneeling position and had another go at me, whacking me across the back with their rods and kicking, always kicking, until I fell over. They pulled off my spectacles and crushed them into the ground. They screamed at me. Then they took me behind a stone lion guarding the gate. Their first thought was that I was an American. One man who spoke some English realised I wasn't. They put two guards beside me.

If this is the People's Army, God spare China. They behaved like the Red Guards, with a systematic and frenzied brutality. They were the very institution that was once called out to protect China from the Red Guard exesses. Now they are killing civilians.

The smooth face of the Chinese Communist establishment appeared two hours later, dressed in cream flannels and a pastel T-shirt, the very image of "moderation" that the Foreign Office has come to believe is the new China and whom it can trust over Hong Kong. 'You have committed an unfriendly act,' he said. I thought that was a bit much. 'You fell over, didn't you? That's why you have that bruise on your arm.' I also had bootmarks, and bloodstains on my shirt from a baton blow. My right knee was swollen, my hips were aching, my trousers were ripped. He confiscated my notebook and gave me a receipt and a written pass to get beyond the army lines into a side street.

All the while the lorries kept rumbling forward, stopping from time to time until the citizens of Peking were pushed back from the northern end of the square by the entrance to the Forbidden City. Andrew Higgins was by now crawling in the mud in front of the vermillion-painted grandstands beside Mao's portrait at the Gate of Heavenly Peace, as bullets whizzed over his head. At first, he said, there was some panic among the young soldiers when they saw the huge crowd. But they were ordered to open fire. An APC was set alight by a youth who climbed on to it when it stopped. The crew were pulled out and beaten, but students intervened and rescued them.

The army had nabbed me at 2 a.m. By 4 a.m. when they let me go, the gunfire could still be heard from the square. At one stage some students came from the side streets, shouting 'Go home, go home,' to stalled lorries outside the leadership compound. They were scattered by militiamen with clubs like axe-handles, which cracked a few skulls. It was probably the one occasion during the night when they did not use guns.

Along the tree-lined streets beside the Forbidden City, groups of people were talking softly, scared but curious. They treated me as a bit of a hero when they saw my bruises and carried me on the backs of their bicycles for about a mile to the rear entrance of the Peking Hotel, on the other end of the square. Soon after I arrived, about 10 tanks and 20 APCs rumbled past the hotel. About half an hour later some of the armour returned again from the square, and in a continuing moving circle, they opened fire all around. Two buses were smouldering outside the hotel.

It was a battlefield. It was a lesson in brute power. I blubbed when I got back to my hotel near midday. I couldn't stop. Perhaps it was shock, or maybe it was because of the carnage, I was weeping for the people of Peking. I cannot see how they are ever likely to trust their leaders again.

Michael Fathers, The Independent, June 5th 1989

1 Since this article was being printed within twenty-four hours of the events it describes, it would seem that Michael Fathers must have written it with the blood still on his shirt and the tears still in his eyes. That being so, do you think this piece lacks detachment and objectivity? Are there signs that in spite of his experiences, Fathers is exercising a certain degree of literary skill in order to convey these events with vividness?

2 Are the previous questions irrelevant or even callous? If so, why? And if not, why not?

3 Newspaper articles are almost by definition ephemeral; it is likely that for you reading this now the events that took place in Peking in 1989 are just a distant memory, and maybe not even that. If Michael Fathers were to write the above piece into a novel or a memoir, how do you think he might do it differently, with the benefit of hindsight and detachment? Or would hindsight and detachment be a benefit? Do you think this piece *would* be improved by being written from a 'cooler' point of view?

Soldiers Plundering a Village

Down the mud road, between tall bending trees,
Men thickly move, then fan out one by one
Into the foreground. Far left, a soldier tries
Bashing a tame duck's head in with a stick,
While on a log his smeared companion
Sits idly by a heap of casual loot –
Jugs splashing over, snatched-up joints of meat.

Dead centre, a third man has spiked a fourth –
An evident civilian, with one boot
Half off, in flight, face white, lungs short of breath.
Out of a barn another soldier comes,
Gun at the ready, finding at his feet
One more old yokel, gone half mad with fear,
Tripped in his path, wild legs up in the air.

Roofs smashed, smoke rising, distant glow of fire,
A woman's thighs splayed open after rape
And lying there still: charred flecks caught in the air,
And caught for ever by a man from Antwerp
Whose style was 'crudely narrative', though 'robust',
According to this scholar, who never knew
What Pieter Snayers saw in 1632.

Anthony Thwaite

1 Were you surprised to discover at the end of the poem that it is describing a painting by Pieter Snayers? What phrases earlier in the poem might have been clues?

2 What can you say about the pace of this poem? Do you find differences in the kind of violence and the way violence is described in each stanza?

3 Pick out two lines in which you think Thwaite uses rhythm effectively, and comment briefly on what these rhythms achieve.

4 What unspoken comments does the poem make about the 'scholar' and his critical comments on the painting in the last stanza?

The next extract is from a novel. It is 1857, and the British Residency at Krishnapur is at the sharp end of the Indian Mutiny. The British, under the command of the senior official, the Collector, have been besieged for many weeks, and are on their last legs. They are starving, diseased, and almost out of ammunition. The rebelling Indian forces, the sepoys, are mounting what must be their final attack.

'Get under cover!' yelled the Collector from the roof, not that anyone could possibly hear him. He and Ford had a cannon on the roof loaded with everything that they had been able to lay their hands on: stones, penknives, pieces of lightning-conductor, chains, nails, the embossed silver cutlery from the dining-room, and even some ivory false teeth, picked up by Ford who had seen them gleaming in the undergrowth; but the greater part of the improvised canister was filled with fragments of marble chipped from The Spirit of Science Conquers Ignorance and Prejudice. Naturally they were anxious to fire this destructive load before it was too late; the angle of the chase was depressed to such an extent that they were afraid that in spite of the wadding the contents of their canister might dribble out ... already a fountain of glass marbles commandeered from the children had cascaded about the ears of the defenders. By this time the last of the garrison had fought their way back into the buildings and were trying to defend doors and windows against a swarm of sepoys. The Collector nodded to Ford who was standing by with the portfire. Ford touched it to the vent. There was a flash and a deep roar, followed by utter silence ... a silence so profound that the Collector was convinced he could hear two parakeets quarrelling in a tamarind fifty yards away. He peered over the parapet. Below, nothing was moving, but there appeared to be a carpet of dead bodies. But then he realised that many of these bodies were indeed moving, but not very much. A sepoy here was trying to remove a silver fork from one of his lungs, another had received a piece of lightning-conductor in his kidneys. A sepoy with a green turban had had his spine shattered by The Spirit of Science; others had been struck down by teaspoons, by fish-knives, by marbles; an unfortunate subadar had been plucked from this world by the silver sugar-tongs embedded in his brain. A heart-breaking wail now rose from those who had not been killed outright.

'How terrible!' said the Collector to Ford. 'I mean, I had no idea that anything like that would happen.'

But Ford's only reply was to clutch his ribs and stagger towards the parapet. He had toppled over before the Collector had time to catch his heels.

But already a fresh wave of sepoys was pouring over the ramparts and bounding forward to the attack over that rubbery carpet of bodies. The Collector knew it was time he hurried downstairs ...

J. G. Farrell: The Siege of Krishnapur

1 How would you describe the tone of this passage, and what contribution to its overall effect do the following words make:

'commandeered from the children' (end of first paragraph)

'plucked from this world by the silver sugar-tongs embedded in his brain' (second paragraph)

'rubbery carpet' (last paragraph)?

2 Why does Farrell itemise the contents of the ammunition canister of the cannon? What do you think is the significance of the name of the statue that has been broken up for ammunition?

Now for some nasty business from Latin America:

What you have heard is true. I was in his house. His wife carried a tray of coffee and sugar. His daughter filed her nails, his son went out for the night. There were daily papers, pet dogs, a pistol on the cushion beside him. The moon swung bare on its black cord over the house. On the television was a cop show. It was in English. Broken bottles were embedded in the walls around the house to scoop the kneecaps from a man's legs or cut his hands to lace. On the windows there were gratings like those in liquor stores. We had dinner, rack of lamb, good wine, a gold bell was on the table for calling the maid. The maid brought green mangoes, salt, a type of bread. I was asked how I enjoyed the country. There was a brief commercial in Spanish. His wife took everything away. There was some talk then about how difficult it had become to govern. The parrot said hello on the terrace. The colonel told it to shut up, and pushed himself from the table. My friend said to me with his eyes: say nothing. The colonel returned with a sack used to bring groceries home. He spilled many human ears on the table. They were like dried peach halves. There is no other way to say this. He took one of them in his hands, shook it in our faces, dropped it into a water glass. It came alive there. I am tired of fooling around, he said. As for the rights of anyone, tell your people they can go f— themselves. He swept the ears to the floor with his arm and held the last of his wine in the air. Something for your poetry, no? he said. Some of the ears on the floor caught this scrap of his voice. Some of the ears were pressed to the ground.

Carolyn Forché: The Colonel

1 Why, do you think, does Carolyn Forché use so many short, simple sentences to recount this incident?

2 This piece is taken from an anthology of poetry. Does this puzzle you at all? After all, it is written in prose, apparently. What is there about the piece that makes it 'poetic'?

3 'Something for your poetry, no?' says the colonel – rightly, it would seem. But what makes him say this? And how do you interpret the last two sentences, which follow his remark?

4 Which of the four pieces you have just read is, in your opinion, the most violent, and why?

Now try one of these exercises:

1 Write two short prose pieces which describe a violent incident – an incident which you have witnessed, or read about, or heard about, or one that is entirely imaginary. Use a different narrative method for each one. For instance, write one from the first person point of view of someone involved, the other from the point of view of omniscient third person narrator. (If you're feeling a bit vague about narrative positions, check Chapter 10 again.) When you have written the two pieces, ask yourself which was the easier to do, and what different demands the different narrative methods made upon you as a writer.

2 Take any two of the above four pieces and compare them in terms of

a) their narrative point of view and technique

b) the 'tone of voice' and what this tells you about the writer's attitude towards what he or she is describing

c) the kind of response you think the writer is seeking from the reader.

Make specific references to the texts when you do this, and if you think that one piece is in some way better than the other, say why.

3 Write a discursive essay about what you consider to be the problems inherent in writing about violence and the demands the subject makes upon the writer. You might discuss the technical and the moral issues involved. Use the four pieces in this chapter to discuss and compare possible approaches to the subject.

22

The Year in Brief

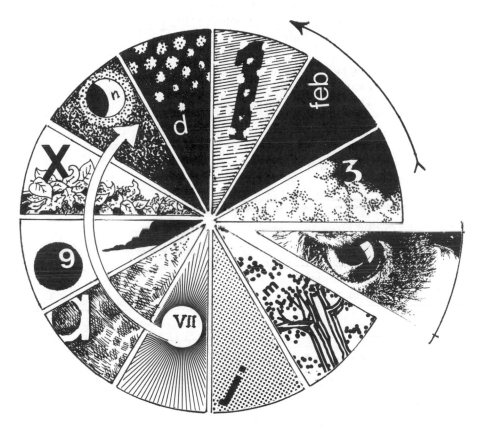

This exercise involves reading just one poem. When you have read it, see if you can work out the two formal devices it employs. (The answers involve counting.) The poem is by Patricia Beer.

January to December

The warm cows have gone
From the fields where grass stands up
Dead-alive like steel.

Unexpected sun
Probes the house as if someone
Had left the lights on.

Novel no longer
Snowdrops melt in the hedge, drain
Away into spring.

The heron shining
Works his way up the bright air
Above the river.

Earth dries. The sow basks
Flat out with her blue-black young,
Ears over their eyes.

The early lambs, still
Fleecy, look bulkier now
Than their mothers.

In this valley full
Of birdsong, the gap closes
Behind the cuckoo.

Fields of barley glimpsed
Through trees shine out like golden
Windows in winter.

Though nothing has changed –
The sun is even hotter –
Death is in the air.

Long shadows herald
Or dog every walker
In the cut-back lanes.

A crop of mist grows
Softly in the valley, lolls
Over the strawstacks.

Meadows filmed across
With rain stare up at winter
Hardening in the hills.

Patricia Beer

Patricia Beer's subject here is an immense one – the changes in a rural landscape throughout an entire year. It's a subject that could take up a weighty tome by a naturalist, or a glossy coffee-table book by a photographer. Beer has set herself a challenge, and she has met it in a way that might seem, at first glance, perverse – she has imposed on herself very strict formal constraints. She allows herself only one stanza for each month, and each stanza has only three short lines. Each of these stanzas is itself rigorously disciplined. Each has a total of only seventeen syllables: five in the first line, seven in the second, and five in the third. These 'stanzas' are, in fact, versions of the traditional Japanese haiku, which is built in this 5-7-5 syllable pattern. In one other respect, Patricia Beer has conformed to the haiku tradition: the haiku should provide a glimpse of the world as seen at a certain time of year.

If you took on board the gist of the things we discussed and quoted in the chapters on form (Chapters 13 to 16), you will have realised that it was misleading of us to have said just now that Patricia Beer has 'imposed formal constraints' upon her subject and herself. The haiku form is not, as far as this poem is concerned, a restrictive device, but an *enabling* one: it is the means by which the poet brings a large and potentially unwieldy subject under control. It is 'a means of getting a thing said'. In practical terms, limiting yourself to a repeating pattern of seventeen syllables means that you can ruthlessly weed out words and phrases and images which are non-essential, thus working towards a single image which, for you, expresses the essence of a place at a particular time. In a moment, we will suggest ways in which you could try this yourself; before that, try answering these questions about Patricia Beer's poem:

1 How does she use variations in sentence structure and punctuation to find flexibility within the haiku form? (Give examples.)

2 Take a close look at any three of Beer's metaphors. How does she use them to concentrate meaning into the haiku's small space?

3 Do you think that some months come across more concretely or vividly than others? Which, and why?

4 The idea that a year begins on the first day of January and ends on the last day of December is a very artificial and local one; the Jews and the Chinese and the Inland Revenue, for instances, do not see it that way. You may think of the year as beginning with your birthday, rather than with a hangover on New Year's Day. Years are cycles, in other words, and where these cycles begin and end (*if* they 'begin' and 'end') is a fairly subjective matter. Do you think that Patricia Beer's poem allows or actually encourages such a cyclical reading? How?

Here's an exercise for your inventiveness. Pick a subject which is dauntingly huge as a subject for a short poem. You can, if you wish, pinch Beer's – the seasonal changes in your own locality. Other suggestions: the last five years of your life; the alleged evolution of humankind from a form of aquatic jelly into the splendid creatures we now are; all the families that live in your street; the animals in the zoo. Now choose a tight poetic form in which to write about your subject. You could try haiku, since you have twelve fine examples in front of you. Or you could try an English form, such as the rhyming pentameter couplet (ten syllables per line – see page 148) or alliterative, four-beat stress verse (see page 151), or you could adopt a reorganised form of the haiku in which the syllables are arranged 5-5-7; or, if you are on good form, you could invent one of your own. Write as many of these miniature stanzas as you feel are necessary for your whole poem to feel 'finished', or go on writing until you feel in danger of going insane. Your aim should be to produce concrete, vivid and self-sufficient little images in a very economical way.

23
The Back Room

In the previous exercise chapter, Patricia Beer – and you too, perhaps – took on a big subject. In this chapter, a poet called Albert Goldbarth is even more ambitious, if the title of his poem is anything to go by.

A History of Civilization

In the dating bar, the potted ferns lean down
conspiratorially, little spore-studded
elopement ladders. The two top buttons
of every silk blouse have already half-undone all
introduction. Slices of smile, slices of sweet brie,
dark and its many white wedges. In back

of the bar, the last one-family grocer's is necklaced
over and over: strings of leeks, greek olives, sardines.
The scoops stand at attention in the millet barrel,
the cordovan sheen of the coffee barrel, the kidney beans.
And a woman whose pride is a clean linen apron polishes
a register as intricate as a Sicilian shrine. In back

of the grocery, dozing and waking in fitful starts
by the guttering hearth, a ring of somber-gabardined grandpas
plays dominoes. Their stubble picks up the flicker like filaments
still waiting for the bulb or the phone to be invented. Even their
coughs, their phlegms, are in an older language. They move the simple
pieces of matching numbers. In back

of the back room, in the unlit lengths of storage, it's
that season: a cat eyes a cat. The sacks and baskets
are sprayed with the sign of a cat's having eyed a cat, and
everything to do with rut and estrus comes down to a few
sure moves. The dust motes drift, the continents.
In the fern bar a hand tries a knee, as if unplanned.

Albert Goldbarth

Notes
'cordovan' means 'like Spanish leather'
'estrus' means season – the kind that dogs and cats etc. can be 'in'

In *January to December*, you may recall, Patricia Beer used the tight formal discipline of the haiku to bring a potentially unmanageable subject under control. Albert Goldbarth's method seems to be to use metaphor for this purpose. But then, how big *is* Goldbarth's subject? Is it really a 'history of civilization'? In what sense is it? Is his title ironic, in a way that Patricia Beer's is not?

Write a detailed study of *The History of Civilization*. In doing so, pay particular (but not exclusive) attention to the following:

a) the overall metaphorical structure of the poem

b) the way that other metaphors work within this general design

c) the way that each stanza comments on and relates to the other stanzas

d) Goldbarth's use of ambiguity and irony.

24
Damn Yankees

British politicians are fond of talking about the 'Special Relationship' which is supposed to exist between Britain and the United States. To some extent, this idea springs from two quite false assumptions which we British, in particular, like to cling to: that Americans are of British descent, and that both countries speak the same language. Historically speaking, the Special Relationship has been characterised by mutual distrust, disdain and hostility. The traditional British (English, especially) view of Americans is that they are crude, materialistic and philistine; they in turn have regarded us as decadent, aloof and reactionary. In defiance of all knowledge and experience, these outrageous generalisations still have considerable power. An IBM sales rep, zooming down the M4 in his Ford Granada, a lunchtime cheeseburger playing hell with his digestion and his favourite Soul tape playing on the stereo, will somehow yet contrive to feel culturally superior to the average 'Yank'. Equally curious is the fact that each year Americans with names like Schuster, da Costa, Zimmerman and O'Hagan visit England and queue to see Shakespeare's birthplace, or stand in a crowd to catch a glimpse of some Royal or other; and they do so with a sense of having a cultural affinity with these things.

The purpose of this little preamble to the four passages that follow has to do (again) with the nature of your response to the texts. If you have no prejudices of any sort towards America and American culture (and these prejudices need not, of course, be hostile) then you are a very rare creature indeed. Almost all of us have been subjected – courtesy of television and the movies – to a great deal of vicarious experience of American life. This means that your response to any piece of writing about the USA is almost certain to be more 'contaminated' than your respose to a piece about, let's say, Patagonia or Chad. For this reason, we would like you to monitor your reactions to the passages that follow. Ask yourself to what extent your appreciation (that is, your understanding and enjoyment) of them depends upon their appeal to those ideas and feelings about America which you already have.

Passage A comes from a book published in 1832. Passage B is from a book published in 1843. (They are therefore close in terms of time and place to the settings of cinema Westerns.) Extracts C and D are both from books which were published in the 1980s. A and C are taken from autobiographical accounts of travels in America, B and D are from novels. All four pieces are by English writers; they are all, in their different ways, critical of aspects of American life; they all employ forms of irony. (If ages have elapsed since you read Chapter 19, we suggest you run through it quickly again now, looking out for words in heavy type.) We have appended a couple of textual questions to each extract, and at the end of the selection you will find a couple of exercises which involve broadening out some of the issues which these passages raise.

A   One of these families consisted of a young man, his wife, two
      children, a female slave, and two young lads, slaves also. The farm
      belonged to the wife and, I was told, consisted of about three hundred
      acres of indifferent land, but all cleared. The house was built of wood,
      and looked as if the three slaves might have overturned it, had they
      pushed hard against the gable end. It contained one room, of about
      twelve feet square, and another adjoining it, hardly larger than a closet:
      this second chamber was the lodging-room of the white part of the
      family. Above these rooms was a loft, without windows, where, I was
      told, the 'staying company' who visited them were lodged. Near this
      mansion was a 'shanty', a black hole, without any window, which served
      as a kitchen and all other offices, and also the lodging of the blacks.
         We were invited to take tea with this family, and readily consented
      to do so. The furniture of the room was one heavy huge table, and about
      six wooden chairs. When we arrived, the lady was in rather a dusky
      dishabille, but she vehemently urged us to be seated, and then retired
      into the closet-chamber above mentioned, whence she continued to
      address to us from behind the door all kinds of 'genteel country visiting
      talk', and at length emerged upon us in a smart new dress.
         Her female slave set out the great table, and placed upon it cups of
      the very coarsest blue ware, a little brown sugar in one, and a tiny drop
      of milk in another; no butter, though the lady assured us she had a
      'deary' and two cows. Instead of butter, she 'hoped we would fix a little

relish with our crackers'; in ancient English, eat salt meat and dry biscuits. Such was the fare, and for guests that certainly were intended to be honoured.

I could not help recalling the delicious repasts which I remembered to have enjoyed at little dairy farms in England, not possessed, but rented, and at high rents too; where the clean, fresh coloured, bustling mistress herself skimmed the delicious cream, herself spread the yellow butter on the delightful brown loaf, and placed her curds, and her junket, and all the delicate treasures of her dairy before us, and then, with hospitable pride, placed herself at her board, and added the more delicate 'relish' of good tea and good cream. I remembered all this, and did not think the difference atoned for by the dignity of having my cup handed to me by a slave.

The lady I now visited, however, greatly surpassed my quondam friends in the refinement of her conversation. She ambled through the whole time the visit lasted, in a sort of elegantly mincing familiar style of gossip, which, I think, she was imitating from some novel; for I was told that she was a great novel reader, and left all household occupations to be performed by her slaves. To say she addressed us in a tone of equality will give no adequate idea of her manner; I am persuaded that no misgiving on the subject ever entered her head. She told us that their estate was her divi-dend of her father's property. She had married a first cousin, who was as fine a gentleman as she was a lady, and as idle, preferring hunting (as they call shooting) to any other occupation. The consequence was that but a very small portion of the divi-dend was cultivated, and their poverty was extreme. The slaves, particularly the lads, were considerably more than half-naked; but the air of dignity with which, in the midst of all this misery, the lanky lady said to one of the young negroes 'Attend to your young master, Lycurgus' must have been heard to be conceived in the full extent of its mock heroic.

Mrs Frances (Fanny) Trollope: Domestic Manners of the Americans

1 Why, do you think, does Mrs Trollope describe the building and its contents in so much detail?

2 What strikes you about the way that Mrs Trollope 'translates' and comments upon American speech?

3 What do you learn about the writer from the sentence 'To say she addressed us in a tone of equality will give no adequate idea of the matter; I am persuaded that no misgiving on the subject ever entered her head'?

B   Martin Chuzzlewit and his faithful companion Mark Tapley have travelled to America in search of fortune. They have been conned into buying a plot of land in 'New Eden', which turns out to be a desolate and disease-ridden swamp. With Martin half-dead of fever, Mark is visited by Mr Hannibal Chollop, an archetypal New American Man.

Mr Chollop was, of course, one of the most remarkable men in the country; but he really was a notorious person besides. He was usually described by his friends, in the South and West, as 'a splendid sample of our na-tive raw material, sir,' and was much esteemed for his devotion to rational Liberty; for the better propagation whereof he usually carried a brace of revolving-pistols in his coat pocket, with seven barrels a-piece. He also carried, amongst other trinkets, a sword-stick, which he called his 'Tickler'; and a great knife, which (for he was a man of a pleasant turn of humour) he called 'Ripper', in allusion to its usefulness as a means of ventilating the stomach of any adverary in a close contest. He had used these weapons with distinguished effort in several instances, all duly chronicled in the newspapers; and was greatly beloved for the gallant manner in which he had 'jobbed out' the eye of one gentleman, as he was in the act of knocking at his own street door.

Mr Chollop was a man of roving disposition; and, in any less advanced community, might have been mistaken for a violent vagabond. But his fine qualities being understood and appreciated in those regions where his lot was cast, and where he had many kindred spirits to consort with, he may be regarded as having been born under a fortunate star, which is not always the case with a man so much before the age in which he lives. Preferring, with a view to the gratification of his tickling and ripping fancies, to dwell upon the outskirts of society, and in the more remote towns and cities, he was in the habit of emigrating from place to place, and establishing in each some business – usually a newspaper – which he presently sold: for the most part closing the bargain by challenging, stabbing, pistolling, or gouging the new editor before he had quite taken possession of the property.

He had come to Eden on a speculation of this kind, but had abandoned it, and was about to leave. He always introduced himself to strangers as a worshipper of Freedom; was the consistent advocate of Lynch law, and slavery; and invariably recommended, both in print and speech, the 'tarring and feathering' of any unpopular person who differed from himself. He called this 'planting the standard of civilisation in the wilder gardens of My country'.

There is little doubt that Chollop would have planted this standard in Eden at Mark's expense, in return for his plainness of speech (for the genuine freedom is dumb, save when she vaunts herself), but for the utter desolation and decay prevailing in the settlement, and his own approaching departure from it. As it was, he contented himself with showing Mark one of the revolving-pistols, and asking him what he thought of that weapon.

'It ain't long since I shot a man down with that, sir, in the State of Illinoy,' observed Chollop.

'Did you, indeed!' said Mark, without the smallest agitation. 'Very free of you. And very independent!'

'I shot him down, sir,' pursued Chollop, 'for asserting in the Spartan Portico, a tri-weekly journal, that the ancient Athenians went a-head of the present Locofoco Ticket.'

'And what is that?' asked Mark.

'Europian not to know,' said Chollop, smoking placidly. 'Europian quite!'

Charles Dickens: Martin Chuzzlewit

1   In what terms would you describe Dickens' use of irony in this passage? Give three specific examples and discuss them.

2   What do the words 'rational' and 'liberty' mean to you? How do your ideas about these concepts compare with Hannibal Chollop's?

C   With the sole exception of Olen's ten-gallon affair, everyone in our crowd was wearing a plastic forage-cap with a long shovel-brim. The hats gave the cavalcade a vaguely military air, as if we were off to sack a city. The fronts of the hats were decorated with insignia and slogans. Oh Boy! Oh Beef! advertised a kind of cake which cows ate. Others peddled farm machinery, Holsum Bread, chemical fertilisers, pesticides, corn oil, cement and root beer. Under these corporation colours, the owners of the hats looked queerly like feudal retainers riding round wearing the arms of their barons. A few self-conscious individualists wore personalised beanies announcing "I'm from the boondocks" and "You can kiss my ... " followed by a picture of an ass in a straw bonnet. Butch's beanie said "John Deere". I took this for his own name, and only gradually noticed that several hundred men at the fair were also called John Deere, which turned out to be a famous brand of agricultural tractor.

The state fair sprawled across a hillside and a valley, and at first glance it did indeed look like a city under occupation by an army of rampaging Goths. I'd never seen so many enormous people assembled in one place. These farming families from Minnesota and Wisconsin were the descendants of hungry immigrants from Germany and Scandinavia. Their ancestors must have been lean and anxious men with the famine of Europe bitten into their faces. Generation by generation, their families had eaten themselves into Americans. Now they all had the same figure: same broad bottom, same buddha belly, same neckless join between turkey-wattle chin and sperm whale torso. The women had poured themselves into pink elasticated pantsuits: the men swelled against every seam and button of their plaid shirts and dacron slacks. Beneath the brims of the forage-caps, their food projected from their mouths. Foot-long hot dogs. Bratwurst sausages, dripping with hot grease. Hamburgers. Pizzas. Scoops of psychedelic ice cream. Wieners-dun-in-buns.

Stumbling, half-suffocated, through this abundance of food and flesh, I felt like a brittle matchstick-man. Everytime I tried to turn my head I found someone else's hot dog, bloody with catsup, sticking into my own mouth.

On either side of us the voices of the freak-show barkers quacked through the loudspeakers.

"Ronny and Donny. The only living Siamese twins on exhibit in the

world today. Now grown men, Ronny and Donny are joined at the
breastbone and the abdomen, facing each other for every second of their
lives."

"We carry the most deadly and dangerous of any in the world. Don't
miss it. All alive!"

"Can you imagine being permanently fastened to another person for
your entire life?"

"You see the deadly Monocle Cobra from Asia, the Chinese Cobra and
the Black-Necked Spitting Cobra. All alive."

"Ronny and Donny, the Siamese twins, are fascinating to see,
interesting to visit, and completely unforgettable. The Siamese twins
are alive, real and living."

"You'll see the giant, one hundred pound pythons. They're alive, and
they're inside. Don't miss it. Everything's alive."

"You will remember your visit with the Siamese twins for the rest of
your life – "

Crushed between the bust of the woman behind and the immense
behind of the man in front, I did not find it hard to imagine what it
might be like to be Ronny or Donny. There was no chance of visiting
with them, though. As the sluggish current of the crowd passed them
by, I was carried with it, deep into the heart of the state fair. I was
going down fast. The air I was breathing wasn't air: it was a compound
of smells: of meat, sweat, popcorn, cooking fat and passed gas.
Wriggling and butting my way out of the crowd, I found myself in the
sudden blessed cool of a vaulted cathedral full of cows. They stood
silently in their stalls with the resigned eyes of long-term mental
patients. The straw with which the stadium was carpeted gave the
whole place a ceremonious quiet. Grave men, whom I took for bulk
buyers from the burger industry, padded from stall to stall. The cattle
stared back at them with profound incuriosity. I wondered what they
made of the smell of charred beef. Soon they'd be minced, ground up
with cereal and soybeans, and turned into Whoppers or Kingburgers.
For now, though, the animals had a lugubrious dignity which put the
people at the fair to shame. They were the real heroes of the day.
Washed sleek as seals, they were the scions of the finest stock of
Minnesota, aristocrats in their world. They looked temperamentally
unsuited to the garish democracy of the fast food business.

Jonathan Raban: Old Glory

1 Can you identify particular sentences or phrases which seem to you to
   convey especially well the grotesque or surreal nature of this State Fair?

2 What contribution to the overall effect of the passage is made by the
   shouts of the sideshow barkers?

3 Raban doesn't seem to be making any overt political comments here, but
   do you think he is making covert, ironic ones? (Remember that he is an
   Englishman at an American event.) What do you make of the use of the
   word 'democracy' in the last sentence?

D   Henderson Dores, an English expert on Impressionist paintings, is on a business trip to Georgia, in the Southern States. Here he is checking in at the Monopark 5000 hotel in Atlanta.

He found himself in a tall brilliant lobby. Thick wands of sunlight shone through vast overhead windows onto a marble floor. There appeared to be numerous entrances. The one through which he had emerged was clearly not the most significant. Various doormen and bellhops stood around in stylised cavalry uniforms: boots, hats, gold epaulettes, even dinky sabres at their belts. At the rear of the lobby was what appeared to be a dense wood of twenty-foot high trees. In front of this forest was a long reception desk. This Henderson approached with due reverence and awe. The experience was, he thought, akin to appearing at Heaven's gate with the sin-virtue equation still in balance.

'Dores,' he said to the tanned cavalryman. 'D,O,R,E,S. I have a reservation.'

'Good afternoon, sir,' he said. 'Welcome to Monopark 5000.' He tapped out the name on a computer keyboard. There was a whirring and clicking and the machine fed out a piece of plastic with holes punched in it.

'What's this?' Henderson asked. 'A credit card?'

'Your key, sir. Need some help with your case?' The smile never budged.

'No thanks. I can manage.'

'You are in suite 35J. Follow this path,' he gestured at an opening in the forest wall, 'go through the atrium and take the scenic elevator to the thirty-fifth floor. Enjoy your stay in Monopark 5000.'

'Right.' Henderson picked up his bag and looked dubiously at the path, which was signposted 'To the atrium'. He felt like an explorer leaving base camp. 'Goodbye,' he said to the man and set off.

He had imagined that the trees were merely a decorative screen but he was wrong. He found himself in a copse, a grove, a veritable spinney of weeping figs, silver birches and stands of bamboo. A soft greenish light filtered down from above, xylophonic music burbled from hidden speakers. Other paths bifurcated from his. 'Convention reservation' he saw, 'To the Indian village' and 'Swimming Creek'. These signs were deliberately 'olde west': chunks of varnished wood with the message burnt on with a branding iron. The frontier theme was enhanced by the sudden appearance from behind a tree of a waitress in fringed buckskin waistcoat and miniskirt. Henderson gave a shrug of alarm. There were stripes of warpaint on her cheeks and forehead.

'Cocktails, sir?' she asked. 'At the Indian village.'

'What? Oh, no. I'm looking for the atrium.'

'Keep right on to the end of this path.' She slipped away into the trees. He followed her instructions and broke out into a towering atrium some twelve or fourteen stories high. Before him stretched a lake, blocking his way, some thirty yards across, dotted with islands furnished with seats and sprouting plants. Over on the left of the far bank was a cluster of wigwams which on closer inspection turned out to be a large restaurant and bar area. On the balconied far wall, a dozen scenic elevators rose up and down, some of them disappearing into holes in the roof like silent glass scarabs.

Henderson let out a spontaneous gasp of surprise. He had heard of this new breed of American hotel: the hotel as wonderland, as secular cathedral, as theme park – but his imagination had been deficient. Plants grew everywhere, fountains splashed, the light was pale, neutral and shadow-free.

A cowboy wandered over and handed him a wooden paddle.

'Good God, what's this for?'

'For the canoe, sir.'

Henderson looked to his right. Sure enough, a dozen canoes were tethered to the concrete bank.

'Do you mean I've got to paddle my way across to the elevators?'

'I can do it for you, sir, but a lot of our guests like to make their own way.'

He saw an intrepid couple set off, little shrieks of delight coming from the wife.

'Oh. Right.'

The cowboy let him down to a canoe, deposited his bag in the bow and helped him in. Henderson settled down.

'Listen are you sure these things are stable? Perhaps you'd better – '

The cowboy pushed him off. 'Enjoy your stay at Monopark 5000, sir.'

William Boyd: Stars and Bars

1 What is the effect of the phrases

'thick wands of sunlight'

'dinky sabres'

'fed out'

'silent glass scarabs?'

2 Do you think that the hotel Monopark 5000 is meant to be metaphorical or even symbolic in some way? Of what? And what makes you think so? What does Henderson Dores find so disturbing about it, and the people in it?

Now try one of these two exercises:

1 Write an essay which discusses the narrative methods of these four pieces, and in doing so, try to deal with these questions:

What is the narrative position in each passage? What advantages does the narrative position give the writer in each case? (A quick re-read of Chapter 10 might help you here.)

Are the writers being ironical? If so, what are they saying 'without saying it'? What relationship, what shared point of view, is each writer assuming exists between himself or herself and the reader?

What conventional attitudes towards Americans is the writer exploiting? To what extent are they your attitudes? Is the writer trying to change or manipulate your attitudes, do you think?

Which piece did you like best, and why?

2 Compare one of the travelogue excerpts (A or C) with one of the novel extracts (B or D). In the process, try answering these questions:

Is there a distinct difference, in terms of style and content, between the two? If we had not said that one was autobiographical and the other was fiction, would you have been able to tell? How?

Do you get a distinct impression of the personality of the Englishwoman or Englishman in each piece? How would you describe him or her? What attitude towards his or her material is conveyed by the tone of voice? Is it an attitude you instinctively sympathise with? If so, why, and if not, why not?

Each piece describes individuals and/or places; but does the writer somehow expand these local observations into observations of a wider, social or political kind? How does the writer do this – by direct comment, by irony, or by insinuation? If such socio-political comments are to be found in the piece, do they strike you as being vivid, or forceful, or convincing? If so, why?

25
Ghost Ships and Gruesomeness

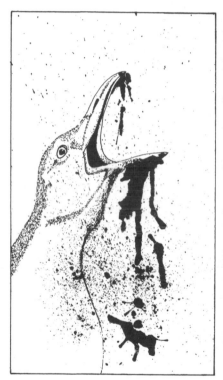

The three pieces of writing in this chapter are surrealistic, phantasmagorical and downright horrible, in that order. They have certain things in common: in each there is a central complex metaphor; in each that metaphor has symbolic qualities; and in each the metaphorical object is a ship, or ships. But in terms of style, they are extremely different. We are therefore concerned here with two things: the possible meanings of metaphor, and the possible ways that metaphor can be expressed.

In Chapter 8, you may remember, we spoke about 'existential' metaphors – metaphors for human life and death. Since 'life' and 'death' are abstract nouns, metaphors for them tend to be symbolic. Writers who write about symbolism sometimes talk about **primary** and **secondary** symbols. Primary symbols are 'elemental'; that is, they are drawn from the elements: earth, water, fire and air. Because such symbols are universal and timeless, their meanings are complicated, and changeable. This may seem a difficult and abstract idea, but is actually not too difficult to grasp. For instance, the 'meaning' of water to a desert dweller will inevitably be different from the meaning of water to an island dweller who goes out on a boat every day to catch fish. 'Earth' will mean different things to an Australian Aborigine and an East Anglian farmer. Even within the same culture, elemental symbols are capable of many different meanings. Fire can signify purification or destruction or energy or transformation. And this is one reason why writers are attracted by symbols – they are very rich in meaning; they come with their own pre-packaged ambiguities. A writer may use the sea as a metaphor for something specific, but that writer knows full well that in so doing he is 'plugging in' to all the other possible meanings of 'sea' as a metaphor. This can, of course, be a cheap trick: if you want to 'add meaning' to a scene of emotional crisis, then slap your characters down in the middle of a violent thunderstorm in the middle of an ocean.

Let's think about the sea for a minute. The sea can be all sorts of things. It can be the ultimate symbol for danger; it is unstable, unpredictable, something you can drown in, the place where sharks live. Death, in short. It can also be the opposite: free, untamed, far from the trappings of civilisation, a place you can run away to. Life, in other words. The sea generates a great range of 'secondary symbols'. If the sea represents danger, then the shore, the harbour, the port, represent safety and peace. If the sea is a symbol for everything which is untameable and unpredictable and vast and shapeless, then a ship must almost inevitably become a symbol of security and order and control and human management of nature. The expression 'ship of state' implies that political order keeps us afloat on the great sea of anarchy which would drown us if we 'rock the boat'. If, on the other hand, the sea is a metaphor for freedom and a life free of maps, then ships are a means of liberation.

And as well as all that, these symbols can be looked at ironically, and this can complicate things still further. Keeping all this stuff afloat in your minds, enjoy the following pieces.

First stop is an imaginary village in an imaginary country somewhere in Central America, perhaps, or northern South America. The inhabitants of the village, Macondo, are none too sure where they are either. One man is very anxious to find out where he would be on the map, if the map existed. He initiates an expedition to make contact with civilisation.

> José Arcadio Buendía was completely ignorant of the geography of the region. He knew that on the east there lay an impenetrable mountain chain and that on the other side of the mountains there was the ancient city of Riohacha, where in times past – according to what he had been told by the first Aureliano Buendía, his grandfather – Sir Francis Drake had gone crocodile hunting with cannons and that he repaired them and stuffed them with straw to bring to Queen Elizabeth. In his youth, José Arcadio Buendía and his men, with wives and children, animals and all kinds of domestic implements, had crossed the mountains in search of an outlet to the sea, and after twenty-six months they gave up the expedition and founded Macondo, so they would not have to go back. It was, therefore, a route which did not interest him, for it could only lead to the past. To the south lay the swamps, covered with an eternal vegetable scum, and the whole vast universe of the great swamp, which, according to what the gypsies said,

had no limits. The great swamp in the west mingled with a boundless extension of water where there were soft-skinned cetaceans that had the head and torso of a woman, causing the ruination of sailors with the charm of their extraordinary breasts. The gypsies sailed along that route for six months before they reached the strip of land over which the mules that carried the mail passed. According to José Arcadio Buendía's calculations, the only possibility of contact with civilisation lay along the northern route. So he handed out clearing tools and hunting weapons to the same men who had been with him during the founding of Macondo. He threw his directional instruments and his maps into a knapsack, and he undertook the reckless adventure.

During the first days they did not come across any appreciable obstacle. They went down along the stony bank of the river to the place where years before they had found the soldier's armour, and from there they went into the woods along a path wild with orange trees. At the end of the first week they killed and roasted a deer, but they agreed to eat only half of it and salt the rest for the days that lay ahead. With that precaution they tried to postpone the necessity of having to eat macaws, whose blue flesh had a harsh and murky taste. Then, for more than ten days, they did not see the sun again. The ground became soft and damp, like volcanic ash, and the vegetation was thicker and thicker, and the cries of the birds and the uproar of the monkeys became more and more remote, and the world became eternally sad. The men on the expedition felt overwhelmed by their most ancient memories in that paradise of dampness and silence, going back to before original sin, as their boots sank into pools of steaming oil and their machetes destroyed bloody lilies and golden salamanders. For a week, almost without speaking, they went ahead like sleepwalkers through a universe of grief, lighted only by the tenuous reflection of luminous insects, and their lungs were overwhelmed by a suffocating smell of blood. They could not return because the strip they were opening as they went along would soon close up with a new vegetation that almost seemed to grow before their eyes.

'It's all right,' José Arcadio Buendía would say. 'The main thing is not to lose our bearings.' Always following his compass, he kept on guiding his men towards the invisible north so that they would be able to get out of that enchanted region. It was a thick night, starless, but the darkness was becoming impregnated with a fresh and clear air. Exhausted by the long crossing, they hung up their hammocks and slept deeply for the first time in two weeks. When they woke up, with the sun already high in the sky, they were speechless with fascination. Before them, surrounded by ferns and palm trees, white and powdery in the morning light, was an enormous Spanish galleon. Tilted slightly to the starboard, it had hanging from its intact masts the dirty rags of its sails in the midst of its rigging, which was adorned with orchids. The hull, covered with an armour of petrified barnacles and soft moss, was firmly fastened into a surface of stones. The whole structure seemed to occupy its own space, one of solitude and oblivion, protected from the vices of time and the habits of the birds. Inside, where the expeditionaries explored with careful intent, there was nothing but a thick forest of flowers.

The discovery of the galleon, an indication of the proximity of the sea, broke José Arcadio Buendía's drive. He considered it a trick of his whimsical fate to have searched for the sea without finding it, at the cost of countless sacrifices and suffering, and to have found it all of a sudden without looking for it, as it lay across his path like an insurmountable object. Many years later Colonel Aureliano Buendía crossed the region again, when it was already a regular mail route, and the only part of the ship he found was its burned-out frame in the midst of a field of poppies.

Only then, convinced that the story had not been some product of his father's imagination, did he wonder how the galleon had been able to get inland to that spot. But José Arcadio Buendía did not concern himself with that when he found the sea after another four days' journey from the galleon. His dreams ended as he faced that ashen, foamy, dirty sea, which had not merited the risks and sacrifices of the adventure.

'God damn it!' he shouted. 'Macondo is surrounded by water on all sides.'

Gabriel Garcia Marquez: One Hundred Years of Solitude
(translated by Gregory Rabassa)

1 What is there in this passage that suggests that José Arcadio Buendía's expedition is more than a journey in the literal sense? What is he looking for? And why is he so angry when he comes to believe that Macondo is surrounded by water?

2 How would you describe the style of this piece of writing? What do you like or dislike about it?

3 What might the Spanish galleon represent? What might it have been doing there in the first place? (If your history is a bit shaky, look up 'Conquistadores' in an encyclopaedia.) Is there anything in Marquez' rather beautiful description of it that hints at a symbolic meaning? Why, do you think, does Marquez mention it again as a 'burned-out frame', many years later, marooned in a field of poppies? Why would anybody want to clear the jungle to cultivate a field of poppies?

The next piece is part of a longer poem. The narrator is Shabine, a West Indian seaman serving on a ship called the Flight. The Middle Passage is the name given to the middle part (that is, the sea journey) endured by slaves on their way from Africa to the plantations in the West Indies.

Shabine encounters the Middle Passage

Man, I brisk in the galley first thing next dawn,
brewing li'l coffee; fog coil from the sea
like the kettle steaming when I put it down
slow, slow, 'cause I couldn't believe what I see:

where the horizon was one silver haze,
the fog swirl and swell into sails, so close
that I saw it was sails, my hair grip my skull,
it was horrors, but it was beautiful.
We float through a rustling forest of ships
with sails dry like paper, behind the glass
I saw men with rusty eyeholes like cannons,
and whenever their half-naked crews cross the sun,
right through their tissue, you traced the bones
like leaves against the sunlight; frigates, barkentines,
the backward-moving current swept them on,
and high on their decks I saw great admirals,
Rodney, Nelson, de Grasse, I heard the hoarse orders
they gave those Shabines, and the forest
of masts sail right through the Flight,
and all you could hear was the ghostly sound
of waves rustling like grass in a low wind
and the hissing weeds they trailed from the stern;
slowly they heaved past from east to west
like this round world was some cranked water wheel,
every ship pouring like a wooden bucket
dredged from the deep; my memory revolve
on sailors before me, then the sun
heat the horizon's ring and they was mist.

Next we pass slave ships. Flags of all nations,
our fathers below deck too deep, I suppose,
to hear us shouting. So we stop shouting. Who knows
who his grandfather is, much less his name?
Tomorrow our landfall will be the Barbados.

Derek Walcott: The Schooner 'Flight'

1 In the poem from which this extract is taken, Shabine's voice is not
consistent. In some sections he speaks 'standard' English, in others he
speaks in dialect. Can you suggest why in this section, describing this
experience, Shabine speaks in dialect?

2 This passage has three parts. The first two are long single sentences; the
third is a separate stanza. Comment briefly on the different ways that
rhythm and rhyme are used in these sections. Shabine's voice changes,
too; where and how and why does it change?

3 What are these ghost ships, and why should they haunt Shabine? Where
do ghosts come from? Where have Shabine's ghosts come from? Who does
'our' refer to in the last line?

The final extract appears to belong to a particular literary genre – that of the
horror story. In fact, it is from a very strange novel, published in 1837, which claims
to be the first person account of the very unpleasant adventures of a man who,
through a series of calamities, ends up at the South Pole. In this extract, the
narrator, along with three other men, is adrift on the hulk of their wrecked ship.

They are half mad with hunger and thirst and exposure. And then they see another ship approaching.

No person was seen upon her decks until she arrived within about a quarter of a mile of us. We then saw three seamen, whom by their dress we took to be Hollanders. Two of these were lying on some old sails near the forecastle, and the third, who appeared to be looking at us with great curiosity, was leaning over the starboard bow near the bowsprit. This last was a stout and tall man, with a very dark skin. He seemed by his manner to be encouraging us to have patience, nodding to us in a cheerful though rather odd way, and smiling constantly, so as to display a set of the most brilliantly white teeth. As his vessel drew nearer, we saw a red flannel cap which he had on fall from his head into the water; but of this he took little or no notice, continuing his odd smiles and gesticulations. I relate these things and circumstances minutely, and I relate them, it must be understood, precisely as they appeared to us.

The brig came on slowly, and now more steadily than before, and – I cannot speak calmly of this event – our hearts leaped up wildly within us, and we poured out our whole souls in shouts and thanksgiving to God for the complete, unexpected, and glorious deliverance that was so palpably at hand. Of a sudden, and all at once, there came wafted over the ocean from the strange vessel (which was now close upon us) a smell, a stench, as the whole world has no name for – no conception of – hellish – utterly suffocating – insufferable, inconceivable. I gasped for breath, and turning to my companions, perceived that they were paler than marble. But now we had no time left for question or surmise – the brig was within fifty feet of us, and it seemed to be her intention to run under our counter, that we might board her without putting out a boat. We rushed aft, when, suddenly, a wide yaw threw her off full five or six points from the course she had been running, and, as she passed under our stern at the distance of about twenty feet, we had a full view of her decks. Shall I ever forget the triple horror of that spectacle? Twenty-five or thirty human bodies, among whom were several females, lay scattered about between the counter and the galley in the last and most loathsome state of putrefaction. We plainly saw that not a soul lived in that fated vessel! Yet we could not help shouting to the dead for help! Yes, long and loudly did we beg, in the agony of the moment, that those silent and disgusting images would stay for us, would not abandon us to become like them, would receive us among their goodly company! We were raving with horror and despair – thoroughly mad through the anguish of our grievous disappointment.

As our first loud yell of terror broke forth, it was replied to by something, from near the bowsprit of the stranger, so closely resembling the scream of a human voice that the nicest ear might have been startled and deceived. At this instant another yaw brought the region of the forecastle for a moment into view, and we beheld at once the origin of the sound. We saw the tall stout figure still leaning on the bulwark, and still nodding his head to and fro, but his face was now turned away from us so that we could not behold it. His arms were extended over the rail, and the palms of his hands fell outward. His knees were lodged upon a stout rope, tightly stretched, and reaching from the heel of the bowsprit to a cathead. On his back, from which a portion of the shirt had been torn, leaving it bare, there sat a huge seagull, busily gorging itself with the horrible flesh, its bill and talons deep buried, and its white plumage spattered all over with blood. As the brig moved further round so as to bring us close in view, the bird, with much apparent difficulty, drew out its crimsoned head, and, after eying us for a moment as if stupefied, arose lazily from the body on which it had been feasting, and, flying directly above our deck, hovered there a while with a portion of clotted and liver-like substance in its beak. The horrid morsel dropped at length with a sullen splash immediately at the feet of Parker. May God forgive me, but now, for the first time, there flashed through my mind a thought, a thought which I will not mention, and I felt myself making a step towards the ensanguined spot. I looked upward, and the eyes of Augustus met my own with a degree of intense and eager meaning which immediately brought me to my senses. I sprang forward quickly, and, with a deep shudder, threw the frightful thing into the sea.

Edgar Allan Poe: The Narrative of Arthur Gordon Pym

We hope you have already had your lunch.

1 Clearly, Edgar Allan Poe is trying to evoke powerful responses from us – responses centred on generally unpleasant feelings. Leaving aside for a moment the question of *why* he should want to do this, *how* does he?

2 Where and how in this extract is Poe trying to use such things as prose rhythm, punctuation, sentence structure and phrasing in order to achieve maximum effect? (Have a look at the last four sentences in each paragraph.)

3 The horror genre was relatively new when Poe was writing, and he is still recognised as one of its masters; but how horrifying was that piece for you? If you give it a low mark for shudders and horrors, is that because you've become hard-boiled, living in a world of horror movies, video nasties and Stephen King? Or are there stylistic failures in the passage itself?

4 On a more general note, why, do you suppose, are horror stories always popular (as films as well as books)? What is it in us that they appeal to? Why is it that they can 'work' even though they are often very badly written – or, in the case of films, badly made and acted? And why, do you think, are we so willing to be scared or shocked or thrilled by things that are so obviously not real?

26
Flagwaving

In this chapter, we are going to consider two prose passages which take a rather sideways look at patriotism. The first describes a peculiar local ritual enacted in a Mid-Western American town so small that no-one seems at all sure where it is; the place is Lake Wobegon, and the ritual is 'The Living Flag'.

Flag Day, as we know it, was the idea of Herman Hochstetter, Rollie's dad, who ran the dry goods store and ran Armistice Day, the Fourth of July, and Flag Day. For the Fourth, he organized a double-loop parade around the block which allowed people to take turns marching and watching. On Armistice Day, everyone stepped outside at 11 a.m. and stood in silence for two minutes as Our Lady's bell tolled eleven times.

Flag Day was his favourite. For a modest price, he would install a bracket on your house to hold a pole to hang your flag on, or he would drill a hole in the sidewalk in front of your store with his drill gun powered by a .22 shell. Bam! And in went the flag. On patriotic days, flags flew all over; there were flags on the tall poles, flags on the short, flags in the brackets on the pillars and the porches, and if you were flagless you could expect to hear from Herman. His hairy arm around your shoulder, his poochlike face close to yours, he would say how proud he was that so many people were proud of their country, leaving you to see the obvious, that you were a gap in the ranks.

In June 1944, the day after D-Day, a salesman from Fisher Hat called on Herman and offered a good deal on red and blue baseball caps. 'Do you have white also?' Herman asked. The salesman thought that white caps could be had for the same wonderful price. Herman ordered two hundred red, two hundred white, and one hundred blue. By the end of the year, he still had four hundred and eighty-six caps. The inspiration of the Living Flag was born from that overstock.

On June 14, 1945, a month after V-E Day, a good crowd assembled in front of the Central Building in response to Herman's ad in the paper:

> Honor 'AMERICA' June 14 at 4 p.m. Be
> proud of "Our Land & People". Be part of
> the "Living Flag". Don't let it be said
> that Lake Wobegon was "Too Busy". Be on
> time. 4 p.m. "Sharp".

His wife Louise handed out the caps, and Herman stood on a stepladder and told the people where to stand. He lined up the reds and whites into stripes, then got the blues into their square. Mr. Hanson climbed up on the roof of the Central Building and took a photograph, they sang the national anthem, and then the Living Flag dispersed. The photograph appeared in the paper the next week. Herman kept the caps.

In the flush of victory, people were happy to do as they were told and stand in place, but in 1946 and 1947, dissension cropped up in the ranks: people complained about the heat and about Herman – what gave him the idea he could order them around? 'People! Please! I need your attention! You blue people, keep your hats on! Please! Stripe number 4, you're sagging! You reds, you're up here! We got too many white people, we need more red ones! Let's do this without talking, people! I can't get you straight if you keep moving around! Some of you are not paying attention! Everybody shut up! Please!'

One cause of resentment was the fact that none of them got to see the flag they were in; the picture in the paper was black and white. Only Herman and Mr. Hanson got to see the real Flag, and some boys too short to be needed down below. People wanted a chance to go up to the roof and witness the spectacle for themselves.

'How can you go up there if you're supposed to be down here?' Herman said. 'You go up to look, you got nothing to look at. Isn't it enough to know that you're doing your part?'

On Flag Day, 1949, just as Herman said, 'That's it! Hold it now!' one of the reds made a break for it – dashed up four flights of stairs to the roof and leaned over and had a long look. Even with the hole he had left behind, it was a magnificent sight. The Living Flag filled the street below. A perfect Flag! The reds so brilliant! He couldn't take his eyes off it. 'Get down here! We need a picture!' Herman yelled up at him. 'Unbelievable! I can't describe it!' he said.

So then everyone had to have a look. 'No!' Herman said, but they took a vote and it was unanimous. One by one, members of the Living

Flag went up to the roof and admired it. It was marvellous! It brought
tears to the eyes, it made one reflect on this great country and on Lake
Wobegon's place in it. One wanted to stand up there all afternoon and
just drink it in. So, as the first hour passed, and only forty of the five
hundred had been to the top, the others got more and more restless.
'Hurry up! Quit dawdling! You've seen it! Get down here and give
someone else a chance!' Herman sent people up in groups of four, and
then ten, but after two hours, the Living Flag became the Sitting Flag
and then began to erode, as the members who had had a look thought
about heading home to supper, which infuriated the ones who hadn't.
'Ten more minutes!' Herman cried, but ten minutes became twenty and
thirty, and people snuck off and the Flag that remained for the last
viewer was a Flag shot through by cannon fire.

In 1950, the Sons of Knute took over Flag Day. Herman gave them
the boxes of caps. Since then, the Knutes have achieved several good
Flags, though most years the attendance was poor. You need at least
four hundred to make a good one. Some years the Knutes made a 'no-
look' rule, other years they held a lottery. One year they experimented
with a large mirror held by two men over the edge of the roof, but when
people leaned back and looked up, the Flag disappeared, of course.

Garrison Keillor: Lake Wobegon Days

In the next passage, the protagonist, Bertram, has returned to the Caribbean
island where he was born after a long voluntary exile in England. He thinks of the
place as 'home', but it doesn't quite feel that way. The island is celebrating its
independence from British colonial rule, and Bertram is on his way to join in the
festivities.

The bus hurtled in the direction of the capital as though being
sucked in by the excitement of what was about to happen. Once in
Baytown Bertram tried to make his way quickly to the park, but like a
bent pipe the streets were clogged with latecomers. Line upon line of
cars jammed every road and junction, but after much tedious waiting
the people and vehicles began to thin out.

When he arrived at Stanley Park, Bertram craned his neck and
looked down at the countless rows of assembled guests. Their
innumerable heads looked like a huge basket full of minature moons,
and their moon-faces were painted with a dreamlike benevolent
austerity. Then Bertram looked beyond them and saw that the
platforms for the dignitaries had been constructed where the cricket
square usually was. But, to his left and to his right, above, below and
around him were the people, their faces gleaming, the tops of their
heads dry and brittle, though some were slicked and greasy for this
special occasion.

Bertram was late and the state service already under way. Then,
barely a few minutes after his arrival, he listened as the Doctor
delivered the climactic line of his speech.

'I have squatted three hundred and fifty years in another man's
house, now that house is mine own!'

The applause was thunderous, and Bertram watched the new flag slide up the pole and cross the old one slithering down. In the distance he heard the cracked report as the guns of the British Royal Navy fired their salute, and overhead a cloud of doves flew in all directions, glad to have escaped their independence baskets. As the church clock struck midnight, and the cheering and celebratory noises grew even louder, Bertram heard raindrops beginning to slap against the leaves of the trees above him. Then as the wheels of History turned, and Mount Misery became Mount Freedom, and Pall Mall Square became Independence Square (although the island had decided to keep its old colonial name), someone punched a hole in the sky and everybody ran for cover as the rain broke through. As they did so the police band started to play the new national anthem in G major like the old British one, but they struggled to find the notes to this new tune. Bertram listened to their waterlogged and unmusical rendering of what seemed an otherwise pleasant composition, but before the band could rescue the anthem the heavens opened wide. The musicians now ran for cover, and all around the umbrellas bloomed like flowers, and the sharp bullets of rain joined the sky to the earth.

Bertram ran quickly but aimlessly, and as he did so he noticed that the dignitaries now had little choice but to mix with the ordinary people in this teeming confusion. He recognized the tall figure of a radical leader from a neighbouring island. He was flanked by gunmen, their jackets bulging. And then he saw a woman leader popularly known as the Iron Woman of the Caribbean. Her umbrella had been peeled inside out by the high wind, and a civil servant nobly held his coat above her head. As she turned, presumably to thank him, Bertram noticed that her upper plate slipped and kissed its partner. A simple pursing of the lips retrieved the situation.

Gradually the drumroll of rain on the car roofs eased to a pitter-patter, and the cars rubbered along in the wet throwing up thin sheets of water. Bertram found himself in a steady stream of people pouring down towards Independence-ville, where the wooden booths were now dazzlingly lit. He prepared himself, ready to drink until dawn on this first day of a new era in his island's history.

Caryl Philips: State of Independence

1 Both these pieces use irony, that much is fairly obvious, but:

   a) How would you describe the different ways that they use irony?

   b) How would you describe the 'tone of voice' in each passage? (The first passage was originally a radio broadcast; is there anything about the text that suggests this?)

   c) What do these tones of voice tell you about the attitude of each writer to his subject? To what extent is this attitude ambivalent?

2 Flags are by their very nature symbolic. What games is Garrison Keillor playing, and what jokes is he making about symbolism in the extract from *Lake Wobegon Days*? Can you work out a way in which this passage could

be read as an allegory or parable about American patriotism and group identities? And what metaphorical interpretation might be made of the last sentence in this passage?

3 What is there in the text of the second passage which suggests that Bertram doesn't 'belong'?

4 What do you think Caryl Philips is suggesting about the concept of 'independence' (political or otherwise)? What is there in the passage that suggests that it might not be so wonderful after all?

5 Finally, a larger question requiring a more discursive answer: why are modern writers usually hostile towards enthusiastic patriotism? Do you feel there is anything about patriotism which is inherently incompatible with good writing?

27
Dead Sentimental

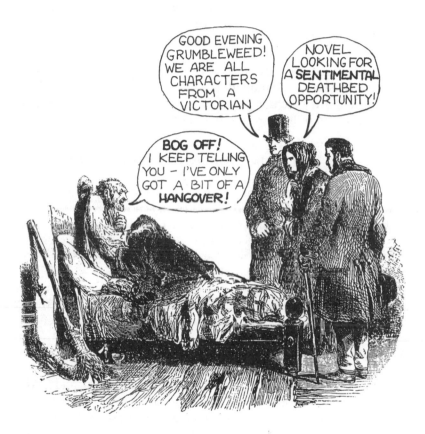

For most modern readers and critics, the word 'sentimental' is a term of condemnation and abuse. It's worth wondering why this is so. The word 'sentiment' is more or less neutral in its meaning: it signifies feeling, but in the sense of *mental* feeling as opposed to *sensation*; if we agree with someone about something, we 'share' that person's 'sentiments'. Yet the adjective 'sentimental', is usually used pejoratively; my dictionary gives the meaning 'addicted to indulgence in superficial emotion'. It is a word which, like a great many others, has changed in meaning over the years. In the latter half of the eighteenth century, it meant 'characterised by or exhibiting refined and elevated feeling', and there is a definable literary genre of the period – the sentimental novel – which concerns itself with characters whose exquisite sensibilities make the rude and cruel world hard to bear. As far as we know, such works were not greeted with jeers; on the contrary, they were exceedingly popular. They continued to be popular for most of the nineteenth century, too; but by then rather more objections could be heard. Although the most famous of all nineteenth century sentimentalists was a man – Charles Dickens – it was generally believed by other men that sentimentality was something purveyed by women, by 'a damned mob of scribbling women', to quote the American writer Nathaniel Hawthorne. And sometime during the nineteenth century, so it seems, sentimentality became identified as a feminine characteristic, one that is incompatible with masculinity. Generally, this remains the male view; sentimentality is one of the elements in the 'softness' of the feminine character. Boys don't cry, in other words. Needless to say, this view of things is highly suspect. However, we digress: the point we were making is that sentimentality is one of those concepts that are relative, historically speaking. M. H. Abrams says that

> Since what constitutes emotional excess or overindulgence is relative both to the judgment of the individual and to large-scale changes in culture and in literary fashion, what to the common reader of one age is a normal expression of humane feeling may seem sentimental to many later readers.

> *M. H. Abrams: A Glossary of Literary Terms*

One of the things this means is that whereas it was not considered unmanly, two hundred years ago, to be moved to tears by a book, it is now.

Already, then, we have three ways of responding to sentimentality in literature: we can look at it more or less objectively as a characteristic of certain kinds of writing from certain periods in history; we can see it as one of those 'gender constructs' put about by men; or we can simply find it offensive.

The following three pieces are all about people dying. This is not because we are hopelessly morbid, but because if the subject is sentimental writing, then death naturally crops up. The first piece is probably the most famous 'sentimental' death scene in English literature: the death of Little Nell from Dickens' *The Old Curiosity Shop*. This novel was first published episodically, in magazine form, beginning in April 1840. When the episode featuring Nell's death appeared, the country was, by all accounts, ankle-deep in tears, and there was widespread wailing and gnashing of teeth. But in harder-boiled times the death of Little Nell has met a frostier reception. Oscar Wilde is reported to have said that 'one must have a heart of stone to read the death of Little Nell without laughing.' Aldous Huxley, in a book called *Vulgarity in Literature*, was very hard indeed:

> ... whenever he is in the melting mood, Dickens ceases to be able and probably ceases even to wish to see reality. His one and only desire on these occasions is just to overflow, nothing else. Which he does, with a vengeance and in an atrocious blank verse that is meant to be poetical prose ... Mentally drowned and blinded by the sticky overflowings of his heart, Dickens was incapable, when moved, of re-creating, in terms of art, the reality which had moved him.

> *Aldous Huxley: Vulgarity in Literature*

You may disagree. Here's part of the rather protracted episode. The 'old man', by the way, is Nell's grandfather, himself very far gone in poverty and misery:

Little by little, the old man had drawn back towards the inner chamber ... He pointed there, as he replied, with trembling lips, 'You plot among you to wean my heart from her. You will never do that – never while I have life. I have no relative or friend but her – I never had – I never will have. She is all in all to me. It is too late to part us now.'

Waving them off with his hand, and calling softly to her as he went, he stole into the room. They who were left behind drew close together, and after a few whispered words – not unbroken by emotion, or easily uttered – followed him. They moved so gently, that their footsteps made no noise; but there were sobs from among the group, and sounds of grief and mourning.

For she was dead. There, upon her little bed, she lay at rest. The solemn stillness was no marvel now.

She was dead. No sleep so beautiful and calm, so free from trace of pain, so fair to look upon. She seemed a creature fresh from the hand of God, and waiting for the breath of life; not one who had lived and suffered death.

Her couch was dressed with here and there some winter berries and green leaves, gathered in a spot she had been used to favour. 'When I die, put near me something that has loved the light, and had the sky above it always.' Those were her words.

She was dead. Dear, gentle, patient, noble Nell, was dead. Her little bird – a poor slight thing the pressure of a finger would have crushed – was stirring nimbly in its cage; and the strong heart of its child-mistress was mute and motionless forever.

Where were the traces of her early cares, her sufferings, and fatigues? All gone. Sorrow was dead indeed in her, but peace and perfect happiness were born; imaged in her tranquil beauty and profound repose.

And still her former self lay there, unaltered in this change. Yes. The old fireside had smiled upon that same sweet face; it had passed like a dream through haunts of misery and care; at the door of the poor schoolmaster on the summer evening, before the furnace fire upon the cold wet night, at the still bedside of the dying boy, there had been the same mild lovely look. So shall we know the angels in their majesty, after death.

The old man held one languid arm in his, and had the small hand tight folded to his breast, for warmth. It was the hand she had stretched out to him with her last smile – the hand that had led him on through all their wanderings. Ever and anon he pressed it to his lips; then hugged it to his breast again, murmuring that it was warmer now; and as he said it he looked, in agony, to those who stood around, as if imploring them to help her.

She was dead, and past all help, or need of it. The ancient rooms she had seemed to fill with life, even while her own was waning fast – the garden she had tended – the eyes she had gladdened – the noiseless haunts of many a thoughtful hour – the paths she had trodden as it were but yesterday – could know her no more.

'It is not,' said the schoolmaster, as he bent down to kiss her on the cheek, and gave his tears free vent, 'it is not on earth that Heaven's justice ends. Think what it is compared with the world to which her young spirit has winged its early flight, and say, if one deliberate wish expressed in solemn terms above this bed could call her back to life, which of us would utter it!'

Charles Dickens: The Old Curiosity Shop

Stop snivelling. For whatever reason, and whether it is woefully sentimental or not, the emotion that Dickens seems to want to stir up in us would appear to be fairly simple. Or is it? Try these questions:

1 What linguistic and stylistic devices does Dickens use in an attempt to manipulate our feelings?

2 There is a religious content in this scene. To some extent it is clearly stated (in the last paragraph, most obviously). Elsewhere it is hinted at. What are these hints? Does the religious element in this scene cause you to re-assess it in some way? Or do these religious overtones strike you as being merely another emotive device?

3 Do you share the views of Wilde and Huxley about this passage? If, like Wilde, you find it laughable, why do you, exactly?

Huxley says two things about passages like this in Dickens: he says, first, that this is vulgar and sloppy and 'sticky'; he also says that it is lacking in technical merit. He accuses Dickens of using 'atrocious blank verse that is meant to be poetical prose', and he says that when Dickens is in this mood he is incapable of 'recreating, in terms of art, the reality which had moved him'. Is that fair? Leaving aside the question of whether or not this is emotionally sloppy, is it a piece of sloppy *writing*?

The next two pieces seem as keen to avoid pathos as Dickens is to pile it on.

The twins came back from school to find their father greasing the hubs of the trap. Mary, pale but smiling, was sitting in the kitchen with her arm in a sling.

'We've been waiting for you,' she said. 'Don't worry. Do your homework and keep an eye on Grandpa.'

By sunset, the twins were speechless with grief, and Old Sam had been two hours dead. At five in the afternoon, the boys were scribbling their sums at the kitchen table when a creak on the landing made them stop. Their grandfather was groping his way down the stairs.

'Sshh!' said Benjamin, tugging his brother by the sleeve.

'He should be in bed,' Lewis said.

'Sshh!' he repeated, and dragged him into the back kitchen.

The old man hobbled across the kitchen and went outside. There was a high windy sky, and the mare's-tails seemed to dance with the larches. He was wearing his wedding-best – a frock coat and trousers, and shiny patent leather pumps. A red handkerchief, knotted round his neck, made him young again – and he carried the fiddle and bow.

The twins peeped round the curtains.

'He's got to go back to bed,' Lewis whispered.

'Quiet!' hissed Benjamin. 'He's going to play.'

A harsh croak burst from the ancient instrument. But the second note was sweeter, and the successive notes were sweeter still. His head was up. His chin stuck truculently out over the sound-box; and his feet shuffled over the flagstones in perfect time.

Then he coughed and the music stopped. One tread at a time, he heaved himself up the stairs. He coughed again, and again, and after that there was silence.

The boys found him stretched out on the quilt with his hands folded over the fiddle. His face, drained of colour, wore an expression of amused condescension. A bumble-bee, trapped inside the window, was buzzing and bouncing against the pane.

'Don't cry, my darlings!' Mary stretched her good arm around them as they blubbed out the news. 'Please don't cry. He had to die some time. And it was a wonderful way to die.'

Bruce Chatwin: On the Black Hill

1 Is this sentimental?

2 What difference would it make to this passage if the sentence which begins 'By sunset, the twins were speechless with grief ... ' was not there?

3 There are places in this passage where Bruce Chatwin uses linguistic devices more commonly found in poetry. Where and what are they, and what might they be doing there?

Now a poem, written, it would seem, posthumously.

> I heard a fly buzz when I died.
> The stillness in the room
> Was like the stillness in the air
> Between the heaves of storm.
>
> The eyes around had wrung them dry,
> And breaths were gathering firm
> For that last onset when the king
> Be witnessed in the room.
>
> I willed my keepsakes, signed away
> What portion of me be
> Assignable; and then it was
> There interposed a fly
>
> With blue uncertain stumbling buzz
> Between the light and me;
> And then the windows failed; and then
> I could not see to see.

Emily Dickinson

1 Is this sentimental?

2 Take a careful look at the form of this poem. One fairly obvious thing about it is that the third and fourth quatrains are rhythmically very different from the first and second. There is a startling 'shuffle' in line 11 after the word 'Assignable'. Until that semi-colon appears, the poem conveys a sense of calmness and ritual in the death room. It's almost as if that semi-colon *is* the fly, which 'interposes' and unsettles the poem. Comment briefly on the following 'events' in the poem:

a) the use of full stops

b) what those three semi-colons do

c) the sound and meaning of the words in line 13

d) the way that rhyme is used differently in the last stanza from the way it is used in the other three.

3 Who or what is the 'king' in the second quatrain? What is the fly? In the first line of the poem, it seems incidental – it demonstrates, by being audible, the 'stillness ... in the room'. How does it become a different, and bigger, thing in the last six lines? Is this fly possibly a relative of the bumble bee in the passage from Bruce Chatwin's novel?

Finally, some questions of a wider nature:

1 What do the writers of passages B and C do to prevent or limit a sentimental response?

M. H. Abrams suggests that modern readers seem to require 'an ironic counterpoise to intense feeling in poetry' – and presumably this applies to prose as well. What do you think he means by 'ironic counterpoise', and is there such a thing in the passages in this chapter?

2 Charles Dickens and Emily Dickinson both wrote at a time when there was a prevailing orthodoxy about death, this being the Christian orthodoxy that death was not merely the end of mortal existence but also the beginning of immortal, heavenly, life. What, generally speaking, would you expect the effect of this belief to be upon writers depicting death? In what different ways do Dickens and Dickinson respond to the Christian concept of death? And do you think there is anything 'religious' about the death of the grandfather in *On the Black Hill*?

3 There is an interesting article by an American critic, Jane P. Tompkins, (which can be found in *The New Feminist Criticism*, a collection of essays edited by Elaine Showalter and published by Virago) which dissents from the conventional, hostile view of sentimentality in literature. Specifically, she writes about the nineteenth century best-seller *Uncle Tom's Cabin*, by Harriet Beecher Stowe. As you may know, *Uncle Tom's Cabin* is a 'weepie' about slavery, and in recent times it has been roundly condemned because it seems to lack any political edge and paints a 'sentimental' picture of the joys and sorrows of life among Black slaves and their owners. Tompkins argues that to condemn Stowe on these grounds is short-sighted, because pity for the victims of tyranny is essential if tyranny is to be overthrown. Tompkins quotes this statement by Harriet Beecher Stowe:

There is one thing that every individual can do – they can see to it that they feel right. An atmosphere of sympathetic influence encircles every human being; and the man or woman who feels strongly, healthily and justly, on the great interests of humanity, is a constant benefactor to the human race. See, then, to your sympathies in this matter! Are they in harmony with the sympathies of Christ? or are they swayed and perverted by the sophistries of worldly policy?

Whether one is a Christian or not, this seems a forceful argument – that social change only comes when people's *feelings* are changed. It is also the case that those books which have actually led to social change have very often been those books labelled as sentimental. Does this mean, do you think, that there may be sometimes grounds for treating sentimental literature as a special case? Do you think that a writer's motives can sometimes excuse her or him from the attentions of literary critics? How can you distinguish well-intentioned sentimentality from cynical exploitation of raw emotion? Dickens wrote *The Old Curiosity Shop* at a time when children were frequently treated cruelly and neglectfully; does this alter your attitude towards his account of the death of Little Nell?

28
Getting On

As you will know if you have been on the receiving end, bigotry and prejudice depend very much upon generalisation. Racism and sexism are based on the pretence that 'Blacks' or 'Asians' or 'women' are 'all the same', and that therefore the same characteristics can be imposed on every member of such groups. This is the process called **stereotyping**, and we have come across it elsewhere in this book. Basically, there seems to be a choice of only two ways to combat hostile stereotyping. One is to try to change the basis of the generalisation, to make the stereotype positive, rather than negative – to assert, for example, that 'Black is Beautiful'. The other is to insist on individualisation, to assert that the uniqueness of any individual makes the stereotype nonsensical.

Over the past decade or so, the word 'ageism' has entered the lexicon of prejudice, and the process of stereotyping operates against the aged in much the same way as against racial minorities.

Stereotypes are motivated by fear. In most cases this fear is the fear of 'The Other', of those who are mysteriously different. In the case of the aged, this fear is deeper and more complex, because it is not the fear of the outsider, it is the fear of that which we ourselves must almost inevitably become. Before you read the three pieces in this chapter, it would be useful if you thought about or discussed your own feelings about old people; perhaps you might attempt the alarming exercise of imagining yourself at the age of seventy or so.

A   In a week's time, Millicent and Alison, who have lived together in the cottage for nineteen years, will have left it for ever and The New People will have moved in.

It is a summer afternoon and the light in the garden is beguiling, Alison thinks, as she passes and re-passes the small bedroom window, carrying Millicent's things. Millicent is downstairs, dusting the weasel. She has promised Alison that she will 'make a start on the books'. There are more than two thousand of these. When The New People first arrived to look round the cottage they appeared genuinely afraid at the sight of them. They'd imagined thick walls, perhaps, but not this extra insulation of literature. Then, as Millicent led them on into the sitting room and they noticed the stuffed weasel under its glass cloche, their fear palpably increased, as if the long-dead animal was going to dart at their ankle veins. And yet they didn't retreat. They knew the weasel would be leaving with the women; their glances said, 'We can take down all these book shelves'. As they left, they muttered, 'We shall be instructing the agents ... '

After they had gone, Alison had started to cry. 'They'll change it all,' she sobbed, 'I always imagined people like us would buy it.' Millicent reprimanded her. 'Change is good,' she said fiercely, 'and anyway, dear, there are no more people like us.'

But later that evening, Millicent found that she too was looking at the shape and detail of rooms and wondering how they would be altered. After supper, she'd gone out into the garden and stared at the summer night and thought, they will never see it as I see it, those New People, because even if their hands don't change it, their minds will. 'We've got ghosts now!' she announced to Alison, as she went in. 'Ghosts who come before instead of after.'

Now, polishing the weasel, Millicent senses that the ghosts are with her in the sitting room. She turns round. 'What we don't understand,' they say, 'is why you're going.'

'Ah,' says Millicent.

Then she notices that Alison has crept down from sorting the old clothes and is sitting in an armchair, saying nothing.

'Is it a long story?'

'No,' says Millicent. 'I'm going because I've been replaced. I look around, in very many places where I once was and now I not only do not see myself there, I see no one who ever resembled me. It's as if I have been obliterated. And I can't, at the age of sixty-nine, accept my obliteration, so I am simply going somewhere where I shall be visible again, at least to myself.'

The New People look utterly perplexed. They want to say, 'We knew you literary folk were a bit mad, a bit touched, but we thought you tried to make sense to ordinary people. We thought this was common courtesy.'

'No,' snaps Millicent, reading their minds, 'it is not common courtesy, yet what I am saying is tediously simple.'

'Well, I'm afraid we don't understand it.'

'Of course you don't. Of course you don't ... ' Millicent mumbles.

'What you still haven't told us,' say The New People, trying to drag the conversation onto a solid foundation, 'is where you're actually going.'

Millicent looks at Alison. Alison turns her face towards the window and the afternoon sun shines on her hair, which is still reddish and only dulled a little with grey.

'Umbria,' says Millicent.

'Sorry?' say The New People.

'Yes. The house we're buying is by a convent wall. It belonged to the nuns for centuries. It was the place where important guests were put. Now, we shall be the "guests".'

At this point, The New People get up. They say they have to leave. They say they have a great friend who's mad on Italian food and who is starting a local Foodie Society. 'Tonight,' they laugh, 'is the inaugural nosebag!'

Millicent turns away from them and goes back to her polishing. When she looks round again, she finds they've gone.

'They've gone!' she calls to Alison, who is after all upstairs and not sitting silently in a chair.

'What, Millie? Who've gone?'

'Those people,' says Millicent, 'those ghosts. For the time being.'

Rose Tremain: The New People

B   She had been taught that life was a punishment for some crime too terrible to mention, which one either endured with a good grace and was rewarded in the hereafter, or else one went to the bad by kicking against the pricks and earned an eternity in Hell with no remission or parole. Frank believed firmly in the here and now. She had been too formed by her upbringing to change at once, but they had allowed each other their different opinions, and the years had worn away at hers.

Frank had run away from a pretty wife. She, Edith, was not at all pretty, nor had she attained prettiness or allowed it to be thrust upon her, not even by Hetty. The two waist-length plaits, which her mother had removed with scissors while showing her the door, had been thick healthy hair and a lustrous black in colour. They had been sold, she discovered later, to a wig-maker who had paid seven shillings and sixpence for the pair, half a week's wages. Ever since, she had worn her hair short and straight with a straight fringe. It was a muddy silver now, and her skin dark and tough-looking. People had called her skin olive, in an attempt to be kind, but since the only olives she had come across were black or green, she considered the kindness misplaced. In her early middle age the three small bumps on her chin had sprouted hair which, if removed, returned more abundantly. Hair was a plague to her. Her upper lip, although well shaped, also had its thatch of dark oily hair, and the black hair on her legs showed through all but the thickest and most matronly of stockings. She had even become convinced that her back and shoulder blades were only awaiting an opportune moment to sprout. There seemed to be little point aspiring to prettiness unless it could be achieved by fur. The forty-shilling permanent wave she had undergone in 1945 to celebrate VE Day had been her first and last; its permanency had proved a fiction. She was one of life's aunties, created to be mocked or pitied, encouraged to be eccentric, and she no longer cared.

The tea was cold. She placed crockery in the sink, and allowed lukewarm water to cover it. He had certainly worn a bowler; her mind's eye was usually reliable. They had enjoyed physical contact because of the amount of clothing which had required his negotiation, not in spite of it. Toast crumbs and tiny globules of Blue Band margarine floated towards the overflow outlet. When he returned from his thinking walk, he would require her to have decided what she felt about the discovery of his son. She would certainly be expected to feel something. What? If they were allowed to visit, what would they call her? Step-gran? Mrs. Cross? Or by Frank's real name, which was Shawcross? If all these irregularities had occurred a few years later, they could have been blamed on the War. Many strange things happened then. She poked at jam with a sponge on a stick, to loosen its grip on the plate. Her mind's eye showed her the Sewage Farm where Frank had once worked, the sprinklers circling with their fountains of water like rows of small boys, Wolf Cubs, all sitting on a roundabout and peeing, seventy-two arches of liquid from seventy-two giggling outlets.

Dermatitis prevented her from placing her bare hands into washing-up water, and she had never mastered the use of rubber gloves. She cleared away and soaked; Frank washed and rinsed; she stacked the dishes when they had drained, and dried glassware and cutlery. When reading library books she wore cotton mittens with a small hole cut for her left index finger to turn the pages. She had no wish to pass on whatever she had or to contract anything new; one always caught the strangest things from books. Cream which smelt of camomile was applied between her fingers morning and night. It did no good, but couldn't, she supposed, do actual harm, and as punishments for old age go, she considered hers to be light.

Every memory of her life contained within it her conviction that she would never grow old. To be fifty had been unthinkable, and she would certainly never be so inconsiderate as still to be using up air, space and food at sixty. Fifty had come and gone, and sixty, and seventy, but she had not grown old; only her body had done that. Her body had always betrayed her.

David Cook: Missing Persons

1 Why, do you suppose, is the phrase 'The New People' capitalised in passage A? What do they represent, as far as Millicent is concerned?

2 Both Rose Tremain and David Cook make imaginative use of a characteristic we commonly associate with elderly people. What is it, and how do they use it?

3 Both of the above extracts contain an ironic reference to literature. What do these ironies tell you about Millicent's and Edith's different attitudes towards books, and, by extension, their attitudes towards life in general?

4 Briefly, what is the difference between the ways that Edith and Millicent regard themselves as old people?

5 What do you deduce about Millicent's past life as compared to Edith's?

6 Write a paragraph or two about the different ways that Rose Tremain and David Cook individuate their characters. Take into account the different narrative techniques each writer uses. (For instance, why is the first passage mostly in the present tense?) Do you think that as a reader you are being asked to respond differently to these two people? If so, in what ways? Do you find one of them more sympathetic than the other? Do you think that in terms of characterisation one of these passages is more effective than the other? If so, which, and why?

Women at Streatham Hill

They stand like monuments or trees, not women,
Heavy and loaded on the common's edge
Pausing before the leaves' decline; far off
The railway runs through grass and bushes where
Slim girls and interested lovers seem
Another species, not just generation:
Butterflies flitting in the leaves, not stones.

Nobody asks what they have done all day
For who asks trees or stones what they have done?
They root, they gather moss, they spread, they are.
The busyness is in the birds about them.
It would seem more removal than volition
If they were not there when men came home.

Ah giggling creamy beauties, can you think
You will withdraw into this private world
Weighted with shopping, spreading hands and feet,
Trunk gnarling, weatherworn? that if you get
All that your being hurls towards, like Daphne
Your sap will rise to nourish other things
Than suppliant arms and hair that glints and beckons?
Your bodies are keyed and spry, yet do you see
Anything clearly through the grass-green haze
Hear anything but the murmur of desires?

Bargains in bags, they separate towards home,
Their talk a breeze that rustles topmost leaves
Tickles the dust in crannies in the rock:
Beetles that grind at roots it touches not.
The women pull their thoughts in, easing like stones

Where they are set, hiding the cavities.
They care as little now to be disturbed
As flighty daughters urgently want peace.

Jenny Joseph

Note: Daphne, in mythology, was a beautiful creature who attracted the attentions of Apollo, who pursued her intending to have his wicked way. Daphne implored the gods to save her, and they responded by turning her into a laurel tree. A fate worse than a fate worse than death, you might think.

Write an appreciation of this poem which comments on the way that old and young people are presented. Among other things, you might discuss the way that images drawn from nature – stones, plants, creatures – are used as metaphors, and the ambiguities in Jenny Joseph's language. How successful do you think she is in conveying the idea that ageing women somehow become 'invisible'?

Finally, as a more personally creative exercise, you might try this. Think of a memorable incident or experience from your recent life. (If you can't remember a memorable experience, invent one.) Now bravely imagine yourself as a seventy year-old man or woman. Write a short monologue, in the first person, as a seventy year-old, recalling that experience. Ruthlessly omit crude informational signals like 'Well, it must be fifty-odd years ago now ... ' or 'When I was seventeen ... ' Let the information emerge from the way you write. You'll probably find it useful to think about the speech habits of an old person you know. If you want to adopt or adapt any of the ideas or images from the three pieces in this chapter which appeal to you, feel free to do so.

29
The Wind-Up: Some Modern Critical Theories

"I CAME IN FOR A VOLUME OF CRITICISM"

We have tried in this book to help you acquire the specific skills of 'practical criticism' (for want of a better term), because they are the skills you need to produce critical essays using an academic language, or 'code'. We do not think that this is the *only* language that is suitable for writing about literature, but it so happens that for the time being A-Level Literature students need to master this language if they – you – are to emerge smiling from the ordeals of examination and assessment.

We hope it hasn't been too boring.

Although we have been at pains to stress that you, as an individual, will be rewarded by examiners if your written work on literature is perceptive, witty, original, and even a little eccentric, it is still true to say that if you depart radically or heretically from the norms of this academic code you will be penalised. Which is just another way of saying that academic literary criticism is a specific kind of 'discourse', and you will have to learn how to get good at it if you want to end up with a decent grade. But what *this* chapter is about is how, over the past twenty years or so, the definition of 'literary criticism' has undergone some changes.

The first three chapters in this book made an attempt to demystify this academic code and suggest what sorts of writing are 'acceptable'. Writing essays on unseen prose passages and poems can be seen as a kind of game (even if the rules are rather vague); and, as with all games, the best players get the most points. In short, *how* you write seems to be at least as important as what you write. Whether this is right or fair is a very big question. Perhaps, by having a more general look at literary theory, this chapter may help you explore the issue.

Over the past two decades or so, a number of literary critics and educationalists have been saying that there should be more to the study of literature than just practical criticism, or 'close reading'. Indeed, all sorts of literary theories have started to question the importance and the validity of such activities. In particular, they challenge the idea that practical criticism is 'objective' or 'neutral'. This may seem to you to be a very obscure question, but it is closer to home than you think – because the idea that practical criticism is somehow 'pure' or 'objective' is one of the more important justifications for you being taught it in the first place. Many students first discover the existence of this debate about what literary criticism is when they begin to study Literature at a university or polytechnic; they suddenly find themselves on the receiving end of a barrage of confusing and vaguely French-sounding terms that they've never heard before. Possibly, this chapter may make your transition – if you plan one – from school or college to degree-level studies a shade less traumatic.

Early on in this book we said that what is included within the category of 'literature' – and what is excluded – is decided by something we called the Literary Establishment, which is a mostly anonymous collection of writers, critics and educators (some dead, some living, some undecided) who determine, among other things, what is 'suitable' for A-Level study. Exactly what are the criteria for such selection remains a mystery to most teachers and all students. This same body (if something as amorphous as the Literary Establishment can be called a 'body') proceeds on the assumption that literary criticism is something that is worthwhile and valuable for students to do. One other purpose of this chapter is to get you to think about the interesting way in which these assumptions – assumptions about what literature is and why it is good for you – have come to seem 'natural'.

Languages and ideologies

Ideology is one key word that seems to be central to much modern literary theory. An ideology is a set of beliefs which we have come to think are natural or normal but which are not, really. They often hide or disguise where the power actually resides in any given society. Unless you've been studying A-Level Sociology, you are likely to think that the way you lead your life, the way in which you make decisions, the way you see yourself as a member of society, are all 'natural'. Maybe you think, in some vague way, that the English language is natural: you 'naturally' think in English, and of course it's 'natural' to study things that are written using the same stuff. It's natural to go to school or college, it's natural to learn how to drive a car, and naturally you'll end up married and wanting to own a house, and then naturally you'll have children and vote every five years ... No, that won't do. It's obviously not natural to vote every five years. It is easy to see that voting every five years or so is the way that we organise things politically in this country, but you'd have to be daft to think that it's the natural or God-given thing to do. It's harder – much harder –

to see that the same is true of language itself. And maybe this is because language is somehow strangely invisible: it's always 'there'.

What many modern philosophers and literary theorists have stressed is that virtually all of our beliefs, values and attitudes are 'constructs'. In other words, they are the products of ideologies, and not natural at all. One important source of this idea is the increasingly accepted but still startling view that meaning is not *reflected in* language but is *produced by* it. Which is to say that language is not a tool for your mind to use, but rather that your mind, your understanding, is something produced by language. This is a difficult idea to deal with. Using language to discuss the idea that ideas are produced by language is like being lost in a hall of mirrors. We are going to try to break through these mirrors by inventing a fictional character.

Frank is a poet who lives in a wooden shack somewhere in the Outer Hebrides. He doesn't have a telly, or even electricity. He pays no attention to his appearance. He considers himself a total rebel; he writes about Nature, about the landscape, about the sea, and sees himself as being outside society altogether. A modern literary theorist might say that Frank feels he is a 'Romantic' poet, and a free spirit; but even in his most secluded and emotional moments he does not really have private thoughts which he then 'translates' into a public language for our benefit. Without language, Frank can have no thoughts at all going on in his head; and language was around a long time before Frank came along and began thinking with it. This means that Frank, despite his isolated way of life, has no choice other than to be a social being who thinks within an artificial system of signs which we call language. Meaning therefore belongs to society, not to the lonely Frank – no matter how sincerely he believes he has rejected society, no matter how unorthodox and subversive he tries to be.

Perhaps what's more important, as far as we are concerned at the moment, is that Frank doesn't realise that language works in such a way as to force him to see the world around him from within a framework of language which is not controlled by him. Frank's language, and thus his thoughts, are very largely determined by a set of ideologies. These ideologies control the meanings of words which are very important to Frank – words like 'beauty' and 'free' and 'nature'. These ideologies, as we said just now, camouflage the fact that our responses to things (and ideas) are conditioned by powerful institutions and forces within our society. These forces may be political, religious or commercial. And, of course, the more traditional they are, the more natural they seem. So that when Frank poetically celebrates the beautiful hills around him and contrasts them with the ugly decadence of civilisation, he is not being subversive at all – because such comparisons between Good and Evil are conventional, they are 'civilised'.

If Frank stopped to think about it – if *we* stop to think about it – it's quite obvious that there is nothing natural about language at all. When Frank uses the word 'dog' (as opposed to 'dot' or 'bog', say) to signify the animal which is trying to have carnal relations with his left trouser-leg, there is no natural connection between the sound of that monosyllable and the creature he is trying to detach from his shin. This very simple example of the arbitrariness of words helps us to see that language is a construct, a system, an organisation of sounds in the air or marks on a page. To put this another way, words do not get their meanings because they 'belong with' things in the world; they get their meanings by connecting with other words within the system. And unless we want to be labelled as mad or stupid, we have no choice but to accept the system as a way of looking at the world. You are stuck in it, so are we, so is this book. It is language that means, not us.

This is dizzying stuff. Let us try to recap these difficult arguments in a more systematic manner:

1 Meaning is produced by language, and not reflected in it.

2 Language is constructed by society prior to an individual acquiring it. The individual cannot think 'outside of' his received language (or languages).

3 An individual's sense of reality as being something 'out there' is wrong. How Frank sees the world is very largely determined by a language that is not his own, but one that he was born into.

4 The individual, therefore, can think only with a language which already has built into it assumptions and concepts which affect his or her thinking.

5 The more powerful cultural and political institutions in any society tend to control the language of that society. Individuals are persuaded, or persuade themselves, to believe that the way their language presents ideas about the world is natural when in fact it is artificially constructed. These persuasive forces are called ideologies.

6 One of the things that writers or critics or philosophers may be able to do is at least reveal to Frank and the rest of us what points 1 to 5 mean; but *how* they do this is very problematic, because they need to use language to do it.

What it all boils down to is that Frank isn't hopelessly brainwashed. He isn't just a robot with a tape recorder in his head, and neither are we; nevertheless all of us can think only with a conditioned and contaminated language which makes it impossible for us ever to see the world objectively. In order for Frank to escape from the web of language he will need to be very clever indeed (and much, much more alone than he already is). Certainly his poems will inevitably reflect society's values, even if he thinks they don't. Sooner or later a literary theorist will sail over to the Outer Hebrides and tell him all this. Frank's not going to be pleased.

How does all this rather abstract linguistic philosophy relate to the study of literature, and why should you bother your head with it? Well, if you think that literary criticism should do more than witter on about iambic pentameters, and if you think that it ought to challenge and explore society's (and therefore literature's) values and beliefs, then you should be interested in the kinds of literary theories that try to do those things. What's more, the literary theories that grow out of the ideas we've been discussing are slowly but surely beginning to reach out and touch you, personally. In recent years, what counts as literature and what is acceptable as literary criticism has become debatable. (Yes, we've said this before, too.) There is no longer a 'natural' consensus about it. It is not 'natural' to study Shakespeare and to write critical essays which avoid those 'heresies' we spoke of in an earlier chapter. It's unlikely that these activities are actually harmful, and there is a strong case for their being beneficial; but a modern literary critic would urge you to see these tasks as highly unnatural. They are, however, activities which are declared legitimate and necessary by certain ideologies – and these ideologies are those of powerful institutions directly affecting your life: Government Departments of Education, 'Think Tanks', Examination Boards, universities, for examples.

Schools of hard knocks

Three literary theories, or 'schools of thought' (both these terms make them sound more organised than they really are) which question the traditional approach to literary criticism are **Structuralism**, **Deconstruction** and **Reader Response Theory**. All this chapter can hope to do is offer a simplified account of what these theories seem to say and how they relate to what we have already said about meaning and ideologies.

All three of these theories begin by challenging the 'common sense' view of the way that writers create meaning, so let's have a look at that first. It goes something like this: a poet, someone like old Frank, say, looks at the world and his experience of it, and has thoughts about both; then he converts these thoughts into words; these words, on paper, communicate Frank's ideas to us. Basically, one private individual (Frank) is communicating with another private individual (the reader). The idea is that the one gets to understand what the other thinks and feels.

Most of us feel pretty comfortable with this version of events. In fact, we cling to it fairly doggedly, and we get upset if someone tries to take it away or knock it about a bit. The trouble with common sense, though, is that it so often turns out to be wrong. It used to be common sense that the world was flat.

Structuralists, most of them, anyway, believe that all languages are made up of specific sets of patterns, or codes, or systems, and they believe that these can be discovered, analysed and understood. And if it is possible to do this, we may be able to escape from the prison of our conditioned thought-processes. Because language has been constructed by human societies, it should be possible to analyse it rationally, perhaps even 'scientifically', in the same way that other artificial devices can be analysed. In other words, Structuralists are looking for structures. They are interested in the way that language is built. One Structuralist writer, a Frenchman called Roland Barthes, has found fascinating structures (he calls them 'mythologies') hidden within not only forms of language, but also within all sorts of other cultural phenomena, including car design and striptease. Structuralists, it needs to be said, treat all cultural products as equal; poems and novels are just two kinds of product among many. We'll quote a bit of Barthes in just a moment. It's probably fair to say that Structuralist criticism has had more interesting things to say about 'popular culture' in general than about literature in particular, although there are some revealing and valuable writings by Structuralists about the way that myths and literary genres are structured. (This aspect of Structuralism is sometimes called **narratology**.) Early Structuralist thinkers, like the famous anthropologist Claud Levi-Strauss, believed that by studying the structures that underlie language it might even be possible to discover how the human mind is structured and how it operates, and see whether it obeys certain rules or procedures when it is engaged in thinking. A Structuralist looking at the poetry of our Hebridean friend Frank would not be particularly interested in Frank's insights into the effects of sunlight on the colours of the heather, or whatever. He would be much more interested in the way Frank uses the language system that he shares with other writers in English, and the ways in which that language system conditions the way that Frank thinks. Or in other words, he would be interested in the way that reality is seen and organised in Frank's language.

This all sounds very technical and 'scientific', no doubt, and it would be true to say that much Structuralist writing is difficult, even downright impenetrable. And Structuralism is somewhat discredited these days, because to a lot of people it seems to be chasing after the impossible or the unattainable. It's pretty hard to accept, for example, the idea that by deep analysis of language you can find some sort of universal model of the human mind; or that there are so-called 'deep structures' to be discovered in every aspect of our culture. But regardless of whether it is in or out of fashion, Structuralism has had some interesting things to say about the ideologies that control the way we look at all sorts of things, and Structuralists have had a good time upsetting apple-carts and rocking boats. If you would like just to dip your toes into the deep waters of Structuralist thought, Roland Barthes is fairly approachable. In fact, he's pretty entertaining. His book *Mythologies* looks critically into a wide range of things, but in each case Barthes' intention is the same: he wants to get behind things we take for granted – in other words, things we complacently think of as natural. The enemy, says Barthes, is the 'ideological abuse' which hides behind the phrase it 'goes without saying'. Here he is talking about detergents and foam:

> To say that Omo cleans in depth is to assume that linen is deep, which no one had previously thought; and this unquestionably results in exalting it, by establishing it as an object favourable to those obscure tendencies to enfold and caress which are found in every human body. As for foam, it is well known that it signifies luxury. To begin with, it appears to lack any usefulness; then, its abundant, easy, almost infinite proliferation allows one to suppose there is in the substance from which it issues a vigorous germ, a healthy and powerful essence, a great wealth of active elements in a small original volume. Finally, it gratifies in the consumer a tendency to imagine matter as something airy ... Foam can even be the sign of a certain spirituality, inasmuch as the spirit has the reputation for being able to make something out of nothing, a large surface of effects out of a small volume of causes ... What matters is the art of having disguised the abrasive function of the detergent under the delicious image of a substance at once deep and airy which can govern the molecular order of the material without damaging it.

> *Roland Barthes: Mythologies*

In other (less witty) words, what Barthes is saying is that foam is a useless by-product of detergent, but is used to persuade us that that using a particular detergent makes washing clothes into a luxury. He is exposing the advertising method by which we are sold things on the basis of 'myths' which have nothing whatever to do with the function of the product – in fact, they serve to *disguise* the function of the product. If you doubt this, then try breaking the habit of a lifetime and actually watch television commercials; you'll find that the myth of masculine power has somehow got something to do with drinking cans of lager, and that the myth of feminine sweetness is used to persuade you to stuff yourself with chocolate. And on the subject of foam, the most famous of all washing-up liquid commercials claims that using the stuff can actually defeat the ageing process, and thus it plugs you into the greatest myth of them all – immortality.

It would be nice if **Deconstructionists** came along in order to knock down what Structuralists had put up, but unfortunately the terminology doesn't work in quite that way. Deconstructionists, of whom two other French writers, Derrida and

Foucault, are the best-known, also start from the premise that language is dominated and controlled by ideologies, and that these ideologies reflect the power structures in society. In a nutshell, the essence of Deconstructionist thinking is that there is no way that language can be used to get at 'The Truth'. Deconstructionists insist that any literary text can only having meanings, plural, not one single ultimate, pure, meaning. Thus all that critics can do is reveal layer after layer, or version after version, of meaning from a text, never arriving at a central 'core' of truth, because language doesn't generate meaning that way. Texts are built like onions, not like nuts. The most interesting – and perhaps the most useful – idea partly to have come out of Deconstructionism is the concept of **closed** and **open** texts. Closed texts are written works which try to impose or assert one particular meaning on the reader. Open texts are ones which somehow admit the possibility that they can be understood in different ways. To give very crude and general examples, advertisers are in the business of trying to create closed texts (they don't want you to have any doubts about the product) whereas most poets are in the business of creating open texts (they want their poems to mean different things to different people over long periods of time).

A Deconstructionist critic will ignore anything a writer may have to say about his or her own work and what it means. Indeed, Deconstructionists have the most fun with writers whose texts claim to have one particular clear meaning, but which on close examination (i.e. deconstruction) mean something else altogether. Let's whistle up Frank again to see if we can clarify this. Let's imagine that Frank has written yet another poem which celebrates the unspoilt 'natural' scenery of the Hebrides, and which, by implication, condemns the evils of mainland city life. You can imagine the kind of thing; it would start something like this:

> Beinn Mohr: the acid
> tongue of mainland rain
> spreads rumours of your pregnability
> yet speaks in vain ...

and so on. Now, a Deconstructionist would deconstruct Frank's poem fairly ruthlessly. For a start, he or she would point out the inherent absurdity of attacking 'civilisation' by using the most sophisticated (i.e. corrupt) invention of that civilisation – language. Then she would go on to say that the polarity that Frank subscribes to (Nature versus Civilisation, Innocence versus Corruption, call it what you like) says a good deal about the way that Frank has been taught to see things but not very much about the way that things *are*; he's caught up in a series of concepts that society is, in fact, perfectly comfortable with. And then if Frank wants to disturb his readers, why does he offer them the reassuring predictability of *rhyme*? And doesn't it tell us quite a lot about Frank and the way people like him think about Nature and inanimate things that he anthropomorphises them all the time? It's revealing, isn't it, that Frank, a male, sees the landscape as female, as 'pregnable'. She – our Deconstructionist – would also be able to show us that Frank deliberately suppresses some of the possible meanings of words, and insists upon the other possible meanings of the same words, in order to create a very partial and probably fraudulent picture of the world. (In Deconstructionist jargon, Frank is being 'logocentric'). In short, a Deconstructionist would want to show us that Frank's poem possesses many 'meanings', some of which he has suppressed (unconsciously, maybe) because his language is dominated by socially-dictated ideologies of which he, poor chap, is unaware.

From the way we write, let's move on to the way we read, and so to **Reader Response** or **Reader-oriented theory**. This is one of the newer and livelier theories, and it concerns itself with what goes on when a reader reads a given text. Let's go back for a moment to that 'common sense' view of writing, which works something like this:

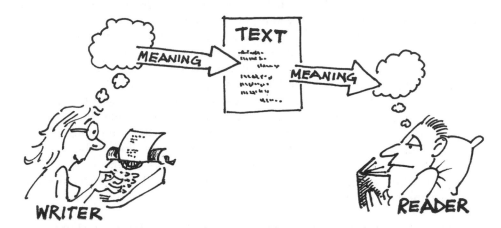

In this formulation, the reader is on the receiving end of the arrow which indicates 'meaning'. This is not to say that the reader's role is a passive one; the early Practical Critics like I. A. Richards were at pains to emphasise the importance of the reader's participation, the imaginative work involved in being a good receiver of meaning. But this mental effort on the reader's part is devoted to receiving meaning which is already *in* the text and which is delivered *by* the text. Reader Response theory re-arranges our diagram in a radical way, something like this:

indicating that the reader is an *active creator of the meaning of the text*.

The key question is this: how far does a text dictate its own meaning, and how far is that meaning dictated by the reader?

If you are hoping that Reader Response theory is a single theory with a single answer to this complex question, we have to disillusion you. Reader Response theorists are a divergent bunch, and approach the question from different angles; all that they seem to agree on is that the reader is a central figure in the process whereby texts get meanings, and that the 'natural' and 'simple' act of reading is, in fact, a very complex business. One approach to reading theory involves looking at what actually goes on when we read. Traditional literary criticism has usually insisted that the text of a poem is an 'organic whole'; but a number of recent theorists (notably the American writer Stanley Fish) have pointed out that this is not actually the way we experience the poem. We read it in bits. Our eyes move from left to right across the page and back again, picking up information. We take in one word, then another, then another; and with each word we add to or revise or eliminate the meanings of the words which preceded it, and, just as importantly, we anticipate what is to come. (And anticipating wrongly may be pleasurable.) In doing this, in accumulating and revising meanings, we are not, according to this way of looking at reading, working towards a 'correct' meaning, we are experiencing a whole range of *potential* meanings; and these meanings do not disappear when a 'correct' one emerges. At the end of one line of the poem we may find the word 'leaves' and read it to mean 'green things growing on trees', only to discover, when we get to the next line, that it means 'departs'. This does not mean that the green things growing on trees disappear; they remain part of our experience of reading the poem. It may be that the poet intended us to experience this ambiguity; but even if he didn't, there's nothing he can do about it. By extension, what this means is that the reader's 'mistakes' become part of the text; and this means that the word 'text' comes to mean something more than just 'the poem as written by the poet' and comes to mean something more like 'the poem as experienced by the reader'.

A rather different, but related, approach to reading theory is to ask what meanings a reader brings, or is likely to bring, to a text. This may strike you as a hopeless line of investigation, since these meanings must differ from reader to reader. This is so, up to a point; but it is an interesting way of looking at, for example, the work of critics, at *why* a critic says what he says about a poet or novelist or whatever. But what is more relevant is that, as we have already said, none of us comes to a text with an 'open' mind; and many Reader Response theorists, echoing the concerns of Structuralists and Deconstructionists, are interested in the extent to which our responses to a text are governed by – yes, you guessed it – ideologies. Since these ideologies can be identified to some extent, we can, with difficulty, be aware of the way they affect our own reading, as well as the way they affect other readers' readings. While these ideologies may well function within us unconsciously, it is also possible to apply them consciously; it is possible to look at a text through a Christian ideology, or a Socialist ideology, or a patriarchal ideology, or any number of other cultural or political 'screens'. Indeed, if you are very impartial and jolly clever, you could write a number of different critiques of the same work from different ideological points of view. This is one reason why many critics now prefer to talk about **readings** of texts, rather than interpretations. 'Interpretation' suggests that a text can be somehow decoded so as to provide a 'real' meaning, whereas 'reading' suggests that such objectivity is not possible, and that variant readings of the same text are equally valid. (It is a term applied to non-literary works, also – one can just as well speak of 'readings' of a film or of a musical score.)

Some Reader Response theorists maintain that if twenty readers were to read one of Frank's poems, then twenty different versions of that poem are thus brought into being. Others maintain that our reading is heavily managed by cultural conditioning and that we define a text in a way that can never be 'free'. In any event, reader-oriented theories have given a new impact to the important truism that a text doesn't mean anything until it is read. No poem – or anything else in writing – can generate meaning except through the mental processes that take it inside a human head. Frank's poems cannot generate any meaning if they remain under his bed quietly humming away to themselves.

If you have only recently got to grips with the mysteries of onomatopoeia and romantic irony and suchlike, you may have found our brief account of these schools of critical thought a bit disturbing. Don't worry too much. These ideas may move the goal-posts an inch or two, but for the time being they are unlikely to change the A-Level game altogether. But it would not be a bad thing if these ideas got you thinking about what you are doing in English lessons and why you are doing it. There are some questions at the end of this chapter that you might like to think about. Also, there are a couple of good books that can give you more detailed and coherent accounts of what literary theorists have been up to in recent years; they are:

A Reader's Guide to Contemporary Literary Theory by Raman Selden, published by Harvester Press in 1985

Literary Theory – an Introduction by Terry Eagleton, published by Blackwell in 1983.

Neither of these books, you will be glad to learn, mention Frank or his poems.

Unless you have remained resolutely asleep during this chapter, it should by now be clear to you that much modern literary theory is as much about politics as it is about literature. Opponents of the schools of thought that we have been discussing have often attacked them on the grounds that they are 'politically motivated'. And as a matter of fact, one of the influences on some modern critical theory is, shock horror, Marxism. This has led the more paranoid of traditional scholars to see Structuralism, for example, as a ghastly Red plot to take over the English Departments of our universities. So let's try to be a little clearer about what 'political' might mean in the context of literary criticism. In the first place, the word does not refer merely to the power struggle between, let's say, the Tory Party and the Labour Party. Having said that, though, it's important to be aware of the fact that party politics has a great deal to do with the manipulation of language. One obvious example is the well-worn phrase 'in real terms', which is a favourite with the government in power at the time we are writing this. It is slipped into sentences like 'In real terms, spending on the National Health Service has increased by 24%.' What this really means is 'Despite the fact that seventeen hospitals had to close last week, we are spending 24% more money on the Health Service according to the way we juggle the figures.' In which case, 'real' means 'unreal'. Politics has a way of reversing the meanings of words, as George Orwell points out in his *Nineteen Eighty-Four*. But this is the language of politics, which is not the same thing as the politics of language. When we talk about the politics of language, the word 'politics' means something like 'the organisation and use of power within a society'. It is the first premise of much modern literary theory that there are political structures which control almost all human activities – the way we eat and what we eat, the way we dress (and undress), and, of course, the way we read and write. This is not an abstract or fanciful idea. We do not decide for ourselves how to do these things. We are taught how to do them. And those who teach us also teach us the 'proper' or 'correct' way to do them; and of course this also involves teaching us that there are inappropriate and incorrect ways of doing these things. The distinction between correct and incorrect, between right and wrong, is the fundamental instrument of social control: we are not allowed to do certain things because they are 'wrong'. And those who have their hands on the social controls are those who have political power. All this applies to language just as much as it applies to anything else. In fact, as many critics would insist, it applies much more crucially to language than to anything else, because language is the stuff we think with and communicate ideas with; and if you can control language, you can control thought. Those in power have always known this. Perhaps the best-known demonstration of it has to do with the Bible. Some four centuries ago, it was a serious criminal offence to translate the Bible from Latin into English. Henry VIII's Lord Chancellor, Sir Thomas More, said in 1530

> It is not necessary the said Scripture to be in the English tongue and in the hands of the common people, but that the distribution of the said Scripture, and the permitting or denying thereof, dependeth only upon the discretion of the superiors, as they shall think it convenient.

It's not hard to work out what that really means. What More was afraid of was that if any old non-Latin-speaking Tom, Dick or Mary got to read for himself or herself what the Bible actually said, then he or she might start to think about, form their own opinions about, what the Christian message meant. And that would never do, because it would mean that the control over the meaning of the Bible would no longer be the exclusive property of the Latin-speaking clergy. Since the clergy were politically powerful, an English Bible could well lead to anarchy: Tom, Dick and Mary might learn from their Scriptures that their 'superiors' were not, in fact, so very superior. We still have a good deal of censorship in this country, of course. We are not allowed to know what government ministers actually say when they are discussing what to do with us, and 'our' laws – the actual Statutes passed by Parliament – are deliberately written in such a way as to make them incomprehensible to most of us. (Which is why the Society for the Promotion of Plain English is possibly the most genuinely subversive organisation around.) But censorship is only one of many ways that language is used, or abused, for ideological purposes. It is probably impossible for any school of criticism – or any number of schools of criticism – to reveal all the ways in which ideologies are built into language. More to the point, most of us would go insane if we tried to carry all that knowledge around in our heads. We'd never get the shopping done. All the same, the best literary criticism, while it may not be able to remove completely the blindfolds from our eyes, may be able to show us where the knots are.

English as he is spoke

The fact that our society and our language are literally man-made is the central issue as far as **Feminist** criticism is concerned. Unless you've spent most of your life living in a cave, you'll know that we live in a society which is patriarchal, or male-dominated. It's a society that seems to believe that all writers and readers are men, if we are to judge by linguistic forms that are habitually used: 'When a poet writes *he* makes conscious decisions ...'; 'The reader will make up *his* own mind about ... ' (And yes, fair enough, this book does it too.) It should by now be clear to you that the literature produced in such a 'phallocentric' society will inevitably be controlled by male ideologies, and that, furthermore, this society will tend to marginalise and trivialise writing by women which tries to question or attack these male ideologies.

Feminist criticism is the most dynamic kind of deconstructive theory to have emerged over the past ten years or so. It is eclectic in that it employs Structuralist methods as well as Deconstructionist scepticism about meaning. Feminist criticism also puts a lot of emphasis on the way that a reader experiences texts and creates meaning from it. (Women very often feel that it is men that writers are addressing, and not women.) Feminist writers and critics are all too aware of the power of disguised male ideologies in language and literature, and they have attempted in their work to produce an alternative or corrective set of ideologies which question this state of affairs. If you have followed this chapter so far, you will understand why women writers know better than to try to make 'correct' or 'proper' accounts of 'the truth'. They tend to be less arrogant than men in this respect, and more aware of the nature of ideologies. It is usually those who suffer from being 'under' an ideology, rather than those who benefit from it, who are the more aware of what that ideology is and how it operates. (If you wanted to know how racism works, you'd find out sooner from a black person than a white one.)

It is a fact that there are many more young women than there are young men studying Literature as an A-Level subject. You may well conclude that this means that English syllabuses should be very different from what they are. (It is hard to imagine, is it not, that if only members of the *male* sex were allowed to study A-Level Literature they would be obliged to study books written almost exclusively by *women*.) It is more than likely that the majority of the writing on your syllabus was produced by men. And it is just as likely that it conforms (in ways both obvious and subtle) to languages which reflect male ideologies. This doesn't mean that they are overtly sexist, of course. Examination boards are rather sensitive about that sort of thing these days.

As long ago as 1929, Virginia Woolf was considering the possibility of escaping from man-made language into a new kind of female literary language. One of the best introductory analyses of this whole debate is her short and famous essay called *Women and Fiction*. In it, she suggests that women writers in the future (which means now) will have to invent a wholly new kind of 'uncontaminated' language because, she says, even the conventional sentence is 'made by men; it is too loose, too heavy, too pompous for a woman's use.' You may or may not accept this rather unsettling idea of there being male and (potentially) female sentences. But there's no question that Virginia Woolf was right when she said that the 'feminist novel' would have to be different from the conventional novel because it will have to 'attempt to alter the current scale of values'. It has indeed turned out that many modern women writers (some of whom accept the term 'feminist', some of whom don't) are great exploders of conventional literary forms and experimenters in new ones. We're thinking of people like Doris Lessing, Margaret Atwood, Angela Carter and Fay Weldon, among many others.

It is a matter of warm debate among women writers and readers and critics as to whether Woolf's vision of a new language, an alternative to 'patriarchal discourse', is attainable or not. As men, and as habitual patriarchal discoursers ourselves, the authors of this book are not in an ideal position to comment. Perhaps it would be best to suggest that you look into the matter for yourself. You may find the following books a good place to start:

Ruth Sherry: *Study in Women's Writing*
Maggie Holmes: *Feminist Criticism*
Elaine Showalter: *The New Feminist Criticism*
Judith Fetterley: *The Resisting Reader*

Closing with an open text

In the preceding two sections of this chapter we have tried to sketch four 'schools' or theories of criticism, and by looking at each one separately we've almost certainly created a wrong impression – which is that these 'categories' have clear boundaries around them and that they are neatly distinguishable one from another. This is not really the case. Critical schools of thought are not separate little tribes, each one camped around its own fire, doggedly refusing to speak the language of the other tribes, and only pausing occasionally to lob a tomahawk at a nearby camp. A certain amount of tomahawk-throwing goes on, of course, and now and again nasty little tribal wars break out in university Literature departments and in the pages of academic journals. But the general, long-term effect of different literary theories is that they feed into and merge with the mainstream of literary criticism and eventually filter down to the likes of us. It is not necessary for you or I to choose to 'become' a Deconstructionist or a Feminist and restructure our thinking accordingly; but the existence of these different ways of looking at literature gives us a wider choice of language and ideas through which and with which we can look at writing. You may find that a particular text will release more meanings if you can approach it in more than one way.

We are going to stick our necks out now, and risk flying tomahawks, by suggesting ways in which the various kinds of literary theory discussed in this chapter might be applied to one text. We are not silly enough, nor skilful enough, to try to impersonate a Feminist or a Structuralist, or whatever – we'll just suggest the kinds of question each might ask, and the issues each might raise.

In 1789 William Blake printed a collection of his illustrated poems under the title *Songs of Innocence*. It included the following short, apparently simple, and very odd little poem:

Infant Joy

'I have no name:
I am but two days old.'
What shall I call thee?
'I happy am,
Joy is my name.'
Sweet joy befall thee!

Pretty joy!
Sweet joy, but two days old!
Sweet joy I call thee:
Thou dost smile,

> I sing the while,
> Sweet joy befall thee.

William Blake

Although we have persisted in calling the critical theories discussed in this chapter 'modern', they may not be as new as they appear; certainly Blake seems to have had some awareness of the ideas behind them when he wrote this poem sometime in the 1780s. He was generally considered mad, of course.

Not so very long ago, the conventional view of this poem was that it was a simple lyric in praise of innocence. After all, the words 'Songs of Innocence' mean exactly that, don't they? The words 'Infant', 'Joy', 'happy', 'sweet', 'smile', and 'sing' add up to a celebration of the uncorrupted nature of the new-born child. The extreme simplicity of the language is appropriate to this theme. There is perhaps something slightly absurd about this simplicity of language, but perhaps it is above criticism because it is so obviously written with such sincere feeling and purity of heart.

This bland and complacent assessment of Blake's poem would not satisfy many critics nowadays. One fault that you might find in it straight away is that it assumes that as far as words are concerned, 'simple' means the same as 'short'; one of the things we have harped on about in this book is that short words are often very complicated. It is true that there are only four words of more than one syllable in the entire poem (one in the title); but this should not delude us into assuming that the poem's *meaning* is simple. In fact, modern literary theory would be particularly interested in the language of this piece. There is a strong case to be made for the poem being *about* language.

A Structuralist might respond to *Infant Joy* by examining the concept of childhood which seems to underlie the poem. Such a critic would argue that childhood is an excellent example of a concept which we take to be natural but which is, in fact, a social construct. We tend to accept that childhood is a natural, inevitable and universal aspect of human life, but as soon as we stop and think about it, it begins to appear quite artificial. The definition of the word is highly negotiable, for a start: when and how is it different from 'infancy' or 'youth'? Linguistically, it is apparently a place as well as a time – we can be 'in' it. Childhood has all sorts of generalised characteristics ascribed to it, despite the fact that no two childhoods can be alike. Although we think that childhood is a universal condition, the Elizabethans, for example, seem never to have heard of it. As a word, childhood depends for its meaning upon being opposed to another word (another social construct): adulthood. Childhood and adulthood together form a **dialectic** – that is, a pair of polarised ideas which depend for their meanings upon each other. Between them, the words suggest a completely artificial division of life into two separate parts (a division which psychologists, among others, would dispute). Perhaps the two voices in the poem are the two parts of this dialectic. Among the more powerful associations of childhood is innocence; and our Structuralist might widen the discussion to include the 'mythology' of this word, too, particularly as it is a word which crops up so frequently in the conventional response to Blake's poem. Although Blake was something of an outsider as far as movements or schools of poetry are concerned, he was writing at the time of the Romantic Revolution. For the Romantic poets (as we have said elsewhere) the concepts of Childhood and Innocence and Nature interlocked, and were seen as being in opposition to Adulthood and Corruption and Civilisation, which also interlocked. It is more than likely that this set of opposed ideas is operating in *Infant Joy*, in which an adult seems anxious to name a child; and naming is the first stage in the 'socialising', or civilising process. In short, then, our Structuralist would probably warn against the temptation to see this piece as a simple poem about a real parent and a real baby: what we have here, actually, is the interplay of two voices which represent ideas, or constructs.

(Incidentally, during the week in which we sat down to hammer out this chapter, the United States Supreme Court ruled that it was legal to execute children for crimes of murder. The Court declared that by 'children' it meant people who were physically, *or mentally*, under the age of eighteen. This would seem a brutally plain indication that childhood and innocence are not natural or God-given entities, but are terms defined – and redefined – by those who have power over us.)

A Deconstructionist would perhaps be able to reveal the most about the actual text of Blake's poem. In Deconstructionist terms, it is an unusually 'open' text, in that Blake doesn't close meanings to the reader; he doesn't strongly insist upon certain kinds of interpretation. In part, this openness is created by the presence of two voices, neither of which is the author's. There is no authoritative voice trying to present us with the 'correct' meaning. What's more, these two voices are involved in a dramatic dialogue of sorts, and the reader has in a way to recreate the poem by imagining the dramatic situation and by supplying bits that are 'missing' (such as 'said the child' and 'said the mother'.) In short, the reader has a fairly high degree of freedom within the text. But at the same time, our Deconstructionist would point out that Blake, like all writers, is in the business of trying to control the way words generate meaning (even though it's more the case that the words control him). The usual way that writers try to do this is by suppressing (i.e. persuading us to ignore) possible meanings which might obstruct or counteract the intended meaning. In this poem, for example, the word 'happy' is problematic: we might reasonably ask how a two day-old child can be happy if it has not experienced sadness. In fact, the poem as a whole is a baffling paradox, because it implies that the infant is happy because it is still free of language – it has not been named, not been labelled – yet Blake makes the child *say* this using the very language of which it claims to be free. (And it is interesting that the word 'infant' evolves from the Latin for 'unable to speak'.) The Deconstructionist might take pleasure in pointing out that *Infant Joy* is a splendid example of a text which deconstructs itself, since its language breaks down its own meaning. The question remains as to whether or not Blake was fully aware of this: perhaps the paradox is the point, and the poem is ironic; perhaps the poem demonstrates the impossibility of expressing innocence in language, since language is the product of experience.

These Deconstructionist comments would also interest a critic looking at the poem from a Reader Response point of view. The traditional interpretation of Blake's poem – that it is a hymn to innocence – is actually a vague aggregate of the usual meanings of words like 'joy', 'happy', 'sing' and 'innocence' itself. But once we start to be aware of what can happen during the process of reading the poem, we soon realise that the way it acquires meaning is really rather enigmatic. If we take the poem as we actually read it – that is, word by word, line by line – meaning does not accumulate in the way that we expect. What happens instead is that our instinctive desire for a coherent meaning or sequence of meanings is continually frustrated; rather than develop meanings, the poem presents us with a sequence of paradoxical notions. The first word of the poem is 'I': so we have an anonymous individual narrator. This is in itself a familiar notion, and we've probably read scores of poems which use the same device. Not knowing exactly who 'I' refers to does not pose a great difficulty – we can understand a poem which begins 'I wandered lonely as a cloud' without needing the name and address of the speaker. But in Blake's poem, the next thing that happens is that we are told that the speaker's anonymity is literal: the 'I' has no name. And this *does* pose a problem, because experience tells us that individuals do have names – how else can they be individuated? There are a number of ways of dealing with this paradox. We can assume that the speaker is concealing or withholding his or her name for some reason. Or we can assume that the speaker is somehow not a 'real' person. Or we can assume that the word 'name' is in some way metaphorical. What we actually do, of course, is go to the next line to seek some sort of solution to this mystery – only to find that the speaker is someone who cannot possibly speak, let alone command concepts like 'name'.

It is not only these semantic paradoxes which defeat our habitual expectations of poetry. The *form* of the poem does this too. Its most obvious formal characteristic is its brevity and the shortness of its lines. In free verse poems, short lines are sometimes used to slow down reading speed so as to elongate the reading experience and emphasise the function of particular words and phrases. (William Carlos Williams does this; there's one of his short poems on page 177.) But Blake's poem employs both rhythm and rhyme, and it is one of the functions of these devices to set up anticipations of what is to come, thus urging the reader onward to find the next part of the pattern – the word which we expect to rhyme with the one we've just read, the line which will echo the rhythm of the line we have just completed. The overall effect of this is to curtail the mental 'space' in which we can generate meaning: we find ourselves at the end before we know 'where we are'.

These semantic and formal peculiarities of Blake's poem – its paradoxical nature, its absence of clear signals as to meaning, its lack of space for developing interpretation – contribute to its being an open text; it demands that the reader actively participates in the creation of meaning. It is, in simple language, very much a poem that is what we make of it. This being so, reader-oriented theory might well be interested in the kind of meanings we are likely to give to it – because, generally speaking, the more open a text is, the more capable it is of being seen from different ideological points of view. It's fairly obvious that one possible reading of this poem is a religious one, and specifically a Christian one. The Mother-and-Child image is, within a Christian culture, almost inseparable from the image of Madonna-and-Child; if you are a Roman Catholic it may be impossible for you not to see the poem through that 'lens' (even though you may not be conscious of it). There is, however, nothing categorically religious in the poem which inhibits many other kinds of reading.

A Feminist critic might well wish to develop these reader-response questions in a more gender-oriented direction. (We are distinguishing here between gender and sex. By 'gender' we mean the concepts of masculinity and femininity, and these are culturally-conditioned constructs; 'sex' merely indicates the separation into male and female according to the different wobbly bits of our anatomies.) You may have noticed that we referred to 'the mother' in this poem. Why is it that most male readers assume that the parent whose voice we hear in this poem is the mother? Does the text justify this assumption in any way? Do male readers react in a hostile way to this poem because they perceive it as incompatible with certain masculine qualities? Is this poem, in fact, some sort of threat to male ideologies? And there are interesting gender questions raised by the text itself. There is nothing in the poem to indicate the infant's gender, and clearly this is deliberate, but why? Is it merely because it is irrelevant, or is it because Blake wants us to be aware that gender is a form of naming, that gender is itself a form of language (the imposed language of role, behaviour, expectation, dress, and so on)? Had you not known that this poem was written by a man, could you have taken it to be the work of a woman?

So it turns out that there are many ways of looking at this poem that take us far beyond a simple celebration of innocence. In any event, most of us would have to conclude that there is a pessimism close to its surface, because we know that the 'Joy' is inevitably short-lived. The traps of language and experience are about to close on this Infant. Pretty soon other adults will be thrusting their faces into its pram and asking 'What's your name, then?' And not long after that the poor creature is going to feel obliged to come up with the right answer.

Blake wrote his own riposte to *Songs of Innocence*: a volume of poems called, you will be unsurprised to hear, *Songs of Experience*. One of the more famous verses in this second book is called *London*, and it is printed below. As the very last critical exercise we shall ask of you in this book, and one of the hardest, try examining it from each of the critical perspectives we have discussed in this chapter. (This is most certainly *not* an exercise you should be asked to do against the clock.)

London

I wander thro' each charter'd street,
Near where the charter'd Thames does flow,
And mark in every face I meet
Marks of weakness, marks of woe.

In every cry of every Man,
In every Infant's cry of fear,
In every voice, in every ban,
The mind-forged manacles I hear.

How the Chimney-sweeper's cry
Every black'ning Church appalls;
And the hapless Soldier's sigh
Runs in blood down Palace walls.

But most thro' midnight streets I hear
How the youthful Harlot's curse
Blasts the new born Infant's tear,
And blights with plagues the Marriage hearse.

William Blake

Notes

'charter'd' is a fairly busy word. In an immediate sense, it means leased or owned (as, in the modern use of the word, planes or boats can be chartered). It may also – since Blake is writing about a city – contain the meaning 'belonging to a borough', since boroughs are corporations which are granted charters. In pronunciation, it is close to 'charted', which means mapped or marked out. An earlier draft of the poem exists, which shows that Blake substituted 'charter'd' for the word 'dirty' (in both the first and second lines). In what way is this a significant revision?

'ban' means curse; but it just might hint at the different meaning of 'proclamation', as in wedding banns – especially when one looks at the last line of the poem.

'manacles': in the earlier version, Blake wrote 'links'. What shift in meaning does 'manacles' achieve?

The 'chimney-sweeper' is not a jolly chap with a bag of brushes and a vacuum cleaner. Blake's chimney-sweeper is one of the wretched children who were sent up chimneys with a scraper. Such children had neither a happy time nor a long life expectancy.

'Blasts': infects with disease

Questions to sleep on

You may recall that we began this book by asking students in our area why they were studying literature, and then we suggested a number of questions that these answers raised. We're going to end the book with another list of questions. Some of these questions relate to matters we have been grappling with in this chapter, others are a little wider in scope. We might as well admit right now that some of these questions are unanswerable. It's perhaps these unanswerable ones that are the most interesting to think about.

1   Who should decide which sorts of writing and which books you study at A-Level? The Government? The Examining Boards? Your teachers? You? Do you think examiners and teachers know best? If *you* were to decide, how would you set about it?

2   How would you define the word 'literature'? Some writers can only manage a definition something like 'language used in special ways'. (This book takes that view, on the whole.) Others have said that literature is any writing which is fictional in some way. Which of these two definitions are you happier with, and why? Or do you think that literature is impossible to define? If so, what do you think you are studying?

3   Which of the following do you think should be accepted as literature?

Journalism
Letters
Biography
Film scripts
History
Advertising copy
Diaries
Photo-romances

If you would include *some* biography, say, but not other sorts, what criteria would you use to make the choice?

4   Do you think that studying literature has, or will, 'improve' you in some way? Are you starting to feel like a better person already? Who would decide if you were a better person at the end of two years, and how would they assess the improvement?

5   Do you think that writing essays in the traditional way is the best way of assessing your understanding and appreciation of other people's writing? Can you think of a better way? Should you be tested at all? Who benefits from the testing? Do you?

6   What would you say to someone who said 'My opinions about literature are entirely my own'?

7   What is a myth? Do you carry any around in your head? Can you identify any myths about literature that you subscribe to? Do you eat any myths? Do you wear any?

8   Which of the books that you have read on your course so far have had political or social 'messages' of some kind? Have these messages been open or disguised? Are there books that give you more space for interpretation than other books? Are there books which seem more 'user-friendly' than others?

9   Does the way that you read an A-Level book differ from the way you read other books? Is it less pleasurable reading A-Level books? If so, how could the activity be made more enjoyable?

10   If a literature class consists mostly of women, should the texts studied by that class be mostly by women? Should there always be books by women among the texts for study, even if the class is entirely male?

11   'Shakespeare was a man; I am a woman. Therefore I should not be obliged to read or watch or study his plays.' Valid argument or not? If not, what's wrong with it?

12   Do women write differently from the way men write, and if so, what's the difference? *Should* women write differently? Do you think that perhaps Writing by Women is a separate category of writing altogether?

13   What do the words 'scientific' and 'creative' mean? Do either or both of them, or neither of them, describe what you do as an A-Level Literature student?

14   If you were given the power to change the way that the A-Level Literature syllabus was organised, what changes would you make? What sorts of values would you want to build into it? What kinds of skill (other than essay-writing) would you want students to have at the end of their studies?

15   Are there any other questions that should be on this list? What are they, and why should they be here?

Solutions to Chapter 13

A   There was an old lady from Kent
Whose tastes were exceedingly bent;
With a rug on her back
(So's to look like a yak)
She lived with a goat in a tent.

B   is an unaltered extract from *Under Milk Wood* by Dylan Thomas.

C   Officious monitors pushed them into a hundred symmetrical rows – dark-haired, dark-suited men alternating with rows of brides all wearing identical white flouncy dresses.

They seemed surprisingly uncurious about each other. There were no sidelong glances through white veils: all eyes were fixed upon the red-carpeted stage where Mr Moon and his wife stood, looking more royal than religious, in ankle-length white and gold gowns and matching crowns.

(newspaper report of a 'Moonie' mass wedding)

D   A touch of cold in the Autumn night –
I walked abroad,
And saw the ruddy moon leap over a hedge
Like a red-faced farmer.
I did not stop to speak, but nodded,
And round about were the wistful stars
With white faces like town children.

T. E. Hulme: Autumn

E   is an unaltered extract from *A Step Away From Them* by Frank O'Hara..

F   is unaltered; Walter Pater writing in 1869 about da Vinci's Mona Lisa.

G   When the sun
falls behind the sumac
thicket the wild
yellow daisies
in diffuse evening shade
lose their
rigorous attention
and

half-wild with loss
turn
any way the wind does
and lift their
petals up
to float
off their stems
and go

A. R. Ammons: Loss

H   I was a Flower of the mountain yes when I put the rose in my hair
like the Andalusian girls used or shall I wear red yes and how he kissed
me under the Moorish wall and I thought well as well him as any other
and then I asked him with my eyes to ask again yes and then he asked
me would I yes to say yes my mountain flower and I put my arms
around him yes and drew him down to me so he could feel my breasts
all perfume yes and his heart was going like mad and yes I said yes I
will Yes.

James Joyce: Ulysses

I   The house is so quiet now.
The vacuum cleaner sulks in the corner closet,
Its bag limp as a stopped lung, its mouth
Grinning into the floor, maybe at my
Slovenly life, my dog-dead youth.
I've lived this way long enough,
But when my old woman died her soul
Went into that vacuum cleaner, and I can't bear
To see the bag swell like a belly, eating the dust
And the woollen mice, and begin to howl
Because there is old filth everywhere
She used to crawl, in the corner and under the stair.
I know now how life is cheap as dirt,
And still the hungry, angry heart
Hangs on and howls, biting at air.

Howard Nemerov: The Vacuum

Acknowledgements

The authors have special debts of gratitude to the following individuals:
Chris Deering; C. S. Brew; Paul and Geoff of Kestrel Data, Exeter.

The authors and publishers would like to thank the following for permission to reprint copyright material:

A. M. Heath and Company Limited on behalf of the estate of the late Henry Wade for extract from *The Three Keys* from *The Fifth Bedside Book of Detective Stories* edited by Herbert van Thal, published by Arthur Barker Ltd
A. P. Watt Limited on behalf of the trustees of the Robert Graves Copyright Trust for *The Cool Web* from *Collected Poems 1975* by Robert Graves
Abner Stein for extract from *Gentlemen Prefer Blondes* by Anita Loos, published by Penguin Books Ltd
André Deutsch Ltd for *Octopus* from *I Wouldn't Have Missed It* by Ogden Nash
The Arts Council and the author for *The Oxfam Coat* by Anna Adams from *New Poetry 23*
Carcanet Press Limited for *January to December* from *Collected Poems* by Patricia Beer
Chatto and Windus for extracts from *Peeping Tom* by Howard Jacobson; *The Kitchen Child* from *Black Venus* by Angela Carter
City Lights Books for extract from *A Step Away From Them* from *Lunch Poems* by Frank O'Hara, copyright © 1964 by Frank O'Hara
Constable and Company Limited for extracts from *Journey Through Britain* and *Journey Through Love* by John Hillaby
Curtis Brown, London on behalf of Random House Inc. for extract from *As I Lay Dying* by William Faulkner
David Higham Associates Limited for extracts from *The Force that through the Green Fuse Drives the Flower* from *The Poems* and *Under Milk Wood* by Dylan Thomas, both published by Dent
Faber and Faber Limited for *Reading Scheme* and *Message* from *Making Cocoa for Kingsley Amis* by Wendy Cope; *Who's Who* from *Collected Shorter Poems* by W. H. Auden; *The Child Dying* from *Collected Poems* by Edwin Muir; extracts from *The New York Trilogy* by Paul Auster; *The Dyer's Hand* by W. H. Auden; *Hugh Selwyn Mauberley* from *Collected Shorter Poems* by Ezra Pound; *Literary Essays of Ezra Pound*; *The Love Song of J. Alfred Prufrock* from *Prufrock and Other Observations* by T. S. Eliot; *Pike* from *Lupercal* by Ted Hughes; *Lake Wobegon Days* by Garrison Keillor; *A State of Independence* by Caryl Phillips
Faber and Faber Limited and Myfanwy Thomas for *Words* from *Collected Poems* by Edward Thomas
George Weidenfeld and Nicolson Limited for extracts from *The Siege of Krishnapur* and *The Singapore Grip* by J. G. Farrell
Albert Goldbarth for his poem *A History of Civilization*
Hamish Hamilton Ltd for extracts from *Farewell My Lovely* and *Pearls Are A Nuisance* by Raymond Chandler; *Men at Work* by Michael Levey; *Stars and Bars* by William Boyd
Harper Collins Publishers Limited for extracts from *Old Glory* by Jonathan Raban
Harvard University Press and the Trustees of Amherst College for *I Heard a Fly Buzz When I Died* from *The Poems of Emily Dickinson* edited by Thomas H. Johnson, Cambridge, Mass.: The Belknap Press of Harvard University Press, copyright 1951, © 1955, 1979, 1983 by the President and Fellows of Harvard College
Holt, Rinehart and Winston, Inc. for extracts from *A Glossary of Literary Terms* (fifth edition) by M. H. Abrams, copyright © 1988 by Holt, Rinehart and Winston, Inc.
Houghton Mifflin Company for extract from *An Aquarium* from *The Complete Poetical Works of Amy Lowell*, copyright © 1955 by Houghton Mifflin Co., copyright © 1953 renewed by

Houghton Mifflin Co., Brinton P. Roberts and G. D'Andelot Belin, Esquire.

Mrs Laura Huxley and The Hogarth Press for extract from *Vulgarity in Literature* by Aldous Huxley

The Independent for *I wept for the people* ... by Michael Fathers (5.6.89.) and cartoon by Neil Bennet (Independent Magazine 17.12.88.)

John Johnson Limited for extracts from *Brazilian Adventure* by Peter Fleming

Jonathan Cape Ltd for extracts from *In Patagonia* and *On the Black Hill* by Bruce Chatwin; *One Hundred Years of Solitude* by Gabriel Garcia Marquez; *The Colonel* from *The Country Between Us* by Carolyn Forché; *The Schooner Flight* from *Star Apple Kingdom* by Derek Walcott; *Soap Powders and Detergents* from *Mythologies* by Roland Barthes

Jonathan Cape Ltd and the Estate of Ernest Hemingway for extract from *A Moveable Feast*

The executors of the estate of James Joyce and The Bodley Head for extract from *Ulysses*

Laurence Pollinger Limited and the estate of Mrs Frieda Lawrence Ravagli for extract from *The Rainbow* by D. H. Lawrence

Martin Secker and Warburg Limited for extracts from *If on a Winter's Night a Traveller* by Italo Calvino, *Missing Persons* by David Cook

Methuen Childrens Books for extract from *The Wind in the Willows* by Kenneth Grahame

Methuen Drama for extract from *Loot* by Joe Orton

Methuen London for extracts from *Titus Groan* by Mervyn Peake; *Metaphor* by Terence Hawkes

W. W. Norton and Company, Inc. for *Loss* from *Collected Poems 1951-1971* by A. R. Ammons, copyright © 1972 by A. R. Ammons

The estate of Wilfred Owen and The Hogarth Press for extract from *Strange Meeting* from *Wilfred Owen: The Complete Poems and Fragments* edited by Jon Stallworthy

Oxford University Press for *The New Hospital* from *A Martian Sends a Postcard Home* by Craig Raine (1979); *By the Boat House, Oxford* from *Selected Poems 1956-1986* by Anne Stevenson; definition of irony from *The Shorter Oxford English Dictionary*;

extract from *The Marvel* from *The Complete Poems of Keith Douglas* edited by Desmond Graham (1978)

Pan Books Ltd for *The Pro-flogging View* from *Generation of Swine* by Hunter S. Thompson

Pavilion Books for extract from *Tales of Witney Scrotum* by Peter Tinniswood

Penguin Books Ltd for two haiku by Matsuo Basho from *The Penguin Book of Japanese Verse* translated by Geoffrey Bownas and Anthony Thwaite (1964), copyright © Geoffrey Bownas and Anthony Thwaite 1964

Peterloo Poets for poems by U. A. Fanthorpe: *After Visiting Hours* from *Side Effects* (Peterloo Poets 1978) and *Selected Poems* (Peterloo Poets and King Penguin 1986) and *Rising Damp* from *Standing To* (Peterloo Poets 1982) and *Selected Poems* (Peterloo Poets and King Penguin 1986)

Peters Fraser and Dunlop for extracts from *The Road to Oxiana* by Robert Byron

The editor of Poetry magazine and the authors for *Books* by Billy Collins and *The Resident Poet* by Thomas Carper: both poems first appeared in the April 1988 edition and were copyrighted in that year by The Modern Poetry Association

Richard Scott Simon Ltd for *The New People* from *The Garden of the Villa Mollini* by Rose Tremain, copyright © 1987 by Rose Tremain, published by Hamish Hamilton/Sceptre

Marie Rodell-Frances Collin Literary Agency and the author for *Villanelle: Late Summer* by Marilyn Hacker from *Separations* copyright © by Marilyn Hacker

The Society of Authors as the literary representative of the estate of Rosamond Lehmann for extract from *The Weather in the Streets*

Extract from the Authorized Version of the Bible (the King James Bible) the rights in which are vested in the Crown, are reproduced by permission of the Crown's patentee, Cambridge University Press

Every effort has been made to trace the copyright holders of the extracts reprinted in this book. The publishers apologise for any inadvertent omissions, which they will be pleased to rectify in a subsequent reprint.